New Directions in Interest Group Politics

Reflecting cutting edge scholarship but written for undergraduates, *New Directions in Interest Group Politics* will help students think critically about influence in the American political system. This volume, comprised of original essays by leading scholars, is designed to summarize and explain contemporary research that helps address popular questions and concerns, making studies accessible to undergraduate students and providing facts to buttress informed debate.

The book covers interest group mobilization and influence. Rather than simply providing a descriptive overview, the chapters are designed to foster critical thinking by getting students to assess the role of interest groups in the American political system and supplying evidence of their effects. The book covers hot topics like the role of SuperPACs in the 2012 elections and interest group use of online social networks as well as perennial questions like when money buys votes in Congress and whether interest groups increase inequality.

Importantly, a set of web resources associated with the book offer instructions for research and writing assignments. Students will be able to collect and analyze data on campaign finance, lobbying, and interest group involvement in governance. The eResource website includes materials for several classroom simulations, such as an interest group legislative battle, a Netroots convention, and a rule-making process. As they read about key questions in democratic government and current research trends, students can practice serving as interest group activists and conduct original research on the topics that most interest them.

Matt Grossmann is Assistant Professor of Political Science at Michigan State University and Director of the Michigan Policy Network. He is the author of *The Not-So-Special Interests: Interest Groups, Public Representation, and American Governance* (Stanford University Press, 2012) and co-author of *Campaigns & Elections: Rules, Reality, Strategy, Choice* (Norton, 2011). His research appears in the *Journal of Politics, American Politics Research,* and twelve other journals. His next book, *Artists of the Possible: Governing Networks and American Policy Change Since 1945* will be published by Oxford University Press. More information is available at www.mattg.org.

New Directions in American Politics

The Routledge series *New Directions in American Politics* is composed of contributed volumes covering key areas of study in the field of American politics and government. Each title provides a state-of-the-art overview of current trends in its respective subfield, with an eye toward cutting edge research accessible to advanced undergraduate and beginning graduate students. While the volumes touch on the main topics of relevant study, they are not meant to cover the "nuts and bolts" of the subject. Rather, they engage readers in the most recent scholarship, real-world controversies, and theoretical debates with the aim of getting students excited about the same issues that animate scholars.

Titles in the Series:

New Directions in American Political Parties
Edited by Jeffrey M. Stonecash

New Directions in the American Presidency
Edited by Lori Cox Han

New Directions in Campaigns and Elections
Edited by Stephen K. Medvic

New Directions in Congressional Politics
Edited by Jamie Carson

New Directions in Public Opinion
Edited by Adam Berinsky

New Directions in Judicial Politics
Edited by Kevin McGuire

New Directions in Media and Politics
Edited by Travis Ridout

New Directions in American Politics
Edited by Raymond J. La Raja

New Directions in Interest Group Politics
Edited by Matt Grossmann

New Directions in Interest Group Politics

Edited by
Matt Grossmann

Routledge
Taylor & Francis Group

NEW YORK AND LONDON

For assignments and simulations on interest group politics, please visit the eResource website at http://www.routledge.com/9780415827553

First published 2014
by Routledge
711 Third Avenue, New York, NY 10017

and by Routledge
2 Park Square, Milton Park, Abingdon, Oxon OX14 4RN

Routledge is an imprint of the Taylor & Francis Group, an informa business

© 2014 Taylor & Francis

Library of Congress Cataloging-in-Publication Data

New Directions in Interest Group Politics / edited by Matt Grossmann.
    pages cm. — (New Directions in American Politics)
    Includes bibliographical references.
    1. Pressure groups—United States—History—21st century. 2. Lobbying—United States—History—21st century. 3. Political action committees—United States—History—21st century. I. Grossmann, Matthew, editor.
JF529.N49 2013
322.4'30973—dc23
2013019502

ISBN: 978-0-415-82753-9 (hbk)
ISBN: 978-0-415-82755-3 (pbk)
ISBN: 978-0-203-52258-5 (ebk)

Typeset in Gill Sans & Minion
by Apex CoVantage

Contents

List of Figures   vii
List of Tables   ix
List of Contributors   x
Preface   xii

1 Group Mobilization from the Economy, Society, and Government   1
   MATT GROSSMANN

2 How Membership Associations Change the Balance of
   Representation in Washington (and How They Don't)   22
   KAY LEHMAN SCHLOZMAN AND PHILIP EDWARD JONES

3 Grassroots Mobilization and Outside Lobbying   44
   EDWARD WALKER

4 The Paradoxes of Inequality and Interest Group Representation   60
   DARA Z. STROLOVITCH

5 Political Parties and Ideology: Interest Groups in Context   86
   HANS NOEL

6 Why Lobbyists for Competing Interest Groups Often Cooperate   105
   THOMAS T. HOLYOKE

7 How Will the Internet Change American Interest Groups?   122
   DAVID KARPF

8 Attack of the Super PACs? Interest Groups in the 2012 Elections   144
   MICHAEL FRANZ

9   When Does Money Buy Votes?:
    Campaign Contributions and Policymaking   165
    CHRISTOPHER WITKO

10 Understanding the Influence of Lobbying in the U.S. Congress:
    Preferences, Networks, Money, and Bills   185
    HOLLY BRASHER AND JASON BRITT

11 Interest Groups, the White House, and the Administration   204
    HEATH BROWN

12 Interest Groups in the Judicial Arena   221
    PAUL M. COLLINS JR.

13 Evaluating Reforms of Lobbying and Money in Politics   238
    LEE DRUTMAN

14 Conclusion   257
    MATT GROSSMANN

    Index   269

Figures

1.1	Distributions of Interest Groups by Category and Year	5
1.2	Distributions of Indicators of Group Prominence and Involvement	7
1.3	Total Reported Lobbying Expenses by Industry Sector, 2012	8
1.4	Factors Contributing to Business Mobilization in Washington	9
1.5	Correlation Coefficients between Characteristics of Public Constituencies and Their Organized Representation in Hearings	11
1.6	Top Issue Areas for Interest Group Lobbying	14
1.7	Distributions of the Average Number of Interest Groups in American States by Category and Year	17
2.1	Active Membership in a Political Group and Socio-economic Status	25
2.2	Affiliations with and Involvement in Political Organizations by SES Quintile	32
2.3	Involvement in Political Organizations among Members by SES Quintile	33
2.4	Feeling Represented by a Political Organization by SES Quintile	34
3.1	Clients of Grassroots Lobbying Consultants	53
4.1	Policy Typology	63
4.2	Predicted Probability of Activity and Inactivity, by Issue Type and Level of Impact (Membership Organizations Only)	66
4.3	Importance of Each Branch as a Target of Organizations' Activity	70
4.4	Institution Targeted, by Policy Type	70
4.5	Predicted Probability of Targeting Each Branch, by Issue Type	71
4.6	Tactics Used to Pursue Disadvantaged-subgroup Issues	74
4.7	Participation in Coalitions, by Issue Type	75
4.8	Predicted Probability that Respondent Reported an Issue Became More Difficult, by Issue Type	79
5.1	Donor Name Trades among Groups in 2004	99
6.1	Interest Group Competition over Bank Reserve Requirements	106

6.2   Coalition Formation Based on the How Strongly Group
      Members Collectively Feel about Issues and the Similarity of
      Member Collective Positions on Issues   109
6.3   Bargaining between the ABA and PIRG   114
6.4   Coalition of Competing Interest Groups Created
      under Lawmaker Pressure   117
7.1   Total Messages Ordered by Group   133
7.2   Total E-mails by Category   134
7.3   Action Requests by Type and Audience   134
7.4   Fundraising Appeal by Organization Type   135
8.1   PAC Contributions to Congressional Candidates in 2012   146
8.2   Advertising in 2012 House and Senate Media Markets   154
8.3   Rankings of Ads and Videos by Users of SuperPACapp, 2012   156
8.4   Issues Mentioned by Candidates and Groups in Ads, 2012   159
9.1   Labor's Proportion of Labor and Corporate/TMH
      Contributions to Democratic Congressional Candidates   176
9.2   The Gap between Labor and Corporate/TMH PAC
      Expenditures and Policy Liberalism   177
10.1 Network of State and Local Governments with Closeness and
      Betweenness Measures for Lobbying Organizations   193
10.2 Connections between Registrants and Clients for Corporations:
      Corporations Network   195
10.3 Corporation Subnetwork   196
10.4 FECA Campaign Contributions for New Lobbying
      Registrants and All Contributors   197
10.5 The Relationship between Sums of Campaign Contributions and
      Lobbying Expenditures   198
10.6 The Relationship between the Number of Campaign Contributions
      and Lobbying Activity   199
11.1 Senate Confirmation Hearing Exchange between
      Senators Hatch and Leahy   209
11.2 Screenshot from Obama Transition Public Website   215
11.3 Post-Transition Appointments   217
12.1 The Percentage of Cases with Amicus Curiae Briefs, 1995–1998 227
12.2 The Percentage of U.S. Supreme Court Majority
      Opinions from Amicus Curiae Briefs, by Justice (2004 Term)   232

Tables

1.1	Categories of Social Groups with Organized Representation	10
2.1	Participation in Various Forms of Political Activity	24
2.2	Washington Organizations with Different Forms of Membership Status: A Few Examples	26
2.3	Examples of Citizens Groups with Different Forms of Membership Status	27
2.4	Membership Status of Washington Organizations	28
2.5	Interests Represented by Organizations in Washington Politics	30
2.6	Political Capacity of Organized Interests: Average Number of In-house Lobbyists and Outside Firms Hired	36
2.7	Spending on Lobbying	37
2.8	Distribution of Political Activity by Organized Interests	38
4.1	Specific Policy Issues Used in SNESJO Questions, by Organization Type and Issue Category	64
4.2	Mean Level of Activity and Percent of Organizations Active on Each Issue Type, by Type of Organization	67
4.3	Perceived Change in Difficulty in Ability to Achieve Specific Policy Goals Listed by Respondent, by Organization Type, 2000–2006	78
5.1	Groups and Policy Positions	87
5.2	Interest Group Endorsements in Presidential Elections	92
7.1	Fundraising Appeal by Organization Type	136
7.2	Media Agenda Propensity Scores by Organization	138
8.1	Interest Group Contributions and Electioneering, 1980–2012	148
8.2	Partisanship in Interest Group Television Advertising, 2010–2012	152
9.1	The Effect of Campaign Contributions on Voting and Outcomes across Different Contexts	171
10.1	Distribution and Chi Square Test of Action Words by New Registrants and All Lobbying Organizations for 2007–2008	191
11.1	Specific Transition Tactics (from 2008 Survey), n = 72	215

Contributors

Holly Brasher is Associate Professor of Government at the University of Alabama at Birmingham. Her research covers interest groups and the U.S. Congress. She has published in the *American Journal of Political Science* and is co-author of *Organized Interests and American Government* from Waveland Press.

Jason Britt is a graduate student in the Department of Computer and Information Science at the University of Alabama at Birmingham. His research covers knowledge discovery and data mining focusing on computer security and political science data.

Heath Brown is Assistant Professor of Political Science and Public Administration at Seton Hall University. He is the author of *Lobbying the New President: Interests in Transition* (from Routledge) and has published research on interest groups in several journals.

Paul M. Collins Jr. is Associate Professor of Political Science at the University of North Texas. He is the author of *Friends of the Supreme Court: Interest Groups and Judicial Decision Making* from Oxford University Press. He has published work on interest groups in the courts in several journals.

Lee Drutman is Senior Fellow at the Sunlight Foundation. He also teaches at Johns Hopkins University and the University of California Washington Program. He is co-author of *The People's Business: Controlling Corporations and Restoring Democracy* and has published articles on lobbying reform.

Michael Franz is Associate Professor of Government and Legal Studies at Bowdoin College. He is co-author of *The Persuasive Power of Campaign Advertising* and *Campaign Advertising and American Democracy* and author of *Choices and Changes: Interest Groups in the Electoral Process* from Temple University Press.

Matt Grossmann is Assistant Professor of Political Science at Michigan State University. He is the author of *The Not-So-Special Interests: Interest Groups, Public Representation, and American Governance* (Stanford University Press, 2012). His research appears in the *Journal of Politics, American Politics Research,* and twelve other journals.

Thomas T. Holyoke is Associate Professor of Political Science at California State University, Fresno. He is author of *Competitive Interests: Competition and Compromise in American Interest Group Politics* from Georgetown University Press. His research on interest groups has appeared in many journals including the *American Journal of Political Science* and *Political Research Quarterly.*

Philip Edward Jones is Assistant Professor of Political Science and International Relations at the University of Delaware. His recent research focuses on how voters hold politicians accountable for policy representation and has appeared in the *American Journal of Political Science,* the *Journal of Politics,* and *Political Behavior.*

David Karpf is Assistant Professor of Media and Public Affairs at George Washington University. He is author of *The MoveOn Effect: The Unexpected Transformation of American Political Advocacy* from Oxford University Press. He has also published research on interest groups, media, and technology.

Hans Noel is Assistant Professor of Government at Georgetown University. He is co-author of *The Party Decides: Presidential Nominations Before and After Reform.* His research on party coalitions and networks has appeared in the *Journal of Politics* and several other journals.

Kay Lehman Schlozman is J. Joseph Moakley Professor of Political Science at Boston College. She has authored or edited eight books and won several prizes. Her work has appeared in the *American Political Science Review,* the *American Journal of Political Science,* and the *Journal of Politics.* Her latest book (with Sidney Verba and Henry Brady) is *The Unheavenly Chorus: Unequal Political Voice and the Broken Promise of American Democracy* (Princeton University Press).

Dara Z. Strolovitch is Associate Professor of Gender & Sexuality Studies and Affiliated Faculty, Department of Politics, at Princeton University. She is author of *Affirmative Advocacy: Race, Class, and Gender in Interest Group Politics* (University of Chicago Press). Her work appears in journals such as the *American Journal of Sociology* and the *Journal of Politics.*

Edward Walker is Assistant Professor of Sociology at the University of California, Los Angeles. He is author of *Grassroots for Hire: The Reshaping of Participation and Policy* (Cambridge University Press). His work appears in venues such as the *American Journal of Sociology* and the *American Sociological Review.*

Christopher Witko is Associate Professor of Political Science at the University of South Carolina. His research focuses on the role of money in American politics and public policy. His articles have appeared in many journals, including the *American Journal of Political Science* and the *Journal of Politics.*

Preface

There is no shortage of fear about "the special interests" in American political debate, but reliable information about what interest groups do, whom they represent, and how they influence government is often lacking. This book is designed to encourage readers to use empirical research to answer just these questions. Each chapter in the volume summarizes and explains contemporary research that helps address popular questions and concerns, making studies accessible and providing facts to inform public debate.

The book covers the mobilization of interest groups, their activities, and their influence. Each chapter reviews research on a central question of scholarship. Many focus on a particular empirical project designed to shed light on the topic while others compile findings from several research projects. Each author elaborates theories and highlights original research. Rather than listing and explaining types of interest group behavior, the chapters are designed to assess the role of interest groups in the American political system and supply evidence of their effects.

Three goals lie at the heart of this book. First, you should gain an understanding of American interest groups, including their history and structure as well as their strategies and behaviors. Second, you should develop a practitioner's sensibility regarding the strategic considerations and constraints of American interest groups. Third, you will become familiar with political science research and be motivated to conduct your own investigations. Interest groups play important roles in American government, even though their behavior does not always match our best hopes or our worst fears. This book provides an update on the state of our knowledge about interest group politics, enabling more informed participation in democratic government.

The book highlights a third generation of interest group research. During the first generation, scholars saw interest groups in society as the primary actors in the political process—but found that their mobilization and influence was not as automatic as they had expected. The second generation of scholarship moved the focus to the population of organizations in Washington, their resources, and their strategies—but found no reliable relationship between the money that groups raised and their policy influence. The contemporary generation of scholarship highlighted in this volume accepts that interest group behavior and influence is highly conditional. It seeks to identify the circumstances under which interest groups make a difference in American government, specify their relationships to the other parts of the political system, and evaluate their role in democratic decision making.

The chapters cover the classic topics of interest group research: mobilization, operations, and influence. Yet each topic is covered with a unique viewpoint. Rather than focus on theoretical models of interest mobilization, the chapters investigate which social and economic groups are advantaged in the mobilization process and how much organizations seek to directly mobilize citizens to participate in politics. Rather than detail organizational bureaucracy and behavior, the chapters focus on how interest groups relate to other parts of the political system and how they respond to political change. Rather than expecting influence to be a direct product of how many resources organizations can mobilize, the chapters investigate the particular circumstances under which group influence is more and less likely.

The focus of the volume has several advantages that should appeal to readers. First, it analyzes interest groups as interdependent actors rather than in isolation. The chapters cover how groups relate to one another as well as political parties, social groups, economic industries, professional lobbying and grassroots mobilization firms, media outlets, political candidates, and policymakers and institutions in all three branches of government. Second, it evaluates evidence of the effects of interest groups rather than merely their activities. The chapters cover influence on political campaigns and election outcomes, congressional votes and lawmaking, administrative organization, and court decisions. Contributors also tackle the consequences of interest groups for democratic accountability as well as social and economic inequalities. Third, the book draws primarily from political science but features an interdisciplinary approach. Contributors use research from sociology, economics, law, and communications as well as many subfields and theoretical frameworks in political science.

The book uses numerous recent examples and interesting descriptive statistics, even as contributors demonstrate their research craft and note the difficulties associated with reaching definitive answers to important questions. Rather than focus on basic information found in primary textbooks, each chapter situates particular research projects within a broader tradition and provides an example of how a scholar conducts their work.

The book is organized topically but can be read out of order, based on reader preferences and interests. Chapters 1–4 investigate where interest groups come from and whom they represent. The authors investigate how people, businesses, and governments mobilize organizations and resources to find out who gains and loses in the process. Chapters 5–7 investigate how interest groups operate, including how they relate to parties and other groups and how they respond to technological change. Chapters 8–12 investigate interest group influence. The authors review the relative importance of campaign contributions and lobbying for policymaking in the legislative, administrative, and judicial branches of government.

Chapter 13 reviews potential reforms to make interest group politics more consistent with democratic values.

As you read the chapters, please also take advantage of the additional online resources associated with the text. The resources include original research modules for collecting and analyzing data on the issues and groups of most interest to you, and ideas for assignments, projects, and simulations. As you read about interest group research, you can practice conducting your own studies and playing the role of interest group leaders.

Chapter I

Group Mobilization from the Economy, Society, and Government

Matt Grossmann

Before President Obama formulated and passed his national health care reform legislation, he consulted with dozens of interest group leaders; he claimed that they represented the breadth of the American people and the American economy. Organizations attending the 2009 White House Forum that kicked off the health care debate included the American Hospital Association, the Service Employees International Union, the AARP (formerly the American Association of Retired Persons), the National Association of Manufacturers, PhRMA (an association of pharmaceutical companies), the American Medical Association (the main professional association of doctors), the Center for American Progress (a liberal think tank), and the National Council of La Raza (a Latino rights group). It is no surprise that interest groups like these play a central role in American politics. How these particular groups were invited to share their views with Obama is less well known. Not everyone who cares about health care has a permanent spokesperson residing in the nation's capital or an ally with an invitation to the White House.

Where do American interest groups come from? What parts of our economy and society generate organizations and lobbyists to speak on their behalf? These questions have traditionally been at the heart of research on interest group mobilization. Scholars look at the composition and dynamics of the interest group population, dividing the interest group community into sectors in order to establish which companies, industries, social groups, and advocates participate most in the political process. Researchers consider both the number of interest groups and their relative capacity. Longstanding, but largely separate, strands of research investigate either (1) economic mobilization by corporations and trade associations (like the manufacturers, hospitals, and pharmaceutical companies at the White House meeting) or (2) societal mobilization by social groups or public interest concerns (like the groups representing retirees, Latinos, and liberals at the same meeting). Yet recent studies have found that the entire community of interest groups mobilizes in response to the agendas of government officials: all of these groups mobilize because the government is discussing health care.

This chapter reviews the most general and systematic findings that scholars have uncovered about interest group mobilization and relays some key lessons from these investigations. First, I sketch the history of theoretical perspectives on interest group mobilization. Second, I report information on the growth of the national interest group community and its distribution by type: how many groups are in Washington and what are they doing there? Third, I detail the distribution of involvement across interest groups: do all groups have equal chances to become active participants? Fourth, I compile research on why some businesses and industries mobilize more than others: for instance, why is the medical industry so well represented? Fifth, I present some data on which public constituencies generate the most organized representation: why are doctors better represented than patients? Sixth, I review findings from research on the role of government in stimulating interest group mobilization and directing its issue focus: does Obama's agenda explain why and when these groups mobilize? Next, I describe interest group mobilization in state capitals: to what extent does it mirror the national picture? Finally, I address the bigger picture: what can we take away from studies of interest group mobilization?

Several intriguing findings appear consistently. The national interest group community is growing, but the share of business interests is falling. State interest group communities are also expanding, but business remains dominant. Larger businesses that have something to gain from government (like sales contracts) or something to lose (like regulation) participate the most and tend to stay engaged once they become politically active. Advocacy groups better represent the most civically engaged ethnic, religious, occupational, and ideological constituencies (groups like Jews, lawyers, and gun owners mobilize more than groups like students and hairdressers). When government creates new programs, more organizations appear and increase their involvement. The agenda of government officials shapes what these groups lobby about.

For students of American politics, these findings show the promise of interest group mobilization research but also suggest caution in interpreting scholarly debates. Even though thousands of interest groups have mobilized, policymaking involvement is highly concentrated among a small number of organizations. Group mobilization responds to the actions and concerns of government, but there is striking consistency in the types of economic sectors and social groups that tend to be best positioned to organize politically. Even though the interest group universe is responsive to changes in the society, economy, and government, opportunities for regular participation are afforded quite disproportionately to different social and economic groups. Scholars study group mobilization to understand not only how a population of organizations maintains resources but also why some parts of the society and economy are better positioned to have their leaders earn an invitation to the White House.

Theoretical Perspectives on Interest Group Mobilization

The first scholars of American interest groups tended to see social and economic groups as the base units of political competition: people acted collectively to pursue their shared interests and agendas, competing with other groups that had opposing interests and often organizing to influence decisions in government institutions.[1]

This perspective, originally associated with Arthur Bentley and David Truman, developed into a theoretical framework called pluralism, usually associated with Robert Dahl. Although it had many variants, the framework had several basic tenets: (1) many different social and economic groups are likely to compete to influence public policy; (2) these groups often develop formal organizations to speak on their behalf before government; (3) a different subset of these organizations is active in each issue area; (4) government institutions and policy outcomes reflect the preferences of well-organized groups; and (5) new groups regularly mobilize in response to social and economic change and government action.[2]

Bentley and Truman focused mostly on how these groups developed and organized in social and economic life, whereas Dahl focused on who possessed resources to help influence government and who was most active in political decision-making. Dahl added two important caveats to pluralist tenets. First, ambitious government officials often mobilize support from groups for their own goals rather than adjudicating among groups. Second, political professionals dominate decision-making, even as they claim to be acting on the public's behalf, because most citizens are uninvolved.[3]

Critics of pluralism tend to invoke a further set of maximalist claims supposedly associated with pluralist scholars: (1) mobilized interest groups are broadly reflective of American society, especially individual citizens; and (2) these interests are each amply represented and effectively balanced against one another.[4] E. E. Schattschneider argued that interest groups would instead benefit mainly the most educated and highest-income citizens and that every step in the political process, from organizational mobilization to government decision-making, would tend to be biased in favor of similar elites.[5] Others argued that these elites would conspire to prevent the poor from realizing and acting on their grievances and manipulate the political process to prevent their concerns from becoming political issues.[6]

Yet Mancur Olson made the critique that had the most influence on the direction of interest group scholarship. He argued that individuals with shared interests or ideas will not usually act collectively to pursue shared goals. To promote mobilization, leaders of large groups need to provide benefits that are only available to members to incentivize participation; otherwise, most will decide to free ride on the work of others and no one will build, support, or maintain an organization to speak for the group.[7] As a result, the interest group system will consist of organizations that have substantial side benefits (like health insurance discounts from the AARP), require participation (such as unions), or represent small industries or groups.

Most evidence collected by interest groups scholars rejects the claim that groups must provide "selective" incentives, those available only to members, to stimulate support for broad causes.[8] Olson's model of collective action nevertheless helped inspire two important conclusions in subsequent interest group research. First, Jack Walker found that most interest organizations form and survive via financial support from patrons like foundations, governments, or rich individuals.[9] Most organizations do not need to stimulate much public support. Second, Robert Salisbury found that most interest organizations are institutions like corporations, charities, and staff-led organizations, rather than membership associations; they do not even have any members to mobilize.[10]

Several scholars have attempted to revive and reformulate traditional pluralism to take account of these findings.[11] Few contemporary interest groups resemble broad social group mobilizations, but changes in the size and diversity of the interest group community may be reflective of changes in the economy and society.[12] Interest groups representing public concerns have fewer resources than corporations, but they may have substantial influence on the government agenda.[13] Other scholars have attempted to refine the Olson model of interest mobilization, adding other types of incentives for participation, emphasizing the dominance of institutions, and focusing on the implications for inequalities in the interest group system.[14] Overall, interest group scholars have moved away from broad pronouncements about how sectors of the economy and society will compete in government and toward an analysis of the population of interest organizations and their lobbying behavior.[15]

The National Interest Group Population

The most important finding in analysis of American interest groups is the tremendous growth in the number of organizations. The number of interest groups listed in the *Washington Representatives* directory doubled from 1981 to 2006 and continues to grow.[16] Figure 1.1 visualizes this growth, dividing the community into five categories of organizational types: (1) corporations and their associations, (2) government organizations, (3) occupational associations and unions, (4) public interest, identity, and issue advocacy groups, and (5) other groups. The number of organizations of each type has grown over time, but advocacy groups and government organizations have grown at a faster rate than corporate and occupational interests. The fastest growth has come from state and local governments and health and education advocates.

Compared to the population of interest groups residing in Washington, businesses account for a much greater share of registered lobbyists, clients of lobbying firms, reported lobbying spending, and total lobbying reports.[17] Yet lobbying disclosure regulations are designed to apply more readily to corporations and for-hire lobbying firms; both may be overrepresented in lobbying data. Regardless of how the business share is measured, two facts are apparent: corporations and their associations represent the largest share of groups and yet their share is declining.

Interest group scholars have paid considerable attention to the "advocacy explosion," the increasing number of groups representing social groups or policy issue perspectives.[18] The aftermath of the 1960s social movements, the rise of funding opportunities from foundations and rich patrons, the availability of direct mail for easier organizing, and the learning process from the success of early advocates all contributed to increased advocacy group mobilization.[19] The rise of organizations lobbying on behalf of state and local governments has received less attention,

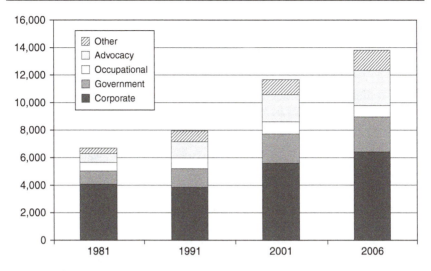

Figure 1.1 Distributions of Interest Groups by Category and Year

The figure reports the number of organizations in each category listed in the Washington Representatives directory in each year. The data are from Schlozman, Verba, and Brady, *The Unheavenly Chorus*, Table 12.2. I combined corporations and trade associations (corporate); occupational associations and unions (occupational); education, health, social welfare, public interest, and identity (advocacy); state and local and foreign governments (government); and other and don't know (other).

but seems just as apparent. A constellation of factors likely contributed: the United States has an increasing number of units of local government (including regional arrangements and single-purpose entities), subnational governments began to rely more on federal funding and were subject to more federal demands and constraints, and other officials learned from the success of governors and mayors.[20]

Researchers have also posited more general explanations for the growth of interest group organizing. The federal government has grown; its responsibilities, budget, and regulatory structure have expanded, leaving more at stake in policy decisions. The society and economy have diversified, increasing the number of industries, occupations, and social groups available for potential organizing. Interest groups have found it easier to raise funds from their supporters and from new institutional sources. All of these explanations find some support in studies of national change as well as analysis of state-level differences in the size of interest group populations.[21] The different rates of growth for different sectors of the interest group population should warn us against a one-size-fits-all solution. After all, organizing by some categories of groups (such as foreign governments, unions, and professional associations) has recently declined.[22] Some factors, such as government expansion, have led to general increases in the interest group population. Others, like the aftermath of social movements, have influenced only some sectors of groups.

The Skew of Interest Group Participation

Despite the growth of the interest group community, the relative participation of interest groups in lobbying activities is remarkably constant. Interest group activity reported on lobbying disclosure forms is very stable from year to year. One study found that 98% of the variation in lobbying across groups and issue areas in any given year could be accounted for by lobbying activity in the previous year.[23] Each year, the population of active lobbying organizations will look just about the same as the year before.

The concentration of lobbying across issue areas is also stable across time. A small number of issues account for the bulk of interest group lobbying activity. In one study, 5% of issues accounted for 45% of all lobbying; most issues involved approximately 15 groups, whereas a few involved more than 300 groups.[24] The issue areas with a lot of interest group activity in one year tend to be the same as those with considerable lobbying in the next year.

Another constant in the interest group system has important implications for American democracy. A small number of organizations account for the bulk of opportunities to participate. Even though the interest groups that get invited to congressional hearings or the White House tend to include many different types of interest groups, the same specific organizations are repeatedly invited to participate and take up most of the opportunities to share views with policymakers.[25] In other words, the cast of characters at the White House Forum on Health Reform was typical: there were some corporate interests, some public interest groups, some unions, and some occupational associations but the most prominent groups in each category got a seat at the policymaking table. A similar subset of groups was invited to relevant congressional hearings and administrative agency discussions, whereas most groups were largely absent from any of the discussions.

In my book, *The Not-So-Special Interests: Interest Groups, Public Representation, and American Governance,* I study the prominence of advocacy groups in political debates in the news media and their involvement in policymaking venues.[26] I measure the number of references to each group in Washington print publications (the main sources of information for political elites) and television news broadcasts (the primary political information source for the public). I also use four indicators of involvement in national policymaking: (1) the number of times that each organization testified in congressional committee hearings, (2) the number of times that they were mentioned in the executive orders, proclamations, and other materials issued by the White House, (3) the number of times they were mentioned in the final rules and administrative decisions issued by executive branch agencies, and (4) the number of times they were mentioned in federal court proceedings.

Figure 1.2 illustrates the distributions of these indicators across the interest group population. In each box-plot, the median is marked with a black diamond and the scores of the middle 50% of the distribution are within the grey box. Each indicator tells the same story: 75% of advocacy groups have very few opportunities for political participation. Three out of four groups receive no more than one Washington

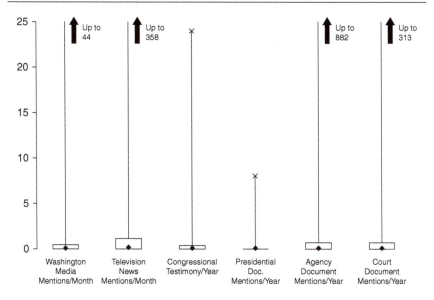

Figure 1.2 Distributions of Indicators of Group Prominence and Involvement

The figure illustrates box plots of each indicator of interest group media prominence and policymaking involvement. The diamonds represent the median, while the boxes cover the 25th to the 75th percentile. The minimum is zero for each indicator. The maximums (44, 358, 24, 8, 882, and 313) are not visible for most indicators. The data are from Grossmann, *The Not-So-Special Interests.*

media mention per month and they give testimony no more than one time per year and never appear at the White House; they receive only a few mentions per year in administrative agency or court documents and no more than three mentions per month on the television news. In all cases, one-quarter of the groups account for the vast majority of opportunities for participation. The graph actually understates the case so that the reader can see the boxes; the actual maximums are much higher for four of the indicators. The top groups are mentioned 44 times per month in the Washington media, 358 times per month on television broadcasts, 882 times per year in administrative agency documents, and 313 times per year in court documents.

These distributions are all incredibly skewed. A small subset of organizations is much more prominent and involved than most other groups in Washington. In some cases, the differences between the middle group and the top group are several orders of magnitude. Investigating the number of organizations mobilizing in each category may be a poor method of identifying the sectors of the economy and society that have a chance to influence policy. The organizations that do account for large shares of opportunities for participation tend to be the oldest and largest groups in each category.[27] Even if the total interest group population doubles, therefore, that may not change which groups have regular opportunities for influence. The vast majority of the newly mobilized groups—along with most of the old groups—do not play a prominent role in policymaking.

Business Mobilization

Rather than look only at organizational populations, some interest group research looks at levels of participation associated with each interest group. In research on business mobilization, this typically takes the form of measuring spending on Washington lobbying, political staff, or campaign contributions. Scholars measure which companies and businesses invest the most in political activities and why some corporate interests are more involved than others.

Economic industries participate at dramatically different rates. Figure 1.3 divides business interests into 12 industry sectors and illustrates the amount each reported spending on lobbying during 2012.[28] The health and finance sectors top the list, with more than $350 million in lobbying spending in one year. The energy and communications sectors also spend more than $200 million. The food, retail, construction, and services sectors each spend less than $50 million, despite all employing sizable proportions of the American workforce.

Why do some corporations and some industries mobilize so much more than others in national politics? There have been at least 24 published academic studies that attempt to answer this question; each study tests the influence of many potential determinants of firm political participation. Figure 1.4 illustrates the factors that may influence corporate mobilization. For each factor, I report both the number of findings of significant influence and the number of findings of no influence; the total length of the bars thus indicates how many times scholars have

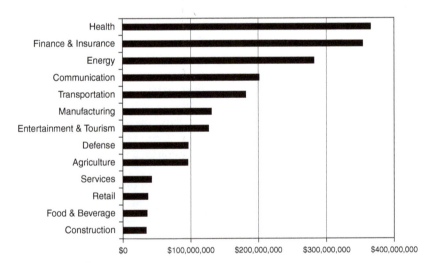

Figure 1.3 Total Reported Lobbying Expenses by Industry Sector, 2012

The figure reports the total lobbying expenses of each industry sector. Data are from The Center for Responsive Politics and are available at opensecrets.org. I added the entertainment & tourism, retail, food, manufacturing, and services categories from general business and re-categorized music/TV/movies as entertainment.

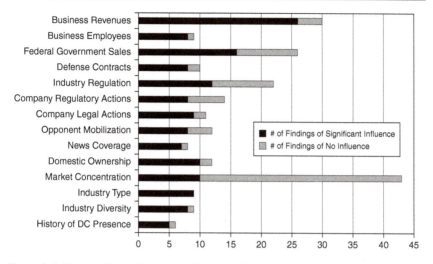

Figure 1.4 Factors Contributing to Business Mobilization in Washington

The figure illustrates factors associated with the mobilization of business interests in Washington. The bars report the total number of studies that examined each factor, divided into studies finding statistically significant influence and those not finding influence. The data are from Brady, Drutman, Schlozman, and Verba, "Corporate Lobbying Activity in American Politics," Table 2.

studied each factor.[29] Following a famous theoretical model of collective action by Mancur Olson, scholars initially concentrated on evaluating the claim that concentrated industries may be better equipped to mobilize politically.[30] Although this factor has been studied the most, there is only limited evidence that it matters.

Instead, the factors that are most consistently related to business mobilization relate to the size of the firm (employees and revenues), its use of the government as a client (federal sales and defense contracts), its reason to fear government oversight (regulatory and legal actions), or its role in Washington (previous presence and domestic ownership). Industries with more diverse products and clear political opponents also mobilize more in Washington. Industries that gain attention from news coverage spend more on political activities as well. There are also consistent differences across industries, even controlling for these factors; only some of the gaps between industry lobbying expenses illustrated in Figure 1.3 are explained by the factors listed in Figure 1.4. Large firms with the government as a potential client or adversary consistently mobilize more than others. Likewise, industries that have something to gain or lose from government actions are the ones that mobilize for political participation.

The consistent story from these studies is that individual businesses and multi-business industries mobilize when they want something from the government, either because they want to avoid regulation or because they want to sell directly to the government. It also matters whether corporate interests have the resources to participate and whether they have done so in the past. Rather than the full diversity of the American economy, business interest groups tend to represent those with the most stakes in government action who have the means to affect it.

Social Constituency Mobilization

In addition to corporations and industry associations, the Washington interest group community is full of organizations that presume to speak on behalf of public constituencies like social groups or supporters of particular issue perspectives. Nearly every kind of public group or perspective has some organization claiming to be its representative. Table 1.1 lists several categories of public constituencies, along with the number of different constituencies within each category associated with Washington interest groups.[31] For each constituency type, I list an example public group and an example organization that claims to speak on their behalf. For instance, African Americans have many different organizations representing them in Washington (including the NAACP), and 39 other ethnic groups also have organizations that claim to speak for them.

Occupational representation is the most diverse, but ethnic and religious representation is also broad. There are 78 other social groups like veterans, skiers, and

Table 1.1 Categories of Social Groups with Organized Representation

Type of Constituency	# of Groups Represented	Example Constituency	Example Organization
Ethnic Groups	40	African Americans	NAACP
Religious Groups	23	Catholics	U.S. Conference of Catholic Bishops
Occupational Groups	254	Appraisers	Appraisers Association of America
Other Social Groups	78	College Students	United States Student Association
Intersectional Groups	64	Blind Veterans	Blinded Veterans Association
Ideological	9	Economic Conservatives	National Taxpayers Union
Liberal Single Issue	53	Drug Policy Reform	Drug Policy Alliance
Conservative Single Issue	27	Pro-Life	National Right-to-Life Committee
Foreign Policy Issue	25	Aid to Africa	Aid for Africa
Other Single Issue	14	Child Welfare	Children's Defense Fund

The table reports the number of social groups in each category that have at least one interest organization speaking on their behalf in Washington, with an example of each type of constituency and organization associated with that constituency. The data are from Grossmann, *The Not-So-Special Interests*.

college students associated with interest groups. I also categorize 64 constituencies as intersectional, meaning that many interest groups speak for the intersection of two social categories (e.g., blind veterans or African American doctors). At least 128 issue perspectives also have their own organizational sector in Washington. Although many constituencies only have one organization speaking on their behalf, some have substantially more. For example, 54 organizations represent women and 87 organizations speak on behalf of environmental concerns; each of these groups is counted as a single constituency in Table 1.1, even though they have plenty of organizational representation.

Not all organizations are created equal. Recall that in each sector, a small number of organizations tend to dominate opportunities to be involved in public debate or policymaking. In order to find out why some public groups are better represented than others, I compared the organized representation of 140 groups. I assessed the characteristics of each organizational sector and their constituencies. For example, I compared the average characteristics of Latinos and Jews in the American public and compared the prominence of Latino and Jewish organizations in Washington to see if there might be a connection; I did the same for 138 other groups.[32]

Figure 1.5 compares characteristics of public constituencies that might influence their level of organized representation in Washington. For each group trait, I report

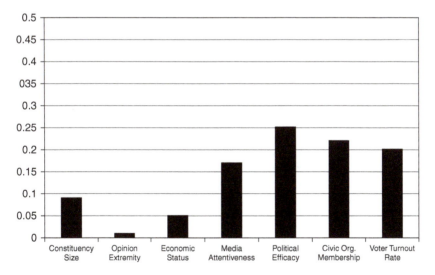

Figure 1.5 Correlation Coefficients between Characteristics of Public Constituencies and Their Organized Representation in Hearings

The figure illustrates the correlation coefficients between the characteristics of public constituencies (as measured in public opinion surveys) and the extent to which their organizational representatives testify before Congress. N = 140 groups where data was available. The first three relationships are not statistically significant. The data are from Grossmann, *The Not-So-Special Interests*, Table 2.1.

its correlation coefficient with the aggregate participation level of the group's representatives, in this case measured by the number of times organizations representing each group appear in congressional committee hearings. Higher columns indicate that the public group trait is more positively associated with the involvement of their organized representatives. This provides a sense of what kinds of groups have their voices heard in Congress, but most of the same associations are evident in public group representation in the other branches of government as well.

Some common theories of why some public groups are better represented than others are not born out. First, group size is not highly associated with organized representation: larger groups do not receive much credit for being larger. Mancur Olson's model of collective action instead suggested that small groups would do better, but this is also untrue.[33] Most public constituencies with high levels of organized representation, like doctors and lawyers, make up small proportions of the public; some large groups, like women, are also well represented. Second, politicians sometimes allege that interest groups represent only extremists. I find that the extremity of opinions in a group is not associated with their levels of representation. I measured how each group feels about five different policy issues; groups with more moderate opinions were not advantaged or disadvantaged when it came to organized mobilization. Third, socio-economic status does not appear to be as influential as some once thought. Social groups that are better off in terms of income, education, and occupational status do not benefit overwhelmingly from organized representation. Higher status groups do mobilize substantially more organizations and political staff to speak on their behalf, but the differences are not as apparent when it comes to the involvement of their organizations.

That hardly means that interest group representation is not associated with public constituency characteristics. The amount of attention that the average constituency member pays to news coverage and the number of local civic organizations that they join is associated with the success of the interest group sector that represents them. The average level of political efficacy (the extent to which one believes they can influence government decisions) in a group is also associated with organized mobilization: groups who believe in the power of political organizing take the steps to overwhelm their opponents.

For example, groups like gun owners are more politically motivated and interested than supporters of gun control, even though they make up a smaller share of the population and are less well off financially. This shows up in the much more prominent role of the National Rifle Association (NRA) compared to the Brady Campaign to Prevent Gun Violence: the NRA's supporters are much more active in politics and members of Congress hear from them more often. Engineers and lawyers are another useful comparison. Both are small and high-income occupations, but lawyers developed substantially more prominent interest groups; one reason is that they care more about politics and participate more in civic life because their careers are tied to government.

The voter turnout rate of a constituency is also significantly related to their organized representation: groups that participate disproportionately in elections are also overrepresented by interest groups. Yet it may make more of a difference in interest group organizing than in elections. Jews and lawyers vote and organize at high rates, but neither group is large enough to swing many election outcomes. In contrast, their interest groups are more successful than those associated with much larger groups. Patients would win an election against doctors, even if doctors vote at higher rates, but they are less likely to win an organizing battle against the American Medical Association.

Although these relationships are descriptive, they suggest that the interest group system has pre-mobilization biases. Organizations that seek to represent a disengaged group like community college students will face a lot more trouble than organizations that seek to represent hospital administrators, even given the same resources. The hospital administrators are much more engaged in civic and political life, and it will help to encourage their interest group organizing. Advocacy groups represent many different public constituencies, but not equally: the politically engaged groups in the American electorate also benefit most from interest group representation.

Government Action and Interest Mobilization

Interest group mobilization can be stimulated by government action. Interest groups organize in order to lobby government officials and influence public policy. The issues that government chooses to address determine what is at stake in these conflicts. The changing capacity of government affects how much economic and social groups can expect to gain or lose from organizing to influence its actions. Economic industries and public constituencies provide the resources that determine the supply side of interest group organizing, but government determines the demand side—why forming interest groups might be necessary or advantageous.

Government programs often stimulate interest groups to support the continuation or expansion of existing policies. After government enacted Social Security and Medicare, groups like the AARP mobilized in Washington and became a prominent force in national politics.[34] After the G.I. Bill enabled World War II veterans to obtain a college education, those soldiers became more active in political life and helped to create supportive interest groups.[35]

Government also acts directly as a patron for a portion of the interest group community, either by providing government contracts or by empowering groups to serve official roles in policymaking and administration.[36] The AARP and the American Legion have both helped with policy implementation and public education, for example, using government support.

State and local governments are also a large and growing share of the interest group community. These tend to be mobilized directly by government policy, often because lower-level governments face mandates from the federal level or are the designated implementers of federal policy. A sizeable share of state budgets also now comes initially from the federal government and may be passed on to local governments. When the national government mandates that metropolitan areas create regional transportation planning organizations, for example, it is directly creating a new category of interest groups. These groups then organize to gain more support from Washington.

Recent political science research has attempted to demonstrate that the choices government officials make about which issues they want to address also affects interest group mobilization by every kind of economic, social, and government constituency. Most of the new studies rely on lobbying registration data from Congress, which requires organizations to report their lobbying activities if they devote considerable time to directly conveying their views to policymakers.

When registering, interest groups are required to check off the issue areas where they are active. Figure 1.6 reports the most common issue areas associated with lobbying activity.[37] The top issue areas are taxes and health care, with a substantial drop off in lobbying after the first few areas. The form includes 56 issue areas; most are associated with a much smaller number of interest groups registered to lobby than the ten issues listed here. Below the 24th most popular issue area, fewer than 100 interest groups are involved in an average six-month period. Beyond the 39th most popular issue area, fewer than 50 groups participate. The least popular issue area (minting and money) averaged only 3.6 participating organizations.

This distribution is usually taken as evidence that interest group lobbying is highly concentrated in a few areas. Yet many of the categories on the list are logically subsets of a larger sector (such as the Medicare category, one aspect of health policy). In addition, some of the names used on the registration forms are

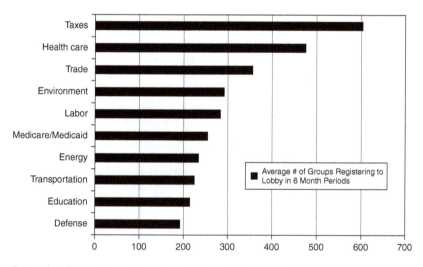

Figure 1.6 Top Issue Areas for Interest Group Lobbying

The figure illustrates the average number of groups registering to lobby on each issue area per six-month period from 1996 to 2003. The data are from Baumgartner et al., "Congressional and Presidential Effects on the Demand for Lobbying," Table 2.

industries rather than policy areas, such as "food industry" and "computer industry." It is unclear how the Office of Public Records even arrived at these categories. Nevertheless, there is some initial evidence of cross-over between the highly represented business industries in Figure 1.3 and the most common issue areas associated with lobbying in Figure 1.6: health, energy, defense, and transportation are frequent concerns of lobbyists and the relevant industries are all highly mobilized to participate.

The primary finding of recent studies using lobbying registration data is that when government is active in an issue area, it draws more interest groups to lobby on that issue. Lobbying is concentrated in the same issue areas that are consistently at the heart of the congressional agenda (usually measured by assessing the topics of congressional hearings). Changes in the congressional agenda are also a better predictor of reported lobbying activity than the number of firms active in each area of the economy.[38]

A few other findings from the literature also merit mentioning. Government spending increases lobbying in related areas but to a more limited extent than government regulations.[39] When a president focuses on an issue area of traditional executive branch concern (such as foreign relations and defense) in his State of the Union address, fewer interest organizations lobby Congress in that issue area (possibly because they begin to lobby the executive branch).[40] State-level lobbying is also more common in issue areas that generate attention in state legislatures. The legislative agenda (in this case, the number of bills considered in each issue area) is a strong predictor of the types of organizations that lobby state government, in addition to the share of the economy dedicated to each industry.[41] More interest groups also report lobbying on legislation that makes it further through Congress. In addition to more lobbying associated with issue areas on the congressional agenda, there is also more lobbying directly related to the minority of bills that make it out of committee or through the House or Senate.[42]

The extensive evidence scholars have collected demonstrating that lobbying follows the government agenda is sometimes seen as support for the idea that the "demand side" of lobbying is more important than the "supply side." The evidence, which is largely based on lobbying registrations in Congress, is not sufficient to prove this case. The relationships between reported lobbying and congressional activity could be a function of the data gathering process; firms register if they spend resources directly lobbying legislators. A recent analysis of a sample of policy advocates in Washington finds that only 47.7% reported lobbying activity; in other words, half of the people most observers would consider lobbyists fail to register. Advocates that previously worked in Congress were much more likely to register than those who worked in the executive branch.[43] Lobbying data cover lobbying attempts, rather than mobilization or success at influencing policy. Some interest groups stay mobilized without lobbying. Others pay firms to lobby on their behalf to influence small provisions of legislation without having much chance to affect broader policy development.

Attempts to compare supply- and demand-side factors tend to focus on business organizations and assume a fairly direct path. Most use the number of firms in an industry or the economic weight of a sector to predict lobbying. This does not assess the influence of any of the other factors found important in the business mobilization literature and entirely excludes most of the factors that influence public constituency mobilization. The "demand for lobbying" models cannot rule out the possibility that group mobilization initially caused government to focus on new issues. Most of the models simply assume that government attention comes before mobilization, and none go back far enough to observe the dynamics that led to the expansion of the government agenda in the 1960s and 1970s. Furthermore, most of the studies look at lobbying registrations within issue area categories. Yet a small number of organizations account for the bulk of opportunities to influence policymaking in each issue area. There may be one prominent organization speaking for each constituency; only a small subset of lobbying registrations may be attached to organizations with real involvement in decision-making.

State-Level Interest Mobilization

Social and economic groups also mobilize interest organizations to lobby state government. Just as Washington has seen an explosion of interest group activity since the 1960s, state capitals have also seen increasing interest group activity. Figure 1.7 uses data from state lobbying registration to analyze the growth of interest groups in the American states.[44] The categories are not identical to those used in the federal data in Figure 1.1, but I combined state interest groups into four large categories to enable comparison: business interests, advocacy organizations, governmental interests, and other groups.

The end of the data series is less recent than for the federal data, but some important trends are evident. Like at the national level, the total number of interest groups is growing over time. The average grew from 338 per state in 1980 to 692 per state in 1997. Also similar to national trends, the advocacy and government sectors are growing at high rates. Unlike at the national level, however, state business mobilization continues to grow just as quickly and business maintains a much larger share of the interest group community (69%) than at the federal level.

These categories miss important changes within the business and advocacy sectors as well as tremendous variation across states. Disaggregating the data shows that business interest group growth has been concentrated in the communications, manufacturing, health, legal, and banking industries. Advocacy organization growth has been most pronounced among groups promoting social welfare and good government. Interest groups in both the business and advocacy sectors are now much less likely to be membership organizations; many more are staff-led institutions.[45] Missouri and Illinois saw the largest increases in organizational mobilization in the 1980s and 1990s.

The primary theory used to analyze state interest group mobilization is based on the population ecology framework. Virginia Gray and David Lowery argue that

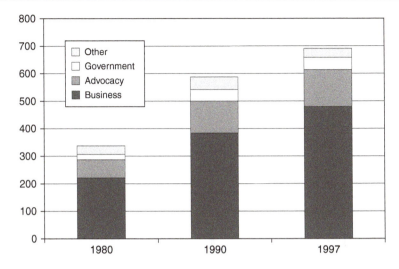

Figure 1.7 Distributions of the Average Number of Interest Groups in American States by Category and Year

The figure reports the total number of lobbying organizations in each category in each year divided by the number of states where lobbying data was available (44 in 1980 and 50 in the other two years). The data are from Virginia Gray and David Lowery, "The Institutionalization of State Communities of Organized Interests," *Political Research Quarterly* 54 (2): 265–84, Table 1. I combined all for-profit categories except utilities (business), intergovernmental and police/fire (government), and all other not-for-profit (advocacy).

the number of interest groups in each category is dependent on the resources available for organizing (such as membership and financial backing) and the amount of government services and regulations on offer. They analogize the resources to "the area" that animal species have to roam and the government activity to "the energy" available for the animals to compete over.[46] Their view is that considering mobilization only from the point of view of the economic industry or social group misses half of the story: the availability of government policies stimulates the need for lobbying government, just as the energy in an ecosystem increases the population of species. Studies do indeed find relationships among the issues addressed in national and state policymaking and the mobilization of state-level interest groups.[47] Gray and Lowery also find that the composition of the interest group community changes with additional mobilization; institutions come to dominate as the density of groups grows.

Social, Economic, and Political Mobilization

American interest groups can arise from the economy, society, or government. Many different social groups, economic industries, occupations, and governments have mobilized interest groups to influence national policymaking. Both the supply of public constituencies, institutions, and businesses as well as the demand for addressing policy issues influence the size of the interest group community and its composition.

The interest group community has grown dramatically since the 1970s, especially with groups representing governments and public concerns. The corporate sector is still the largest, but its share is declining at the federal level. Yet the population dynamics only tell a small part of the story. Scholars also look at the issue areas where interest groups lobby and the resources they mobilize in Washington. A small subset of interest groups accounts for the bulk of opportunities to play an important role in public debate and policymaking. Some types of economic industries and social groups consistently generate and sustain more prominent and involved interest groups.

Unfortunately, in considering both business and social group mobilization, scholars tend to begin with a poor model of mobilization based on collective action: the Olson critique of pluralism.[48] Neither group size nor industry concentration turned out to be consistently important factors in driving interest group mobilization. Research on both business and social group mobilization has nonetheless advanced, leading to increased knowledge about the factors that govern interest group formation and maintenance.

The latest turn in the mobilization literature toward the influence of government agendas has led to important insights. Yet the perspective that this demand-side literature offers may be replicating the worst aspects of the theory that collective action models were designed to remedy (known as pluralism) without gaining from its strengths. Positing that when government addresses an issue area, interest groups will appear on the scene to fight it out in that issue area seems curiously close to the initial view (attributed to pluralism) that interest group mobilization was automatic. The benefits of the pluralism perspective were that it concentrated attention on the factors that led some groups to mobilize more extensively than others, but this seems to be of less concern in recent research. By moving to lobbying registration as an outcome, scholars prize evidence of any group lobbying activity, rather than differences in the potential influence of different sectors of the society and economy.

Fortunately, the distinct literatures on business mobilization and social group mobilization already offer reasonable models of what parts of the economy and society are likely to be best represented. Two features of these literatures are especially important. First, they tend not to focus on the same factors promoting mobilization; social group and corporate mobilization are not properly equated. Public interest groups are not best viewed as another "industry" competing with the others. Research that treats all interest groups as responding similarly to the same dynamics is at best incomplete. Second, both literatures already incorporate the back-and-forth process by which government action stimulates mobilization and then interest groups mobilize for more government action. Research on business political participation points to the importance of industry regulation and government sales. Public mobilization research includes analysis of how single-issue groups develop out of policy debates and how constituencies come to feel efficacious as government responds to their concerns. In other words, the demand side of lobbying is already productively incorporated into these research programs. The largest hole in the mobilization literature concerns government mobilization; we have some understanding of why subnational governments have become more numerous and active as interest groups, but the process does not seem to match either corporate or social group mobilization.[49]

As the interest group population has expanded, it has become tempting to treat it as an amorphous mob of policy demanders responding to the growth of government. Scholars should not give in to this temptation because it misses the bulk of the story. Corporations, governments, and public groups mobilize in response to different dynamics. The factors that govern their relative mobilization are also somewhat distinct. In all cases, having an organization present in Washington is only the first step in the very long process of becoming a major player with the capacity to influence policy. It is time we move beyond models of interest group populations and toward models of who gets what, when, and how. Understanding the relative mobilization of different economic sectors, social groups, and governments is certainly an important part of the answer.

Notes

1 Arthur F. Bentley, *The Process of Government: A Study of Social Pressures* (Evanston, IL: Principia Press, 1935); David B. Truman, *The Governmental Process: Political Interests and Public Opinion* (New York: Knopf, 1951).

2 Truman, *The Governmental Process;* Matt Grossmann, "American Pluralism, Interest Group Liberalism, and Neopluralism," in *Guide to Interest Groups and Lobbying in the United States,* eds. Burdett A. Loomis, Peter L. Francia, and Dara Z. Strolovitch (Washington, DC: CQ Press, 2011).

3 Robert A. Dahl, *Who Governs? Democracy and Power in an American City* (New Haven: Yale University Press, 1961); Andrew S. McFarland, *Neopluralism: The Evolution of Political Process Theory* (Lawrence: University of Kansas Press, 2004); Grossmann, "American Pluralism." Dahl focuses on an initiative in urban redevelopment by the mayor of New Haven, Connecticut, arguing that he gained the acquiescence of business leaders rather than waiting for business mobilization. Dahl also emphasized the low level of involvement by most citizens of the city, famously observing that for most people, "politics is a sideshow in the great circus of life."

4 E.E. Schattschneider, *The Semisovereign People: A Realists View at Democracy in America* (New York: Holt, Rinehart, and Winston, 1960); Robert H. Salisbury, *Interests and Institutions: Substance and Structure in American Politics* (Pittsburgh: University of Pittsburgh Press, 1992).

5 Schattschneider, *The Semisovereign People.*

6 Peter Bachrach and Morton Baratz, "Two Faces of Power," *American Political Science Review* 56, no. 4 (1962): 947–52; John Gaventa, *Power and Powerlessness: Quiescence and Rebellion in an Appalachian Valley* (Urbana: University of Illinois Press, 1980).

7 Mancur Olson, *The Logic of Collective Action: Public Goods and the Theory of Groups,* 2nd ed. (Cambridge, MA: Harvard University Press, 1971).

8 Jack L. Walker, *Mobilizing Interest Groups in America: Patrons, Professions, and Social Movements* (Ann Arbor: University of Michigan Press, 1991); Virginia Gray and David Lowery, *The Population Ecology of Interest Representation: Lobbying Communities in the American States* (Ann Arbor: University of Michigan Press, 2000).

9   Walker, *Mobilizing Interest Groups in America.*

10   Salisbury, *Interests and Institutions.*

11   This usually takes the label of "neopluralism." David Lowery and Virginia Gray, "A Neopluralist Perspective on Research on Organized Interests," *Political Research Quarterly* 57, no. 1 (2004): 164-75; Andrew McFarland, *Neopluralism: The Evolution of Political Process Theory* (Lawrence, KS: University Press of Kansas, 2004); Grossmann, *The Not-So-Special Interests.*

12   Gray and Lowery, *The Population Ecology of Interest Representation.*

13   Jeffrey M. Berry, *The New Liberalism: The Rising Power of Citizen Groups* (Washington, DC: Brookings Institution Press, 1999).

14   Salisbury, *Interests and Institutions;* Kay Lehman Schlozman and John T. Tierney, *Organized Interests and American Democracy* (New York: Harper and Row, 1986); Frank R. Baumgartner and Beth L. Leech, *Basic Interests: The Importance of Groups in Politics and Political Science* (Princeton, NJ: Princeton University Press, 1998).

15   Baumgartner and Leech, *Basic Interests.*

16   Kay Lehman Schlozman, Sidney Verba, and Henry E. Brady, *The Unheavenly Chorus: Unequal Political Voice and the Broken Promise of American Democracy* (Princeton, NJ: Princeton University Press, 2012), Table 12.2.

17   Frank R. Baumgartner and Beth L. Leech, "Interest Niches and Policy Bandwagons: Patterns of Interest Group Involvement in National Politics," *Journal of Politics* 63, no. 4 (2001): 1191–213.

18   Jeffrey M. Berry and Clyde Wilcox, *The Interest Group Society,* 5th ed. (New York: Pearson, 2009).

19   Walker, *Mobilizing Interest Groups in America.*

20   Anne Marie Cammisa, *Governments as Interest Groups: Intergovernmental Lobbying and the Federal System* (Westport, CT: Praeger, 1995).

21   Gray and Lowery, *The Population Ecology of Interest Representation;* Berry and Wilcox, *The Interest Group Society;* Walker, *Mobilizing Interest Groups in America.*

22   Schlozman, Verba, and Brady, *The Unheavenly Chorus.*

23   Beth L. Leech, Frank R. Baumgartner, Timothy M. La Pira, and Nicholas A. Semanko, "Drawing Lobbyists to Washington: Government Activity and the Demand for Advocacy," *Political Research Quarterly* 58, no. 1 (2005): 19–30.

24   Baumgartner and Leech, "Interest Niches and Policy Bandwagons."

25   Matt Grossmann, *The Not-So-Special Interests: Interest Groups, Public Representation, and American Governance* (Stanford, CA: Stanford University Press, 2012). The book does not cover businesses or governments but the same concentration of opportunities for participation also likely appears among these sectors of interest groups. See Schlozman, Verba, and Brady, *The Unheavenly Chorus;* Cammisa, *Governments as Interest Groups.*

26   Grossmann, *The Not-So-Special Interests.* The book only addresses a subset of interest groups, those that claim to represent public interests or concerns. It does not include an analysis of business policy offices or trade associations. Some descriptions used here are from the book.

27   Grossmann, *The Not-So-Special Interests.*

28   The data is from the Center for Responsive Politics and is available at opensecrets.org.

29   The data are from Henry E. Brady, Lee Drutman, Kay Lehman Schlozman, and Sidney Verba, "Corporate Lobbying Activities in American Politics" (paper presented at the Annual Meeting of the American Political Science Association, Chicago, August 2007).

30   Olson, *The Logic of Collective Action.* Olson's collective action model predicted that small groups would find it easier to organize because no individual member would have an incentive to free ride, gaining public goods by relying on the activities of others.

31   Grossmann, *The Not-So-Special Interests.*

32   Grossmann, *The Not-So-Special Interests.*

33   Olson, *The Logic of Collective Action.*

34 Andrea Louise Campbell, *How Policies Make Citizens: Senior Political Activism and the American Welfare State* (Princeton, NJ: Princeton University Press, 2005).
35 Suzanne Mettler, *Soldiers to Citizens: The G.I. Bill and the Making of the Greatest Generation* (New York: Oxford University Press, 2005).
36 Jack L. Walker, *Mobilizing Interest Groups in America.*
37 These data are from Frank R. Baumgartner, Heather A. Larsen-Price, Beth L. Leech, and Paul Rutledge, "Congressional and Presidential Effects on the Demand for Lobbying," *Political Research Quarterly* 64, no, 1 (2011): 3–16, Table 2.
38 Leech et al., "Drawing Lobbyists to Washington."
39 Baumgartner et al., "Congressional and Presidential Effects on the Demand for Lobbying;" Leech et al., "Drawing Lobbyists to Washington."
40 Baumgartner et al., "Congressional and Presidential Effects on the Demand for Lobbying."
41 Virginia Gray, David Lowery, Matthew Fellowes, and Jennifer L. Anderson, "Issue Agendas and Interest Advocacy: Understanding the Demand Side of Lobbying," *American Politics Research* 33, no. 3 (2005): 404–34.
42 Matt Grossmann and Kurt Pyle, "Lobbying and Congressional Bill Advancement," *Interest Groups & Advocacy* 2, no, 1 (2013): 91–111.
43 Timothy M. LaPira and Herschel F. Thomas III, "Just How Many Newt Gingrich's Are There on K Street? Estimating the True Size and Shape of Washington's Revolving Door," presented at the Midwest Political Science Association Annual Meeting, Chicago, 2013. The estimates are based on a sample of 285 professional advocates in the lobbyists.info database.
44 The data are from Virginia Gray and David Lowery, "The Institutionalization of State Communities of Organized Interests," *Political Research Quarterly* 54, no. 2 (2001): 265–84, Table 1. I combined all for-profit categories except utilities (business), intergovernmental and police/fire (government), and all other not-for-profit (advocacy).
45 Gray and Lowery, "The Institutionalization of State Communities of Organized Interests," Figure 3. Business groups are less likely to have membership.
46 Gray and Lowery, *The Population Ecology of Interest Representation.*
47 Frank R. Baumgartner, Virginia Gray, and David Lowery, "Federal Policy Activity and the Mobilization of State Lobbying Organizations," *Political Research Quarterly* 62, no. 3 (2009): 552–67.
48 Olson, *The Logic of Collective Action.* Olson's work served as the basis for the market concentration hypothesis used in the business mobilization literature, the most commonly studied factor but far from the most consistently important. It also encouraged the focus on group size and, to a lesser extent, socio-economic status as the determinants of social group mobilization; these factors again turn out to be inconsistently important.
49 Lowery et al., "Explaining the Anomalous Growth of Public Sector Lobbying in the American States," attribute the growth of government lobbying in state legislatures in part to the increasing dominance of the Republican Party in state government. It is possible that Republican gains in Congress have also stimulated state and local government lobbying at the national level.

Chapter 2

How Membership Associations Change the Balance of Representation in Washington (and How They Don't)

Kay Lehman Schlozman and Philip Edward Jones

Americans are often characterized as "a nation of joiners." But Americans do not just come together in collective enterprises that range from holding bake sales to support the local schools to distributing groceries at the food pantry to playing softball; they also join together to further their shared political goals. In fact, according to a once-dominant analysis of American politics, interest group pluralism, competition among such interest groups for policy influence is central to understanding public outcomes. For several good reasons, that theory is now discredited. Among them, not all of the organizations that advocate on behalf of Americans' shared political concerns are even groups, much less groups of individuals. For that reason, when referring to the organizations that get involved in politics, political scientists tend to use locutions like "advocacy organizations" or "organized interests" that encompass such politically active entities as ExxonMobil Corporation, the Children's Hospital of Philadelphia, or the City of Los Angeles.

In this chapter, we entertain a counterfactual, and ask what the pressure system would look like if it were composed only of "interest groups" or voluntary associations that have individuals as members.[1] Specifically, we consider how their presence expands the kinds of interests represented in Washington politics and how their internal dynamics and the level of their resources affect the kinds of voices that are heard in politics. What we find is not a simple story: on one hand, membership associations of individuals broaden the set of people and concerns that have political representation; on the other, a closer look at whose interests they represent, the experiences of their members, and the personpower and dollars they mobilize makes clear the limitations of that broadening.

To investigate these matters we use data from two national surveys of individuals: the Tracking Survey conducted by the Pew Internet and American Life Project in August 2008, and, because it contains a set of measures about individuals' experiences in membership associations that have not since been replicated, the 1990 Citizen Participation Study.

In addition, we use the Washington Representatives Study, an extensive data archive containing information about the characteristics, organizational histories, and political activities of organizations involved in national politics including the kinds of interests they represent and the nature of their members, if any. This data base covers the more than 27,000 organizations listed in the 1981, 1991, 2001, or 2006 *Washington Representatives* directory as having a presence in national politics—either by maintaining an office in the capital or by hiring Washington-based consultants or counsel to manage their government relations activities. A crucial part of the construction of the Washington Representatives data base was to place each organization into one or more of 96 categories designed to capture the nature of the interest being represented—business, an occupation, a foreign government, a group of universities, a religious or ethnic group, a conservative think tank, and so on—as well as something about its organizational structure. In contrast to most studies of organized interests that rely on highly aggregated categories, the number of categories was deliberately proliferated in order to capture fine distinctions.[2] Together, these data sets allow us to explore the type of organizations active in politics and the interests on behalf of which they advocate.

Putting Interest Groups at the Center: Interest Group Pluralism

As a point of departure for understanding the place of interest groups within the politics of organizational advocacy, we consider the postulates of interest group pluralism, an approach associated with Arthur Bentley and David Truman. They placed interest groups—that is, organizations with individuals as members—at the center of policy making and emphasized the low barriers to entry to the organized interest system and its fluid nature.[3] Thus, interest groups supposedly emerge more or less automatically when individuals whose interests are affected respond to disturbances in the political environment. Interest groups regularly enter and leave the pressure system as dictated by their concerns about the particular issues at stake in politics at any given time. Because of the ease of entry and exit from pressure politics, the absence of advocacy for a particular point of view in a political controversy was sometimes interpreted as an indication of a corresponding absence of political concern on the part of those who might be expected to articulate a collective opinion on a policy matter—but, in fact, do not.

These axioms have been criticized from numerous directions. For one thing, policy outcomes are shaped by a host of factors other than the conflicting preferences of contending interest groups—ranging from public opinion to the media to the ideological preferences and political ambitions of policymakers—and government hardly functions in the role of passive referee that it was assigned by interest group pluralists.

For another, a number of observers, most notably E. E. Schattschneider and Mancur Olson, argue that the barriers to entry to the political fray are higher than would be expected on the basis of interest group pluralist analysis. Schattschneider argued that two kinds of interests—those of broad publics seeking public goods and those who lack political and economic resources—are less likely to achieve organized representation.[4] In an influential formal analysis, Mancur Olson reached through logical deduction the same conclusion about advocacy on behalf of public interests that Schattschneider had reached by empirical observation. Olson pointed out that large, diffuse groups lacking the capacity to coerce cooperation or to provide selective benefits often face severe collective action problems that prevent them from organizing on behalf of their joint political concerns.[5] Thus, organizations do not emerge automatically to advocate on behalf of groups of people who might be expected to have joint interests. The corollary of this observation is that the absence of group activity is not necessarily prima facie evidence of satisfaction with the policy status quo but may reflect the barriers, including a deficit of resources, to interest group formation and political activity.

A related but sometimes overlooked critique of interest group pluralism is that many people are not even affiliated with politically active organizations. Although politically involved organizations are extremely numerous, empirical studies of individual activity in politics make clear that affiliation with and activity in organizations that take stands in politics are anything but universal. Table 2.1 presents data from a 2008 survey conducted by the Pew Internet and American Life Project about a number of forms of political participation—individual and collective, formal and informal. Only 15 percent of respondents indicated that, in the past 12 months, they had been an active member of any group that tries to influence public policy or government, not including a political party. It is well known that voting is the only political activity in which a majority of Americans engage. Still, the proportion of those active in a politically active group is lower than the proportion who indicated having contacted a national, state, or local official about an issue; having worked with fellow citizens to solve a problem in their communities; having attended a political meeting on local, town, or school affairs; or, even, having contributed money to a political candidate or party, or any other political organization or cause.[6]

Table 2.1 Participation in Various Forms of Political Activity

	Percent Active
Registered to vote	79.7
Worked for a political party or candidate	8.1
Made a political contribution	18.3
Contacted a government official	29.7
Worked with others to solve a community problem	28.2
Attended a local meeting	24.2
Attended a protest	3.7
Active in a group that takes stands in politics	15.2
N	2,250

Source: Pew Internet and American Life Project (August 2008)

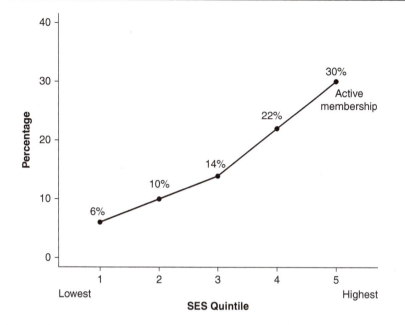

Figure 2.1 Active Membership in a Political Group and Socio-economic Status

Source: Pew Internet and American Life Survey (2012)

Moreover, as is well known, active members of voluntary associations are not a random sample of citizens: they are more likely to be well-educated and afflu- ent. Figure 2.1 divides respondents into five equal groups or quintiles based on a combined measure of their education and income—or what is often called "socio- economic status" (SES)—and shows that those active in voluntary associations are drawn disproportionately from the ranks of those with high levels of education and income.[7] Just 6 percent of those in the lowest fifth of the SES distribution, as opposed to 30 percent of those in the highest fifth, reported being active in a voluntary association. That is, as education and income increase, so does active or- ganizational membership—with the result that membership associations mobilize an unrepresentative group into politics.

Organizational Membership Status and Representation in Washington

One further objection to the assumptions of interest group pluralism is that, to an extent that is perhaps surprising, the pressure system is not composed solely or even largely of membership associations of individuals. The thousands of organizations in the pressure community are not all groups—especially, groups of individuals. In fact, of the 13,786 organizations listed in the 2006 Washington Representatives Directory, only 1,711 were membership associations of individuals.

In addition to organizations of individuals, several other kinds of organizations get involved in politics. Robert Salisbury pointed to the significance for interest representation of a large group of for-profit and not-for-profit economic entities—for example, corporations, universities, hospitals, and museums—which, in a specialized use of the term, he called "institutions."[8] Such institutions—which do not have members in the traditional sense—not only are active in politics on their own but come together in organizations like trade associations that have institutions as members. In addition, an important set of organizations that are active in Washington politics are subnational governments: state and local governments and their agencies acting on their own or in consortia of governments. For each of these four organizational membership statuses—associations of individuals, associations of institutions, institutions, and state or local governments—Table 2.2 presents a few examples of organized interests active in politics. With a few exceptions like the American Legion (a veterans' organization) and the Communications Workers of America (which organizes workers in such industries as telecommunications, broadcasting, and cable TV), most of these organizations have names that are recognizable or that give clues to their nature.

A number of the major categories of organized interests are defined by a particular membership status. For example, corporations like Microsoft are institutions. The various kinds of organizations that represent people on the basis of how they make a living—among them, most notably, unions and professional associations—are membership associations of individuals.

Table 2.2 Washington Organizations with Different Forms of Membership Status: A Few Examples

Associations of Individuals

American Legion
American Medical Association
Communications Workers of America

Associations of Institutions

American Hospital Association
National Automobile Dealers Association
United States Chamber of Commerce

Institutions

Metropolitan Museum of Art
Microsoft Corporation
University of Michigan

State and Local Governments

City of Las Vegas, Nevada
Port Authority of New York and New Jersey
State of South Carolina

In contrast, there is a mix of membership statuses in the organizations within the several categories of what are sometimes called "citizen groups": identity groups, organizations representing racial, ethnic, or religious groups, the elderly, women, or LGBT sexual orientation; public interest groups, which seek broadly shared interests or such public goods as wilderness preservation, safe consumer products, safe streets, gun rights, or gun control; and organizations for social welfare and the poor.[9]

To illustrate this blend of organizational membership statuses for these three kinds of citizen groups, Table 2.3 gives, for each of these three categories of citizen groups, an example of a membership association of individuals, a membership association of institutions, and an institution. Consider, for example, the three organizations listed for identity groups. These organizations have complementary goals and use many of the same tactics; yet they are organized differently. The League of United Latin American Citizens, which seeks to "advance the economic condition, educational attainment, political influence, housing, health and civil rights of the Hispanic population of the United States," is a voluntary association with individuals as members. The Leadership Conference on Civil and Human Rights, the umbrella organization bringing together civil and human rights organizations in a "coalition charged by its diverse membership of more than 200 national organizations to promote and protect the civil and human rights of all persons in the United States," has organizations as members. The National Women's Law Center is a staff-driven institution, organized as a public interest law firm and think tank, which focuses on "getting new laws on the books and enforced, litigating groundbreaking cases all the way to the Supreme Court, and educating the public about ways to make laws and public policies work for women and their families."[10]

With respect to the balance among these different organizational forms, the set of organizations that represent people on the basis of an identity such as race, nationality, or gender tilts toward membership associations of individuals. Even so, only 42 percent of identity organizations are membership associations

Table 2.3 Examples of Citizen Groups with Different Forms of Membership Status

	Associations of Individuals	Associations of Institutions	Institutions
Identity Groups[a]	League of United Latin American Citizens	Leadership Conference on Civil and Human Rights	National Women's Law Center
Social Welfare or Poor	Volunteers of America	Coalition on Human Needs	Center on Budget and Policy Priorities
Public Interest Groups	American Civil Liberties Union	Endangered Species Coalition	Accuracy in Academia

a   Includes associations representing racial, ethnic, or religious groups, elderly, women, or LGBT

Table 2.4 Membership Status of Washington Organizations[a]

Associations of individuals	12.7%
Associations of institutions	14.8
Institutions[b]	54.0
State and Local Governments[c]	13.4
Mixed/Other	5.0
	99.9%
	13,455

Source: *Washington Representatives Study* (2006)

a   Includes all organizations listed in the 2006 *Washington Representatives* directory
b   For example, corporations, universities, or hospitals
c   Includes foreign as well as domestic governments and associations of governments

of individuals, compared to the 23 percent that are institutions. Among social welfare organizations and organizations for the poor, the modal organization is an institution like the Center on Budget and Policy Priorities—a think tank that does research and analysis with respect to such issues as the impact of the federal budget on low-income Americans—rather than a membership association of individuals. Among social welfare organizations and organizations for the poor, institutions outweigh the membership associations of individuals 34 percent to 21 percent.[11] Among the public interest groups that advocate for liberal and conservative public goods like environmental preservation, low taxes, clean government, and national security, there is parity between these types: 35 percent are institutions, and 35 percent are membership associations of individuals.

When we consider all the organizations listed in the *Washington Representatives* directory for 2006 in Table 2.4, it turns out that only a small fraction, about 13 percent, of the organizations in the directory were associations of individuals; about 15 percent were associations of institutions such as trade and other business associations; and fully two-thirds were governments (13 percent) or institutions like corporations, hospitals, or universities (54 percent). To repeat, under a third of the organizations listed were membership associations of any kind, and only about one in eight was a classic membership association composed of individual members.

What Kinds of Interests Are Represented by Membership Associations of Individuals?

Although membership associations of individuals constitute only a very small share of the organizations active in Washington, they make an important contribution to broadening the set of interests represented by advocacy organizations. In the aggregate, the set of organized interests that get involved in national politics is organized principally around economic matters. Among organized interests in the economic domain, the representation of business is dominant. Moreover, a number of other kinds of organizations—in particular, state and local governments in the United States and a variety of kinds of foreign interests—that are less often featured in discussions of Washington pressure politics also have a substantial organizational presence. In contrast, the economically disadvantaged are underrepresented in pressure politics. In addition, organizations representing broad public interests (whether of the right or the left) and identity groups are relatively rare—each accounting for 4 percent of the organizations active in Washington in 2006.[12]

The profile is quite different when we consider membership associations of individuals only. Most fundamentally, although a majority of membership associations of individuals bring together members on the basis of their relationship to the economy, business interests weigh much less heavily among membership associations of individuals than they do in the pressure community in the aggregate. In 2006, 52 percent of all organizations involved in Washington politics—including 75 percent of institutions, 79 percent of all membership associations of institutions, but only 5 percent of membership associations of individuals—represented business.[13]

If not business interests, then what kinds of interests are represented by membership associations of individuals? Table 2.5 shows the distribution for 2006. Just over half, 53 percent, represent members on the basis of the way they make a living. The organizations in the other portion are a mix in terms of the causes on behalf of which they advocate. The public interest groups that advocate on behalf of such public goods as auto safety, religious freedom, electronic privacy, or an end to capital punishment and the identity groups that represent people on the basis of common racial, ethnic, or religious background, or of sexual orientation as well as women and the elderly together account for roughly a quarter of the membership associations of individuals and thus figure considerably more importantly among such associations than they do within the pressure community as a whole. In short, the relatively small number of membership associations of individuals add significantly to the diversity of interests represented in Washington politics.

Closer inspection makes clear, however, that there are important limits to that diversity. Four kinds of organizations represent people on the basis of their occupation: occupational associations; unions; military associations comprising current members of the military, reservists, and veterans; and farm groups. On balance, they tilt strongly in the direction of providing representation to those whose occupations demand high levels of formal education and skill. Traditionally, unions organize blue-collar workers, including unskilled ones. As is well known, however, rates of union membership, which are currently much higher for workers in the public than the private sector, have plunged over the last generation. Interestingly, because public-sector professional workers like teachers are relatively likely to be unionized, professionals have, overall, higher rates of union membership than do service, sales, or production workers.

There are several kinds of occupational associations of which a substantial majority, 70 percent, bring together people in managerial or professional occupations—for example, criminal defense lawyers, architects, cell

Table 2.5 Interests Represented by Organizations in Washington Politics[a]

	Membership Assns of Individuals	All Organizations
Corporations[b]		36.0%
Trade and other business assns		10.6
Occupational Associations	40.6%	5.1
Unions	5.9	.8
Education	2.6	5.4
Military Associations[c]	2.7	.4
Farm Groups	2.8	1.0
Social Welfare or Poor	1.6	.9
Disabled or Health Advocacy[d]	3.6	1.4
Public Interest Groups	11.7	4.1
Identity Groups[e]	12.9	3.8
State and local governments		11.8
Other	15.5	18.6
Total	99.9%	99.9%
N	1,711	13,786

Source: *Washington Representatives Study* (2006)

a   Distribution of membership associations of individuals and all organizations listed in the 2006 *Washington Representatives* directory

b   Includes U.S. corporations, U.S. subsidiaries of foreign corporations, and for-profit firms of professionals such as law and consulting firms

c   Includes associations of current members of the military, reservists, and veterans

d   Includes associations that engage in advocacy and research regarding disability, in general, as well as particular illnesses or kinds of disability

e   Includes associations representing racial, ethnic, or religious groups, elderly, women, or LGBT

biologists, and human resource managers.[14] Even the associations that enroll non-professional and non-managerial workers tend to represent those in occupations that demand relatively high levels of skill, pay, such as realtors, master printers, meeting planners, travel agents, medical sonographers, and pilots. What this means is that, unless they are union members, those who make their living as office receptionists, Wal-Mart associates, parking lot attendants, bellhops, telemarketers, laundry workers, van drivers, and bartenders have no occupational associations at all to represent their interests in Washington. In fact, other than unions, not a single occupational organization represents the shared concerns of those whose work is unskilled.

The representation of the economic interests of those who are not in the work force is very uneven. Representing the retired are numerous organizations of the elderly—one of which, AARP, has, according to its website, 37 million members. There are also organizations that engage in advocacy and research regarding disability, in general, as well as particular illnesses or kinds of disability. In contrast, there are no membership associations at all that bring together people who are out of the work force because they are unemployed or because they are at home full time caring for children, the infirm, or the elderly. Furthermore, a small number of membership associations of individuals advocate for the poor; however, there is not a single organization that brings together recipients of means-tested government benefits such as Medicaid or SNAP (formerly food stamps) acting on their own behalf. Similarly, there are no organizations that bring together parents of children in Headstart programs, criminal defendants awaiting trial, or workers whose company pensions are in jeopardy. Clearly, then, the voluntary associations of individuals that represent members' economic concerns differ from other kinds of organized interests in that they do not give overwhelming representation to business organizations. Still, the extent to which they represent those further down the economic ladder is quite limited.

In contrast, the public interest groups and identity groups among membership associations of individuals broaden the set of issues, perspectives, and publics that have voice in American politics. Still, scholars point to the extent to which they represent the priorities and preferences of the relatively advantaged. A number of observers—in particular, Theda Skocpol—have commented upon the extent to which increasing numbers of such membership organizations are professionally managed national organizations, requiring little of their members other than financial support and drawing their members very disproportionately from among the well-educated.[15] In a pressure system dominated by economic organizations, most of them representing the interests of economic haves, such checkbook organizations clearly broaden the set of interests represented, bringing into the political conversation points of view that might otherwise go unvoiced. Nevertheless, more often than not, such citizen groups reinforce the class bias in organized political voice.[16] Furthermore, Dara Strolovitch's research on the organizations that advocate on behalf of those who are disadvantaged on the basis of a shared identity—for example, race or ethnicity, gender, sexual orientation—makes clear that such organizations are more vigorous in their efforts to represent the interests of the more advantaged subgroups, as opposed to the less advantaged subgroups, within their differentiated constituencies.[17]

Inside Membership Associations: Who Is Active? Who Gets Mobilized? Who Feels Represented?

We can gain additional perspective on who is being represented in pressure politics by looking not just at the names and purposes of organization but at the internal operations of the organizations for which questions of who is being represented should be easiest to answer, membership associations of individuals.[18] Analysts of organizational life have long been aware that members of organizations are not uniform in their opinions and interests and that they differ in their activity and influence over organizational matters.[19] In order to assess whether what goes on inside organizations replicates or alters the representation of members' preferences and interests, we return to survey data about individuals from the 1990 Citizen Participation Study—both respondents' activities and experiences of being mobilized within political organizations and their perceptions of the extent to which they feel represented by those organizations.[20]

We have already seen in Figure 2.1 that the well-educated and affluent are more likely to be active members of voluntary associations. We can investigate that finding further in the 1990 data. Figure 2.2 presents information for five SES quintiles—that is, for five equal groups arrayed on the basis of a combination of education and income—about several measures of affiliation with and activity in organizations that take stands in politics.[21] Whatever the specific measure of activity, there is a strong relationship to socio-economic status: those at the top of the SES ladder are much more likely than those lower down to be affiliated with a political organization and to indicate that they have attended a meeting, that they have been active (that is, that they have served on a committee, given time for special projects, or helped organize meetings), and that they have served as a board member or officer of an organization that takes stands in politics.

That attendance at meetings, organizational activity, and service on the board of political organizations rise with socio-economic status follows naturally from

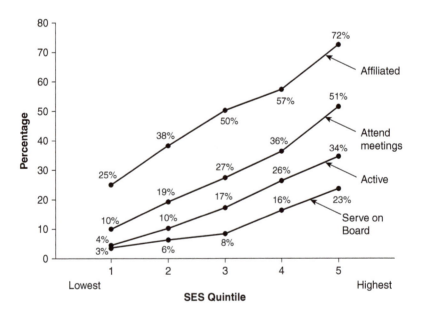

Figure 2.2 Affiliations with and Involvement in Political Organizations by SES Quintile

Source: Citizen Participation Study (1990). Note: Affiliated: either was a member of or contributed money to an organization that takes stands in politics; Meetings: attended a meeting of an organization; Active: served on a committee, gave time to special projects, or helped organize meetings; Board: served as a member of the board or an officer of an organization.

the way that affiliation with political organizations is structured by SES. What is equally striking is the way that the internal processes within these organizations give further advantage to those with higher levels of education and income. Figure 2.3 repeats the data in Figure 2.2 just for those who are affiliated with a political organization. The association between socio-economic status and activity in organizations that take stands in politics is not driven solely by the relationship between SES and affiliation with such organizations. Restricting our purview to members of political organizations, we find that, compared to members in the lowest SES quintile, members in the highest SES quintile are nearly twice as likely to have attended a meeting, three times as likely to have been active, and more than three times as likely to have served on the board or as an officer. In short, compared to lower-SES members, higher-SES citizens are not only more likely to affiliate with an organization in the first place, but once affiliated, more likely to take active roles in the organization. It is not only the selection processes that operate to bring a disproportionately affluent and well-educated group into organizations but also what happens within organizations that produces the outcomes we saw in Figure 2.2.

Who Feels Represented by Political Organizations?

We can get additional purchase on the thorny issue of who is represented by the membership organizations that take part in politics by considering the extent to

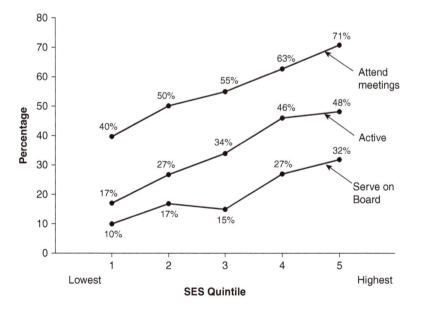

Figure 2.3 Involvement in Political Organizations among Members by SES Quintile

Source: Citizen Participation Study (1990).

which the perception of being represented by those organizations is correlated with SES. After respondents had been asked about all the organizations with which they were affiliated, they were asked to choose one organization as the most important to them.[22] A series of follow-up questions were asked, including four about their views about how well this organization represents them: whether the organization has asked the respondent's opinions on issues, whether the respondent agrees strongly with the organization's policies, whether the respondent feels at least some control over the organization, and whether the respondent has volunteered opinion about issues confronting the organization at a meeting. Just over a third, 35 percent, of those whose most important organization takes stands in politics agree with at least three of these four items—which measure what members perceive and not necessarily what organizations actually do—and feel themselves to be represented by the organization.

Figure 2.4 presents striking data about the probability that organization members feel well represented—within the subset of respondents who chose a political organization as their most important, a group that is already highly skewed in the direction of the affluent and well-educated. The bottom line on Figure 2.4—which shows the percentage who feel well represented among all who chose an organization that takes political stands as their most important—rises sharply with socio-economic status. Only 14 percent of those in the lowest quintile, compared

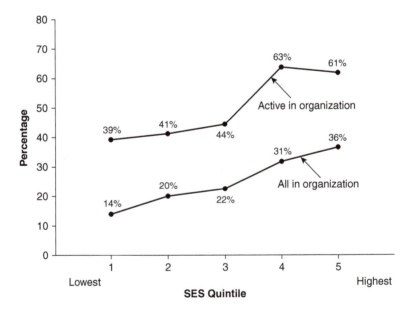

Figure 2.4 Feeling Represented by a Political Organization by SES Quintile

Source: Citizen Participation Study (1990). Note: The table reflects the percentage who reported feeling represented among only those respondents who chose as their most important organizations one that takes stands in politics.

to 36 percent of those in the highest quintile, indicated feeling represented by the organization.[23] Thus, compounding the impact of selection processes such that upper-SES individuals are substantially more likely to be affiliated with political organizations in the first place are processes within these organizations that leave their upper-SES members substantially more likely to feel well represented. The upper line in Figure 2.4 shows the percentage who feel well represented for the smaller group of those who are organizational activists. Even within this group of organizational activists—which, as we saw in Figures 2.2 and 2.3, over represents upper-SES individuals even more substantially—those in the lower three SES quintiles are much less likely than those in the top two SES quintiles to feel well represented.

In short, these data show the interaction between individual and organizational data and demonstrate how what happens within the voluntary associations of individuals that take stands in politics operates to reinforce political voice by the well-educated and affluent. Not only are those of upper-socio-economic status more likely to be affiliated with political organizations but, even among members, they are more likely to be active in those organizations and to serve on the board or as officers. Consequently, they are more likely to feel that these organizations speak for them.[24]

How Much Do They Say?

Organizations that get involved in politics have many options for seeking to inform and persuade various audiences. However, when it comes to the techniques they marshal in pursuit of political influence, there are actually striking similarities among organizations that differ in membership status. For example, while voluntary associations of individuals—especially those that fall under the rubric of "citizen groups"—emphasize grassroots lobbying and other techniques of public mobilization, institutions like corporations also make substantial efforts to shape public opinion and encourage sympathetic constituencies to communicate with public officials.[25]

Politically active organizations differ not only in what but in how much they do. Organizations with intense political concerns and deep resources are likely to do more in pursuit of political influence. Therefore, the political voice of any category of organizations depends on both the number of organizations in that category and the amount of their activity. However, determining the weight of voluntary associations of individuals in the totality of political input turns out to be complicated. That different tactics of political advocacy entail different metrics—for example, the number of communications with policymakers, the number of advertisements broadcast, the number of testimonies at congressional hearings, or the number of amicus briefs filed in Supreme Court cases—implies that it is difficult to compare organizations with respect to the volume of their political activity. We can, however, get some purchase on how much organizations actually do by considering two important resources that can be used in numerous ways in the quest for policy influence: people and dollars.

The *Washington Representatives* directories contain a valuable measure of an organization's political capacity, the number of in-house lobbyists it has on staff in an office in Washington and the number of outside law, public relations, or consulting firms it hires.[26] A number of factors might predispose an individual organization to choose in-house or outside representation: the limitations it faces in locating its headquarters; the extent to which political representation is central, or peripheral, to its mission; and the volume of its business with the federal government.[27] Table 2.6 presents data about the political capacity of organized interests, measured in terms of the average number of in-house lobbyists on the staff of the Washington office and the average number of outside law, public relations, or consulting firms retained as listed in the directory for 2001. It suggests that the number of inside lobbyists and outside firms hired also varies with whether or not an organization has members. Membership associations are likely to have their own offices in Washington and to rely on in-house lobbyists. While membership associations with institutions as members are likely to use both kinds of advocates, associations of individuals are relatively unlikely to hire outside firms. In contrast, institutions such as hospitals, museums, or corporations, rely in large part on outside firms.

An alternative measure of the capacity for policy influence is spending on lobbying. For the organizations in the 2001 *Washington Representatives* directory, we recorded the amount spent on lobbying in 2000 and 2001 as reported in the lobbying registrations filed under the Lobbying Disclosure Act of 1995 (LDA).[28] Spending on lobbying permits an organization to use its financial resources at its own initiative—constrained only by the registration requirements under the LDA and the restrictions on lobbying by non-profits.[29] Data from lobbying registrations show that, even when we omit organizations that registered no lobbying expenses, the vast bulk of lobbying spending is concentrated among a very small share of political organizations. Of the nearly $3 billion spent on lobbying during 2000 and

Table 2.6 Political Capacity of Organized Interests: Average Number of In-house Lobbyists and Outside Firms Hired[a]

	In-house Lobbyists	Outside Firms
Associations of individuals	1.79	0.69
Associations of institutions	1.48	1.18
Institutions[b]	0.77	1.25
State and Local Governments[c]	0.21	1.14
All	0.94	1.14

Source: *Washington Representatives Study* (2001)

a   Figures are the averages, for all the organizations in each category that were listed in the 2001 Washington Representatives directory, of the number of in-house lobbyists and outside firms hired.
b   For example, corporations, universities, or hospitals.
c   Includes foreign as well as domestic governments and associations of governments.

2001 by the registered organizations listed in the 2001 *Washington Representatives* directory, 33 percent was spent by the top 1 percent of lobbying spenders. Fully 75 percent was spent by the top 10 percent of lobbying spenders and a mere 3 percent by the bottom 50 percent of lobbying spenders. Had we been able to include in the denominator the organizations that did not register because their lobbying expenses fell below the threshold in the LDA, these figures would have shown even greater concentration of lobbying spending.

Table 2.7 shows the proportion of organizations in the 2001 directory that spent at least $10,000 on lobbying over the two-year period and the average amount spent—both for all organizations and for those that spent more than $10,000. Average lobbying spending for associations of individuals is quite close to the average for all organizations, an outcome that reflects that membership associations of individuals are, on average, fairly big spenders among those organizations that spent at least $10,000, but they are somewhat less likely than other kinds of political organizations to have done so.

We can put these data together to characterize the relative weight of old-fashioned interest groups—that is, membership associations of individuals—when it comes to the personnel and lobbying dollars deployed by advocacy organizations in national politics, a function of the number of organizations of each membership type and the average number of people or dollars for each type. In interpreting the figures in Table 2.8, it is important to keep in mind that, only in the left-hand column, which shows the distribution of organizations in the 2001 *Washington*

Table 2.7 Spending on Lobbying[a]

	Percentage Spending at Least $10,000 on Lobbying	Average Spent	
		All	Organizations Spending at Least $10,000
Associations of individuals	52%	$246,000	$472,000
Associations of institutions	62%	$335,000	$538,000
Institutions[b]	64%	$254,000	$399,000
State and local governments[c]	62%	$ 86,000	$140,000
All[d]	61%	$241,000	$394,000

Source: *Washington Representatives Study* (2001)

a   Figures are the percent of organizations that spent at least $10,000 on lobbying and the average spent per year in the 2000–2001 period for all the organizations in each category that were listed in the 2001 Washington Representatives directory and for those organizations that spent at least $10,000 in one or both years.
b   For example, corporations, universities, or hospitals.
c   Includes foreign as well as domestic governments and associations of governments.
d   Figures for all organizations also include organizations of mixed membership status, organizations with other membership structures, and organizations for which membership status could not be ascertained.

Representatives directory, is the organization the unit of analysis. The other columns show the distribution of the number of in-house lobbyists on staff in organizations' Washington offices; outside lobbying firms hired; and dollars spent on lobbying.[30]

The bottom line is that, for all these measures—whether in-house lobbyists, outside firms, or lobbying spending—the relative share for any kind of organization reflects, first and foremost, the number of such organizations and, thus, their weight in the overall distribution of organizations. Nonetheless, some types of organizations account for a greater share of political activity than would be expected from their population size alone.

With a higher proportion of in-house lobbyists, outside firms hired, and lobbying expenditures than their proportion among all organizations, associations of institutions—almost all of which are trade or other business associations—punch above their weight. Voluntary associations of individuals have roughly a proportionate share both of hired advocates—a relatively higher share of in-house lobbyists and a relatively lower share of outside firms—and of dollars spent on lobbying. Although they have a relatively lower share of in-house lobbyists and a relatively higher share of outside firms, institutions are also roughly proportionally represented. The catch is that there are so many more—more than four times more—institutions than membership associations of individuals.

The result is that associations of individuals field only a small fraction of the people and dollars devoted to political advocacy. To put a substantive face on these data, the business organizations that figure so heavily among institutions and associations of associations account for 53 percent of all organizations in the 2001 directory, 53 percent of the in-house lobbyists, 64 percent of the outside firms, and 72 percent of the spending on lobbying. Adopting a very expansive definition, organizations that represent the economic interests of those below the top

Table 2.8 Distribution of Political Activity by Organized Interests[a]

	All Organizations	In-house Lobbyists	Outside Firms	Lobbying Expenditures
Associations of individuals	12%	23%	7%	12%
Associations of institutions	17	27	18	24
Institutions[b]	53	43	58	55
State and local governments[c]	12	3	12	4
Mixed/Other/Unknown	6	5	5	4
	100%	101%	100%	100%

Source: *Washington Representatives Study* (2001)

a   Distributions for all organizations listed in the 2001 *Washington Representatives* directory
b   For example, corporations, universities, or hospitals
c   Includes foreign as well as domestic governments and associations of governments

economic tier account for just 2 percent of organizations in the directory, 5 percent of the in-house lobbyists, 2 percent of the outside firms, and a mere 2 percent
of the money spent on lobbying.[31]

Conclusion

Studies of organized interests usually focus on a single organization, a single category of organization—say, unions or advocates for the elderly—or the organizations involved in a particular political controversy. Less often they encompass the
entire set of politically active organizations. In this chapter, we have instead sliced
the pressure system on the basis of organizational membership status, focusing
attention on the organizations at the intersection of individual political participation and political organization, membership associations of individuals, and asking what the pressure system would look like if such organizations were—as they
were once assumed to be—the dominant organizational form.

Perhaps most unexpected is the finding that voluntary associations of individuals, which are only one of several kinds of politically active organizations, form
only a small fraction, about one-eighth, of the organizations in the pressure community. Although few in number, they are much less likely than institutions, most
of which are corporations, or voluntary associations of institutions, most of which
are trade or other business associations, to represent business. In consequence,
membership associations of individuals bring into politics perspectives that are
otherwise underrepresented, in particular, those of broad publics advocating on
behalf of public goods, identity groups, and those with limited resources. Without
voluntary associations of individuals, pressure politics, a domain dominated by
well-paid professional advocates, would be even more skewed in the direction of
narrow policy concerns and the advantaged.

Nevertheless, there are severe limits on the extent to which they broaden the
voices heard. Voluntary associations of individuals are relatively few in number,
and the personnel and dollars they are able to invest in pursuit of political influence are commensurate only with their small numbers. Besides, when we considered what kinds of individuals affiliate with membership associations and, among
those who are affiliated, who is likely to be active, to attend meetings, to serve on
the board, or to feel represented, we saw the extent to which the well-heeled and
well-educated are overrepresented. In short, without membership of associations
of individuals, pressure politics would be quite different but not quite as different
as was once assumed.

Notes

1 This chapter draws from the arguments and analysis in Part III of Kay Lehman
  Schlozman, Sidney Verba, and Henry E. Brady, *The Unheavenly Chorus: Unequal
  Political Voice and the Broken Promise of American Democracy* (Princeton, NJ: Princeton
  University Press, 2012), of which Philip Edward Jones is a co-author of Chapters 11 and

14. Material from *The Unheavenly Chorus,* including Figures 13.1–13.3 (Figures 2.2–2.4 in this chapter), is reprinted by permission.

2 The directory, *Washington Representatives* (Washington, DC: Columbia Books), is published annually. Although the *Washington Representatives* directory contains extensive listings, it includes neither organizations that drop in on Washington politics on an occasional basis but do not maintain an ongoing presence nor organizations whose participation is confined to writing checks to campaigns or filing amicus briefs. In addition, the directory does not list organizations active only in state or local politics, an omission with possible consequences for our concern with inequalities of political voice. For more information about the directory and the data base constructed from it, see Schlozman, Verba, and Brady, *Unheavenly Chorus,* 317–18 and Appendix E.

3 Among the most significant works from an interest group pluralist point of view are Arthur F. Bentley, *The Process of Government* (Chicago: University of Chicago Press, 1908); David B. Truman, *The Governmental Process: Political Interests and Public Opinion,* 2nd ed. (New York: Knopf, 1951); Earl Latham, *The Group Basis of Politics* (Ithaca, NY: Cornell University Press, 1952); and Robert A. Dahl, *A Preface to Democratic Theory* (New Haven, CT: Yale University Press, 1956). The authors of these works differ from one another in important respects, and no single work serves as the definitive text for interest group pluralism. Thus, the brief rendition of the interest group pluralist perspective in this paragraph is a caricature that, while frequently set up as a straw man by detractors, was never espoused by interest group pluralists. In particular, Robert A. Dahl, in *Who Governs?* (New Haven, CT: Yale University Press, 1961), gave a less central place to interest groups in his understanding of political contestation and never subscribed to the belief that the competing pressures comprise the sum total of political forces in making policy. For a discussion of the many uses of the term "pluralism," see Andrew S. McFarland, "Neopluralism," *Annual Review of Political Science* 10 (2007): 53–57.

4 E. E. Schattschneider, *Semi-Sovereign People* (New York: Holt, Rinehart and Winston, 1960), chap. 2.

5 Mancur Olson Jr., *The Logic of Collective Action: Public Goods and the Theory of Groups* (Cambridge, MA: Harvard University Press, 1965).

6 The figure from the Pew study would seem to be considerably lower than the 48 percent of respondents in the 1990 Citizen Participation Study who indicated that they were affiliated with an organization that takes stands in politics. (See Sidney Verba, Kay Lehman Schlozman, and Henry E. Brady, *Voice and Equality: Civic Voluntarism in American Politics* [Cambridge, MA: Harvard University Press, 1995], p. 62.) There are several factors that would contribute to the discrepancy. First, the Pew survey asked about being "active"; the figure for the Citizen Participation Study is based on a lower threshold of commitment, being a member or making a financial contribution (or both). In addition, while the Pew survey posed a general question about organizations that seek to influence public policy, the Citizen Political Study asked one by one about membership in or contributions to twenty different recognizable categories of membership associations and then followed up for those affiliated with a particular kind of organization with a question about whether that particular organization takes stands in politics. Naturally, it is easier to key into such affiliations when the referent is more concrete. Furthermore, as Robert D. Putnam makes clear in *Bowling Alone: The Collapse and Revival of American Community* (New York: Simon and Schuster, 2000), there has been a decline in memberships in membership associations since the Citizen Participation Study was conducted.

7 The SES quintiles are based on a measure constructed to give equal weight to family income and respondent's educational attainment. For details on the construction of this measure, see Schlozman, Verba, and Brady, *Unheavenly Chorus,* p. 123.

8 Robert H. Salisbury, "Interest Representation: The Dominance of Institutions," *American Political Science Review* 78 (1984): 64–76.
9 The procedures used to ascertain the membership status of organizations are described in Schlozman, Verba, and Brady, *Unheavenly Chorus,* Appendix E.
10 The language describing these organizations' objectives was taken from their Web sites on April 30, 2013. Note that in January 2010, the Leadership Conference changed its name from the Leadership Conference on Civil Rights to emphasize is embracing human rights mission.
11 It is worth noting that, among the organizations representing the economically disadvantaged, the overwhelming share of those classified as membership associations of individuals bring together donors who write checks rather than members who take part in organizational activities and governance.
12 Schlozman, Verba, and Brady, *Unheavenly Chorus,* p. 356. For extensive discussion of the kinds of interests represented in Washington pressure politics, see chaps. 11–14.
13 Organizations representing business include corporations, both domestic and foreign; the multiple kinds of business associations, again both domestic and foreign; occupational associations of business executives; and business-oriented think tanks and research organizations.
14 The specific characteristic that differentiates unions from occupational associations is that the former bargain collectively. The various sub-categories of occupational associations are distributed as follows:

Professional associations	54%
Associations of business professionals, managers, and executives	12
Associations of administrators and managers of non-profits	4
Associations of public employees	20
Other occupational associations	10
	100%

15 See Theda Skocpol, "Voice and Inequality: The Transformation of American Civic Democracy," *Perspectives on Politics* 2 (2004): 3–20, Figure 3.
16 A similar point is made by Jeffrey M. Berry, *The New Liberalism: The Rising Power of Citizen Groups* (Washington, DC: Brookings, 1999), pp. 57, 169.
17 See Dara Z. Strolovitch, *Affirmative Advocacy: Race, Class, and Gender in Interest Group Politics* (Chicago: University of Chicago Press, 2007), especially chap. 3.
18 This section draws directly from Schlozman, Verba, and Brady, *Unheavenly Chorus,* pp. 375–80.
19 See Robert Michels, *Political Parties: A Sociological Study of the Oligarchical Tendencies of Modern Democracy,* trans. Eden and Cedar Paul (New York: Dover, 1959); and Grant McConnell, *Private Power and American Democracy* (New York: Knopf, 1966), chap. 5.
20 We use the 1990 Citizen Participation Study, which contains an unusually extensive battery of questions about organizational membership and activity. It should be noted that, because it encompasses organizations that take stands in state and local politics, the set of membership associations referenced by these survey data is quite different from the set of organizations included in the Washington Representatives Study.
21 With respect to the measures of organizational affiliation and activity, for each of 20 categories of organizations, respondents were asked whether they were members of or make contributions to an organization of that type. (If respondents indicated affiliation with more than one organization in a particular category, they were asked the follow-up questions about the single organization in that category with which they were most involved.) Then they were asked about attending meetings, being active, and having served on the board or as an officer of that organization.

Respondents were also asked whether that organization ever takes stands in politics. It should be noted that the designation of an organization as political, therefore, does not depend upon the substantive category into which it fell. This strategy has the advantage that politically active organizations in seemingly non-political categories— for example, the local gun club that lobbies on the state level for the relaxation of gun laws, discussed by a respondent under the rubric of "hobby clubs"—are appropriately construed as political. It has the disadvantage that respondents did sometimes made mistakes.

22 The "most important" or "main" organization was selected as follows: respondents who reported affiliation with only one organization were asked the follow-up battery about that organization; respondents affiliated with more than one organization were asked to choose the one in which they are most active and the one to which they give the most money; if the two organizations were different, they were asked which organization is most important to them. For a full explanation of the selection of the most important organization, see Sidney Verba, Kay Lehman Schlozman and Henry Brady, *Voice and Equality* (Cambridge, MA: Harvard University Press, 1995), pp. 542–49.

23 The following data show the proportion of all respondents (including those who had no organizational affiliations at all) in each SES quintile who chose an organization that takes stands in politics as their most important organization:

Lowest SES	1	2	3	4	5	Highest SES
	16%	24%	28%	40%	40%	

24 Melissa K. Miller demonstrates the joint effect of stratification in citizen choices to join and become active in organizations coupled with the actions of organizational leaders in privileging their stratified members in "Membership Has Its Privileges: How Voluntary Groups Exacerbate the Participatory Bias," *Political Research Quarterly* 63 (2010): 356–72.

25 For relevant, if dated, evidence on this point, see Kay Lehman Schlozman and John T. Tierney, *Organized Interests and American Democracy* (New York: Harper and Row, 1986), pp. 172–78.

26 Because we do not have data about lobbying for 2006, in this section we use data from the 2001 *Washington Representatives* directory.

27 On the decision whether to open an office in Washington or to hire outside counsel or consultants, see Lee Drutman, "The Business of America is Lobbying" (PhD dissertation, University of California, Berkeley, 2010), ch. 3.

28 We coded lobbying expenses for 2000 and 2001 of all organizations listed in the 2001 *Washington Representatives* directory as presented on the publicly accessible Web site of the Center for Responsive Politics, opensecrets.org. For discussion of sources and coding methods used by the Center, see http://www.opensecrets.org/lobbyists/methodology.asp. If opensecrets.org did not have any information about the lobbying spending of an organization, we also consulted the data contained at PoliticalMoneyLine. For discussion of our methods, the reasons why data could be found for only two-thirds of the organizations in the directory, and the regulations in the Lobbying Disclosure Act of 1995, see Schlozman, Verba, and Brady, *Unheavenly Chorus*, pp. 406–11.

29 Unless they establish a parallel, non-tax-deductible 501(c)4 arm, organizations that fall into the 501(c)3 designation under the tax code—that is, non-profits for which contributions are tax deductible—are legally enjoined from undertaking significant lobbying, though not from engaging in many other kinds of political activity. See Jeffrey M. Berry (with David F. Arons), *A Voice for Nonprofits* (Washington, DC: Brookings, 2003). They demonstrate (pp. 54–65) that "H election" can permit nonprofits to ignore lobbying limits.

30 It is critical not to reify the distribution of organizations in the left-hand column of Table 2.8. Although a census of organizations, it cannot be considered any kind of natural population. For many reasons, it is impossible to specify what a representative distribution of organizations would look like. Still, the existing distribution is anything but representative.

31 This category encompasses all unions including white-collar unions, all occupational associations representing non-professional and non-managerial employees, and all organizations that either advocate for the poor or provide social services.

Chapter 3

Grassroots Mobilization and Outside Lobbying

Edward Walker

A widely accepted tenet of political and social thought is that the advantaged prefer to quietly maintain the status quo, whereas the disadvantaged are forced to engage in mass mobilization efforts (lest their concerns be ignored entirely in the political process). This working assumption is present in E. E. Schattschneider's classic theorizing on democratic politics and the interest of the relatively disadvantaged in widening the "scope of conflict" to gain political attention.[1] It is also present in sociological theorizing in the Resource Mobilization tradition, which hypothesizes that whereas the relatively advantaged need not engage in social movement activity, those lacking in resources and organization do need to take such action, yet they still require the sponsorship of more advantaged patrons in order to generate real social change.[2] In the generations since these early works, scholars have brought diverse evidence to bear in support of the distinction between the "quiet politics" of elites versus the noisy politics of the masses.[3]

But mass politics are not just for the disadvantaged, as the repertoire of grassroots mobilization—organizing large-scale public participation campaigns aimed at either changing or maintaining a particular policy—is favored not only by social movement organizers and community organizations but also by elites in corporations, industry groups, think tanks, foundations, and other relatively advantaged sectors. Although structurally advantaged, these actors at times find themselves on the losing end of policy battles and must adopt a populist posture and find ways to galvanize activism on their behalf. And, as I will explain, the rise of an industry of consultants who specialize in mobilizing grassroots participation on behalf of paying organizational clients has made it much easier for elites to facilitate participation than it was before the field of professional grassroots lobbyists took off in the 1970s and 1980s.

One such prominent example was the recent mobilization of for-profit colleges in response to the Obama administration's proposed "gainful employment" rule, which would have imposed severe penalties on for-profit colleges whose students graduate with heavy debt loads and relatively low chances of repaying those loans in their chosen career. With the help of consultants, companies and trade associations for the for-profit colleges facilitated large-scale campaigns to mobilize their students and employees in response to the proposed regulations. Although there were multiple factors at play in shaping these regulations, the adopted rules were significantly less stringent than those initially proposed.

Consistent with the overarching theme of *New Directions in American Politics*, this chapter highlights major research findings on grassroots mobilization by advocacy groups and other organizations, highlighting how changes in American politics, new communications technologies, and shifts the political activity of business all helped to transform grassroots politics in the United States since the regulatory and political upheavals of the late 1960s and early 1970s.

I begin by providing background on the politics of grassroots mobilization in the United States and the evolution of thinking about such strategies in political science and sociology. I then consider how such forms of political engagement are facilitated by a range of types of advocacy groups and firms. Studies of grassroots participation facilitated by parties and electoral campaigns, while important, have been covered extensively in other research and are generally outside the scope of this chapter.[4] I then move on to consider how the "interest group explosion" of the 1970s and 1980s helped to transform grassroots mobilization and facilitate its commercialization through the rise and institutionalization of the field of grassroots lobbying consultants, thus further widening the use of grassroots strategies by business groups. I conclude by considering how best to interpret the shifting terrain of grassroots politics in the United States.

Defining Grassroots Lobbying and Mobilization

Grassroots participation is seen as a source of authentic citizen voice in American politics, or the place in which the true voice of the people is articulated in a fashion independent of the pressures of state administration and the influence of business and the marketplace. William Safire's famous *Political Dictionary* once defined the grassroots as "the ultimate source of power, usually patronized, occasionally feared"; although tongue-in-cheek, Safire's definition reinforces the idea that the political grassroots are endowed with a distinct legitimacy in the representative politics of the United States.[5] Legislators often view the grassroots communications they receive from constituents "as a sort of hyper-concentrated version of what people are thinking back [in their] home [district],"[6] given that presumably only the most motivated citizens will make the effort to send communications or visit their office.

I use the terms "grassroots lobbying" and "grassroots mobilization" interchangeably in this chapter. Grassroots (or "outside") lobbying is set in distinction to "inside" lobbying, the latter of which focuses on making private contacts with policymakers and their assistants, deploying expert knowledge through circulating position papers and offering testimony in hearings, and offering campaign or other financial contributions. Grassroots lobbying, by contrast, involves "the identification, recruitment, and mobilization of constituent-based political strength capable of influencing political decisions."[7] Those seeking to bring about policy change often make judgments regarding whether to take an inside versus an outside lobbying strategy, in part, on the basis of the public accessibility of an issue. For overly technical issues that are not amenable to framing for a non-expert audience, inside lobbying alone is likely to be the favored strategy; for issues that can be framed as having a potentially broad and interested audience, and for which it would benefit the claimant to expand the scope of conflict, outside strategies may be more appealing, often in simultaneous combination with inside strategies.[8] Advocacy groups often combine inside and outside strategies, finding that these strategies complement one another when sufficient resources and organization make both options simultaneously feasible.[9]

Taking this more expansive definition of grassroots lobbying avoids unnecessarily restricting analysts' investigation to forms of participation that are strictly local, lacking in formal organization/professionalization, and/or carried out without much resource expenditure. It also allows for the recognition that much mass participation is indeed prompted by well-heeled interest groups, political and corporate elites, and political professionals including consultants, lobbyists, and PR specialists; the ambiguity in ferreting out how heavy a role the latter groups play in mobilizing participation is the terrain on which many today debate the distinction between "astroturf" lobbying and truly "grassroots" campaigns.

Analysts tend to define astroturf as participation that (1) is quite heavily incentivized, (2) involves the deception of activists by the campaign's sponsor or engages in fraud by misrepresenting citizens' views to policymakers, or (3) features recruitment efforts that willfully conceal the disproportionate resources provided to a mass mobilization effort by an elite patron or group of patrons.[10] New technologies, organizational forms, and fields of consultants have made such strategies more accessible to those seeking to mobilize participation, and policymakers accordingly tend to distrust the authenticity of many of the communications they receive from citizens.[11] In addition, given that grassroots lobbying is generally unregulated at the federal level, much of this activity remains off the radar of scholars, journalists, and members of the general public. Nonetheless, campaigns that engage in fraud or deception are regularly exposed by critical publics and media observers, and the most egregious astroturf campaigns are generally much less effective than those that take a more traditional grassroots organizing strategy. My research also provides evidence that the most effective elite-sponsored grassroots campaigns are those that are transparent about the identity of their sponsor, while also making partnerships with local stakeholders who have an authentic and independent interest in the campaign's issues. In short, they look more like traditional grassroots campaigns.

Although the focus of most research on grassroots lobbying—and, indeed, lobbying more generally—has been political action targeted at federal (and to a lesser extent state and local) legislatures,[12] the concept need not be restricted to legislative policy. Agency decisions often mandate windows of public comment prior to rulemaking, and such periods tend to attract substantial volumes of lobbying activity during these concentrated periods.[13] My forthcoming book describes one such instance, in which a decision on whether to allow a corporate acquisition by a major railroad company—that was to be decided by the U.S. Surface Transportation Board—galvanized fierce public mobilization both by supporters and opponents. While grassroots advocates did indeed lobby their legislators to add indirect pressure on the STB to support their side in the decision, the primary focus of their lobbying was the STB itself. Grassroots lobbying also plays a role in the courts, although one that is much smaller; such influence occurs primarily in an indirect fashion through lobbying of legislators to support or oppose the appointments of judges, and more directly through, for example, inviting members of the lay public to testify in court hearings.

Grassroots lobbying is also used as a strategy when seeking change outside the three branches of government, such as when mass activists target a corporate practice or the policy of an educational or medical institution, or when working to facilitate change in a professional or civic association. A number of recent studies have examined how, for instance, activists inside major corporations have successfully lobbied such companies to begin offering health and other benefits to the same-sex domestic partners of a company's employees.[14] Other research has shown how mass mobilization practices have changed medical institutions' research practices and understanding of particular health conditions such as AIDS and breast cancer.[15] And media accounts have revealed that grassroots political efforts have challenged membership associations ranging from the Augusta National Golf Club over its exclusion of women to the American Psychiatric Association on its former definition of homosexuality as a mental disorder. Research on grassroots political action targeted against organizations outside government has become a central area of investigation in sociology and management studies.[16] Still, governments remain the fundamental guarantors of new benefits for those seeking social change in advanced democratic societies,[17] and the theory and practice of mass participation continue to reflect this reality.

I now shift attention to the sources of mass mobilization by describing processes of organizing among seven unique organizational forms, shifting from those most traditionally associated with these practices (interest groups, labor unions, and community organizations) to those less well known for outside lobbying (trade associations, professional associations, and corporations). I then describe how studying the field of grassroots lobbying consultants offers additional insights into how the context of mass participation has changed since the 1970s. I conclude by discussing future directions for research on grassroots advocacy.

Associational Sources of Mass Participation

The participation of lay citizens in policymaking has, of course, quite deep roots in the habits, traditions, and institutional designs of American politics and governance as envisioned by the founders and remarked upon by Tocqueville. Although concerns about the decline of such participation are a hardy perennial in scholarly commentary about the American project,[18] mass participation in American governance is nonetheless still relatively high in comparative perspective,[19] even if the concern remains that the associations in which Americans engage today may not be quite as effective as those of past generations in creating and maintaining thick and durable ties between their participants.[20]

Studies of the sources of mass participation tend to classify the associational sources of citizen participation into a distinct set of organizational types.[21] Some further differentiate between associations that have members versus those that are "non-membership" and are driven entirely by the efforts of paid staff.[22] Most studies group corporations separately, and trade associations and labor unions are often provided with their own category; some analyses additionally break out professional associations, government associations (e.g., mayors' associations), identity groups (e.g., ethnic groups), religious associations, and nearly all studies retain a residual category for general public interest or citizen associations.

A commonplace finding in these studies is that grassroots mobilization tactics—including organizing letter-writing campaigns, protesting, holding press conferences, and/or calling critical attention to the voting record of a legislator—are deployed to a great extent by labor unions and general citizen advocacy groups, a moderate extent by trade associations, and generally less often by professional associations or corporations, consistent with elite scope-of-conflict assumptions.[23] Still, my study of the clients of professional grassroots lobbyists suggests that although most businesses do not engage in heavy amounts of grassroots lobbying through their own internal mechanisms, the largest firms do engage in such efforts regularly and with the assistance of a professional firm. I found, in fact, that nearly 40% of the Fortune 500 appear on the client list of at least one such lobbying firm in the United States.[24]

National Interest Groups. General citizen associations active at the national level—and especially federated organizations that span federal, state, and local boundaries through their own internal mechanisms—are central sources of public participation in American politics and continue to be active in generating requests for engagement. Even though those who that are recruited into participation by associations are generally not representative of the public at large because they tend to be more highly educated and well-resourced,[25] there is evidence that benefits accrue regardless to groups that are most organized and active.[26]

A core strength of mass membership organizations is their capacity for turning out large volumes of participatory action, although a quality/quantity trade-off is inherent. Internet and social media technologies have further lowered the costs of collective action for mass membership groups and have made it even easier than it was during the early years of mass mailings for centralized, professional, and non-federated groups with far-flung memberships to generate communications with policymakers.

While it is clear that national associations are often quite effective in stimulating citizen action, some raise critical questions about the ability of contemporary civic and political associations to meaningfully "connect people to politics."[27] It is widely recognized that the "interest group explosion" of the 1970s and early 1980s fundamentally reorganized the interest group sector, but interpretations of the consequences of these changes vary.[28] On one side are those who echo Theda Skocpol's influential argument that the advocacy field has transformed with a decline of fraternal associations and other types of (often federated) membership-based advocacy groups that instill rich civic traditions and thick social capital in their members, and which have been effectively replaced by distant, single-issue, Washington-based checkbook-and-mailing-list associations.[29] On the other are those who find evidence that even though membership organizations may not be quite as effective in instilling social capital in their members as they once were, nonetheless substantial organizational form diversity continues to exist in the sector of national advocacy associations in the United States.[30] Further, there is evidence of a complementary and supportive division of labor between the most professionalized associations and those that engage members in participatory action, suggesting that caution is merited in assuming deleterious representative consequences of a changed advocacy field.[31]

Non-Membership Advocacy Organizations (NMAOs). Although not typically understood as sources of mass mobilization—indeed, even held by some as the antithesis of participatory engagement—it nonetheless remains true that advocacy groups without memberships help to stimulate mass participation in the political process. Such non-membership groups include foundations, institutes, centers, policy planning organizations, think tanks, and advocacy affiliate networks. Such groups have seen a considerable numeric increase in the U.S. political system since the late 1960s, but this increase has been roughly proportional to the expansion of membership-based associations and has not involved the displacement of the latter.[32]

NMAOs support grassroots participation both directly and indirectly, although they tend toward the latter. Most commonly, NMAOs serve to support and reinforce the mass advocacy efforts of grassroots membership groups. The NAACP Legal Defense and Education Fund, for instance, served as a crucial legal support to the mass advocacy of the NAACP and other civil rights movement organizations, just as Earthjustice Legal Defense Fund plays a complementary role for the Sierra Club today. Non-membership affiliate networks such as the contemporary Industrial Areas Foundation help to provide essential technical support and organizing resources to low-income faith-based community organizations across the United States. And foundations, of course, provide resources that make organizing possible in many social movements and other advocacy organizations, while think tanks and policy planning groups help to promote their ideas and reinforce the ground game of membership groups. Indeed, the founding of new membership organizations like those described above provided a strong support for the founding of new NMAOs in a variety of policy domains.[33] Still, NMAOs do, at times, mobilize participation directly, although it is mainly in their ability to engage in mass fundraising efforts or in the generation of communications through mass mailings, email, and/or telephone technologies.

Labor Unions. Unions have seen major declines in the U.S. context since the 1970s, with questions about what this decline will mean for the political capacity of organized labor.[34] The capacity of management to fight back against unions in aggressive fashion has been made possible by policy changes within the NLRB, especially under the Reagan administration,[35] and recent state-level policy changes have also provided support for such employer efforts to counter unions. Despite these changes, unions remain a significant force in mobilizing working Americans to provide a voice in the workplace and as voters and constituents. They also arm themselves with a muscular in-house lobbying force, retaining proportionally more inside lobbyists than corporations do, according to one study.[36] Other evidence suggests that two-thirds of union members report being asked directly to take part in political activity by their union, and that it is nearly universal for unions to engage in grassroots tactics such as organizing letter-writing campaigns, mobilizing members, and protesting.[37]

Local Community-Based Organizations. The local community mobilizations of the late 1970s and early 1980s came to be known as the "Backyard Revolution," as a wave of activism swept many low- and moderate-income communities across the United States during that period.[38] Cities like Cleveland were central to this, and public participation by disadvantaged groups has suffused urban politics there in the years since.[39] Community-based organizations were influential in shaping the passage of the 1977 Community Reinvestment Act, and myriad new community groups were established in the 1980s in order to secure benefits for communities on its basis. Local community-based organizations, whether of the congregation-based or the individual-membership variety, continue to represent a significant countertrend against the professionalization of advocacy politics in other domains,[40] and are helping disadvantaged communities today on issues including housing and foreclosure policy, covering the uninsured, and providing social supports for undocumented immigrants, in addition to general community issues such as policing, economic development, and public services.

Trade Associations. While more often understood as a powerful inside lobbying force or a source of cultural integration among business elites,[41] trade associations are also active in grassroots lobbying on issues of pressing concern to their corporate members. Ken Kollman, for instance, finds that although trade associations do not engage in protest, they engage in other grassroots strategies about as often as nonbusiness citizen interest groups do.[42] Still, trade association members are less likely to be asked to take political action than union members or those active in neighborhood groups.[43] Thus, what grassroots advocacy trade associations do is apparently more selective and targeted. Further, trade associations spend more on inside lobbying expenditures than unions or most other kinds of public interest groups, and at the same time they are less likely to claim to represent women, the poor, or disadvantaged minorities than unions or professional associations are.[44]

Professional Associations. Sociologists and organizational theorists tend to see professional associations as key sources in the normative institutionalization of practices within fields.[45] But professional associations do more than just certify certain practices as legitimate, in that they also occasionally facilitate the expression of the political voice of their members. The American Medical Association, for instance, has a long history as a powerful lobbying force on behalf of physicians, and myriad professional associations within other sectors of medical practice are also regularly mobilized when federal, state, and/or local health policy reforms are proposed or enacted.[46] Although less active in supporting grassroots participation given that, like trade associations, the role of professional groups is primarily for networking and sharing best practices within an occupational community, nonetheless professional groups often become politically mobilized when policy changes threaten the interests of their members.

Corporations. As I describe below, corporations outsource much of their grassroots lobbying to consultants and other outside professionals, given that they lack the internal capacity for substantial advocacy possessed by advocacy groups. In addition, grassroots participation directly sponsored by corporations (i.e., without a proxy) may, under certain circumstances, be more likely to be discredited by the public and the media as being outside the public interest. Nonetheless, as scholars of corporate political activity have recognized, the in-house corporate public affairs function has expanded considerably in the past four decades,[47] and companies regularly engage in constituency-building efforts that mobilize their employees, shareholders, distributors, executives, and local community stakeholders as a political force.[48] Corporations' interest in taking an issue to the public (as compared to 'quiet' inside lobbying) is generally conditioned on the extent to which the issue is one that is salient to the broader public; certain issues, such as the regulation of hostile corporate takeovers, fall outside this purview.[49]

Consultants and the Restructuring of Grassroots Political Engagement Since the 1970s

Grassroots political engagement can be facilitated directly by associations or firms, as described above, or can take place through the supplementary efforts of consultants and other political professionals. Political consultants have become an essential part of electoral campaigns and corporate public affairs strategies, and consultants have also become major players in the mobilization of mass participation in the contemporary United States. (There is also some initial evidence that the U.S. models of professional grassroots lobbying are beginning to diffuse internationally).[50] Although they often refer to themselves as "public affairs consultants" rather than grassroots or outside lobbyists, what they share in common is an ability to generate demonstrations of mass support or opposition to a policy on behalf of a paying client. This may involve partnering with existing advocacy groups, the creation of new structures for facilitating activism, ad hoc strategies for targeting particular demographic groups, or, often, all of the above.

In a series of studies, I have investigated the founding patterns, client bases, strategies, resources, and a variety of other features of the field of consulting firms active in providing grassroots lobbying services to paying clients.[51] While in the 1970s the industry was relatively tiny and comprised mainly of a small number of electoral consultants searching for additional issue advocacy revenue during campaign off-seasons, today this consultant industry is a well-institutionalized player in the advocacy field, with hundreds of active firms providing services ranging from patch-through calls to personalized targeting services, and from direct mail to data mining to uncover new sources of support for a client's policy interests. Such consultants have become a one-stop-shopping source for mobilizing grassroots support under circumstances in which a corporation or advocacy group needs to show a groundswell of backing for their policy interests but lacks sufficient internal capacity, organizational structure, data, and/or strategic knowledge to carry it out on their own.

Using evidence culled from a variety of sources including political consultant directories, surveys of lobbying firms, client lists, consultant interviews, and searches of public records about each firm, my studies of these public affairs consultants reveals a picture in which considerable volumes of grassroots participation are being generated on the basis of commercial contracts between organizations and grassroots lobbyists. Contemporary grassroots participation, in a context where new technologies have lowered costs of mounting collective action, has taken on some somewhat new meanings now that professional grassroots lobbying services are widely available.

Companies appear to be the primary users of consultants' services, but they are not the only ones to do so. Corporations, which lack associations' inherent capacities for mobilizing participation (and often face certain legal restrictions against it, such as in state laws against paying employees to lobby on the firm's behalf), represent a plurality of the clients of consultants (29%), and an additional 10% of their aggregate clients are trade associations. Other common client types include candidate campaigns—who often hire grassroots consultants for support in get-out-the-vote (GOTV) efforts—which are 26% of clients, and citizen advocacy groups are 18%. Less common clients are government agencies (7%), political party organizations (5%), labor unions (3%), and other types of clients such as universities or individuals (3%).[52] A strong plurality of grassroots lobbyists have a background in either electoral consulting, campaign staffing, or legislative staffing, and relatively few got their start in corporate PR or public affairs, thus providing further indication that these consultants apply practical knowledge of how to run a political campaign to their work for diverse clients who lack their own capacities to mount a campaign.

My study of the founding patterns of these consulting firms revealed that the founding of new grassroots lobbying firms between the early 1970s and the early years of the new century was associated most closely with the dramatic

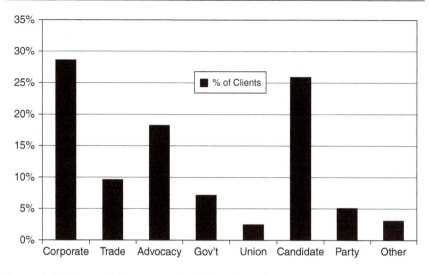

Figure 3.1 Clients of Grassroots Lobbying Consultants

expansion of the field of organized advocacy groups in the 1970s and 1980s—what has come to be known as the "advocacy explosion"—as well as with the widening collective action of business through industry trade groups. In addition, the founding of new consulting firms was also strongly associated with the substantial increase in political partisanship seen in the United States over this period, as consultants draw upon highly partisan citizens as activists who are more likely to be successfully moved to action on behalf of political requests coming from strangers through cold calls, mass emails, and/or advertisements. These models also showed that the founding of new firms was not significantly associated with changes in the rate of political participation, trust in government, citizens' interest in public affairs, or their feelings of political efficacy, nor did economic conditions or corporate taxes play much of a role in influencing foundings. Also, this study of founding patterns revealed somewhat uneven evidence regarding how party control of governorships and legislative offices related to the founding of firms.[53]

The story about foundings, then, suggests that the opening of new grassroots lobbying firms in the closing decades of the twentieth century was primarily a response to a new market opportunity in the changing advocacy field, which allowed the exploitation of new information and communications technologies by professionals on behalf of citizen and business advocacy groups. Seeing this opportunity, electoral consultants and staffers familiar with the workings of political campaigns began to broaden their efforts into issue advocacy. Contemporary evidence from my research suggests that corporations, trade groups, and unions pay relatively better on a per-client basis than political candidates do, thus suggesting that the promise of doing less work for more pay was at least part of the draw for new consultants, not to mention that such revenue would even out the unstable peaks and valleys associated with election season revenues. One of my interviewees, a prominent West Coast consultant whose firm followed precisely this path, said that the reason for taking on more corporate issue advocacy over the years was little more than to "make money and have year-round business."

Grassroots lobbying consultants active today are predominantly non- or bipartisan (47%), with a roughly even distribution of partisan firms split between those that are either Republican-affiliated (26%) or Democratic (28%); consistent with this finding, my studies have not revealed an overwhelming dominance of firms' engagement in either conservative or progressive issue advocacy. Still, my study did reveal some partisan differences in client bases, in that firms with more of a citizen advocacy group clientele tended to work with Democrats at higher rates, whereas those working with electoral campaigns were more Republican.[54] Corporate clients seemed to prefer nonpartisan firms, and my interviews also revealed a preference on the side of corporate-serving consultancies to keep their options open by not having strong partisan allegiances (even in those cases where consultants cut their teeth on partisan electoral campaigns).

Grassroots lobbying consultants, like other types of political recruiters, tend to operate as rational actors who seek to be effective in their requests for participation, and therefore target would-be activists most likely to acquiesce; this may reinforce participatory inequalities and exacerbate the over-representation of those who are already most politically active. My research revealed that consultants focus their efforts most heavily on recruiting those who are strongly partisan and have a history of activism in political organizations and who have voted regularly in Congressional elections. They also disproportionately target civic activists and the college educated, although these factors are less central in consultants' campaigns than citizens' partisanship and past activism. The most commonly reported "secondary target" in grassroots lobbyists' campaigns are minority groups; this undoubtedly reflects a degree of political tokenism. For example, Wal-Mart's consultant-backed campaign to open a store in the East New York neighborhood of Brooklyn has emphasized that the proposed location is otherwise a supermarket desert and that the predominantly low-income and minority population near the proposed site is unfairly harmed by its lack of access to quality food.[55] Similarly, reports about the flame-retardant chemical manufacturers' industry front group Citizens for Fire Safety Institute (CFSI) illustrated that CFSI's campaign sought to mobilize minority groups as supporters of their chemicals, given their claim that minority groups may be disproportionately likely to die from fires in the home.[56]

These consultants report the greatest degree of success in their work helping to qualify ballot measures at the state level, modest success in legislative and electoral campaigns, and somewhat less success in shifting the decisions of administrative agencies. Importantly, they report a quality-quantity tradeoff across the types of participation they request. That is, high-cost practices like encouraging attendance at public events or meeting directly with a policymaker (or their staff) are seen as most effective but can only be expected of a very limited subset of resourceful constituents; low-cost tactics like petitioning, emailing, phone calling, and letter-writing, can, of course, be executed at a large scale but are also easily ignored (or dismissed as "astroturf").

On a broader level, consultants campaigns seem to be most effective when they can closely mimic the strategies of traditional grassroots campaigns organized by associations; by contrast, they are less likely to be effective to the extent that the campaign can be dismissed as "astroturf" due to a lack of transparency and an inability to make partnership with genuine supporters who engage for their own independent purposes. To the extent that campaigns fail to be transparent and lack these partnerships, critical advocacy groups and organized opponents may be able to more effectively discredit a consultant's campaign and the client. Such was the case, for instance, in labor unions' efforts to discredit Wal-Mart in its Working Families for Wal-Mart campaign, organized with the support of PR behemoth Edelman.[57] On the other hand, it is worth noting that more effective campaigns often look similar to the well-known "Baptist and bootlegger" coalitions described by public choice economists; these are tacit partnerships in which groups with opposing social values lobby for the same policy outcome. Consulting firms often seek to facilitate the grassroots activism of those who support their client's cause but do not have the same pecuniary interests behind their lobbying.

Conclusion

Considering the associational and professional sources of grassroots participation and outside lobbying activity in the closing decades of the twentieth century and opening decades of the new century, this chapter found both areas of stability and change. What remains common is that insider strategies of traditional lobbying and deploying expert knowledge continue to be favored by corporations and advocacy groups without members; by contrast, outsider strategies of mass mobilization still tend to be the purview of labor unions, community organizations, and mass membership organizations. Nonetheless, new communications technologies and the development of a field of professional grassroots lobbying firms have meant that grassroots strategies are more often deployed by corporations and other professionalized interest groups than they were in generations past. The example of mobilization by for-profit colleges, as described at the outset of this chapter, illustrates just one case of this strategy.

As a consequence, volumes of public participation today are mediated by consultants, who disproportionately mobilize those who are already overrepresented in the political system. Ironically, then, much grassroots participation today may be reinforcing representative inequalities rather than challenging them.

Nonetheless, there are reasons to temper this argument a bit, in that the campaigns of grassroots lobbying consultants face many of the same constraints as grassroots organizers of all stripes: they must contend with opposing forces, locate political allies, frame their message persuasively, and build effective organizing structures (or co-opt existing ones). And, because of their elite sponsorship, they face an additional hurdle that other organized advocates may not, in that they often contend with the charge of being inauthentic "astroturf" if they fail to connect with independent supporters of their client's cause. Thus, there is reason for caution against the simplistic argument that grassroots political influence can simply be purchased in the modern context. The power of organized civil society continues to serve as a primary force in American civic life and politics.

Notes

1 E. E. Schattschneider, *The Semisovereign People* (New York: Holt, Rinehart, and Winston, 1960).
2 John D. McCarthy and Mayer N. Zald, *The Trend of Social Movements in America* (Morristown, NJ: General Learning Press, 1973); John D. McCarthy and Mayer N. Zald, "Resource Mobilization and Social Movements: A Partial Theory," *American Journal of Sociology* 82, no. 6 (1977): 1212–41; Jack L. Walker,. *Mobilizing Interest Groups in America* (Ann Arbor: University of Michigan Press, 1991).
3 See, for example, Frank R. Baumgartner, "Independent and Politicized Policy Communities: Education and Nuclear Energy in France and in the United States," *Governance* 2, no. 1 (1989): 42–66; Pepper Culpepper, *Quiet Politics and Business Power* (New York: Cambridge University Press, 2011); Mark Smith, *American Business and Political Power* (Chicago: University of Chicago Press, 2000).; Edward T. Walke, "Industry-Driven Activism," *Contexts* 9, no. 2 (2010): 44–49.
4 See, for instance, Margaret Weir and Marshall Ganz, "Reconnecting People and Politics," *The New Majority* (1997): 149–71; Daniel Kreiss, *Taking Our Country Back* (New York: Oxford University Press, 2012); Rasmus Kleis Nielsen, *Ground Wars* (Princeton, NJ: Princeton University Press, 2012).
5 William Safire, *Safire's Political Dictionary* (New York: Random House, 1978), p. 289.
6 Ken Kollman, *Outside Lobbying* (Princeton, NJ: Princeton University Press, 1998), p. 155.
7 Kenneth Goldstein, *Interest Groups, Lobbying, and Participation in America* (New York: Cambridge University Press, 1999), p. 3.
8 See Smith, *American Business and Political Power.*
9 Edward T. Walker, *Grassroots for Hire: Public Affairs Consultants in American Democracy* (Cambridge and New York: Cambridge University Press, forthcoming).
10 Walker, *Grassroots for Hire*, chap. 2.
11 For example, Brad Fitch and Kathy Goldschmidt, *Communicating with Congress* (Washington, DC: Congressional Management Foundation, 2005); Kathy Goldschmidt and Leslie Ochreiter, *Communicating with Congress* (Washington, DC: Congressional Management Foundation, 2008).
12 Marie Hojnacki, David C. Kimball, Frank R. Baumgartner, Jeffrey M. Berry, and Beth L. Leech, "Studying Organizational Advocacy and Influence: Reexamining Interest Group Research," *Annual Review of Political Science* 15, no. 1 (2012): 379–99.
13 Daniel Carpenter, Jacqueline Chattopadhyay, Susan Moffitt, and Clayton Nall. "The Complications of Controlling Agency Time Discretion: FDA Review Deadlines and Postmarket Drug Safety," *American Journal of Political Science* 56, no.1 (2012): 98–114.

14 Forrest Briscoe and Sean Safford, "The Nixon-in-China Effect: Activism, Imitation, and the Institutionalization of Contentious Practices," *Administrative Science Quarterly* 53, no. 3 (2008): 460–91; Nicole Raeburn, *Changing Corporate America from Inside Out* (Minneapolis: University of Minnesota Press, 2004).

15 Steven Epstein, *Impure Science* (Berkeley, CA: University of California Press, 1998); Maren Klawiter, *The Biopolitics of Breast Cancer* (Minneapolis: University of Minnesota Press, 2008).

16 See Edward T. Walker, "Social Movements, Organizations, and Fields: A Decade of Theoretical Integration," *Contemporary Sociology* 41, no. 5 (2012): 576–87.

17 Edward T. Walker, Andrew W. Martin, and John D. McCarthy, "Confronting the State, the Corporation, and the Academy: The Influence of Institutional Targets on Social Movement Repertoires," *American Journal of Sociology* 114, no. 1 (2008): 35–76.

18 Michael Schudson, *The Good Citizen* (New York: Martin Kessler, 1998).

19 Evan Schofer and Marion Fourcade-Gourinchas, "The Structural Contexts of Civic Engagement: Voluntary Association Membership in Comparative Perspective," *American Sociological Review* 66, no. 6 (2001): 806–28.

20 Theda Skocpol, *Diminished Democracy* (Norman, OK: University of Oklahoma Press, 2003); Edward T. Walker, John D. McCarthy, and Frank R. Baumgartner, "Replacing Members with Managers? Mutualism among Membership and Non-Membership Advocacy Organizations in the U.S." *American Journal of Sociology* 116, no. 4 (2011): 1284–1337.

21 For example, see Goldstein, *Interest Groups, Lobbying, and Participation in America*, p. 9; Kollman, *Outside Lobbying*, p. 20; Kay Lehman Schlozman and John T. Tierney, *Organized Interests and American Democracy* (New York: Harper and Row, 1986); Frank R. Baumgartner, Jeffrey M. Berry, Marie Hojnacki, David C. Kimball, and Beth L. Leech, *Lobbying and Policy Change* (Chicago: University of Chicago Press, 2009); Matt Grossmann, *The Not-So-Special Interests* (Stanford, CA: Stanford University Press, 2012); Christine Mahoney, *Brussels versus the Beltway* (Washington, DC: Georgetown University Press, 2008).

22 Skocpol, *Diminished Democracy*; Walker et al., "Replacing Members with Managers?"; Grossmann, *The Not-So-Special Interests*, pp. 31–32; Dara Z. Strolovitch, *Affirmative Advocacy* (Chicago: University of Chicago Press, 2007) p. 54.

23 Kollman, *Outside Lobbying*, p. 48.

24 Walker, *Grassroots for Hire*, chap. 5.

25 Henry E. Brady, Kay Lehman Schlozman, and Sidney Verba, "Prospecting for Participants: Rational Expectations and the Recruitment of Political Activists," *American Political Science Review* 93, no. 1 (1999): 153–68; Kay Lehman Schlozman, Sidney Verba, and Henry E. Brady, *The Unheavenly Chorus* (Princeton: Princeton University Press, 2012).

26 Grossmann, *The Not-So-Special Interests*.

27 Weir and Ganz, "Reconnecting People and Politics."

28 Walker, *Mobilizing Interest Groups in America*; Jeffrey M. Berry, *The Interest Group Society* (New York: Longman, 1997); Debra C. Minkoff, *Organizing for Equality* (New Brunswick, NJ: Rutgers University Press, 1995).

29 Skocpol, *Diminished Democracy*; Christopher J. Bosso, *Environment, Inc.* (Lawrence: University Press of Kansas, 2005).

30 Debra Minkoff, Silke Aisenbrey, and Jon Agnone, "Organizational Diversity in the U.S. Advocacy Sector," *Social Problems* 55, no. 4 (2008): 525–48.

31 Walker et al., "Replacing Members with Managers."

32 Ibid.

33 Ibid., p. 1313.

34 Andrew W. Martin and Marc Dixon, "Changing to Win? Threat, Resistance, and the Role of Unions in Strikes, 1984–2002," *American Journal of Sociology* 116, no. 1 (2010): 93–129.

35 Schlozman et al., *Organized Interests and American Democracy*, pp. 92–93.

36 Ibid., p. 399.

37 Respectively, Sidney Verba, Kay Lehman Schlozman, and Henry Brady, *Voice and Equality* (Cambridge: Harvard University Press, 1995), p. 386; Kollman, *Outside Lobbying*, p. 18.

38 Harry Boyte, *The Backyard Revolution* (Philadelphia: Temple University Press, 1980).

39 Michael McQuarrie, "Nonprofits and the Reconstruction of Urban Governance: Housing Production and Community Development in Cleveland, 1975–2005," *Politics and Partnerships* (Chicago: University of Chicago Press, 2010).

40 Edward T. Walker and John D. McCarthy, "Legitimacy, Strategy, and Resources in the Survival of Community-Based Organizations," *Social Problems* 57, no. 3 (2010): 315–40.

41 Howard E. Aldrich, Catherine R. Zimmer, Udo H. Staber, and John J. Beggs, "Minimalism, Mutualism, and Maturity: The Evolution of the American Trade Association Population in the 20th century," in *Evolutionary Dynamics of Organizations,* ed. Joel A. C. Baum and Jitendra V. Singh (New York: Oxford University Press, 1994): pp. 223–39; Lyn Spillman, *Solidarity in Strategy* (Chicago: University of Chicago Press, 2012).

42 Kollman, *Outside Lobbying*, p. 18.

43 Verba et al., *Voice and Equality*, p. 376.

44 Schlozman et al., *Organized Interests and American Democracy*, pp. 409, 386.

45 Paul J. DiMaggio and Walter W. Powell, "The Iron Cage Revisited: Institutional Isomorphism and Collective Rationality in Organizational Fields," *American Sociological Review* 48, no. 2 (1983): 147–60; Royston Greenwood, C. R. Hinings, and Roy Suddaby, "Theorizing Change: The Role of Professional Associations in the Transformation of Institutionalized Fields," *Academy of Management Journal* 45, no. 1 (2002): 58–80.

46 Jill Quadagno, "Why the United States Has No National Health Insurance: Stakeholder Mobilization against the Welfare State, 1945–1996," *Journal of Health and Social Behavior* 45 (2004): 25–44; Paul Starr, *The Social Transformation of American Medicine* (New York: Basic Books, 1982).

47 Martin B. Meznar and Douglas Nigh, "Buffer or Bridge? Environmental and Organizational Determinants of Public Affairs Activities in American Firms," *The Academy of Management Journal* 38, no. 4 (1995): 975–96.

48 D. M. Hart, "'Business' Is Not an Interest Group: On the Study of Companies in American National Politics," *Annual Review of Political Science* 7 (2004): 47–69; Michael Lord. "Constituency-based Lobbying as Corporate Political Strategy: Testing an Agency Theory Perspective," *Business and Politics* 2, no. 3 (2000): 289–308; Barry Baysinger, Gerald D. Keim, and Carl P. Zeithaml, "An Empirical Evaluation of the Potential for Including Shareholders in Corporate Constituency Programs," *Academy of Management Journal* 28, no. 1 (1985): 180–200.

49 Culpepper, *Quiet Politics and Business Power*.

50 Phil Harris and Craig S. Fleisher, *Handbook of Public Affairs* (Thousand Oaks, CA: Sage, 2005).

51 Edward T. Walker, "Privatizing Participation: Civic Change and the Organizational Dynamics of Grassroots Lobbying Firms," *American Sociological Review* 74, no. 1 (2009): 83–105; Edward T. Walker, "Putting a Face on the Issue: Corporate Stakeholder Mobilization in Professional Grassroots Lobbying Campaigns," *Business and Society* 51, no. 4 (2012): 619–59; Walker, "Industry-Driven Activism"; Walker, "Social Movements, Organizations, and Fields"; Walker, *Grassroots for Hire*.

52 Totals exceed 100% due to rounding.

53 See Walker, "Privatizing Participation," p. 96.

54 Many Democratic firms work with groups founded during the "advocacy explosion," and these are predominantly left-leaning associations. The conservative firms tend

to have relatively fewer advocacy clients and continue to rely on revenue from right-leaning candidate campaigns.

55 Walker, *Grassroots for Hire*, chap. 5.
56 Michael Hawthorne, "Higher Levels of Flame Retardants Found in Minority Children," *Chicago Tribune,* May 23, 2012.
57 Walker, *Grassroots for Hire*, chap. 7.

Chapter 4

The Paradoxes of Inequality and Interest Group Representation

Dara Z. Strolovitch

Contemplating the relationship between interest groups and inequality suggests a somewhat paradoxical situation regarding the role of such organizations as representatives of disadvantaged groups: On the one hand, national advocacy organizations have long provided vital representation to women, people of color, and low-income people—groups that are marginalized in national politics; under-served by two-party, winner-take-all elections; and under-represented in legislative bodies. In addition, the last five decades have witnessed an explosion in the number of organizations that represent these and other marginalized groups in national politics. On the other hand, for all of their growth, organizations advocating on behalf of groups such as women, people of color, low-income people, and lesbian, gay, bisexual, transgender, and queer (LGBTQ) people continue to make up only a small portion of the broader interest group universe that counts more than 17,000 national organizations representing much wealthier and more powerful interests.[1] Moreover, organizations representing marginalized groups have also been criticized for focusing mostly on the needs of the relatively advantaged members of their constituencies.

To explore how well contemporary American advocacy groups represent marginalized constituencies, this chapter draws on surveys of interest groups that I fielded in 2000 and 2007 and on evidence from a series of in-depth interviews that I conducted between 2000 and 2010. The evidence makes clear that advocacy groups are a crucial source of compensatory representation. That is, such organizations provide extra representation that helps to offset the unequal voice afforded marginalized groups in political institutions and policy-making processes. Contextualizing evidence from these studies within a framework that scholars have come to call "intersectionality," however, also reveals that organizations do indeed prioritize the interests of advantaged members while giving short-shrift to disadvantaged subgroups of their constituencies. Moreover, such biases have been exacerbated in the wake of 9/11 and the War on Terror. The evidence also makes clear, however, that while such trends are widespread, they are not ubiquitous. In fact, many advocacy groups work to remedy these biases using a set of principles that I call *affirmative advocacy*—a framework that aims to counteract the biases against issues that affect people at the intersection of more than one marginalized group.

A Question with Deep Roots

Writers since Alexis de Tocqueville have recognized that civic organizations are a key component of American democracy, but they have also long disagreed about whether such organizations alleviate or exacerbate inequalities in American politics and public policy. Indeed, such questions are among the most longstanding and fundamental debates about the role of interest groups and civil society organizations in American politics.[2] Many of the scholars and political observers who first considered such questions were quite sanguine about the role of pressure groups in the United States. Scholars who came to be called "pluralists" such as David Truman and Robert Dahl, for example, were optimistic that societal groups would form organizations when their interests were at stake in the policy process, and they were also confident that no single such interest would win or lose all of time.[3] And, in fact, for many years, one form of civic organization—national advocacy organizations—offered some of the only representation available to groups such as Southern blacks and women of all races, who were denied formal voting rights until well into the twentieth century. Long before women won the right to vote, for example, organizations such as the National American Woman Suffrage Association mobilized women and lobbied legislators on their behalf. Similarly, the National Association for the Advancement of Colored People provided representation for African Americans in the South.

But although such organizations often were the only voice for these groups, they were nonetheless comparatively weak, greatly outnumbered and outresourced by business, financial, and professional interest groups. Because relatively few formal political organizations represented the interests of groups such as women, people of color, and low-income people in national politics before the 1960s, critics such as E. E. Schattschneider argued that interest groups exacerbated rather than eased inequalities in political access.[4] Through the process that he termed the "mobilization of bias," the concerns of weak groups were "organized out" of politics by elites who manipulated the agenda toward their own interests.[5] As a consequence, he asserted, the interests of weak groups were not merely opposed but were actually excluded from the political agenda. "The flaw in the pluralist heaven," he wrote, "is that the heavenly chorus sings with a strong upper-class accent." He estimated that approximately 90 percent of the population could not access what he called "the pressure system," the informal but extensive system of organizations mobilized to influence national politics.[6]

True as this was when he wrote it, the movements of "long 1960s" mobilized historically marginalized and excluded groups, in particular women, people of color, and low-income people, and led to an explosion in the number of organizations speaking on behalf of disadvantaged populations.[7] Organizations advocating on their behalf pursued lawsuits, regulations, and legislation to end *de jure* (that is, legally defined) racial and sex-based discrimination and to increase resources and opportunities for those groups, and many of the resulting policies and programs themselves spawned organizations. By the beginning of the twenty-first century, more than seven hundred organizations represented women, people of color, and low-income people were active in national politics, including more than forty African American organizations, more than thirty Asian-Pacific American organizations, and well over one hundred women's organizations.[8]

Although the increase in the number of organizations has helped usher in significant legal and policy gains for these and other marginalized groups, decades later, important questions remain about how well such organizations represent their less privileged constituents. And while some of the debates about these questions echo the longstanding concerns of scholars such as E. E. Schattschneider who were concerned with biases inside the broader pressure group system that favored wealthy and powerful interests, some also express concerns about the development of biases among the very organizations that claim to represent marginalized populations.[9] Feminist groups have been criticized by some as organizations of and for affluent white women, for example, and civil rights organizations are sometimes said to focus too much on "middle-class" issues. Organizations championing economic justice are said to fall short when they overlook or downplay the multiple disadvantages suffered by low-income women, immigrants, LGBTQ people, or people of color.[10] Legal scholar and critical race theorist Kimberlé Crenshaw has termed the multiply disadvantaged subgroups of marginalized groups such as women, people of color, and low-income people "intersectionally marginalized."[11] Intersectional frameworks contend that economic and social injustices are not mutually exclusive and that no particular form of domination or social relation—be it race, class, patriarchy, or heteronomativity—is the primary source of oppression.[12] Recognizing that important inequalities persist *among* racial, gender, and economic groups, intersectional approaches highlight inequalities *within* marginalized groups. These approaches also emphasize the consequent unevenness in the effects of the political, economic, and social gains made by marginalized groups since, and as a result of, the social movements and policy gains of the "long 1960s."[13] For example, low-income women constitute an intersectionally disadvantaged subgroup of women, as they face marginalization both economically and based on gender.

To examine how well advocacy organizations represent intersectionally disadvantaged subgroups of their constituencies, my book, *Affirmative Advocacy,* explored how advocacy organizations decide which battles to prioritize in an era marked by subsiding de jure discrimination but often heightened de facto inequalities, both *between* their marginalized constituencies on the one hand and dominant racial, gender, and income groups on the other hand as well as *within* the marginalized populations they claim to represent. Faced with limited resources but encompassing large and internally complex constituencies, how do advocacy organizations decide which groups and subgroups warrant the most attention? To explore these issues, I asked three key questions fundamental to evaluating the representation of marginalized groups in the United States: First, how active are advocacy organizations when it comes to policy issues that affect intersectionally marginalized subgroups of their constituencies? Second, when they are involved with such issues, in what ways are they active—in particular, at which political institutions do they target their advocacy, and what kind of coalitions do they form? Third, how do organizations define their mandates as representatives, and what are some of the steps that can be taken by organizations to strengthen representation for intersectionally marginalized groups?

To answer these questions, in 2000 and 2001, I collected new quantitative and qualitative data using a survey of 286 organizations as well as in-depth face-to-face interviews with officers and professional staff at 40 organizations. To collect the survey data, I designed the first large-scale study focusing on the organizations that together make up the social and economic justice interest community, the 2000 Survey of National Economic and Social Justice Organizations (hereafter referred to as the SNESJO). Coupled with the information that I collected through the in-person interviews and analyzed in light of insights based in theories of intersectionality as well as theories of representation, these data allow for the first broad and in-depth examination of the extent to which these advocacy organizations represent disadvantaged subgroups of their constituents.

Respondents were asked a series of questions about the levels and targets of their advocacy activities on four domestic policy issues. The four issues were assigned to different types of organizations based on a four-part policy typology that I created to operationalize key aspects of intersectional theories about power and marginalization and to test them against competing explanations (see Figure 4.1): (1) Universal issues, which affect, at least in theory, the population as a whole, regardless of race, gender, sexual orientation, disability, class, or any other identity or axis of marginalization; (2) Majority issues, which affect an organization's members or constituents relatively equally; (3) Disadvantaged subgroup issues, which affect a subgroup of an organization's constituents that is intersectionally marginalized (i.e., it is *disadvantaged* economically, socially, or politically compared

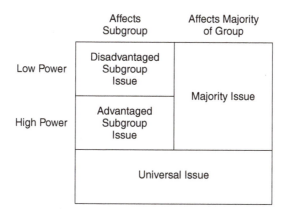

Figure 4.1 Policy Typology

Note: From *Affirmative Advocacy* (Strolovitch 2007).

Table 4.1 Specific Policy Issues Used in SNESJO Questions, by Organization Type and Issue Category

Organization Type	Majority Issue	Advantaged Subgroup Issue	Disadvantaged Subgroup Issue	Universal Issue
Asian Pacific American	Hate crime	Affirmative action in government contracting	Violence against women	Social Security
Black/African American	Racial profiling	Affirmative action in higher education	Welfare	Social Security
Latino/Hispanic	Census undercount	Affirmative action in higher education	Welfare	Social Security
Native American/American Indian	Tribal sovereignty	Affirmative action in higher education	Violence against women	Social Security
Civil rights – Other[a]	Hate crime	Affirmative action in higher education	Discrimination against LGBT people	Social Security
Immigrants' rights	Green-card backlog	Availability of H1B visas	Denial of benefits to immigrants	Social Security
Labor[b]	Minimum wage	White-collar unionization	Job discrimination against women and minorities	Social Security
Economic justice[c]	Welfare	Minimum wage	Public funding for abortion	Social Security
Public interest[d]	Campaign finance reform	Internet privacy	Environmental racism	Social Security
Reproductive rights/women's health	Late-term abortion	Abortion coverage by insurance/HMOs	Public funding for abortion	Social Security
Women's rights/feminist[e]	Violence against women	Affirmative action in higher education	Welfare	Social Security

Sources: Issues were selected by the author based on information from *Congressional Quarterly* (1990, 1993, 1996, and 1999); the *Congressional Record* (1990–2000); the *New York Times* "Supreme Court Roundup" (1990–2000); and the *Federal Register* (1990–2000).

a   Includes broadly civil rights and civil liberties organizations; lesbian, gay, bisexual, and transgender (LGBT) rights organizations; criminal justice organizations; Arab/Muslim organizations; antiracist organizations; some religious minority groups; and multiculturalism organizations.

b   Includes unions.

c   Includes antipoverty, welfare rights, anti-homeless, and anti-hunger organizations.

d   Includes consumer, environmental, and "good government" organizations that advocate in the areas of racial, gender, or economic justice. From *Affirmative Advocacy* (Strolovitch 2007).

e   Includes women of color organizations.

to the broader constituency); and (4) advantaged subgroup issues, which also affect a subgroup of an organization's constituents, but a relatively advantaged or privileged minority compared to the broader constituency (though, it is important to note, they are nonetheless disadvantaged compared to the general population).

So, for example, I asked respondents from women's organizations about their advocacy efforts regarding violence against women (VAW) as a majority issue, as all women are, theoretically, equally likely to be victims of VAW, even if not every women is in fact a victim. I asked them about affirmative action in higher education as an advantaged subgroup issue, as it affects primarily college educated women, a relatively privileged subgroup of all women. Finally, I asked these same respondents about welfare reform as a disadvantaged subgroup issue, as it intersects gender and class and affects low-income women, an intersectionally disadvantaged subgroup of women. Respondents from all organizations in the study were asked about Social Security as a "universal" issue. Based on this typology, respondents from different kinds of organizations were asked a series of questions, including one that asked them to estimate the proportion of their constituency that was affected by each of four designated policy issues, and how active, on a scale of 1–5, their organization was on each one between 1990 and 2000.

Levels of Activity

To answer the first question about levels of activity, Table 4.2 shows the percentage of organizations that were active and inactive on each issue type, as well as the mean levels of activity on each one (based on the 1–5 scale of activity). As the data in the table make clear, the organizations in the study were involved in many of the issues about which they were asked, thereby confirming that advocacy groups are a critical source of compensatory representation for marginalized groups. The variations in these patterns of involvement also demonstrate, however, that these organizations devote considerably *less* attention to issues affecting intersection-ally disadvantaged constituents than they do when it comes to issues affecting more advantaged ones. In the case of women's organizations, for example, approximately 85% of organizations were active on the majority issue, violence against women. Slightly fewer, about 77%, were active on affirmative action in higher education, an issue affecting an advantaged subgroup of women. However, a significant but far smaller proportion of these organizations—just over 65%— were at all active on welfare reform, an issue affecting a *disadvantaged* subgroup of women.

The effects of these disparities are illustrated in Figure 4.2. Probabilities of activity that simulate the contingent effects of the proportion of constituents affected as they vary by policy type (while holding the values of all variables at their means) show that there is a 23.3% chance that an organization will be very active (4 or 5 on the 1–5 scale of activity) on a majority issue with a low level of impact on an organization's constituents ("1" on the 1–5 scale of impact). This probability increases to 78.8% in the case of a majority issue with a *high* level of impact ("5" on

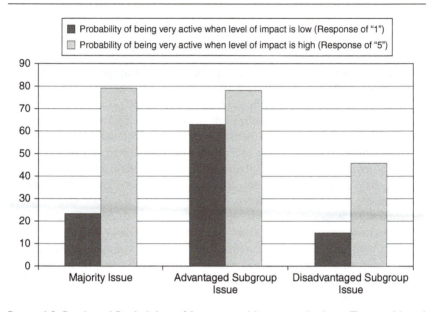

Figure 4.2 Predicted Probability of Activity and Inactivity, by Issue Type and Level of Impact (Membership Organizations Only)

Note: Organization officers were asked, "Please tell me, on a scale of 1 to 5, where 1 is not active, and 5 is very active, how active has your organization been on each of the following policy issues in the past ten years?" The black columns reflect the probability of giving the answer "4" or "5" (holding the other variables in the model constant) when they judge the level of impact on their constituency to be low (1). The shaded columns reflect the probability of giving the answer "4" or "5" (holding the other variables in the model constant) when they judge the level of impact on their constituency to be high (5) (Source: SNESJO). From *Affirmative Advocacy* (Strolovitch 2007).

the 1–5 scale of impact). In the case of disadvantaged subgroup issues, the chances of high level of activity increase from 14.6% to 45.6% as we move from low to high levels of impact. The simulation also demonstrates, however, that levels of activity for *advantaged-subgroup* issues are likely to be very high (62.8% chance of a high level of activity) even when impact is at its *lowest* level. Moreover, the probability of a high level of activity on an advantaged subgroup issue increases much less starkly (to 78%) as we move from low to high levels of impact. In fact, the probability that an organization will be active at a high level is greater in the case of an advantaged-subgroup issue with a very low level of impact on its constituents than it is for a disadvantaged-subgroup issue that affects "almost all" of its constituents. In addition, while activity on both majority and disadvantaged subgroup issues is sensitive to levels of impact, levels of activity on advantaged subgroup issues do *not* increase or decrease as the proportion of constituents affected by an issue increases, suggesting that these issues are almost immune to strategic considerations about breadth of impact. Instead, it is often the case that the broader the potential impact of an issue, the *less* attention it receives.

Table 4.2 Mean Level of Activity and Percent of Organizations Active on Each Issue Type, by Type of Organization

Organization Type	Majority Issue		Advantaged Subgroup Issue		Disadvantaged Subgroup Issue		Universal Issue	
	Mean	%	Mean	%	Mean	%	Mean	%
Asian Pacific American	3.7	76.9	3.0	84.6	2.4	69.2	1.6	30.8
Black/African American	4.1	85.0	4.5	90.0	3.7	90.0	2.1	45.0
Latino/Hispanic	4.6	100.0	4.3	100.0	2.9	62.5	2.1	50.0
Native American/ American Indian	4.0	100.0	3.8	69.2	2.9	69.2	1.7	15.4
Civil Rights – Other[a]	3.3	74.4	2.9	64.1	2.7	64.1	1.6	23.1
Labor[b]	3.8	78.6	4.0	78.6	3.5	71.4	2.9	54.8
Economic Justice[c]	3.4	69.7	3.4	71.2	1.2	12.1	1.9	30.3
Public Interest[d]	3.3	72.7	2.4	45.5	2.1	63.6	1.8	27.4
Women's Rights/ Feminist[e]	3.6	84.8	3.4	77.3	2.9	65.2	2.1	39.4

Source: 2000 Survey of National Economic and Social Justice Organizations (see Strolovitch 2007 for details). Organization officers were asked, "Please tell me, on a scale of 1 to 5, where 1 is not active, and 5 is very active, how active has your organization been on each of the following policy issues in the past ten years?

Note: Data reflect the percentage of respondents giving answers between 2 and 5.

a   Includes broadly based civil rights and civil liberties organizations; lesbian, gay, bisexual, and transgender (LGBT) rights organizations; criminal justice organizations; Arab/Muslim organizations; antiracist organizations; some religious minority groups; and multiculturalism organizations. Also includes immigrants' rights organizations.

b   Includes unions.

c   Includes antipoverty, welfare rights, anti-homeless, and anti-hunger organizations.

d   Includes consumer, environmental, and "good government" organizations that advocate in the areas of racial, gender, or economic justice.

e   Includes women of color, reproductive rights, and women's health organizations. From *Affirmative Advocacy* (Strolovitch 2007).

Institutional Targeting

Advocacy organizations use a wide array of tactics aimed at many institutions as they represent their constituents and pursue their policy goals. When they target Congress, for example, they can lobby legislators directly, organize letter-writing campaigns among their constituents, testify at committee hearings, or provide policy makers with information and research. Advocacy organizations can also attempt to influence the executive branch by lobbying the president and presidential advisers regarding pending legislation or by providing agencies with comments and testimony about proposed regulations. Organizations can also target the courts by filing amicus curiae briefs or bringing test cases and class action suits to represent their constituents.

Organizations' decisions about tactics and institutional targets depend on many factors, including their general preferences for one institution over another, the political party in control of each branch, and whether there are preexisting opportunities to address an issue in a given branch.[14] In addition to these influences on their decisions, it is important to consider whether organizations' choices about which political branch to target—legislative, judicial, or executive— vary on the basis of the issue type or the status of the affected group. In other words, another measure through which we can evaluate inequality and interest group representation is to assess the *ways* in which organizations advocate on behalf of marginalized groups. Particularly telling in this regard is the extent to which advocacy organizations target the court compared to their targeting of the legislative and executive branches.

As I explain at greater length in *Affirmative Advocacy*, the judiciary is the branch of the federal government that is most explicitly (though by no means exclusively) charged with protecting rights and with checking the powers and actions of the majoritarian, electorally based legislative and executive branches. As a consequence, the courts are often called upon to protect unpopular minorities from the tyranny of majority rule. Some have argued (most notably Charles Beard) that the minorities the framers likely had in mind were wealthy landowners who, they thought, needed protection from the masses that might wield their populist power against them in the new democracy.[15] However, questions about the policy-making activities of the courts, while of broad concern, have particular implications for the protection and representation of disadvantaged groups as well as for the organizations that advocate for and represent them. Proponents of a "legal mobilization" paradigm, such as Michael McCann, argue that legal strategies are crucial for outsider groups because they "help movement activists to win voice, position, and influence" in the policy process and give them a way to "formalize" their roles in policy formulation and implementation processes.[16] Sally Kenney argues similarly that courts are essential conduits for pursuing women's grievances because the judicial branch plays an important constitutive role in framing issues for policy makers.[17] Paul Frymer explains that the courts play an important role when it comes to marginalized groups because Congress often delegates responsibility for their representation and for redressing their grievances to the courts.[18] In these and other ways, the courts provide outsider groups with unique opportunities to make claims and to shape the discourses about the policy issues that concern them.[19] As such, although the record of the courts in protecting disadvantaged groups has been inconsistent, advocacy groups and organizations have targeted the judicial branch when other political opportunities have been absent, particularly when they have been unsuccessful in the legislative and executive branches, or in conjunction with these other branches.[20]

While advocacy groups might invite the courts to decide such questions, and while the courts might accept the invitation to do so, many critics argue that this virtue of the courts is also its vice. Echoing Alexander Bickel's concern about "counter-majoritarian difficulty" of judicial review, they worry that the same insulation from the will of the majority that allows judges to rule on behalf of unpopular minorities also lays the basis for portrayals of their decisions in such cases as undemocratic, antimajoritarian, and therefore illegitimate.[21] Many such critiques of judicial activism are lodged by opponents of reproductive rights, gay rights, and affirmative action, most of whom would object to these policies from whatever institution they were to emanate.[22] However, ambivalence also emanates from some who support these policies and who sympathize with the goals of the marginalized groups. Many liberal legal scholars have taken issue with what they perceive as an overreliance on court-based strategies by the organizations that represent marginalized groups, arguing that the nonmajoritarian character of the courts entails political costs that make judicial strategies a poor means of representing marginalized groups.[23] The ranks of such critics have grown markedly in recent years, at least in part in response to "the conservative entrenchment of federal courts" since the late 1960s.[24]

Because of these high costs, however, when an organization targets the judiciary to pursue an issue, it sends strong signals about the issue's importance and about its own willingness to go to bat for the constituents affected by it.[25] As a consequence, we might think of judicial strategies as "big guns" that are kept in reserve and brought in when other approaches have failed or are futile. From this perspective, understanding how willingly advocacy organizations expend these scarce resources on behalf of intersectionally disadvantaged groups can be a way to assess the robustness of the representation they provide to them.

To explore the extent to which organizations that represent marginalized groups target the court relative to their targeting of other political institutions, Figure 4.3 summarizes responses to a question asking respondents to rate how important each branch is as a target of their organization's activity on a 1-to-5 scale. The pattern of responses departs quite strikingly from the image of profligate litigation by liberal organizations conjured up by critics, as the judicial branch is the least popular target of advocacy activity, while the legislative branch is again the most popular target.[26] The legislative branch was ranked "very important" by 48.6% of the respondents; the executive branch, by 37.5%. However, the federal courts were identified as "very important" by a mere 20% of the respondents.

Even though organizations target the judicial branch at rates far lower than the ones at which they target the legislative and executive branches, they may still not use the courts in the "right" way—to protect the most vulnerable and unpopular groups when other branches fail to do so, saving the associated resources and political and social capital for the constituencies that need them the most. To examine what proportion of court-related resources and energy organizations devote to addressing issues that affect intersectionally disadvantaged subgroups of their constituencies and whether their decisions about which political branch to target—the legislative, the judicial, or the executive branch—vary based on the power of the affected group, Figure 4.4 summarizes responses to a series of questions in the SNESJO that asks respondents to select the federal-level political institution (legislative, executive, or judicial branch) that is the most frequent target of their efforts on each of the four policy issues designated for their organization.[27]

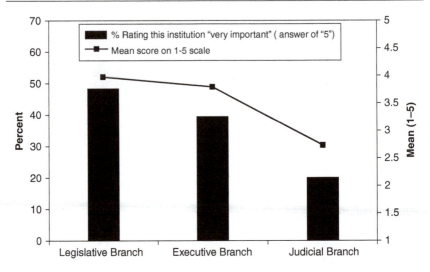

Figure 4.3 Importance of Each Branch as a Target of Organizations' Activity

Note: Organization officers were asked, "On a scale of 1 to 5, if 1 is not important and 5 is very important, how important is each of the following as a target of your organization's activity?" Data in the columns reflect the percentage of respondents giving the answer "5" (Source: SNESJO). From *Affirmative Advocacy* (Strolovitch 2007).

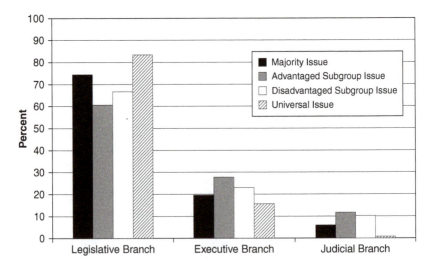

Figure 4.4 Institution Targeted, by Policy Type

Note: Organization officers were asked, "Which of the following political institutions is the most important target of your efforts in trying to influence policy on [the issue in question]?" Data in the columns reflect the percentage of respondents selecting that branch for the policy issue in question. The question was posed so that respondents had to select only one of the institutions (Source: SNESJO). From *Affirmative Advocacy* (Strolovitch 2007).

As is the case with the general levels of institutional targeting, the answers to the policy-specific questions reveal that the percentage of organizations targeting the courts is quite low regardless of the issue type in question. However, looking at these results more closely reveals greater complexity. In particular, the data show that rates of court use vary markedly by issue type: while the legislative branch is the most frequent target of activity for all issues, organizations target the courts approximately twice as often when it comes to issues affecting advantaged or disadvantaged subgroups than they do when comes to majority issues. Indeed, there is a clear progression in the extent of this activity that increases steadily as we move from universal issues on the low end to advantaged-subgroup issues on the high end.

Probabilities predicting the chances that an organization will target each branch and to examine these chances as they vary by issue type confirm that Congress is, overwhelmingly, the most likely target of advocacy activity for each of the four types of public policy issues (see Figure 4.5). However, when issues affect subgroups, weak or strong, organizations are more likely to use the courts to pursue their goals than they are when issues affect a majority of their constituents. Specifically, there is a 44% chance that an organization will target the legislative branch when it is working on a majority issue. This chance decreases to 43% if the issue in question affects an intersectionally disadvantaged subgroup of their constituency and decreases even further to 39% is the issue in question affects an advantaged

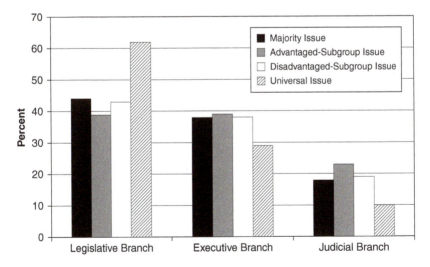

Figure 4.5 Predicted Probability of Targeting Each Branch, by Issue Type

Note: Organization officers were asked, "Which of the following political institutions is the most important target of your efforts in trying to influence policy on [the issue in question]?" The columns represent the probability of targeting each branch while holding the other variables in the model constant (Source: SNESJO). From *Affirmative Advocacy* (Strolovitch 2007).

subgroup of the constituency. Conversely, there is about a 23% chance that the judicial branch will be the focus of attention in the case of an issue that affects an advantaged subgroup. The probability of focusing on the courts in cases when an issue affects a disadvantaged subgroup is only about 19%, which further decreases to 18% in the case of a majority issue. As such, court tactics are most prevalent when it comes to advantaged-subgroup issues. Even though organizations still direct the bulk of their efforts at Congress when it comes to these issues, legislative activity constitutes a far smaller proportion of their activity and judicial activity a far greater proportion of their activity for advantaged-subgroup issues than for any of the other issue types.

These disparities between the probabilities of targeting the courts in the case of advantaged-subgroup issues and disadvantaged-subgroup issues make a bigger difference than we might appreciate at first glance. As I showed above, a great deal of attention is devoted to advantaged-subgroup issues—and very little attention is devoted to disadvantaged-subgroup issues—in the first place. As a consequence, the 23% chance of court activity in the case of advantaged-subgroup issues is 23% of a very high level of activity, while the 19% chance of court activity in the case of disadvantaged-subgroup issues is 19% of a very low level of activity. In this context, the substantive implications of these probabilities are quite striking: organizations are more likely to target the courts when issues affect subgroups within their constituency, but even so, they expend a far greater proportion of their court-oriented resources on behalf of advantaged subgroups of their constituencies. That organizations save their use of court tactics for subgroups is understandable and might be considered congruent with the constitutional role of the courts as protectors of minority rights within a majoritarian democracy. However, it is the fact that organizations are most likely to target both the courts and the executive branch on behalf of advantaged subgroups of their constituencies than they are when it comes to disadvantaged subgroups that is most remarkable. In fact, once we take other factors into account, disadvantaged-subgroup and majority issues are almost equally likely to be pursued through the courts. As such, the concentration of judicial targeting on behalf advantaged subgroups reinforces, rather than alleviates, the low levels of representation for intersectionally disadvantaged groups.

Coalitions

Coalitions offer an array of benefits to all types of organizations, but their advantages are particularly pronounced among organizations that represent marginalized groups because they allow these organizations—which typically have few resources or limited political clout—to consolidate and share scarce material resources such as funds and staff, to compound the strength of their numbers, to increase their credibility with both political elites and grassroots constituents, and to increase their joint political influence.[28] In light of these advantages, it not surprising that coalitions are by far the most popular tactic among organizations that represent marginalized groups, with 98% of the organizations surveyed in the SNESJO indicating that they have worked in coalitions at some point and approximately two-thirds reporting that they have done so "frequently."

In addition to providing ways for organizations that represent marginalized groups to compound their strength and maximize their influence, they may also provide a way for them to pursue issues affecting intersectionally disadvantaged subgroups of their constituencies. Coalitions are ideally suited to pursuing such issues because they have the capacity and indeed the objective to work on issues that intersect the interests and goals of many organizations and movements. By allowing organizations to pursue issues that cut across the constituencies of a range of organizations, they might, in turn, alleviate the inequities that favor advantaged subgroups at the expense of disadvantaged ones by giving organizations the opportunity to work on issues and to service constituencies that they might otherwise overlook.

Evidence from the survey and interviews confirms that this is indeed the case. As Figure 4.6 makes clear, although organizations make extensive use of coalitions when it comes to all issue types, they are the most frequently reported activity for issues affecting intersectionally disadvantaged subgroups. Coalitions are therefore the source of a very high proportion of the activity that is devoted to disadvantaged-subgroup issues and are consequently a fertile source of representation for intersectionally disadvantaged subgroups.

The popularity of coalitions as a way to address disadvantaged-subgroup issues is understandable because such partnerships offer a low-cost, low-profile way to get involved in an issue. By allying with others, organizations can take part in policy activity on issues about which they would otherwise likely be inactive, and they can do so without expending extensive resources or calling too much attention to their efforts.[29] Alliances can be particularly useful when it comes to disadvantaged-subgroup issues that tend not to be popular among constituents. In fact, many of the officers I interviewed made repeated references to channeling activity on such issues into coalition work. For example, the executive director of an economic justice organization told me that when her members are ambivalent about an issue or when the organization does not want to take the lead on it is "exactly why we enter into coalitions. Our name might be on a sign-on letter, or we might be doing some visits on a particular issue, but . . . we aren't seen as the one out in front on it."

Similarly, the executive director of an Asian-Pacific American organization explained that her organization often restricts its work on issues that are controversial among its constituents to coalition efforts. Doing so, she said, is one way to show support for an issue and for the organizations that are working on it, but in a low-profile way. For example, she explained that violence against women (an issue that affects an intersectionally disadvantaged subset of her group's constituency) is a "touchy" subject within the community she represents. As a consequence, she told me, "rather than being out there as an organization" when it comes to addressing this issue, her organization "sign[s] on with some other groups."

Although the foregoing statements demonstrate some of the ways in which coalitions can promote intersectional understandings about issues and

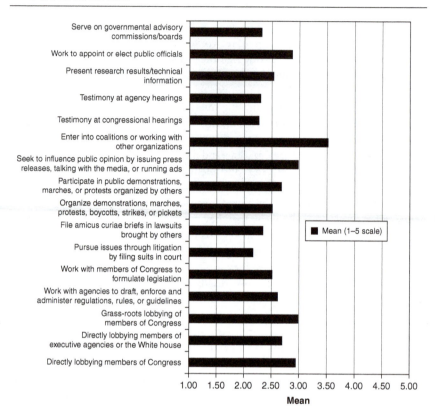

Figure 4.6 Tactics Used to Pursue Disadvantaged-subgroup Issues

Note: Organization officers were asked, "On a scale of 1 to 5, where 1 is never and 5 is frequently, how often does your organization engage in the following activities in pursuing its policy goals on the issue of [the issue in question]?" Data in the bars represent the mean response for each tactic (Source: SNESJO). From *Affirmative Advocacy* (Strolovitch 2007).

constituencies and can therefore correct many of the inequities in representation for intersectionally disadvantaged subgroups, they also underscore the extent to which coalitions can also present their own challenges to effective advocacy and representation by reproducing many of the same problems associated with advocacy on behalf of these subgroups that have been on display in the analyses of the levels and targets of activity.

These unequal efforts are evident in respondents' answers to survey questions about their participation in coalitions when it comes to particular policy issues. The proportion of organizations engaging in coalition work is relatively equal over each of the four types of public policy issues, ranging from 90% in the case of advantaged-subgroup issues to 95% in the case of majority issues (see Figure 4.7). However, while the percentage of organizations working in coalitions does not vary much by issue type, the average level of participation in coalitions varies a fair bit, and participation levels are lower when disadvantaged-subgroup issues are

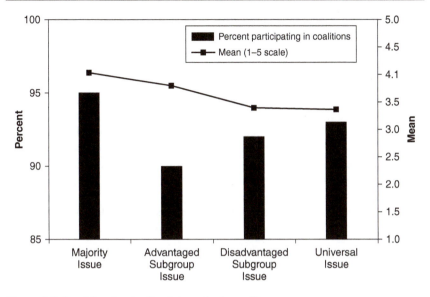

Figure 4.7 Participation in Coalitions, by Issue Type

Note: Organization officers were asked, "On a scale of 1 to 5, where 1 is never and 5 is frequently, how often does your organization engage in the following activities in pursuing its policy goals on the issue of [the policy issue in question]?" Data in the columns reflect the percentage of respondents giving answers of 2 to 5 for each issue type. The trendline shows the mean response for each issue type (Source: SNESJO). From *Affirmative Advocacy* (Strolovitch 2007).

concerned than they are for either majority or advantaged-subgroup issues. The disparity between the two measures also demonstrates that although organizations are somewhat less likely to join coalitions when it comes to advantaged-subgroup issues than they are for other issues, when they do join coalitions on such issues, they are very active. On the other hand, while a higher proportion of organizations join coalitions as part of their advocacy on disadvantaged-subgroup issues, the resources and energy that they devote to coalition work on such issues is lower than it is when they work in coalition on other issues. As a consequence, one defining limitation of coalitions when it comes to advocacy on disadvantaged-subgroup issues is that organizations often devote only symbolic efforts to issues affecting these groups, reserving their "best efforts" in coalition work for the issues that they see as central to their main policy goals.

In spite of these challenges, the evidence shows that many organizations do exploit the opportunities presented by coalitions to more effectively advocate on behalf of intersectionally disadvantaged groups. Under some circumstances, for example, coalitions compel organizations to expand their agendas by taking part in advocacy on issues that they might otherwise ignore. In addition, the relationships that are fostered by coalitions allow organizations to act as mediators for their constituents within their interest community. But while coalitions are a key source of activity on such issues, they do not prevent the more general tendency of organizations to give short shrift to the issues that affect their intersectionally disadvantaged constituents. As such, although coalitions account for a disproportionately large share of the activity devoted to disadvantaged-subgroup issues by advocacy organizations, coalitions often mirror and perpetuate the very problems associated with advocacy on such issues that permeate the broader political universe. Many of these disparities originate in reasonable considerations about maintaining access to policy makers, organizational maintenance, reputation, and scarcity of resources. Nonetheless, their cumulative effect is that coalitions frequently marginalize issues affecting intersectionally disadvantaged subgroups, thereby reinforcing the mobilization of bias in representation observed in other aspects of the work of interest groups and reproducing many of the biases in politics and policy making more generally.

Taken together, the analyses I have presented make clear that although advocacy organizations are a critical source of representation for marginalized groups, they are considerably less active, and active in substantially different ways, when it comes to issues affecting disadvantaged subgroups than they are when it comes to issues affecting more advantaged subgroups. These disparities are not due to strategic concerns, nor are they due to tradeoffs between economic issues on the one hand and social issues on the other. Rather, they stem from failures to address issues that intersect multiple disadvantages. As such, these analyses reveal what I characterize as a double standard on the part of advocacy organizations that represent women, people of color, and low-income people in U.S. politics—a double standard in which issues affecting *advantaged* subgroups receive more attention not only than disadvantaged subgroup issues but also than *majority* issues. Thus, although they constitute a critical source of representation for their intersectionally marginalized constituents, advocacy organizations are considerably less active, and active in substantially different ways, when it comes to issues affecting disadvantaged subgroups than they are when it comes to issues affecting more advantaged subgroups.

Advocacy in Not-So-Good Times

Such evidence of inequalities in representation even among those organizations most concerned with advocating on behalf of marginalized groups is particularly sobering in light of the fact it is based on data that were collected between June 2000 and August 2001, when times were, by many accounts, relatively good. Though the survey and interview questions asked respondents to reflect upon their organizations' activities and priorities going back to 1990—an era that encompassed, among other things, an economic recession and Operation Desert Storm—the period under examination in *Affirmative Advocacy* was one that has come to be characterized as a decade of relative "peace and prosperity." While that era was by no means a utopian one for marginalized groups— the wealth and income gaps between rich and poor widened dramatically; and Congress passed and President Clinton signed the 1994 Omnibus crime bill, the

1996 welfare reform legislation, Don't Ask Don't Tell, immigration reform, and the Defense of Marriage Act—it is normally remembered as having been markedly untumultuous.[30]

Even during such an ostensibly peaceful and prosperous period, respondents had claimed that, as organizations and movements speaking on behalf of weak, minority, and marginalized groups, they first needed to secure their place at the political table before they could be expected to pay attention to what they characterized as "narrow" issues affecting their intersectionally marginalized constituents. Framing such issues as narrow and particularistic "special" interests allowed them to justify both their lack of attention to them as well as their extensive attention to issues affecting advantaged subgroups. Others argued that the concerns of intersectionally marginalized subgroups were not central to their organization's mission, and that other groups were therefore better suited to address them. Still others claimed that the crosscutting issues of race, class, gender, or sexuality would be taken care of by addressing whatever the organization in question considered the more "fundamental" issue. Most centrally, when I probed respondents about their organizations' lack of attention to issues affecting intersectionally disadvantaged subgroups of their constituencies, they often gave answers such as that "the time wasn't right" to address such concerns because resources were scarce, that there were "bigger issues" at stake, or that such issues were divisive in ways that threatened their ability to present a united front to dominant groups.[31]

That these responses justifying meager representation for intersectionally marginalized groups were articulated during what are typically characterized as relatively good times leads to questions about what we might expect during the "hard times" that followed 9/11. At the same time, while 9/11 undoubtedly and unalterably changed the political terrain, the issues at the core of *Affirmative Advocacy* were not unique to the 1990s. Rather, as scholars have noted in other contexts, these issues are related to enduring and deeply entrenched structural inequalities, as embedded in continuities as they are subject to change[32] Contemplating the advocacy organization officers' responses from this perspective leads to two additional question: First, how would organizations that represent groups for whom times are "always hard" respond to and be affected by the nexus of crises in the midst of the persistent inequalities that impact their constituents?[33] Second, what would happen to advocacy on behalf of intersectionally disadvantaged subgroups of these constituencies?

To explore these questions, I use data from "Public Interest Organizations in the New Millennium" (PIONM), a survey of 626 advocacy organizations that I conducted in 2007, as well as information from 45 face-to-face interviews with organization officers that I conducted in 2006, 2007, and 2010.[34] To examine how the political terrain changed for advocacy organizations in the wake of 9/11 and in the context of the War on Terror, PIONM respondents were first asked to list up to five policy issues that had been most important to their organization in 2000. They were then asked whether their organization had experienced changes in the difficulty of pursuing its goals on the issues they mentioned between 2000 and 2006—that is, had they found that these goals had become harder, become easier, or remained the same during this period? Table 4.3 summarizes the responses to this question and reveals that a plurality of respondents from most types of organizations felt that it had become more difficult to pursue their goals on the issues that were most important to their organizations. Civil liberties, American Indian, women of color, and HIV/AIDS groups were particularly likely to report that it had become more difficult for them to achieve their policy goals. The responses also reveal provocative outliers. In particular, immigration and LGBT organizations both stand out—immigration organizations because they were most likely to report that their policy goals had become more difficult (71.1%), and LGBT groups because, at 64.5%, they were more likely than any other organization type in the survey to report that their goals on the issues they named had become easier.

Table 4.3 Perceived Change in Difficulty in Ability to Achieve Specific Policy Goals Listed by Respondent, by Organization Type, 2000–2006

	Easier	No Change	Harder
AIDS/HIV	22.2	16.7	61.1
Arab/Muslim	25.0	25.0	50.0
Asian American	25.8	22.6	51.6
Black/African American	31.4	20.0	48.6
Civil Liberties	16.1	12.9	71.0
Civil Rights – General	29.2	19.8	51.0
Criminal Justice/Anti-Death Penalty	31.6	31.6	36.8
Disability Rights	19.0	25.9	55.2
Environment/Ecology/Animal Rights	17.3	25.3	57.4
Farm Workers/Migrant Workers	27.8	22.2	50.0
Healthcare	33.3	6.7	60.0
Immigration	7.9	21.1	71.1
Labor Organization or Union	17.3	25.3	57.4
Latino/Hispanic	36.4	25.0	38.6
LGBT/Queer	64.5	9.7	25.8
Native American/American Indian	14.3	20.4	65.3
Peace, Anti-Militarism, Anti-Nuclear	25.7	14.3	60.0
Poverty and Social Justice	22.3	27.2	50.5
Progressive Social Change – General	25.0	37.5	37.5
Public Interest	8.7	30.4	60.9
Senior Citizens	13.3	26.7	60.0
Women of Color	29.2	12.5	58.3
Women's Health/Reproductive Rights	21.8	29.1	49.1
Women's Rights/Feminist – General	22.3	27.7	50.0

Source: 2007 PIONM.

To understand this pattern, it helps to return to the question about intersectional marginalization that I asked above. To do so, I coded the issues that respondents listed using the four-part policy typology that I developed in *Affirmative Advocacy* (with the help of two research assistants) to distinguish among majority issues, advantaged subgroup issues, disadvantaged subgroup issues, and universal issues. The bars in Figure 4.8 depict the predicted probability that a respondent reported that an issue became more difficult, as this varies by issue type, and show that the landscape after 2000 was particularly bad for issues affecting intersectionally marginalized groups. Holding all other variables at their means, there is a 78% chance that a respondent said that an issue affecting an intersectionally disadvantaged subgroup had become more difficult, but this was about half as likely to be true of an advantaged subgroup or universal issue. While there is about a 20% chance that a majority issue was perceived to have become easier and about 30% chance that this was true of an advantaged subgroup or universal issue, this probability declines to 8% in the case of intersectionally disadvantaged subgroup issues. In other words, the issues affecting intersectionally marginalized groups that had received substantially less attention in good times became even more difficult in bad ones.

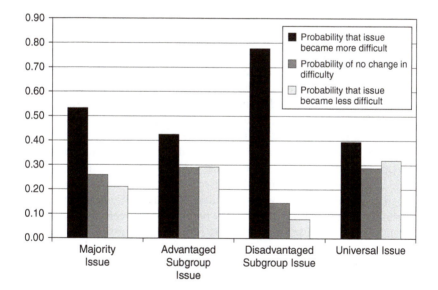

Figure 4.8 Predicted Probability that Respondent Reported an Issue Became More Difficult, by Issue Type

Note: Organization officers were asked, "During the years 2000–2006 was there any change in the difficulty of pursuing your organization's goals on this issue?" The black columns reflect the probability of giving the answer "Harder to pursue," the white columns reflect the probability of giving the answer, "No change," and the shaded columns reflect the probability of giving the answer "Easier to pursue." (Source: 2007 PIONM).

Conclusion: Affirmative Advocacy in Good Times and Bad

Although the trends that I have described are widespread, they are not ubiquitous, nor are they intentional. Indeed, the story of interest groups as representatives of intersectionally marginalized groups is more one of possibility than it is one of failure, and some organizations do speak extensively and effectively on behalf of intersectionally disadvantaged subgroups of their constituencies. Evidence from the survey and interviews demonstrates that what separates these organizations from those that fail to provide extensive representation for intersectionally disadvantaged groups is their commitment to a set of practices and principles that together constitute a framework of representational redistribution that I call *affirmative advocacy.*

Like affirmative action in education or employment, which is intended to redistribute resources and level the playing field for disadvantaged individuals in these arenas, the principle of affirmative advocacy recognizes that equitable representation for disadvantaged groups requires proactive efforts to overcome the entrenched but often subtle biases that persist against marginalized groups in American politics. This recognition compels those organizations that appreciate it to redistribute resources and attention to issues affecting intersectionally disadvantaged subgroups in order to level the playing field among groups. Among the practices they adopt to accomplish this redistribution are creating decision rules that elevate issues affecting disadvantaged minorities on organizational agendas; using internal processes and practices to improve the status of intersectionally disadvantaged groups within the organization; forging stronger ties to state and local advocacy groups; promoting "descriptive representation" by making sure that staff and boards include members of intersectionally marginalized subgroups of their constituencies; resisting the silencing effects of public and constituent opinion that is biased against disadvantaged subgroups; and cultivating among advantaged subgroups of their constituencies the understanding that their interests are inextricably linked to the well-being of intersectionally disadvantaged constituents. Through procedures and mores such as these, organizations engage in a form of redistributive representation that blurs the boundaries between advocacy and representation and that is itself a prefigurative form of social justice.[35] In these ways, organizations advance an innovative conception of representation that has great potential to equalize both representation and policy outcomes by offsetting the power of relatively advantaged subgroups. Doing so is particularly important during hard times, when, as the PIONM data show, disadvantaged subgroup issues become even more difficult to pursue. During such periods, they should not lose sight of or neglect the longer-term, quotidian, and structural problems that affect intersectionally marginalized constituents.

In sum, America's contemporary advocacy groups do often speak most loudly and effectively for the relatively advantaged members of historically underrepresented groups. But such biases are not intentional—and they are not universal. Advocacy leaders often know they need to do better, and they have developed special practices to help them speak effectively for the most marginal.

Notes

1 Kay Lehman Schlozman and Traci Burch. 2009. "Political Voice in an Age of Inequality," in America at Risk: Threats to Liberal Self-Government in an Age of Uncertainty, ed. Robert Faulkner and Susan Shell (Ann Arbor: University of Michigan Press).

2 Frank R. Baumgartner and Beth Leech, *Basic Interests: The Importance of Groups in Politics and Political Science* (Princeton, NJ: Princeton University Press, 1993).

3 David Truman, *The Governmental Process* (New York: Knopf, 1958); Robert A. Dahl, *Pluralist Democracy in the United States* (Chicago: Rand McNally, 1967). See also Arthur F. Bentley, *The Process of Government* (Chicago: University of Chicago Press, 1908); E. Pendleton Herring, *Group Representation before Congress* (Baltimore: Johns Hopkins University Press, 1929); Earl Latham, *The Group Basis of Politics* (Ithaca, NY: Cornell University Press, 1952). James Q. Wilson, *Political Organizations* (Princeton, NJ: Princeton University Press, [1974] 1995), p. 3.

4 I use the terms "advocacy organization," "interest group," political organizations, and "social movement organization" relatively interchangeably.

5 E. E. Schattschneider, *The Semisovereign People* (New York: Holt, Rinehart, and Winston, 1960).

6 Ibid., 35. See also Robert Michels, *Political Parties* (New York: Free Press, 1911); C. Wright Mills, *The Power Elite* (New York: Oxford University Press, 1956); Charles Lindblom, *The Intelligence of Democracy* (New York: Free Press, 1963); Theodore Lowi, *The End of Liberalism*, 2nd ed. (New York: Norton, 1969). These and other authors have noted that it is not only disadvantaged populations that are often poorly represented by their leaders. Michels's "iron law of oligarchy," for example, refers to the lack of activist-member belief congruence in left political parties. See also David Knoke,"Associations and Interests Groups." *Annual Review of Sociology*(1986) 12: 1–21.; Paul A. Sabatier and Susan M. McLaughlin. "Belief Congruence between Interest-Group Leaders and Members: An Empirical Analysis of Three Theories and a Suggested Synthesis." *The Journal of Politics* (1990) 52: 3: 914–35.; and Maryann Barakso and Brian Schaffner, "Exit, Voice, and Interest Group Governance." *American Politics Research* (2008) 36: 2: 186–209.

7 Schlozman, "What Accent the Heavenly Chorus?"; Berry, *Lobbying for the People*; Anne Costain, *Inviting Women's Rebellion: A Political Process Interpretation of the Women's Movement* (Baltimore: Johns Hopkins University Press, 1992); Rodney E. Hero, *Latinos and the U.S. Political System: Two-Tiered Pluralism* (Philadelphia: Temple University Press, 1992); Douglas R. Imig, *Poverty and Power: The Political Representation of Poor Americans* (Lincoln: University of Nebraska Press, 1996); Alvin M. Josephy Jr., Joane Nagel, and Troy Johnson, *Red Power: The American Indian's Fight for Freedom* (Lincoln: University of Nebraska Press, 1999); Doug McAdam, *Political Process and the Development of Black Insurgency, 1930–1970* (Chicago: University of Chicago Press, 1982); Debra Minkoff, *Organizing for Equality: The Evolution of Women's and Racial-Ethnic Organizations in America, 1955–1985* (New Brunswick, NJ: Rutgers University Press, 1995); Aldon Morris, *The Origins of the Civil Rights Movement: Black Communities Organizing for Change* (New York: Free Press, 1984); Dianne Pinderhughes, "Black Interest Groups and the 1982 Extension of the Voting Rights Act," in *Blacks and the American Political System*, ed. Huey L. Perry (Gainesville: University Press of Florida, 1995); Frances Fox Piven and Richard A. Cloward, *Poor People's Movements: Why They Succeed, How They Fail* (New York: Vintage Books, 1977); Schlozman, "What Accent the Heavenly Chorus?"; Robert C. Smith, *We Have No Leaders: African Americans in the Post-Civil*

Rights Era (Albany: State University of New York Press, 1996); *Latino Social Movements: Historical and Theoretical Perspectives*, ed. Rodolpho D. Torres and George Katsiaficas (New York: Routledge, 1999).

8 Dara Z. Strolovitch, *Affirmative Advocacy: Race, Class, and Gender in Interest Group Politics* (Chicago: University of Chicago Press, 2007).

9 Jeffrey M. Berry, *The New Liberalism* (Washington, DC: Brookings Institution Press, 1999); Donna Cooper Hamilton and Charles V. Hamilton, "The Dual Agenda of African American Organizations since the New Deal: Social Welfare Policies and Civil Rights," *Political Science Quarterly* 107 (1992): 435–53; Theda Skocpol, *Diminished Democracy: From Membership to Management in American Civic Life* (Norman: University of Oklahoma Press, 2003); Strolovitch, *Affirmative Advocacy*.

10 Donna Cooper Hamilton and Charles V. Hamilton, "The Dual Agenda of African American Organizations since the New Deal: Social Welfare Policies and Civil Rights," *Political Science Quarterly* 107 (1992): 435–53.

11 Kimberlé Crenshaw, "Demarginalizing the Intersection of Race and Sex," *University of Chicago Legal Forum* 39 (1989): 139–67. See also Patricia Hill Collins, *Black Feminist Thought* (Boston: Unwin Hyman, 1990); Angela Y. Davis, *Women, Race, and Class* (New York: Random House, 1981); bell hooks, *Ain't I a Woman?* (Boston: South End Press, 1981).

12 Sharon Kurtz, *Workplace Justice: Organizing Multi-Identity Movements* (Minneapolis: University of Minnesota Press, 2002), p. 38.

13 Leslie McCall, "The Complexity of Intersectionality," *Signs: Journal of Women in Culture and Society* 30 (2005): 1771–1800; See Strolovitch, *Affirmative Advocacy*, pp. 22–28.

14 Baumgartner and Jones, *Agendas and Instability in American Politics;* Thomas G. Hansford, "Lobbying Strategies, Venue Selection, and Organized Interest Involvement at the U.S. Supreme Court," *American Politics Research* 32 (2004): 170–97; John W. Kingdon, *Agendas, Alternatives, and Public Policies* (New York: Harper Collins, 1995); Ken Kollman, Outside Lobbying: Public Opinion and Interest Group Strategies, (Princeton, NJ: Princeton University Press, 1998); McAdam, *Political Process and the Development of Black Insurgency, 1930–1970*; David S. Meyer and Debra Minkoff, "Conceptualizing Political Opportunity," *Social Forces* 82 (2004): 1457–92; Kay Lehman Schlozman and John T. Tierney, Organized Interests and American Democracy (New York: Harper and Row, 1986); Jack L. Walker, Jr., *Mobilizing Interest Groups in America: Patrons, Professions, and Social Movements* (Ann Arbor: University of Michigan Press, 1991).

15 Charles Beard, *An Economic Interpretation of the Constitution of the United States* (New York: Macmillan, 1913); Robert Dahl, "Decision-Making in a Democracy: The Supreme Court as a National Policy-Maker." *Journal of Public Law* 6 (1957): 279–95.

16 Michael McCann, "Social Movements and the Mobilization of Law," in *Social Movements and American Political Institutions,* ed. Anne N. Costain and Andrew McFarland (New York: Rowman and Littlefield, 1998), p. 212

17 Sally J. Kenney, "Making the Case for Women on the Bench: Comparative Perspectives" (paper presented at Inequality and Representation in American Politics meeting, Minneapolis, 2005).

18 Paul Frymer, "Distinguishing Formal from Institutional Democracy," *Maryland Law Review* 65 (2006): 125–38.

19 Frymer, "Distinguishing Formal from Institutional Democracy." See also Jonathon D. Casper, "The Supreme Court and National Policy Making." *American Political Science Review* 70 (1976): 50–63; Charles R. Epp, *The Rights Revolution: Lawyers, Activists, and Supreme Courts in Comparative Perspective* (Chicago: University of Chicago Press, 1998); Joel F. Handler, *Social Movements and the Legal System: A Theory of Law, Reform and Social Change* (New York: Academic Press, 1978); Karen O'Connor, *Women's Organizations' Use of the Courts* (Lexington, MA: Lexington Books, 1980); Karen O'Connor and Lee

Epstein, "Sex and the Supreme Court: An Analysis of Support for Gender-Based Claims," *Social Science Quarterly* 64 (1983): 327–31.

20 Lucius Barker, "Third Parties in Litigation: A Systematic View of Judicial Education," *Journal of Politics* 29 (1967): 49–69; Alexander M. Bickel, *The Least Dangerous Branch: The Supreme Court at the Bar of Politics*, 2nd ed. (New Haven, CT: Yale University Press, 1986); Richard C. Cortner, "Strategies and Tactics of Litigants in Constitutional Cases," *Journal of Public Law* 17 (1968): 287–307; Ronald Dworkin, *Taking Rights Seriously* (Cambridge, MA: Harvard University Press, 1977); Ronald Dworkin, *Freedom's Law: The Moral Reading of the American Constitution* (Cambridge, MA: Harvard University Press, 1986); Handler, *Social Movements and the Legal System*; David Manwaring, *Render Unto Caesar: The Flag Salute Controversy* (Chicago: University of Chicago Press, 1962); Michael W. McCann, *Taking Reform Seriously: Perspectives on Public Interest Liberalism* (Ithaca, NY: Cornell University Press, 1986); McCann, "Social Movements and the Mobilization of Law"; O'Connor and Epstein, "Sex and the Supreme Court: An Analysis of Support for Gender-Based Claims"; Frank J. Sorauf, *The Wall of Separation: The Constitutional Politics of Church and State* (Princeton, NJ: Princeton University Press, 1976); Clement E. Vose, "Litigation as a Form of Pressure Group Activity," *Annals of the American Academy of Political and Social Science* 319 (1958): 20–31; Clement E. Vose, *Caucasians Only* (Berkeley and Los Angeles: University of California Press, 1959); Steven L. Wasby, "How Planned Is 'Planned' Litigation?" *American Bar Foundation Research Journal* (Winter 1984): 83–138.

21 Bickel, *The Least Dangerous Branch*. See also John Hart Ely, *Democracy and Distrust: A Theory of Judicial Review*, (Cambridge, MA: Harvard University Press, 1980); Jeremy Waldron, *Law and Disagreement* (New York: Oxford University Press, 2001).

22 Robert Bork, *Slouching towards Gomorrah: Modern Liberalism and American Decline*, (New York: Regan Books, 2003); Antonin Scalia, *A Matter of Interpretation*, (Princeton, NJ: Princeton University Press, 1998).

23 Derrick A. Bell Jr., "Serving Two Masters: Integration Ideals and Client Interests in School Desegregation Litigation," *Yale Law Journal* 85 (1976): 470–516; Alan David Freeman, "Legitimating Racial Discrimination through Antidiscrimination Law: A Critical Review of Supreme Court Doctrine," *Minnesota Law Review* 62 (1978): 1049–1119; Stuart Scheingold, *The Politics of Rights: Lawyers, Public Policy, and Political Change* (Ann Arbor: University of Michigan Press, 1974); Mark V. Tushnet, "Critical Legal Studies: A Political History," *Yale Law Journal* 100 (1991): 1515–44.

24 Frymer, "Distinguishing Formal from Institutional Democracy," 125.

25 Timothy R. Johnson, "The Supreme Court, the Solicitor General, and the Separation of Powers," *American Politics Research* 31 (2003): 426–51; Kollman, *Outside Lobbying*; Rorie Spill Solberg and Eric N. Waltenberg, "Why Do Interest Groups Engage the Judiciary? Policy Wishes and Structural Needs," *Social Science Quarterly* 87 (2006): 558–72.

26 Berry, *Lobbying for the People*; Kay Lehman Schlozman and John T. Tierney, *Organized Interests and American Democracy* (New York: Harper and Row, 1986); Walker Jr., *Mobilizing Interest Groups in America*; see also William Haltom and Michael McCann, *Distorting the Law: Politics, Media, and the Litigation Crisis* (Chicago: University of Chicago Press, 2004).

27 In the book, I explore whether these variations can be explained as matters of jurisdiction, organizational maintenance, or variations in the receptivity or political opportunities associated with each branch. For further discussion of these questions, see Baumgartner and Jones, *Basic Interests*; Thomas G. Hansford, "Lobbying Strategies, Venue Selection, and Organized Interest Involvement at the U.S. Supreme Court." *American Politics Research* 32 (2004): 170–97; John W. Kingdon, *Agendas, Alternatives, and Public Policies* (New York: HarperCollins, 1995); McAdam, *Political Process and the Development of Black Insurgency, 1930–1970*; David S. Meyer and Debra Minkoff, "Conceptualizing Political Opportunity," *Social Forces* 82 (2004): 1457–92.

28 J. Craig Jenkins and Charles Perrow, "Insurgency of the Powerless: Farm Worker Movements (1946–1972)," *American Sociological Review* 42 (1977): 249–68; Constance Cook, "The Washington Higher Education Community: Moving Beyond Lobbying 101," in *Interest Group Politics,* 5th ed., ed. Alan Cigler and Burdett Loomis (Washington, DC: CQ Press, 1998), p. 109; Kevin Hula, "Rounding Up the Usual Suspects: Forging Interest Group Coalitions in Washington," in *Interest Group Politics,* 5th ed., ed. Alan Cigler and Burdett Loomis (Washington, DC: CQ Press 1995), pp. 239–58; Margaret Levi and Gillian Murphy, "Coalitions of Contention: The Case of the WTO Protests in Seattle," *Political Studies* 54:4 (2006): 651–70; David A. Snow and Robert D. Benford, "Master Frames and Cycles of Protest," in *Frontiers of Social Movement Theory,* ed. Aldon Morris and Carol M. Mueller, (New Haven, CT: Yale University Press, 1992), pp. 133–55; Will Hathaway and David S. Meyer, "Competition and Cooperation in Movements Coalitions: Lobbying for Peace in the 1980s," in *Coalitions and Political Movements: Lessons of the Nuclear Freeze,* ed. Thomas R. Rochon and David S. Meyer (Boulder, CO: Lynne Rienner, 1997), pp. 61–79; Holly J. McCammon and Karen E. Campbell, "Allies on the Road to Victory: Coalition Formation between the Suffragists and the Woman's Christian Temperance Union," *Mobilization* 7 (2002): 231–51; David S. Meyer, *A Winter of Discontent: The Nuclear Freeze and American Politics* (New York: Praeger, 1990); David S. Meyer, "Institutionalizing Dissent: The United States Structure of Political Opportunity and the End of the Nuclear Freeze Movement," *Sociological Forum* 8 (1993): 157–79; Bernice Johnson Reagon, "Coalition Politics: Turning the Century," in *Homegirls: A Black Feminist Anthology,* ed. B. Smith (New York: Kitchen Table—Women of Color Press, 1983), pp. 356–68; Suzanne Staggenborg, "Coalition Work in the Pro-Choice Movement: Organizational and Environmental Opportunities and Obstacles," *Social Problems* 33 (1986): 374–90; Nella Van Dyke, "Crossing Movement Boundaries: Factors That Facilitate Coalition Protest by American College Students," *Social Problems* 50 (2003): 226–50; Nella Van Dyke and Sarah A. Soule, "Structural Social Change and the Mobilizing Effect of Threat: Explaining Levels of Patriot and Militia Mobilizing in the United States," *Social Problems* 49 (2002): 497–520; William Browne, *Groups, Interests, and U.S. Public Policy* (Washington, DC: Georgetown University Press, 1998).
29 Staggenborg, "Coalition Work in the Pro-Choice Movement."
30 Larry Bartels, *Unequal Democracy* (Princeton, NJ: Princeton University Press, 2008); Jacob Hacker and Paul Pierson, *Winner-Take-All Politics* (Simon and Schuster, 2010); Corey Robin, *Fear: The History of a Political Idea* (New York: Oxford University Press, 2004).
31 Strolovitch, *Affirmative Advocacy.*
32 See, for example, Gretchen Ritter, "Gender and Politics over Time," *Politics and Gender* 3 (2007): 388; see also Lawrence Jacobs and Desmond King, "America's Political Crisis: The Unsustainable State in a Time of Unraveling," *PS: Political Science & Politics* 42 (2009): 277–85; Patricia Strach and Virginia Sapiro, "Campaigning for Congress in the '9/11' Era: Considerations of Gender and Party in Response to an Exogenous Shock," *American Politics Research* 39 (2011): 264–90.
33 I borrow this formulation from Khalila Brown-Dean, "From Exclusion to Inclusion: Promoting Civic Engagement When Times Are Always Hard" (paper presented at the American Political Science Association Annual Meeting, Washington, DC, September 2010).
34 PIONM was administered by the University of Chicago Survey Lab. The sample is comprised of 626 respondents out of an original list of 1249 organizations, for a response rate of 50.1%. PIONM targeted liberal organizations as well as organizations affiliated with conservative movements, and contained general questions about organizations' constituencies, governance, and funding, as well as more specific questions that asked respondents about changes in their organizations' advocacy targets and policy agendas over time and about the effects of the 9/11 attacks and Hurricane Katrina on

several dimensions of their organizations' work. Respondents could complete the survey by phone, on the internet, or on paper.

35 Nadia Urbinati, "Representation as Advocacy: A Study of Democratic Deliberation," *Political Theory* 28 (2000): 758–86; Nadia Urbinati, *Mill on Democracy: From the Athenian Government to Representative Government* (Chicago: University of Chicago Press, 2002).

Chapter 5

Political Parties and Ideology
Interest Groups in Context

Hans Noel

Political science has long treated political parties and interest groups as related subjects. They share an official section of the American Political Science Association dedicated to their study, and many schools offer courses that integrate them. But scholars often treat them independently. They are both examples of "political organizations," but they are different kinds of organizations, and with important exceptions, they are often studied independently.

That is unfortunate. Interest groups do their work in an environment shaped largely by political parties. And parties mobilize activists who are also organized and mobilized by interest groups. A complete understanding of one requires an understanding of the other. Both parties and interest groups operate in an increasingly ideological world.

All of this implies that the classic model of interest group pluralism simply misses the most important elements of modern politics. Politics is not best understood as a clash of various interests with shifting allegiances across differing lines of conflict. The lines of conflict are well organized and rather consistent, which has consequences for our understanding of interest group politics.

This chapter begins with a theoretical discussion about the place of interest groups in a theory of political parties, and about the role of ideology in organizing both parties and interest groups. I then discuss some areas of scholarship in which this theoretical framework provides some guidance. First, I consider the role of organized interests in electoral campaigns. Second, I explore ways in which interest groups appear to organize into a larger, coordinated force. Before concluding, I discuss a counter-example from history, in which an interest group was particularly successful at avoiding the limitations of the environment created by political parties.

The Partisan and Ideological Environment

We can go a long way in understanding the organization of interests by focusing on individual interests and their efforts at policy advocacy. But there is a forest/trees danger if we never pull back and look at the environment in which interest group activity takes place. Political parties organize interests. So does ideology.

Parties as Interest Group Coalitions

Our modern understanding of political parties views them as long-standing coalitions. The members of parties have diverse, potentially even conflicting preferences, but they manage to set aside their disagreements to accomplish things that they can agree on.

We can describe this conception of parties verbally and get the point across fairly well. But it is helpful to get a little more rigorous about what is implied, as in Table 5.1, which outlines the preferences of three actors over three policy areas. This approach is developed most completely by John Aldrich[1] in his influential book *Why Parties?* The model is ultimately based on a basic distributive politics model developed by Barry Weingast[2] to study norms in legislatures. If we are thinking about distributive politics, the actors are legislators and the policies are projects that will perhaps benefit their home districts. But we can generalize this to any set of actors or policies.

Table 5.1 shows which policies each of the three actors likes and dislikes. Policy 1 is favored by Actor A but not by B or C. Perhaps Policy 1 is a bridge that will be built in Actor A's district but paid for by taxes levied on the citizens of all three legislators' districts. Similarly for Actor B and Policy 2 and for Actor C and Policy 3.

We would expect that each of these policies would fail if they were voted on one at a time. When Policy 1 comes up, A would vote for it, but B and C would vote against it. Even though this is true, any two actors can improve their outcome by allying with each other. If B agreed to support Policy 1 in exchange for A's support on Policy 2, then A and B both get something they want for only the cost of paying for the other's policy. This is a short-term "logroll." One actor does a favor for another, in expectation of a favor in return. But of course, when Policy 3 comes up, C could try to buy off either A or B for some future policy vote, which would help one of the first two actors at the expense of the other.

The central insight of the Aldrich model is that A and B (or any two actors) can make themselves much better off by entering into a permanent alliance. This way, they ensure that they are always in the majority and never have to suffer the consequences of a Policy 3 passing. Such a coalition is no longer a simple logroll. It is a "long coalition," "long" because it extends into future policies rather than being "wide," including everyone in the legislature. Being always in the majority is of course a great advantage for legislators because they can bring policy back to their districts and thus win re-election.

Table 5.1 Groups and Policy Positions

	Actor A	Actor B	Actor C
Policy 1	Likes at lot	Dislikes a little	Dislikes a little
Policy 2	Dislikes a little	Likes at lot	Dislikes a little
Policy 3	Dislikes a little	Dislikes a little	Likes a lot

The examples given by Aldrich and others tend to imagine the actors as legislators and the policies as things enacted by a legislature. But the model need not be restricted to that example. An alternative approach is articulated in Marty Cohen et al.'s *The Party Decides* and Kathy Bawn et al.'s *A Theory of Political Parties*.[3] This approach, sometimes called the UCLA School, treats the actors in the model as societal groups and others who are motivated by policies that they want to see enacted. These "policy demanders" are interested specific policy goals, and so they ally with other policy demanders to form parties and take control of nominations. Instead of supporting a sequence of legislation that benefits coalition members, they back candidates who will commit to embodying their long coalition. Such candidates either themselves want all the policies the diverse policy demanders want individually or are at least committed to advocating for all of those policies. The candidate essentially stands in for the coalition, because the candidate is accountable to all the different policy demanders in the coalition.

By shifting the focus off of legislators, the UCLA School highlights the role of policy goals and especially nominations in the formation of parties. But this approach is rather expansive about exactly what constitutes a "policy demander." It is therefore susceptible to being criticized as vague. Who are these policy demanders, exactly?

One simple way to think about the groups of policy demanders is to imagine that they are, in fact, the same formally organized interest groups discussed in this volume. That is, in Figure 5.1, imagine for example that A is the National Rifle Association, and Policy 1 is an unrestricted right to bear arms, and B and C are other interests with specific policy goals. The interest groups then throw their support behind common candidates for the purpose of winning elections. In this interpretation, we have simply replaced the well-defined legislators of the traditional interpretation of Figure 5.1 with well-defined interest groups.

This would be too simplistic, but it is not far off. The interests that a party organizes are the same underlying interests that interest groups organize. It may even be helpful to look to those interest groups to learn what the interests are demanding of the parties, as David Karol does.[4]

At the same time, interest groups are not simply the constituent parts of a party, like five smaller robots assembling Voltron. Parties can organize interests that do not have official groups to speak for them; even formal interest groups will need to bargain with party leaders. Policy demanders who do form interest groups can also act directly in shaping political parties without going through their interest group apparatus. It is perhaps better to think of interest groups as also made up of the same set of admittedly vaguely defined policy demanders that Bawn et al. discuss. When a policy demander contemplates their options, one natural strategy is to join and work with a political party, as Bawn et al. claim. A different strategy is to go it alone, working with an interest group and focusing only on the more narrow set of policies that the group prefers. In short, policy demanders might join a party, an interest group, or both.

Both of these strategies are reasonable. In that sense, those who study parties are studying one strategy, while those who study interest groups are just studying a different strategy. Sometimes that second strategy is particularly important. That may be especially true for classic unaligned or unorganized issues, such as small industries or the unemployed. If one side of a policy debate is largely unorganized and may not even recognize the importance of the issue, while the other side has strong preferences and is organized, that interest may not need to focus its lobbying attention on one party. Everyone might be receptive to them, because politicians are not representing competing interests. In such a case, the go-it-alone strategy may be more successful.

But these two strategies do not operate independently of one another. Advocating for policy in a non-partisan environment is different from doing so in a partisan environment, and both of these are different from a partisan environment in which most interests are deeply connected to one and not the other political party.

For instance, the resurgence of interest in gun control after the school shooting in Newtown, Connecticut, had a deeply partisan character. Democrats, who had historically been more likely to favor gun control, had largely given up on the issue before the shooting. But it was Democrats who were most likely to advocate for the policy then. Republicans, on the other hand, were generally resistant to such policies.

But in that conflict, the National Rifle Association, and particularly its spokesperson, Wayne LaPierre, were the most vocal voice against new gun restrictions. The standard bearer for the policy is not the Republican Party per se, but one of its allied groups. And that tells us a lot about how the parties will break.

The Ideological Landscape

The model outlined in Table 5.1 does not tell us anything about how different groups ought to be allied. A and B could join forces, but B and C could just as easily decide to make up a long coalition. This flexibility is in some ways the model's strength, because it makes clear that all sorts of arrangements might be possible. Neither the legislator-focused account offered by Aldrich nor the policy-demander account offered by Bawn et al. tells us anything about which groups should be together.

That is indeed one of the strengths of the approach. And it is true that, historically speaking, politics can make very strange bedfellows. Today, allied with the Republican Party, we find both the interests organized on behalf of a larger role for religion in public life and those opposed to redistributive policies. The opposite groups are affiliated with the Democrats.

This arrangement may feel very natural, but it need not be. There was a time when religious groups advocated for redistributive policies, and indeed some religious groups do today. The alignment was very different when William Jennings Bryan represented the Democratic Party.

The groups that are aligned with one party can shift for a variety of reasons. The present alignment, I would argue, has come about because of an increasingly ideological division between the parties. This evolution is complex, and discussed at greater length elsewhere.[5] In short, in the middle part of the twentieth century, there were conservatives and liberals in both the Democratic and Republican parties. This is essentially untrue today.

How exactly this happened is somewhat tangential to the present discussion. Some approaches characterize ideology as the rationalization of party platforms, but the evolution of the past several decades suggest that is not correct. Modern liberalism and modern conservatism emerged in the early part of the twentieth century and then slowly remade the political parties so that they were aligned with those ideologies by the end of the century. We now have a liberal party and a conservative party.

On that account, ideology is at least independent of partisan alignment. It is probably true that strategic partisan concerns also shaped ideologies. The past century has not been a one-way street. But ideology is a real constraining force that is at least more than simply a rationalization of whatever platform the parties put together at the last national convention. Ideological liberals pressure President Obama and the Democratic Party from the left, while conservatives and particularly Tea Party activists pressure the Republicans from the right.

That ideological organization constrains the parties in what groups they can accommodate. Republicans can, for instance, try to appeal to African American voters, but they will find little success without disavowing many conservative policy positions. This same ideological organization also has consequences for interest groups, even those that seek to operate independently of political parties.

Most importantly, ideology helps determine likely allies. Interest groups occasionally find themselves coordinating with other groups. To the extent that those groups are ideologically defined, they are less likely to work with groups from a different ideology. But resources may well be shared among ideological similar groups.

Ideology thus forms the background for the dynamics discussed in the previous section. The next session considers what we learn from looking at patterns of interest group endorsements.

Interest Group Participation in Elections

The broader conception of political parties that is advanced by Cohen et al. relies on endorsements as a measure of the support of party members, including interest groups. Endorsements are only part of the many ways in which policy demanders and other party leaders might indicate their support. The most valuable endorsements are backed up by campaign resources and other efforts.

Labor unions are famous for providing a backbone of campaign support for Democrats. A variety of interest groups are known to engage in campaign activity either directly for a candidate or in get-out-the-vote campaigns that will likely benefit those candidates associated with the group. When African American organized interests get voters to the polls, for example, this helps Democrats.

And yet endorsements are an excellent indicator of interest group support. Simply endorsing a candidate can send a signal to members of an interest group that they should vote for that candidate. Because interest groups are organized around identifiable interests, their endorsements might have more clout than that of a leading party politician. Group identity is often stronger among voters than partisan identity, and is indeed part of what drives partisan identity. If voters see interest groups representing their social group allied with a particular candidate, that will have an impact. Even voters who might not consider themselves members of a particular interest group will still learn about the candidates' policy positions in a way that a politician's endorsement cannot convey.

Table 5.2 reports the endorsements of a large number of interest groups in presidential election from 1988 to 2012.[6] The table includes only those groups for which we have a record of more than one endorsement in that period. Interest groups in Table 5.2 have been sorted into categories. Table 5.2 is based on web searches and is not a random sample, but it is a revealing one.

A number of interesting patterns pop out of Table 5.2. The most obvious is that, with only three exceptions, every group has been loyal to the same party for all of its endorsements since 1988. This tells us a lot, especially if we take the view that interest groups are (or at least can be) the elemental members of the party coalitions.

There is a widespread misconception, not among political scientists but among many citizens and even political journalists, that every candidate is new, and therefore every contest is new. But the major political parties in the United States have been rather stable in their political coalitions for the last several decades. Table 5.2 shows that stability in their relationship to allied interest groups. Labor unions are part of the Democratic Party. So are organized ethnic minorities, environmental activists, women's groups, and gay rights activists. Business groups are part of the Republican Party, along with anti-abortion activists and gun rights activists.

This pattern is stronger than it would be among other political actors. A team of researchers at the University of Maryland,[7] for example, break down political donations by industry sector. While they find many partisan patterns, they find that many sectors are divided between Democrats and Republicans, and sectors that are lock-step for one party are the exception, not the rule. The same is true of voters. Even demographic groups that we know have a strong partisan tilt—gender, race, income, religiosity, etc.—are never 100%. Even among African Americans, whose association with the Democratic Party is the strongest of any demographic group, as many as 10% will vote for Republicans.

The difference between interest groups and political donations or voting is that interest groups are *organized* political action. They are not atomistic. And the first thing that coordinated action does is coordinate with the most important players in politics, political parties.

Table 5.2 Interest Group Endorsements in Presidential Elections

Endorser	1988	1992	1996	2000	2004	2008	2012
Abortion and Women's Groups							
National Right to Life Committee			R	R	R	R	R
Illinois Federation for Right to Life						R	R
Susan B. Anthony List						R	R
NARAL Pro-Choice America				D		D	D
Planned Parenthood					D	D	D
Business and Professional Women/USA PAC		D		D	D	D	
Feminist Majority Political Action Committee						D	D
National Organization for Women						D	D
Business/Professional							
Associated Builders and Contractors		R		R	R	R	R
National Troopers' Coalition		R		R			
Western Growers Association						R	R
Environment							
League of Conservation Voters	D	D	D	D	D	D	D
Sierra Club		D	D	D	D	D	D
Friends of the Earth Political Association	D			D	D	D	
California League of Conservation Voters					D	D	D
Clean Water Action					D	D	D
Defenders of Wildlife Action Fund					D	D	
Environment America						D	D
Environment New Jersey						D	D
Ethnic							
80-20 Initiative				D		D	D
Italian American Democratic Leadership Council		D	D	D			
Irish American Democrats		D		D			
Arab American Political Action Committee				R	D		
Hispanic Business Roundtable				R	R		
Gay Rights							
Human Rights Campaign		D	D	D	D	D	D
Log Cabin Republicans			R	R		R	R

Endorser	1988	1992	1996	2000	2004	2008	2012
Gun Rights							
National Rifle Association	R			R	R	R	R
Law Enforcement Alliance of America			R	R			
Ideological or Partisan							
Americans for Democratic Action			D	D	D	D	D
MoveOn Political Action						D	D
Republican Governors Association			R	R			
Labor							
American Federation of Labor and Congress of Industrial Organizations (AFL-CIO)	D	D	D	D	D	D	D
American Federation of Government Employees, AFL-CIO			D	D	D	D	D
Building and Construction Trades Department, AFL-CIO		D		D	D	D	D
International Association of Fire Fighters	D	D	D	D	D	D	D
National Education Association	D	D	D	D	D	D	D
American Federation of Teachers	D	D		D	D	D	D
American Nurses Association	D	D		D	D	D	D
Fraternal Order of Police	R	R	D	R	R	R	
International Brotherhood of Police Officers		D	D	R	D		
International Brotherhood of Teamsters	R	D		D	D	D	D
United Auto Workers		D	D	D	D	D	D
United Steel Workers	D	D	D	D		D	D
American Federation of State, County, and Municipal Employees (AFSCME)	D	D		D	D		D
American Postal Workers Union	D			D	D	D	D
Communications Workers of America		D	D	D	D		D
International Brotherhood of Boilermakers				D	D	D	D
National Association of Police Organizations				D	D	D	D
National Farmers Union		D		D	D	D	

(continued)

Table 5.2 (Continued)

Endorser	1988	1992	1996	2000	2004	2008	2012
Communications Workers of America				D	D	D	D
Laborers International Union of North America			D	D		D	D
United Farm Workers of America				D	D	D	D
United Food and Commercial Workers Union				D	D	D	D
International Association of Machinists				D		D	D
International Brotherhood of Painters and Allied Trades				D		D	D
United Mine Workers of America, AFL-CIO				D	D	D	
AFSCME Council 5					D	D	D
Amalgamated Transit Union Local					D	D	D
Association of Machinists and Aerospace Workers	D		D	D			
Bakery, Confectionery, Tobacco Workers and Grain Millers					D	D	D
United Association of Journeymen and Apprentices of the Plumbing and Pipefitting Industry					D	D	D
Alabama AFL-CIO						D	D
American Federation of School Administrators					D		D
Flight Attendants Union Coalition						D	D
Health Professionals and Allied Employees						D	D
International Union of Bricklayers and Allied Craft Workers				D			D
Retail, Wholesale, and Department Store Union						D	D
Service Employee International Union (SEIU)						D	D
Other							
Association of Community Organizations for Reform Now				D	D	D	

There are nevertheless exceptions in Table 5.2. Some groups split their support, and other groups representing similar interests nevertheless back different parties. These too are revealing, because they help to illustrate the dynamics at play in the larger pattern.

Law and Order

Let's begin with the deviations of the Fraternal Order of Police (FOP) and the International Brotherhood of Police Officers (IBPO). The FOP has endorsed Republicans in every contest except one, when it endorsed Bill Clinton over Bob Dole in 1996. Meanwhile, the IBPO has endorsed Democrats in every contest except for 2000, when the union endorsed George W. Bush over Al Gore. These two groups together tell us several things. First, note that these are two unions that represent the same population, law enforcement. This is a group that definitely has political policy demands. The problem is that they have conflicting policy demands that are associated with different parties.

On the one hand, the police are responsible for law and order in America's cities. This means they have positions on all manner of policies that affect how easy it is to do their job. Politicians balance the powers of the police against the privacy and due process interests of private citizens, but we should expect the police themselves to advocate for more power, especially in areas where they see restrictions as hindering their mission. The political party that is most associated with a "law and order" platform is the Republican Party. That is, the policy demanders who think that the rights of the accused are abused and that crime is best fought by tough sanctions (including but not limited to police officers who feel that way) are part of the Republican coalition. Policy demanders who feel the police are the ones who abuse their power, and that think crime is best fought by attacking root social causes are part of the Democratic coalition. And so it makes sense that the Fraternal Order of Police is usually affiliated with Republicans.

On the other hand, law enforcement officers are moderately paid public employees whose budgets are often targeted by fiscal hawks in city government. And so they join unions, which are broadly a part of the Democratic coalition. So it makes sense that the International Brotherhood of Police Officers generally favors the Democrats.

The police amount to a group of policy demands that has no safe home in either party coalition. Those that want more police powers are Republicans. Those that want better pay and benefits for public employees are Democrats. As police want both, they are cross-pressured. This points to a limitation of treating interest groups per se as the groups organizing under the dynamic outlined in the last section. Cohen et al. elaborate:

> Many intense policy demanders are identifiable by social, economic, or demographic characteristics, but what is relevant for our theory is that they have the same policy demands. In some cases, intense policy demanders from the same social or demographic category make opposing demands. When this happens, we say that two (or more) groups of intense policy demanders exist. For example, most members of feminist organizations are intense policy demanders for a liberal view of women's rights. But some women do not care much about feminism, and some women actively oppose liberal feminism.

In our theory, the relevant group is not "women," but "feminist women" and "traditional women." So it is with all intense policy demanders: They are defined by their demands, not their social or demographic characteristics.[8]

In this case, not only do two subgroups exist, but they are represented by two organized interests. It would be too simple to just say that the FOP are the police who care about police powers while the IBPO are those who care about public employee benefits. But the two organized interests have largely divided the labor that way, at least as they have engaged in presidential politics. Not all groups are internally divided into liberal and conservative constituencies the way that police are.

Gay Rights

Another, similar anomaly in the table is in the presence of the Log Cabin Republicans and the Human Rights Campaign, two groups advocating for gay rights. Unlike police officers, gay rights activists are not split between the two parties. The Democratic Party (and the liberal ideology that is associated with it) is the more sympathetic to gay rights. The Republican coalition, however, includes social conservatives who are the primary opposition to gay rights. So there is nothing surprising when the Human Rights Campaign endorses and works with Democrats.

But these party coalitions are not set in stone. As noted above, a coalition needs to be large enough to win, but different policy demanders might have different opinions about who their best coalition partners are. The Log Cabin Republicans are a pro-gay rights interest group that wishes the Republican Party had a different coalition. Imagine, in the simple model in Table 5.1, if A and B were in a coalition, but A would really prefer to be in a coalition with C. The A+B coalition is hard to abandon, but a switch would be an improvement for A, or, in this case, some members of group A. This is essentially what the Log Cabin Republicans represent. They are Republicans or conservative on most other issues. They want to see lower taxes, less government spending, and so forth. But they also want gay rights. One might say they represent a "libertarian" ideology, but many homosexuals are socially conservative on other issues. Gay citizens have diverse views on many other issues, and some are conservative on those issues. Those conservatives are advantaged by the Republican coalition, but they would like to see that coalition shift to include those fighting for gay rights.

The existence of the Log Cabin Republicans is further evidence that construing of the policy demanders and being exactly the same as organized interests is too simplistic. Gay rights activists are not quite "in" the Republican coalition. They are fighting to get in. Social conservative groups resist the influence of the Log Cabin Republicans and the similar GOProud. Gay conservatives' participation in the Conservative Political Action Committee generated opposition,[9] and Republican nominee Bob Dole caused a minor controversy when his campaign returned a

Log Cabin donation in the 1996 election cycle.[10] Dole eventually reversed what he characterized as a misunderstanding, but the entire incident highlights the tenuous place that gay conservatives have in the Republican Party.

The Log Cabin Republicans also illustrate the dynamics by which organized interests influence political parties. The decision to endorse has been a central issue for the Log Cabin Republicans, often debating it at its national convention. The group explicitly declined to endorse George H. W. Bush in 1992 because the elder Bush did not denounce anti-gay rhetoric at the Republican National Convention. And they declined to support George W. Bush in 2004 because of the younger Bush's support for the Federal Marriage Amendment, which would have limited marriage to a man and a woman.[11] The logic behind the group's endorsement practices is the same as the logic behind the sometimes conditional support of other interests. The difference is that the Log Cabin Republicans cannot be taken for granted by the coalition, but neither does the party know that it needs their support to win.

Women's Groups

The case of the Log Cabin Republicans and the Equal Rights Campaign is slightly different than that of the National Organization for Women and Susan B. Anthony's List, which also endorse divergent parties. As with gay rights, it is safe to say that many of the issues we tend to think of as "women's issues" are affiliated with the Democratic Party, and there is a gender gap in voting that advantages the Democrats with women voters. And again, there are many women who are conservative and vote for Republicans.

However, Susan B. Anthony's List is not trying to get the Republican Party to accept the policy positions that the National Organization for Women is trying to advance. Rather, the group is interesting in demonstrating that some women support the Republican coalition on every issue, even "women's issues" such as abortion. And in fact among voters, gender is not a particularly strong indicator of support for abortion rights. So this divide is a clean break on policy grounds, as in the example offered in the quotation from Cohen et al. above.

Arab Americans

Another anomaly in Table 5.2 is the endorsement of Republican George W. Bush in 2000 by the Arab American Political Action Committee, followed by a reversal of the group in 2004 to support Bush's opponent John Kerry. Bush was also endorsed in 2000 by the American Muslim Political Coordination Council PAC, but this group does not appear in Table 5.2 because only one endorsement was found.

It is safe to say that, by and large, ethnic minorities tend to be affiliated with the Democratic Party, as that party includes within its coalition those who prefer affirmative action and other policies designed to prevent discrimination. Republicans and conservatives prefer what they would call a "color-blind" approach to policy.

But as with homosexuals and women, ethnic minorities can have a variety of opinions about other issues, and often do. (See, for example, the Hispanic Business Roundtable in Table 5.2, which represents those Hispanics for whom their identity as business leaders is more important than their ethnic identity.) In the late 1990s, the public's attention was not on Arab and Muslim Americans, and they could have easily acted like an unaligned group. Republican politicians had a positive relationship with some Arab regimes, notably Saudi Arabia, and many Muslims were and are conservative on social issues.

After the terrorist attacks of September 11, 2001, that obviously changed. President Bush made efforts to distinguish between Muslims and Arabs broadly and Al-Qaeda, but the rhetoric of many others around the U.S. response did not always make the same distinction. And so Arab and Muslim groups that might have had inroads into the Republican Party found those openings closing. This may be a perfect example of what happens when a generally unopposed group faces a newly organized opposition, and so must pay more attention to the ideological and partisan environment.

Interest Group Coordination

The previous section focused on interest groups interacting with the party, or the party's nominee. But interests interact with one another as well. And ideology and partisan divides shape that interaction. One way to see this is to look for patterns in the ways that interest groups interact with each other. And one approach to that is to use social network analysis techniques to track interest group networks.

For example, Gregory Koger, Seth Masket, and Hans Noel[12] traced the trade in mailing lists among interest groups that solicit donations. In early 2004, they donated small sums to an initial set of politically oriented interest groups, party and candidate committees, and political magazines, using differently spelled names of donors. When those names received solicitation from other organizations, that indicates that the first group sold the name to second group. Those transactions traced out a network of group coordination.

The resulting network is presented in Figure 5.1. Each point in the figure represents a different group. Triangles are formal interest groups, squares are political parties or candidates, and pentagons are magazines. (Circles represent other categories, generally businesses attempting to sell products or services.) An arrow from one point to another indicates that the first organization sold a name to the second.

The emergent pattern is the degree to which political organizations cooperate with like-minded groups. Large solid symbols represent groups traditionally affiliated with conservatives or Republicans, such as the Republican National Committee, the Family Research Council or the National Review. Large open symbols represent groups traditionally affiliated with liberals of Democrats, such as candidates for the Democratic nomination in 2004, the Human Rights Campaign, or *The Nation* magazine. Smaller symbols represent groups that were not origi-nally solicited and that are not political or ideologically affiliated, such as the American Cancer Association or *Time* magazine.

The notable pattern in Figure 5.1 is the degree to which (a) the groups do inter-act, and (b) they do so with their co-partisans. Interest groups and party groups are tightly connected to one another in both the Republican side and the Democratic side of the network. The only bridges between the two partisan sides are through truly non-partisan actors such as general interest magazines. It is easy to distin-guish Democrats from Republicans, but hard to distinguish interest groups from partisan groups from partisan magazines.

At the same time, the connections are much denser on the left. Koger, Masket, and Noel do not offer an explanation for this pattern, although they speculate that it may be because the left relies more on informal coordination, or that liberal and Democratic groups were simply more active in early 2004, when

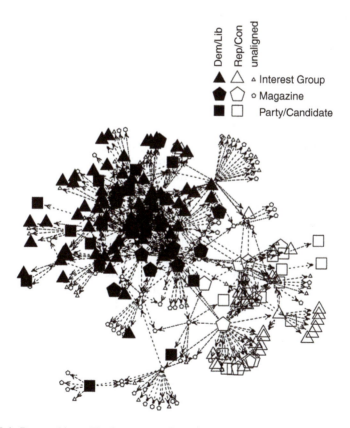

Figure 5.1 Donor Name Trades among Groups in 2004

the Democratic primary was gearing up, but no similar activity was energizing conservatives.

Koger, Masket, and Noel claim that this is evidence for a more expanded notion of a political party.[13] The party, they argue, consists of not only the formal party organs, but also of the interest groups and media outlets that support it. That they share mailing lists is only one aspect of that coordination, and it therefore does not prove the level of coordination that the authors believe exists, but it is suggestive.

Other scholars have applied social network methods to other aspects of this "expanded" party, with similar results. Michael Heaney and Fabio Rojas[14] survey participants in anti-war rallies during the Iraq War and find that these participants tended to be mobilized by a network of groups that were connected to other aspects of the Democratic and liberal partisan network. Heaney also finds that network ties shape the way that members of one organization view the influence of other important organizations in the health care policy area.[15]

The network approach to interest groups shows some promise. If interest groups do represent policy demanders who have also entered into coalitions to form parties, they provide an opportunity to observe that coalition formation in a more concrete domain. Since interest groups are not, themselves, the constituent parts of the party, important coordination may not be captured by observing the formal groups, but it is a useful place to begin.

Going it Alone: The Anti-Saloon League

The organizations discussed in the previous two sections are operating in an ideological and partisan environment. Ideology in particular shapes which groups can ally with other groups. But we have not always had such clearly ideologically divided parties. At the turn of the century, for instance, many issues cross-cut the partisan divide. The prohibition of alcohol, for example, was not an issue well organized into the partisan coalitions. That shaped how anti-alcohol interest groups interacted with political parties.

Some interests were concerned with many issues. The Woman's Christian Temperance Union (WCTU), for example, was animated by founder Francis Willard's aim to "do everything." WCTU activists were concerned with women's issues, urban poverty, prison conditions, international relations, and a host of other issues. This broad agenda may well have had positive consequences, but it was not largely responsible for the eventual passage of the 18th Amendment that prohibited alcohol.

The interest group that played a larger role was the Anti-Saloon League (ASL). While the WCTU was interested in everything, the ASL focused on one thing: prohibition. We do not have the ASL in Table 5.2, of course, but if we did, we would find that the group endorsed both Democrats and Republicans, provided they were "dry" and not "wet." The result was an increase in the number of dry members of Congress from both parties, which in turn resulted in a successful campaign for the 18th Amendment. There were, of course, many other players involved in the drive for Prohibition, but the ASL and especially its focused endorsements were important.[16]

What the story of the ASL tells us is that the nature of the party coalitions matters a great deal. When the coalitions are well-defined, and particularly when they are ideological, interest groups will be part of the policy demanders that make up the parties. But where a set of interests is not organized into the party divisions, then an independent strategy is likely to be easier. (It is worth noting that prohibition was not always a cross-cutting partisan issue. In the mid-1800s, Republicans were more likely to be dry and Democrats wet. But this dichotomy had broken down by the end of the nineteenth century and was not the case when the ASL and the WCTU were most active.)

What are the prospects for the ASL's strategy today? Certainly it works well for low profile issues. Issues with diffuse opposition and organized and powerful advocacy can easily work through both parties. These are the kinds of issues that are the bread and butter of interest group scholarship, precisely because they are hard to understand by reference to popular opinion and partisan conflict.

But prohibition was far from a low-profile issue. It was central to electoral conflict but was not inherently partisan. Among high-profile issues today, questions of national security and civil liberties have a similar character. The most ardent supporters of the PATRIOT Act have been Republicans, but many of its strongest opponents are libertarian activists. Similarly, many have criticized President Obama from the left on his failure to close the detention facility at Guantanamo Bay and the U.S. drone program in Pakistan.

Yet interest groups concerned with civil liberties are constrained by party and ideology. Tea Party activists who are focused on civil liberties would be unlikely to support a Democrat, even if the Democrat opposed Obama on these issues. It is hard to imagine a single-issue interest group in the mode of the Anti-Saloon League putting this issue above partisanship and backing civil liberties candidates regardless of party. Even if we can imagine it, we are not currently observing it.

Future Directions

The analysis presented here does not radically upend most of the findings in the interest group literature. Interest group scholars understand that parties are amenable to some groups, while other interests are unorganized.

But looking at interest groups from the perspective of political parties changes some of the questions that we ask. Instead of studying how interests get their way on policy, we may study how interests reshape the coalitions that are tools for getting one's way on policy. The gay rights activists in the Log Cabin Republicans could just support the Human Rights Campaign. They could even donate their time or money to HRC while also supporting the Republican Party. That might be a good strategy for achieving their final policy goals. But it makes for an awkward and bifurcated effort. It would be easier if they could advocate for their preferred policy from within their preferred party. Since party coalitions are so important, the coalition itself is a subject of conflict.

These motives, in turn, shape what interest groups are doing. If coordinating with like-minded groups is part of a global and long-term strategy, instead of just a strategy for success on specific policy goal, then the nature of that large scale coordination needs to be better understood.

For example, Richard Hall and Alan Deardorff[17] argue that lobbying should be viewed not as vote buying or persuasion but as a legislative subsidy, where interest groups and other lobbyists provide useful information to otherwise like-minded legislators. Of course, ideology and partisanship will shape which legislators will be like-minded and which will not. Legislators from the "opposite" party of an interest group can still be like-minded, of course, but the kinds of information and support they would need from a lobbyist may differ. Seen through the filter of party organization, the Hall and Deardorff framework gives us insights into the different strategies a lobbyist might use with different legislators.

In a working paper, Scott McClurg and Jeremy Philips[18] suggest that interest group strategy may vary with the group's goals. When interest groups want to protect the status quo, they will stick with the party that they are already aligned with. When they want to change policy, they will target members of both parties. This of course depends a great deal on how embedded the group—and its opposition—is in the party system. New issues may afford interest groups more opportunity to reach across the aisle. In any event, it is worth noting that some lobbying does amount to "reaching across the aisle," even for ostensibly non-partisan interest groups.

And that, in a nutshell, is the important point. Some interests can and should try to avoid partisanship and ideology. There are advantages. Other interests do better by allying with one party. Still more importantly, many interests do not have much of a choice.

Notes

1 John Aldrich, *Why Parties? The Origin and Transformation of Political Parties in America*, (Chicago: University of Chicago Press, 1995). See also Kathleen Bawn, "Constructing 'Us': Ideology, Coalition Politics, and False Consciousness," *American Journal of Political Science* 43, no. 2 (1999): 303–34; Thomas Schwartz,. "Why Parties?" research memorandum, 1989; Hans Noel, "The Coalition Merchants: The Ideological Roots of the Civil Rights Realignment," *Journal of Politics* 74, no. 1 (2012): 156–73; and Hans Noel, *Political Ideologies and Political Parties in America* (New York: Cambridge University Press, forthcoming).
2 Barry Weingast, "A Rational Choice Perspective on Congressional Norms," *American Journal of Political Science* 23, no. 2 (1979): 245-262.
3 Marty Cohen, David Karol, Hans Noel, and John Zaller, *The Party Decides: Presidential Nominations Before and After Reform* (Chicago: University of Chicago Press, 2008); and

Kathy Bawn, Marty Cohen, David Karol, Seth Masket, Hans Noel, and John R. Zaller, "A Theory of Political Parties: Groups, Policy Demands and Nominations in American Politics," *Perspectives on Politics* 10, no. 3 (2012): 571–97. For related works, see Marty Cohen, "Moral Victories: Cultural Conservatism and the Creation of a New Republican Congressional Majority" (Ph.D. dissertation, UCLA, 2005); David Karol, *Party Position Change in American Politics: Coalition Management.* (New York: Cambridge University Press, 2009); Seth Masket, *No Middle Ground: How Informal Party Organizations Control Nominations and Polarize Legislatures* (Ann Arbor: University of Michigan Press, 2009); Kathleen Bawn and Hans Noel, "Long Coalitions Under Electoral Uncertainty: The Electoral Origins of Political Parties" (paper presented at the annual meeting of the Midwest Political Science Association, Chicago, Illinois, April 2007); Noel, "The Coalition Merchants"; and Noel, *Political Ideologies and Political Parties in America.*

4 Karol, *Party Position Change in American Politics.*

5 Noel, "The Coalition Merchants" and *Political Ideologies and Political Parties in America.*

6 Table 2 was constructed using lists compiled by Project Vote Smart and Democracy in Action, supplemented by web searches on the groups that turned up in those sources, as well as other interest groups that were found in general searches in election years. It does not represent a random sample.

7 James G. Gimpel, Frances E. Lee, and Michael Parrott, "Business Interests and the Party Coalitions: Industry Sector Contributions to U.S. Congressional Campaigns" (paper presented at the NCAPSA American Politics Workshop at American University, Washington, DC, January 7, 2013).

8 Cohen et al., *The Party Decides*, pp. 30–31.

9 Valerie Richardson, "CPAC Meeting Raises Gay Issue." December 29, 2010, *Washington Times.*

10 Richard Berke, "Dole, in Shift, Says Refund of Gay Gift Was Staff Mistake," *New York Times,* October 18, 1995, accessed February 15, 2013.

11 Lisa Anderson, "Gays Long Loyal to GOP Agonize over Supporting Bush," *Chicago Tribune,* April 19, 2004.

12 Gregory Koger, Seth Masket, and Hans Noel, "Partisan Webs: Information Exchange and Party Networks," *British Journal of Political Science* 39, no. 3 (2009): 633–53; and Gregory Koger, Seth Masket, and Hans Noel, "Cooperative Party Factions in American Politics," *American Politics Research* 38, no. 1 (2010): 33.

13 Jonathan Bernstein, "The Expanded Party in American Politics" (Ph.D. thesis, University of California, Berkeley, 1999); Casey Dominguez and Jonathan Bernstein, "Candidates and Candidacies in the Expanded Party," *PS: Political Science and Politics* 36, no. 2 (2003): 165–69; Richard Skinner, "Do 527's Add Up to a Party? Thinking About the 'Shadows' of Politics," *The Forum* 3, no. 3 (2005): Article 5.

14 Michael Heaney and Fabio Rojas, "Partisans, Nonpartisans, and the Antiwar Movement in the United States," *American Politics Research* 34, no. 4 (2007): 431–64.

15 Michael Heaney, "Multiplex Networks and Interest Group Influence Reputation: An Exponential Random Graph Model," *Social Networks,* http://dx.doi.org/10.1016/j.bbr.2011.03.031.

16 For more detailed discussions of the different strategies of the WCTU and the ASL in the Prohibition fight, see Thomas R. Pegram, *Battling Demon Rum* (Chicago: Ivan R. Dee, 1998); Jack S. Blocker Jr., *American Temperance Movements: Cycles of Reform* (Boston: Twayne, 1989); and Daniel Okrent, *Last Call: The Rise and Fall of Prohibition* (New York: Scribner, 2010).

17 Richard L. Hall and Alan V. Deardorff, "Lobbying as Legislative Subsidy," *American Political Science Review* 100, no. 1 (2006): 69–84.

18 Scott McClurg and Jeremy Philips, "A Social Network Analysis of Interest Group Contributions and Partisan Behavior in the 2006 House of Representatives," Working Paper, 2011. OpenSIUC, http://opensiuc.lib.siu.edu/cgi/viewcontent.cgi?article=1027& context=pnconfs_2011.

Chapter 6

Why Lobbyists for Competing Interest Groups Often Cooperate

Thomas T. Holyoke

It was the very strangeness of the bedfellows that turned heads on March 30, 2013. The AFL-CIO and the U.S. Chamber of Commerce, fierce antagonists and two of the nation's most powerful interest groups, had struck a deal resolving their two major concerns on immigration reform legislation and were ready to lobby together for its enactment.[1] It had not been easy. The chamber's top concern was how many foreign workers needed by a variety of industries would be annually admitted to the United States. Labor's chief concern was how much these workers would be paid and what their working conditions would be. Each cared about the other's major issue as well, just not quite as much. This difference in priorities made it possible to strike a deal, though it also helped that both groups were under enormous pressure from Senator Charles Schumer (D-NY), who brokered the deal, to resolve their differences. While this deal between competing organizations grabbed headlines, such deal-making is not as unusual as many might think. Competing interest groups frequently work together, because they must.

Think about these numbers. There are over 7,000 interest groups in Washington, DC, along with 6,500 corporations or other institutions with lobbying offices.[2] There are at least 19,000 people in and around the capitol city practicing the profession of lobbying, even if they do not print that word on their business cards.[3] Roughly 63% of Americans are members of at least one organization that could be called an interest group.[4] While their membership may amount to little more than writing checks or clicking on "donate now," realize that only about 62% of voters voted in the 2008 presidential election, and that was higher than in previous elections.[5] It seems citizens may believe interest groups are the best form of political representation. Yet there is something peculiar about so much lobbying by so many special interests.

To see why, consider that the number of lawmakers in Congress has not grown since Hawaii became a state in 1959, remaining at 535. That makes 36 lobbyists for every member of Congress! With legislators spending only a few days a week at the capitol, contacts with lobbyists are largely handled by congressional staff, and while several thousand staffers can more easily meet with over 19,000 lobbyists, they too have other responsibilities, like serving constituents. In the executive branch, lobbyists focus their efforts at appointed officials at the top of the hierarchy, not the hundreds of thousands working in the agencies.[6] With so few people available for lobbying, how do all these lobbyists manage to get the job of representation done?

Political scientist Robert Salisbury took a look at all of this and concluded that lobbying in teams was the new norm, teams of lobbyists achieving what one lobbyist could not.[7] But that answer confuses more than it helps. Why would a lobbyist for any special interest want to work with another? Are they not all competitors trying to win policy benefits *just* for their members or clients, the people they represent? With more diverse interests making more demands on government, but limited public budgets and less willingness by lawmakers today to carelessly fund government programs, politics today seems like it should be more zero-sum in that benefits to one interest group's members must be taken from those of another. Why would lobbyists for all of these competing interests ever be willing to compromise member or client interests by working together? Or *are* they compromising those interests? In this chapter I try to untangle this confusion by providing some insights into what lobbyists are lobbying for, what it means for them to compete, and when it is okay to make peace with their opponents.

Competing Interests

Cooperating in a coalition means overcoming competing interests, but what does it mean for interest groups to compete? Look at Figure 6.1. The thick horizontal line is a policy outcome continuum, meaning it is a series of possible policies that lawmakers *could* enact as a solution to a question of how an issue on the government's agenda ought to be solved. While there are many potential policy

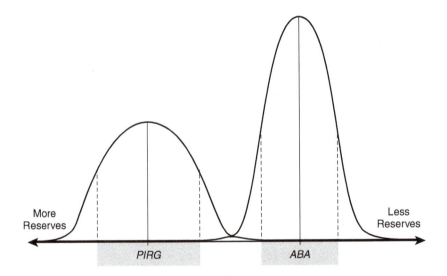

Figure 6.1 Interest Group Competition over Bank Reserve Requirements

solutions on this continuum, only one (if any) can become law.[8] Say the issue is how much of a bank's deposits must be held in reserve to keep it solvent rather than be leant out for profit. The continuum represents a series of possible policies answering the issue question of how great the reserve amount imposed by government bank regulators should be. 10%? 20%? More? No reserve at all? All of these are possibilities in Figure 6.1, with smaller reserve requirements toward the right (it is less government regulation after all) and higher amounts to the left. Lawmakers, though, can only choose one policy position, assuming they choose to enact any at all.

The American Bankers Association (ABA) is a large and, many would say, powerful interest group representing banks big and small. Bank officials, who are ABA's members, probably think about loan-to-reserve ratios every day, but have different ideas of what the ratio ought to be. That is, they have different *preferences* for policy outcomes on the continuum in Figure 6.1. Having said that, their reserve ratio preferences are probably not that far apart from each other, all of them tending toward the less-regulatory side of the continuum. So which position should ABA's lobbyist advocate for on the reserve requirement issue when she goes to Capitol Hill? A plurality of members, possibly even a majority, may prefer the same policy position. That is, ABA has a *distribution* of member preferences on this issue, a distribution that probably looks like the hump on the right side of Figure 6.1.[9] Ethically and practically her best position is under the top of the distribution hump, position *ABA* because more members prefer this position to any other. When your employment depends on keeping members happy, take the position pleasing most of them.

Another interest group, the U.S. Public Interest Research Group, usually just called PIRG, also cares about bank reserve requirements, though for different reasons. A better capitalized bank (one with greater reserves) is less likely to fail because it made careless loans or exploited poor homeowners with high interest mortgage loans. Like ABA, though, PIRG members are not united in their preferences for exactly what the reserve requirement ought to be. Hence the hump representing PIRG member preferences on the left side of Figure 6.1. PIRG's members are less united on what the requirement ought to be than are ABA's members, so the PIRG hump is actually wider than ABA's, with PIRG's lobbyist supporting the plurality position at *PIRG*. Because position *PIRG* is not even close to *ABA*, the members of one group collectively prefer a policy outcome seen as threatening to the members of the other group. These groups are competing.

Both ABA and PIRG lobbyists have a little wiggle-room on what positions they can advocate for on this issue because most group members will tolerate a little deviation from their individually preferred positions, though how much they will tolerate depends on how intensely they feel about the bank reserve issue.[10] Furthermore, even if the lobbyists support points a little to the right or left of *ABA* and *PIRG*, both still have quite a few members who ideally prefer those alternative positions. Just how much wiggle-room each lobbyist has is shown by the distance between the vertical dashed lines under the humps in Figure 6.1, identified by the gray boxes. The amount of available wiggle-room (at the moment) is determined by how great a deviation from their individual preferences members will tolerate. If a lobbyist deviates too much, economist Albert Hirschman lays out two ways members will likely respond.[11] If the PIRG lobbyist publicly supports too low a reserve requirement, members will abandon the group, taking their dues with them. If the ABA lobbyist publicly supports too great a reserve requirement, she will be fired. Neither outcome is particularly good for a lobbyist.

Coalition Conditions

So what does it take for lobbyists from two (or more) competing interest groups to work together? It comes down to two broad factors. First, though, it is worth emphasizing that it would be a rare circumstance indeed if all of the interest groups in a coalition concerned with the same issues were not competing with every other at least a little. If two (or more) groups' members collectively preferred the same policy position, these organizations would be providing exactly the same representational service. One would be redundant. Why would any faction of citizens pay to support two organizations lobbying for the same thing? As political scientist McGee Young showed in the histories of small business and environmental groups, organizations trying to recruit the same potential members strive to distinguish themselves from each other, often by taking different positions on issues, even if the differences are small, to draw people to their group instead of their rival.[12] They do not lobby for the same thing.

The magnitude of the difference between what the collective membership of one group wants from that of one or more competing groups, like the distance between *PIRG* and *ABA* in Figure 6.1, is one of the driving factors of coalition formation. Look at Figure 6.2. The vertical axis on the left represents the distance between the positions of two (or more) groups on issues their members care about. Going further down the axis means there are greater competitive differences between what the memberships of these groups want, which makes it harder for their lobbyists to coalesce around a single position without making too many compromises.[13] And coalitions can only support one position. The closer group positions are on the issues, higher up on the vertical axis, the easier it is for their lobbyists to work together and thus the greater the likelihood that they will.

The horizontal axis on top of Figure 6.2 indicates just how strongly members of these groups feel about *several* of the issues a coalition might lobby. Interest groups are typically concerned with several issues, but all of these issues are usually connected by common themes like banking policy or environmental policy and are called policy domains. If interest group members have really strong feelings about many of the issues in a domain, it will be hard for their lobbyist to make the compromises necessary to work in coalitions with other groups on these issues, even if the collective positions preferred by the members of all of the concerned interest groups are not that far apart (upper right in Figure 6.2). If these lobbyists actually do manage to form a coalition, it will be a tenuous one. Nearly

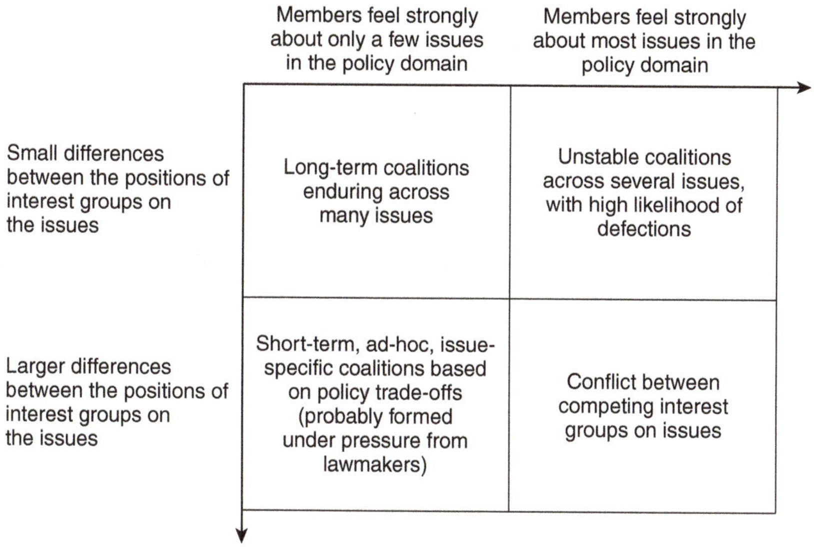

	Members feel strongly about only a few issues in the policy domain	Members feel strongly about most issues in the policy domain
Small differences between the positions of interest groups on the issues	Long-term coalitions enduring across many issues	Unstable coalitions across several issues, with high likelihood of defections
Larger differences between the positions of interest groups on the issues	Short-term, ad-hoc, issue-specific coalitions based on policy trade-offs (probably formed under pressure from lawmakers)	Conflict between competing interest groups on issues

Figure 6.2 Coalition Formation Based on the How Strongly Group Members Collectively Feel about Issues and the Similarity of Member Collective Positions on Issues

any disruptive influence from lawmakers or other lobbyists may shatter it. Thus, what the lower right box in Figure 6.2 shows is that coalitions are nearly impossible to form when there is significant competition between would-be coalition partners (greater distance between group positions) *and* when members of these groups feel so strongly about the issues that compromise is just about impossible to achieve. Instead competition erupts into conflict.

Long-Term Coalitions

Small Differences

As Figure 6.2 suggests, interest group coalitions range from the short-term, ad-hoc variety working only on specific issues to semi-permanent, long-term coalitions lobbying on many issues for many years. Long-term coalitions form when the positions supported by the members of the concerned interest groups are not that far apart on most of the issues in the policy domain (they are not competing much) *and* when there is significant variation in how strongly members of the groups feel about these issues (upper left of Figure 6.2). In other words, the people represented by organizations in long-term coalitions have fairly similar interests on most issues to begin with. They probably have the same general ideological outlook on politics and beliefs regarding the values society ought to prioritize. The difference between members of one group from those of others in the coalition is that they have different ideas regarding which issues are actually most important.

Environmental advocacy is a good example. While it makes sense to think that interest groups always try to expand their membership to include every person who shares the interest defining each group, something else appears to be happening in the environmental community.[14] There are hundreds of thousands of people in America for whom environmental preservation is an overriding issue; this is the tie that binds them together as a common interest. Yet they vary in just what aspects of environmentalism they care about the most. This has made it possible for many interest groups to establish themselves and thrive in the environmental interest "niche."[15] People who feel especially strong about clean water can join Environmental Defense Fund, while those primarily interested in roadless forests can join the Wilderness Society. People interested in limiting public and private land development can join the Nature Conservancy, while those wanting to preserve grey wolves can join Defenders of Wildlife. All of these people care about water, wolves, and wilderness; they just care about one more than others.

Because they peacefully divvy-up the environmental interest niche, these organizations can reinforce each other in coalitions when lobbying issues rather than attack each other in a scramble for members. Because the members of one group care more about one issue than another, their interest group takes the lead for the coalition when that issue comes up. Then the organization steps back and supports another interest group when the environmental issue most important to that group's members arises. Since they all draw members from the same pool of environmentally conscience citizens, the differences in member and therefore group positions on issues is small enough that no interest group will have to demand its members hold their noses as it agrees to support a position staked out by a coalition partner. They are firmly in the upper left of Figure 6.2. Defenders of Wildlife can lead on Endangered Species Act issues with support, but little interference, from other environmental groups. In return, Defenders of Wildlife will back the Wilderness Society in its efforts to designate more national forests as roadless wilderness. Deference and reciprocity make a long-term, semi-permanent coalition of groups work and keep it alive.

To be sure, not all environmental groups are great coalition partners. Those further out on the ideological left, such as EarthFirst!, Earthjustice, and to some extent Greenpeace, tend to be less accommodating of the positions of their more moderate cousins. These groups are trying to appeal to the more radical side of the environmental community, people who feel very strongly about more issues (upper right of Figure 6.2) and are thus less inclined to defer to the less radical environmental groups on any issues. Also, interest groups without a membership base large enough to support them in the long run may feel they need to fight harder to give the appearance that they and they alone are the true representatives of a potential membership. This makes it hard for them to make compromises and share credit in a coalition.[16] Even if they do join a coalition, this need to lead and unwillingness to compromise makes them untrustworthy partners.

Coalition Benefits

Degree of competitive differences and variation in member intensity regarding issues explains why it is possible for some interest groups to work together in long term coalitions, but not why they would want to. Political scientist Kevin Hula lays out the benefits of membership.[17] They include the sharing of information, contacts, credit, and financial resources. Start with information sharing. As mentioned earlier, the number of interest groups active in national politics has become enormous. And that is just the tip of the iceberg. Many ideologically leaning think tanks, consulting firms, public relations agencies, and corporate lobbyists are also trying to push their issues and policies. As the networks of all of these advocates working on the same issues grow increasingly dense, learning who is pushing what position, how successful they are with lawmakers, where individual legislators stand on issues, and generally cutting through the fog of political warfare becomes *very* difficult. No single lobbyist can keep track of what is going on all of the time no matter how well connected they are. Coalitions help lobbyists manage this difficulty.

When lobbyists join stable, long-term coalitions, enough trust is generated from their repeated experiences together for each lobbyist to be comfortable sharing what he or she knows.[18] They contribute to a common pool of knowledge regarding everything happening with an issue, what policies are coming up in the future addressing the issue, how lawmakers are likely to respond, and which competing interest groups are likely to wade into the fight. The result is that coalition members become collectively better informed.

They also share *who* they know. Gaining access to elected lawmakers usually requires some type of constituency connection. All interest group members are somebody's constituents, and people who care enough about public policy to join an interest group also tend to be informed voters and thus important to a legislator's re-election coalition. If group members are concentrated enough and politically active enough in a state or district, their elected officials will want to help them in return for electoral support and are happy to work with the members' lobbyists.[19] Lobbyists not representing people in the districts of important officials will have a much harder time gaining access and will be attracted to coalitions with stronger, better connected groups to alleviate this problem.[20] Groups in the coalition with access will presumably help their partners get some face-time with key legislators and staff. At the very least, well-connected lobbyists will deliver messages to lawmakers on behalf of all coalition members. They have an incentive to do so. The bigger the coalition, the greater the perception on Capitol Hill that there is widespread unity for or against a policy proposal in the constituencies that matter.

The direct benefit of financial resources is obvious. Working in coalitions means an interest group does not have to itself incur the enormous expense of waging a lobbying campaign to get lawmakers' attention and convince them to support a policy solution. If the lone interest group also lacks a clear constituency connection to the lawmakers who matter on an issue, then to have any influence at all they must undertake grassroots advocacy by pressing thousands of members and supporters to call the Capitol to convince lawmakers that there is an electoral reason for paying attention to its interest.[21] Such campaigns are enormously expensive and may not work.

There is also an indirect benefit from coalition cost sharing—it makes it easier for more interest groups to claim more credit for policy successes. Lobbyists must keep their members interested in the group. They have to keep looking impressive, convincing members that their concerns are being well represented in the political arena by the group's lobbyist across a whole array of related issues. Long-term coalitions of groups with similar positions on multiple issues can tackle more issues than any group could realistically hope to by itself unless it was exceptionally large and wealthy. Since most are not exceptionally large and wealthy, coalitions provide the *appearance* of vigorously lobbying on many issues members and potential members care about. In reality the group's lobbyist spends most of his or her time lobbying only the one or two issues his or her group's members care about most. He or she just claims some credit for success on all of the other issues. Unless members and potential members are especially savvy, they will be impressed with their apparently superhuman lobbyist's ability to work so hard on so many issues at once. For members it suggests their dues are being well-spent. For potential members, it suggests the interest group soliciting them is more than worthy of their dues.

Coalition Costs

The costs of joining a long-term coalition are suggested back in Figure 6.1. Remember that on an issue like loan-to-reserve ratios, a coalition can only support one policy position. All interest groups in the coalition must agree on that position, which probably requires significant negotiations. Membership means being willing to support positions on issues other than those ideally preferred by a majority or even a plurality of group members. If members do not feel all that strongly about an issue, then the group's lobbyist probably has little to worry about from some compromise. Unsurprisingly, this makes a lobbyist a popular coalition partner because he or she is not making things difficult for anybody else. But if group members do feel strongly about an issue, and especially if they are fairly united on the positions they want to see enacted into law, then almost any compromise their lobbyist makes to support other groups in the coalition will upset them. If the lobbyist cannot persuade coalition partners to back his or her members' ideal position on this issue, he or she may have to break from the coalition. If this happens too often, the lobbyist may be booted out entirely, his or her credibility with other lobbyists in tatters. If he or she instead compromises member preferences and members find out, they may dissert the group, leaving the organization's reputation in tatters. Or they may just fire the lobbyist.

This gets back to the notion of wiggle-room on an issue identified in Figure 6.1, the flexibility a lobbyist really has for determining what policy outcome he or she can support on an issue to keep members happy and accommodate other interest groups. The benefits and costs the lobbyist must weigh against each other on each and every issue. Sometimes this means deciding who is really more important to serve, group members or coalition allies. I return to discuss that tension later.

Short-Term Issue Coalitions

An arguably better demonstration of the complexities of interest group politics is why lobbyists form short-term coalitions—coalitions only lasting the lifetime of an issue, and sometimes not even that. The alliance between AFL-CIO and the Chamber of Commerce described earlier is an example. It came late in the immigration issue's life, after years of conflict. While they carry many of the same benefits and costs, short-term coalitions are very different from long-term ones in that they are more likely temporary alliances between competitors, groups whose members prefer significantly different policies, but for a variety of reasons support compromises. They fall in the lower left of Figure 6.2. How they sometimes find common ground provides insight into the real give and take of interest group competition and cooperation.

Return for a moment to Figure 6.1 where the American Bankers Association and PIRG are competing to shape policy regarding bank loan-to-reserve ratios. Recall that the dashed vertical lines under each distribution of group member preferences shows just how far each organization's lobbyist can deviate from positions *ABA* and *PIRG* without making members so mad that many will abandon the group. If the shaded areas, determined by member toleration, could extend far enough toward the center to intersect, then lobbyists for these competing groups might find one or more policy proposals both could support. Since the shaded areas do not intersect, cooperation between these competitors is not possible, and may not be as long as they are only concerned about bank reserve requirements. Fortunately, policy-making is more complex than this simple zero-sum trade-off.

Multi-Dimensional Trade-offs

In most political fights, one interest group tends to care more about one facet of an issue than others, making that issue multi-dimensional rather than just uni-dimensional as in Figure 6.1.[22] Although these issue's facets are often contained in the same bill or regulatory proposal, as long as members of one group feel more strongly about one part of the issue than another, and vice versa for the competitor group, compromise is easier to achieve because trade-offs are possible. One group more or less gets its way on its part of the issue, and in return gives way to its competitor on the facet of the issue most important to the competitor's members. Arguably this is just what happened with AFL-CIO and the Chamber of Commerce with wages and number of workers on the immigration issue.

Expanding on the reserve requirement issue example should make this clearer. The policy continuum from Figure 6.1 is now the horizontal axis in Figure 6.3 as the amount of money banks must keep in reserve rather than lend out now becomes one piece of the larger issue of bank regulation. It remains the most important piece to the American Bankers Association. PIRG, however, cares more about how much money banks lend in poor communities, places many bankers tend to avoid for fear of high default rates. This becomes the second facet of the bank regulation issue and is the vertical continuum in Figure 6.3. Members of ABA care about low-income lending as well, just not as much as PIRG members. Because under-capitalized banks are more likely to fail and leave poor communities without any financial services, PIRG cares about loan-to-reserve ratios as well, just not as much as low-income lending. But because neither group prioritizes the same facet of this complex issue of bank regulation, a trade-off might be negotiated and a short term coalition formed to advocate for policy embodying that trade-off.

How much would ABA and PIRG sacrifice on the pieces of the issue less important to their members to make gains on their more preferred policy outcome? Their willingness to trade defines the shapes of the curves winding their way through Figure 6.3. Think about these curves as a series of possible trade-offs both group might support. Bankers really want a low loan-to-reserve ratio and are willing to

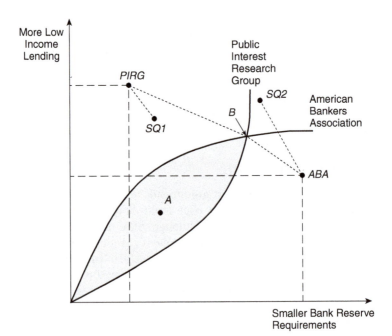

Figure 6.3 Bargaining between ABA and PIRG

give a little on the low-income lending requirements to get it. Some bankers may even believe they *ought* to do some low-income lending out of a sense of social responsibility, though only up to a point. So the ABA trade-off curve initially bends steeply upward as it moves away from 0, indicating a willingness by bankers to agree to quite large increases in low-income lending requirements (starting from the baseline of 0 lending) for every unit decrease in their mandated reserve requirements, but only when the overall amounts of both are still quite low.

This changes for ABA when larger amounts of low-income lending and reserve requirements are considered. Since bankers do not want to be obligated to make too many risky loans in poor neighborhoods, they will only agree to more low-income lending in increasingly smaller increments to gain PIRG's support for further decreases in reserve requirements. ABA's trade-off curve therefore flattens into a horizontal line at the point where bankers still want lower reserves but are unwilling to agree to *any* more low-income lending to get it. The reverse is true of PIRG. Initially PIRG members are willing to support significant reductions in reserve requirements for set increases in low-income lending. Obviously a bank cannot lend in poor communities if all of its assets are locked-up in the vault. But as bankers demand even more free capital to lend, the more PIRG members insist that more slices of it be lent in poor neighborhoods. When PIRG members will agree to no more reductions in reserve requirements, even though they want more low-income lending, their trade-off curve becomes a vertical line.

All of the points on these two curves are potential deals, and so are all of the points in the gray area between them. Only none of them will ever actually be a deal. Why would PIRG's lobbyist advocate for a deal at point *A* when he knows that the banker's lobbyist would support higher low-income lending for exactly the same reserve requirement, and vice versa for ABA? Both lobbyists know their competitor will agree to something better, so *A* is never considered. Neither lobbyist will get their members' ideal trade-offs either, which are points *ABA* and *PIRG*. As you can probably guess, the best possible, realizable deal is at point *B* where the curves intersect. This is the only point where neither lobbyist can get the other to agree to anything better.

Status Quo Sticking Points

A serious impediment to successful bargaining between competitors is an existing policy already on the books, a status quo position. Bank reserve requirements have been in federal law since the passage of the Federal Reserve Act of 1913, and low-income lending requirements since enacting the Community Reinvestment Act of 1977. One or both interest groups might prefer the status quo to any deal their competitor would agree to. Say the status quo policy in Figure 6.3 is at point *SQ1*. The dotted line from *PIRG* to *SQ1* is shorter than from *PIRG* to *B*. This means current policy is closer to what PIRG members would ideally prefer than the bargain proposed with the bankers. If preserving the status quo *is* still a realistic possibility, then there will be no short-term issue coalition because

PIRG prefers the status quo, enacting no new policy, to any alternative the bankers would support. Bankers, on the other hand, prefer the bargain because B is closer to ABA than is $SQ1$, but they may have a harder time getting B because they must expend valuable resources fighting PIRG rather than enjoy the advantages of sharing resources and contacts in a coalition.

But if the status quo is at $SQ2$, then the deal at B makes both interest groups better off than current policy so both will lobby together for it in an issue coalition. They appear to be strange bedfellows to the casual observer—PIRG and ABA together? Somewhere pigs are flying!—but given the structure of this competitive scenario, it makes sense. Competitors become temporary allies, pooling resources, sharing information and contacts, combining their grassroots efforts, all of the benefits mentioned in the last section, and, of course, all of the costs too. Once their deal is enacted, PIRG and ABA can go back to fighting each other on the next banking issue.

Lawmakers and Lobbyists

Pressured to Cooperate

The immigration issue example at the beginning of the chapter suggested that Senator Schumer pushed AFL-CIO and the Chamber of Commerce toward an alliance. Are lawmakers that influential? Can they pressure lobbyists into working together in support of policies their members might not like? Probably. Lobbyists and interest groups are not the same thing, even though they are frequently treated as such by scholars and journalists.[23] And what lawmakers want matters a great deal to lobbyists. Like most everyone, lobbyists are people who are first and foremost interested in pursuing their own interests, which in this case are their careers. What makes for a successful lobbying career? Who you know in Washington, DC, matters. Lobbyists' abilities to represent member or client interests are only as good as the quality of the relationships they have with lawmakers. They ply their trade by building long-term relationships, which means helping lawmakers advance *their* interests. Often lobbyists do this by connecting the needs of the people they represent to the needs of the lawmakers whose favor they hope to garner.

Lobbyists cannot directly influence the lawmaking process. They need government officials to act on their behalf if their group members or clients are to be aided. Contrary to popular belief, lobbyists can rarely threaten lawmakers into supporting or opposing policies against their will. Rather, lawmakers must be convinced that helping a lobbyist's members serves their own interests, that interest usually being re-election.[24] That is why having a lot of group members living in a lawmaker's district, creating a constituency connection, is such a valuable resource for a lobbyist, and why not having one entices lobbyists to join coalitions with groups that do. Helping group members achieve their policy desires helps lawmakers achieve theirs, so they want to help the lobbyist because it means they help themselves.[25] Happy group members are happy constituents and they will vote for legislators who aided their lobbyist, especially after the lobbyist tells them how helpful these legislators were!

But lobbyists' need for these strong relationships has an edge to it. Maintaining portfolios of relationships with powerful lawmakers is so important to lobbyists that when the desires of their allies in Congress do not align with the wishes of their members, and no amount of persuasion can change these lawmakers' minds, lobbyists may well choose to support their legislative allies' positions at the expense of their members' preferences.[26] Furthermore, getting legislation passed Congress requires the acquiescence of a majority of lawmakers in both House and Senate. This necessity also might convince a lobbyist to support a position further away from members' ideal policy preferences on an issue just because nothing else can get enacted (at least as long as the status quo is still the worse outcome). These two pressures also make it more likely that lobbyists will work together in short-term coalitions.

Look at Figure 6.4, a modification of Figure 6.1. The upper horizontal line is the exact same policy outcome continuum for bank reserve requirements as the lower line. The upside-down gray area under it represents the distribution of elected officials' preferences for loan-to-reserve ratios. Liberals are on the left and are lighter in color, while dark-colored conservatives are on the right. Because lawmakers can only enact policy at one position, for a variety of reasons, such as pressure from presidents and party leaders, they coalesce around position B on the lower line. Since there are more liberal than conservative lawmakers, B is a

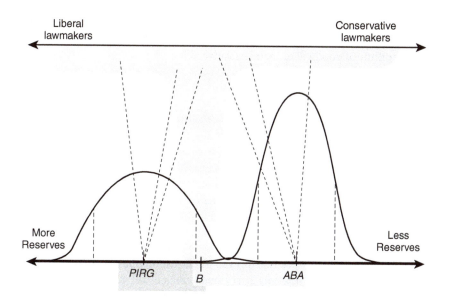

Figure 6.4 Coalition of Competing Interest Groups Created under Lawmaker Pressure

little left of center. The cone stretching down to the lower continuum, however, does not come to a point at *B* because there is still some disagreement among lawmakers as to just what the bank reserve requirement should be within that narrow range. The dashed lines rising from *PIRG* and *ABA* symbolize the connections of these groups' lobbyists to a few lawmakers in Congress, lawmakers these lobbyists have built relationships with and have access to.

Yet *B* is unacceptable to most of ABA's and PIRG's members. After all, what they will tolerate is still the same in Figure 6.4 as it was in Figure 6.1. They have not given their lobbyists any more wiggle-room. Realizing this, the lobbyists may try to convince their allies in Congress that it is really in their interests to support a policy at *ABA* or *PIRG* instead of *B*, but these lawmakers still might not want to change their positions to accommodate the interest groups. Perhaps they are convinced by presidents, party leaders, or other lobbyists that *B*, or some position near it, better reflects their personal interests, or is more likely to pass Congress, than *ABA* or *PIRG*.

Having settled on *B*, lawmakers expect their lobbyist allies to support the compromise as well rather than create trouble by riling-up their members, members who may be these lawmakers' constituents. That would end any lobbyist's relationship with a lawmaker quick. What group member-constituents do not know will not hurt lawmakers or lobbyists. Under such pressure, the range of positions ABA and PIRG lobbyists will support, shown by the gray boxes at the bottom of Figure 6.4, are no longer solely determined by what the bulk of the two groups' members prefer, but now also reflect pressure from lawmaker allies. Thus the shaded areas now shift toward the middle and encompass *B*, the position both lobbyists will support in a short-term coalition. Whatever member anger results from these lobbyists supporting the compromise at *B* is more than compensated by the continued goodwill of their legislative allies.

What Is Really Important?

By now it is clear that coalitions require lobbyists to make all kinds of trade-offs, but not all trade-offs are equally important. The ABA and PIRG lobbyists will support policy proposal *B* in a coalition because not doing so means they (not their interest groups) risk incurring the serious cost of damaging the relationships they have built with congressional allies, the very relationships that make lobbyists valuable in the Washington influence market. The relationship between lobbyists and lawmakers requires both to commit to helping the other achieve their interests and goals.[27] By refusing to support a policy that a legislator ally believes is in his or her interests, the lobbyist is saying that he or she is not going to be there when this ally needs help, even if it is just on one issue. That cracks the relationship, and even if it is only a very small crack it still means the relationship is no longer as dependable (for either party) as it once was. It will take time and work to recover the lost trust, so lobbyists will be very reluctant to ever damage it by defying their legislative patrons.

It is a lot easier for a lobbyist to go against the wishes of group members. Members often have no idea what is going on in Washington, and what they do know usually comes from their lobbyist.[28] This gives the lobbyist a significant advantage. ABA's lobbyist in Figure 6.4 might use her control of information to convince banker-members that it is in their interests to support higher reserve requirements at B rather than *ABA*. Perhaps because she convinces members the only realistic choice is between B and *PIRG*, with B the lesser of two evils. Or she might convince members that they should really *want* higher reserves. If the lobbyist's efforts at member persuasion, and some might say manipulation, is successful, ABA will support position B. If PIRG's lobbyist also agrees to B, both will combine forces in a short-term coalition, enjoying all of its benefits with the added benefit of keeping their patron lawmakers, on whose goodwill they depend, happy.

If one or both lobbyists *cannot* persuade members of the compromise's value, and they cannot hide the compromise from their members, then they must choose whom to anger. If too many members will dissert ABA or PIRG should their lobbyist support B, that hurts the interest group and perhaps even the lobbyist's reputation as an honest representative. This is a very real rock-and-hard place for lobbyists. In 2011 lobbyist John Rother of AARP suggested that the super-powerful organization representing retired Americans might be open to the possibility of increasing the age of retirement, delaying the receipt of Social Security and Medicare benefits, from 65 to 67 under pressure from congressional Republicans. Rother explained, "You want to be perceived as being a strong advocate, but at the same time your long-term interest is in solving a problem. The art, if you will, is to make sure that you are operating and messaging in such a way as to get the best possible result for your members within the context of solving the problem."[29] AARP's 38 million members did not see it that way and Rother no longer works there. Nor, by 2012, was AARP showing any willingness to support any changes to the age of retirement. Whichever way the lobbyist jumps, the deciding factor is what will benefit and hurt the *lobbyist* most. Whether or not lobbyists have read Shakespeare's *Hamlet,* their driving imperative is always "to thine own self be true"!

Summary and Ethics

Coalitions are valuable to lobbyists. Working in coalitions helps them save their organization money because they can collect information, make contacts with more lawmakers, and claim credit for working on more issues more easily and more cheaply than they ever could on their own. Joining coalitions may also carry costs because lobbyists will likely be required to compromise the positions their members care about, making them angry. Long-term coalitions work best when the collective memberships of the involved groups prefer similar policies, and when members do not have strong feelings about all of the issues the coalition lobbies on. Thus there are far fewer trade-offs for the lobbyists to balance, and the coalition endures. Short-term issue coalitions tend to form between interest groups that are competing over how to resolve an issue with policy, meaning that the policies each group's members would like to see enacted are quite different from each other. They form when an issue has many pieces and each group cares more about one piece than the others so that trade-offs are possible, giving each side more of what they want. Lobbyists may also form coalitions under pressure from the very lawmakers they depend on for influence and for having successful careers.

In conclusion, coalition politics clearly brings up the sticky issue of ethics in lobbying, especially when it comes to short-term coalitions of competing interest groups. While many people complain about interest groups and lobbying in terms of campaign contributions and the apparent ability of lobbyists to divert lawmakers from enacting legislation in the public interest, the right to form interest groups and lobby is protected by the First Amendment to the Constitution as "the right of the people peaceably to assemble, and to petition the government for a redress of grievances." Thus they must be considered ethical in our system of government. What lobbyists do to help their peaceably assembled members petition for a redress of grievances, which is what lobbying is, is also ethical as long as lobbyists do not break the law and as long as *they represent the interests of their members before government.* Yet coalition formation often requires lobbyists to do something potentially unethical. They must compromise member interests to work together in coalitions and gain the favor of lawmakers. Furthermore, our system of government, so full of checks and balances and powers separated even more than the founders intended, makes it easy for one or a small number of interests to block the making of new law and preserve an antiquated status quo. Given that there are now so many interest groups in America, coalition formation, and therefore the compromising of the interests of dozens of groups of politically organized Americans, is essential if lawmakers are to get anything done. Only by genuinely convincing members of a compromise's value can a lobbyist remain ethical.

Notes

1 Erica Werner, "Immigration Reform: Business, Labor Get Deal on Worker Program, Source Says," *Huffington Post,* March 30, 2013. http://www.huff ingtonpost.com/2013/03/30/immigration-reform_n_2985521.html.
2 Thomas T. Holyoke, *Interest Groups and Lobbying: Pursuing Group Interests in American Politics* (Boulder, CO: Westview Press, 2014).
3 From the database Lobbyists.info for 2011.
4 Holyoke, *Interest Groups and Lobbying,* the original data from a survey by Zogby of Americans in 2008.
5 Harold W. Stanley and Richard G. Niemi, *Vital Statistics on American Politics, 2011–2012* (Washington, DC: CQ Press, 2012).
6 Interview with agency staff.
7 Robert H. Salisbury, "The Paradox of Interest Groups in Washington: More Groups, Less Clout," in *The New American Political System,* 2nd ed., ed. Anthony J. King (Washington, DC: American Enterprise Institute Press, 1990), pp. 203–30.

8 This is the typical approach in spatial models of politics; see Melvin J. Hinich and Michael C. Munger, *Analytical Politics* (New York: Cambridge University Press, 1997).

9 A nice description of variation in member preferences is in Terry M. Moe, *The Organization of Interests* (Chicago: University of Chicago Press, 1980).

10 Developed from chap. 2 of Thomas T. Holyoke, *Competitive Interests: Competition and Compromise in American Interest Group Politics* (Washington, DC: Georgetown University Press, 2011).

11 Albert O. Hirschman, *Exit, Voice, and Loyalty* (Cambridge, MA: Harvard University Press, 1970).

12 McGee Young, *Developing Interests: Organizational Change and the Politics of Advocacy* (Lawrence: University Press of Kansas, 2010).

13 Thomas T. Holyoke, "Interest Group Competition and Coalition Formation," *American Journal of Political Science* 53, no. 2 (2009): 360–75.

14 See William P. Browne, "Organized Interests and Their Issue Niches: A Search for Pluralism in a Policy Domain," *Journal of Politics* 52, no. 2 (1990): 477–509.

15 Christopher J. Bosso, "Rethinking the Concept of Membership in Nature Advocacy Organizations," *Policy Studies Journal* 31, no. 3 (2003): 397–411.

16 Virginia Gray and David Lowery, "To Lobby Alone or in a Flock: Foraging Behavior Among Organized Interests," *American Politics Quarterly* 26, no. 1 (1998): 5–34.

17 Kevin W. Hula, *Lobbying Together: Interest Group Coalitions in Legislative Politics* (Washington, DC: Georgetown University Press, 1999).

18 Marie Hojnacki, "Interest Groups' Decisions to Join Alliance or Work Alone," *American Journal of Political Science* 41, no. 1 (1997): 61–87.

19 John Mark Hansen, *Gaining Access: Congress and the Farm Lobby, 1919–1981* (Chicago: University of Chicago Press, 1991). Also John R. Wright, *Interest Groups and Congress* (Boston: Little, Brown, 1996).

20 Michael T. Heaney, "Issue Networks, Information, and Interest Group Alliances: The Case of Wisconsin Welfare Politics, 1993–1999," *State Politics and Policy Quarterly* 4, no. 3 (2004): 237–70.

21 Ken Kollman, *Outside Lobbying: Public Opinion and Interest Group Strategies* (Princeton, NJ: Princeton University Press, 1998).

22 Frank R. Baumgartner, Jeffrey M. Berry, Marie Hojnacki, David C. Kimball, and Beth L. Leech, *Lobbying and Policy Change* (Chicago: University of Chicago Press, 2009).

23 Rogan Kersh, "Corporate Lobbyists as Political Actors: A View from the Field," in *Interest Group Politics,* 6th ed, eds. Allan J. Cigler and Burdett A. Loomis (Washington, DC: CQ Press, 2002), pp. 225–48.

24 See Wright, *Interest Groups and Congress.*

25 Scott H. Ainsworth, "The Role of Legislators in the Determination of Interest Group Influence." *Legislative Studies Quarterly* 22, no. 4 (1997): 517–33.

26 See chap. 2 of Holyoke, *Competitive Interests.*

27 See Ainsworth, "The Role of Legislators."

28 Terry M. Moe, *The Organization of Interests* (Chicago: University of Chicago Press, 1980).

29 Michael A. Fletcher and Zachary A. Goldfarb, "AARP Uses Its Power to Oppose Social Security, Medicare Benefits Cuts for Retirees," *Washington Post,* November 17, 2012.

Chapter 7

How Will the Internet Change American Interest Groups?

David Karpf

Some of the largest political organizations in America today are also some of the youngest. In the past 15 years, groups like MoveOn, DailyKos, and the Progressive Change Campaign Committee have become fixtures of the political news cycle. Rather than focusing on a single issue-area, these progressive advocacy organizations galvanize citizen activity around whatever issues appear at the top of the political agenda. Relying primarily on e-mail, websites, and social media, their member lists have swelled into the millions. They have become central actors in myriad issue coalitions, nimbly pivoting attention and resources to pressure legislators and attempt to influence the policy process. These "netroots" (internet/grassroots) organizations share key features: a redefinition of organizational membership that no longer requires any form of annual dues payment, the constant use of analytics tools to identify member sentiment, and multi-issue portfolios that keep them attuned to the fast-paced media environment. These interest groups have jointly been responsible for tactical innovations that have, in turn, spread to peer organizations through conference panels, training seminars, and staff mobility. If we want to understand how interest groups are changing in the face of new media—particularly the large-scale membership associations that play a central intermediary role between active citizens and their government, then we must begin by taking a hard look at these new netroots organizations and asking how, if at all, they differ from their older "legacy" organizational peers.

All interest groups make use of the same communications tools. Netroots organizations do not stand alone in their reliance on e-mail, blogs, YouTube, Twitter, and Facebook. But research shows that these new organizations *employ* these tools (e-mail in particular) differently than more established, single-issue organizations. There is a pronounced generational distinction between how old and new organizations use information technology to promote citizen participation, raise money, and influence the broader political agenda. What's more, the new organizations are promoting a "culture of testing" that helps them optimize mobilization tactics, nimbly respond to the fast-paced media cycle, and identify new forms of *passive democratic feedback* from their membership. By analyzing which issues, actions, and arguments attracted mouseclicks from the membership, netroots organizations gain fresh insights into the preferences and interests of their supporters. New media thus has differential impacts on new organizations than on their older peers.

While their use of new communications technologies elevates the size and scope of these netroots issue campaigns, most of the political landscape remains otherwise unchanged. The new generation of interest groups faces all of the same constraints that the incumbent generation has historically faced.[1] Just as lobbying, petition deliveries, and press conferences often fail to result in new legislation, online petitions and targeted Google advertisements are new modifications to longstanding interest group activities. The Internet has not rendered traditional actors and institutions powerless, nor has it ushered in a brave new era of "organizing without organizations."[2] Instead, the new communications technologies have given rise to a shift at the *organizational layer* of American politics.[3] The tools, strategies, and tactics that interest groups use to mobilize citizen involvement are changing. The overall influence of these organizations remains similar to their legacy peers, though. This chapter discusses findings from the Membership Communications Project, a six-month study of advocacy group e-mail practices among a networked cluster of 70 progressive interest groups in 2010. Drawing upon detailed content analysis and elite interviews, the chapter highlights some important and previously overlooked divisions in how the Internet is used for mobilization by a new generation of digitally based advocacy groups. It offers a clear empirical picture of how e-petitions and tweets support different outcomes than the petitions and fliers they have replaced.

Why Focus on E-mail?

E-mail is the oldest and most mundane element of the "new" media. E-mail predates the World Wide Web by roughly two decades. Despite this grand pedigree, academics and journalists alike have tended to pay far more attention to the latest individual emerging technologies. Yet for the organizations themselves, e-mail communication—not Tumblr pages, not social networking sites, not Twitter posts—remains the primary interface with their large supporter lists. Among the suite of online communications technologies, e-mail remains unique as a "push" medium. Unlike tradition mail, the incremental cost of an additional e-mail recipient is approximately zero. Unlike newer social media tools, e-mail has been universally adopted among the populations that advocacy groups seek to mobilize.

Despite the centrality of e-mail communication to interest group activation strategies, there has to date been little systematic analysis of *how* organizations use the medium. Attention has instead turned to the isolated role of blogs,[4] YouTube,[5] social networking sites,[6] and Twitter.[7] While advocacy professionals have cultivated best-practices in areas like list-building, e-mail fundraising, and online-to-offline engagement, academic researchers have gotten distracted by the latest technological wave and missed the increasingly sophisticated use of what Rasmus Kleis Nielsen terms "mundane mobilization tools."[8]

The research community has recently taken note of the systemic gaps that isolated social media analyses create in our understanding of technology. Bruce Bimber, Andrew Flanagin, and Cynthia Stohl argue in *Collective Action in Organizations* that technology should be treated as "context" for complex organizational and behavioral analysis. Quoting Mark Weiser, they note, "the most profound technologies are those that disappear. They weave themselves into the fabric of everyday life until they are indistinguishable from it."[9] They go on further to argue, ". . . too close a focus on individual technologies is especially limiting in times of rapid change. A theory of e-mail from 1993 or chat rooms from 1995 is hardly adequate to the new dynamism and multiplicity of alternatives for communication available now through our organizations and others. Just as feudalism cannot be understood from a theory of irrigation, or the Industrial Revolution from a theory of threshing machines or looms, understanding the information revolution requires more than a theory of how organizations use Facebook or Twitter."[10] In accordance with their analytic perspective, organizational membership communications through e-mail are of particular interest *because* e-mail is no longer a rapidly changing medium. While newer social media platforms are constantly developing, e-mail has taken on more of an old-fashioned character within the digital media landscape.

Indeed, e-mail defines twenty-first-century advocacy group membership. MoveOn.org boasts a membership list over 8 million; Organizing for Action's reportedly exceeds 13 million.[11] Few of these "members" attend local events, take regular actions, or necessarily donate funds to the organizations. In fact, many of these "members" are unaware that they even qualify as members! This was MoveOn's original innovation: their initial 1998 online petition to "censure Bill Clinton and Move On" went viral, yielding a list of over 500,000 supporters. Founders Wes Boyd and Joan Blades chose to treat these signers as members, following up with them to request further actions. Many legacy advocacy groups, such as the Environmental Defense Fund, have followed suit, redefining membership from a financial-supporter relationship (sometimes derisively termed "armchair activism") to a communication-recipient relationship (sometimes derisively termed "clicktivism"). Particularly in the face of falling direct mail response rates, legacy organizations are pressured to move to keep pace with these looser-and-broader e-mail relationships.[12]

The change in membership definition has an important historical precursor. In her 2003 book, *Diminished Democracy*, Theda Skocpol describes the shift "from membership to management," in which the federated membership organizations that had defined American political associations for centuries were replaced by DC-based professional advocacy organizations. The professionalization of political advocacy was accomplished on the basis of a redefinition of membership, wherein members became small-donor check-writers rather than active local participants. This shift was *itself* technologically mediated, requiring the lowering costs of mainframe computer databases to make large-scale donor management feasible for nonprofit organizations. Skocpol notes that this led not only to the "interest group explosion" of the 1970s, but also to the decline of the previously dominant organizational form—the cross-class membership federation. The (technologically mediated) shift in membership regime presaged a generational displacement in the interest group ecology of American politics.

In a 2010 article, "Mundane Internet Tools: The Coproduction of Citizenship in Political Campaigns," Rasmus Kleis Nielsen argues that "when it comes to mobilization, *mundane internet tools* like e-mail and search are more important than *emerging tools* (like social networking sites) or *specialized tools* (like campaign websites)." Nielsen's evidence is based on detailed ethnographic observation of two campaign sites in the 2008 election. In my own field work observing "netroots" advocacy organizations, I have encountered a similar distinction. The 2010 Netroots Nation convention featured no fewer than six panels and workshops on writing effective advocacy appeals, building e-mail lists, and other e-mail-related skills. Annual technology and politics events like the New Organizing Institute's "Rootscamps," the Institute for Politics, Democracy and the Internet's Politics Online Conference, and the Personal Democracy Forum annual conference all offer multiple sessions on e-mail. Emerging tools and specialized tools attract a lower level of attention from advocacy professionals.

Convergence around e-mail best practices has also launched a new sector in the professional advocacy world. Several large vendors have emerged to offer state-of-the-art e-mail management for legacy interest groups, among them Convio, Blue State Digital, and Democracy in Action. A February 2010 twitter post by Democracy in Action is indicative of the sheer volume of this communication channel: "So I knew we sent a lot of e-mail, but 1.73 Billion e-mails sent last year is crazy."[13] While these groups have a presence on Twitter, Facebook, YouTube, and frequently updated web pages, e-mail remains their chief membership communications tool. Specialized tools and emerging tools are elements of a broad communications strategy, usually aimed at converting readers to take a first action which, in turn, adds those readers to the e-mail list.

Not all observers are so sanguine about this trend toward e-mail based communications. Both Malcolm Gladwell and Micah White have argued at length that "clicktivism" is cheapening political activism, turning it into slick marketing campaigns and oversimplifying complex problems.[14] Often missing from these critiques is the broader strategic context of the interest group campaign, in which an initial petition (digital or analog) serves as the first step in a "ladder of engagement" that promotes more sophisticated forms of member engagement.[15] Advocacy campaigns begin by asking supporters to take part in some simple act of solidarity—signing an (online) petition, displaying a (Facebook) button, or writing (e-mailing) their representative. Those supporters who take part in that first activity are then invited to take on increased responsibilities (attending a rally/ participating in citizen lobbying). The ladder of engagement is a longstanding framework within professional advocacy circles.[16] The easy membership tracking enabled by e-mail has extended the reach of these stratified leadership development practices.

Despite overwhelming interest group e-mail use, to date there has been minimal empirical research on just *how* these groups make use of the new communications tool. Advocacy groups have unleashed a torrential flood of e-mail communications. The junk mail that filled citizen mailboxes through past decades has been replaced by e-mail, arriving daily to tens of millions of inboxes around the world. Beginning in 2010, I sought to remedy this empirical gap through the Membership Communications Project (MCP).

The Membership Communications Project

The MCP dataset relies on a simple, intuitive design, harvesting publicly accessible membership communications from a large cluster of progressive advocacy organizations. On January 21, 2010, I created a dummy e-mail account via Gmail. I then visited the websites of 70 advocacy organizations and signed up for any e-mail lists or outreach efforts provided through those sites. For the first two weeks of data collection, I used a broad descriptive classification scheme, then refined it to a set of seven categories based on observed patterns and commonalities between e-mails—(1) topic, (2) digest/e-newsletter, (3) action ask, (4) fundraising ask, (5) request for member input, (6) event advertisement, and (7) media agenda link. The purpose here is to do the basic descriptive spadework of categorizing what organizations contact their members about, at what frequency, and for what purposes.

I encountered three primary hurdles in designing the dataset: (1) identification of an appropriate sample of political associations, (2) deciding what to do about conservative groups, and (3) accounting for limitations created by proprietary data and important e-mail lists that are left "unseen" by the analytic techniques employed. Each hurdle sheds light on some of the core challenges Internet politics researchers face, so I will describe them below.[17]

Identifying Organizations

As Jack Walker famously demonstrates in *Mobilizing Interest Groups in America*,[18] population-definition is an eternally troubling issue for students of American interest groups. In practical terms, it was virtually impossible even in the 1980s to define the full universe of organizations. The population-definition problem is even more complicated today. Whereas previous scholars have equated the interest group population with DC lobbying organizations, this design choice introduces an implicit bias to interest group research. The vast majority of lobbying organizations and Political Action Committees has always represented business or other private interests. Membership-based advocacy groups, meanwhile, constitute a small-but-vital segment of our political system, what I refer to as the "organizational layer" of American politics.[19] Sampling from directories of Washington lobbying organizations or PAC spending reports thus does not present a solution. Unlike other authors in this volume who focus attention on analyzing the lobbying community as a whole, I am interested in separating out those groups that seek to galvanize a broader issue public to take action around their shared values.

The Internet has facilitated novel structures for netroots political associations. Research on new media and advocacy groups must account for the possibility that such groups assume different forms than we are used to finding in the Washington lobbying directories. MoveOn.org, for instance, has 8 million members, 32 staff, and no office space. It employs no full-time lobbyists. While interest group studies have traditionally been equated with studies of "the DC lobbying community," here we see a disjuncture between lobbying (a tactic) and advocacy (a field of practice). It is unclear whether the traditional indexes of DC interest groups appropriately capture this new generation of infrastructure-poor, communication-rich organizations.

To provide a workaround of sorts, I chose to construct a convenience sample based on publicly available network data. In the aftermath of the America Coming Together 527 effort[20] in the 2004 Presidential election, a large network of progressive/liberal major donors was unhappy with the results of their donations. Rob Stein, Erica Payne, and a few other high-profile individuals connected to the community began presenting a slideshow on "The Conservative Message Machine Money Matrix." Their central argument was that conservative donors had built a set of institutions that helped them achieve greater successes in elections and governance than the single-issue groups prevalent in the American left. This led to the 2005 founding of the Democracy Alliance (DA), an umbrella organization for the major donor community. Altogether, DA donors have provided well over $100 million in funding to the organizations that they have jointly identified as representing important pieces of progressive infrastructure.[21]

The list of groups eventually funded by the DA thus provides a network of interest in its own right. Funding from the alliance not only represents a substantial investment of resources (creating a practical floor for the advocacy groups represented in the MCP—anyone can start an e-petition, but obtaining major donor funding is a stronger indication of long-term viability) but also indicates that the groups are themselves nodes within a progressive advocacy network. Though support from the DA is not a necessary and sufficient condition for including an organization in the list of "public interest political associations," it is an opportune place to start. Though the exact donor list is not public information, the DA's former director, Erica Payne, published a helpful guide to the groups she/they felt were part of the new progressive infrastructure in her 2008 book *The Practical Progressive*.[22] Payne profiles 81 organizations in her book, and this list serves as a proxy for the network of prominent groups that networked progressive donors consider important. Of the 81 organizations in the book, 42 represent elements of progressive infrastructure that do not engage in direct mobilization (*The Nation* magazine and blogs like the *Huffington Post*). In all, 49 of the 81 groups had some form of e-mail list to which a member or supporter could subscribe.

I augmented this list of 49 groups with 21 additional organizations that were either well-known members of the political left (National Association for the Advancement of Colored People, National Organization for Women, Amnesty International, American Civil Liberties Union) or prominent netroots groups that had been founded since Payne's book had been published (Organizing for America/Organizing for Action,[23] Change Congress, Progressive Change Campaign Committee, Courage Campaign). While the findings from this study thus cannot be treated as a representative of the interest group population, they can tell us a great deal about how new media tools are used by the subset of public interest advocacy associations that scholars, journalists, and citizens care the most about. Other researchers—Jennifer Earl, in particular—have pursued alternate research designs, deriving a population of online mobilization efforts through exhaustive keyword-based Google scans, then sampling from that population.[24] Such designs allow for more reliable statistical inference but change the scope of research from interest groups to webpages, thus limiting the types of questions one can answer.

I divide this broad list of progressive organizations into two groups based on founding date. Organizations founded after 1996 are considered members of the "new generation" of political associations, having been created to take advantage of the new communications landscape. Organizations founded prior to 1996 are considered "legacy" political associations.[25] 1996 provides a natural break in the data, as there are several organizations in the dataset founded in 1996, 1997, 1998, and 1999, but only one organization founded in the earlier 1990s. (FairVote was founded in 1992 under the name "Center for Voting and Democracy.") Of 40 organizations that were founded post-1996, 2 contributed no e-mails to the dataset, while of 30 organizations that were founded pre-1996, 4 contributed no e-mails to the dataset. Of the 2,162 e-mails in the dataset, 911 come from legacy political associations, and 1,251 come from the new generation. This produces surprisingly similar averages for the two subsets, with the average legacy organization sending 30.4 e-mails over the 6 months of the study and the average new generation organization sending 31.3 e-mails in that timeframe.

Segmenting the organizations according to founding date relies upon an axiomatic assumption about organizational structure, rooted in Paul Dimaggio and W. Powell's institutional isomorphism theory, which predicts that organizations will seek to mimic the internal institutional practices of their peers.[26] Advocacy groups in a membership and fundraising environment will face pressures to develop similar bureaucratic structures. Groups from the direct mail era maintain large expertise in direct mail operations, for instance. They built these departmental structures over the course of decades and, due to path dependence, do not seamlessly restructure themselves in response to new technological affordances. Rather than classify organizations by subject era—grouping all civil rights organizations under one heading, grouping environmental organizations under another—I instead classify organizations by founding date. The questions I seek to answer specifically concern whether groups founded in the online communications regime operate differently than groups founded in earlier communications regimes (regardless of field of specialization).[27]

The Left-Right Divide in Organizational Communications

Absent from this study is any conservative interest group representation. Particularly during a time period (2010) when conservative grassroots mobilization appeared to be flourishing through the "tea party" movement, this bears discussion. Methodologically, if we are going to study advocacy organizations as networks, then we have to approach left-right comparisons with caution.

Particularly in areas like tactical and communication experimentation and innovation, interest groups learn from one another through four forms of networked communication. First, the staff of like-minded interest groups move from one group to another over the course of their careers, bringing skills and learned organizational habits with them. Former MoveOn staffers have launched their own new organizations and been hired by legacy peer organizations on the left. In the electoral arena, Daniel Kreiss demonstrates that the Obama campaign's vaunted digital infrastructure was built by alumni of the Howard Dean campaign.[28] This staff mobility occurs entirely within ideological sectors. It is common for a staffer from the Sierra Club to move to the National Resources Defense Council, but moving from the National Organization for Women to the National Rifle Association is unheard of.

Progressive advocacy professionals also share knowledge through overlapping conferences, consultants, and data vendors. The New Organizing Institute (NOI) was founded in 2005 by alumni of the Howard Dean campaign and several MoveOn.org leaders. NOI's annual "Rootscamp" conference, along with the Netroots Nation conference, serve as key network forums for the top practitioners to share knowledge and build relationships with one another. While there are a few industry-wide conferences—events like the Institute for Politics, Democracy and the Internet's Politics Online Conference, and the annual Personal Democracy Forum conference—conservatives are in the minority at these events as well. Most progressive organizations employ the same consultants to manage their e-mail programs—primarily SalsaLabs, Blue State Digital, M+R, and Convio. These consultancies cater to the ideological left and create shared understandings about the best uses of e-mail. Finally, organizations learn about new technologies and tactics through coalition work, sustained working relationships between executive directors, and confidential data-sharing agreements with organizations such as Catalist.

These network ties serve as conduits for organizational learning. They are present within the political left. A parallel set of network ties are present within the political right. Organizations like Target Point and Engage DC serve as large e-mail vendors to the right, promoting and selling their technology services.

Cross-ideological ties are absent, however. Republicans have frequently attempted to build a "conservative MoveOn." The resulting organizations bear little similarity to the progressive netroots, though.[29] Their e-mails are far less associated with the dominant issue of the day, are less likely to include a call-to-action, and are significantly more likely to highlight generic "liberal media bias." Conservative interest groups online are developed against the backdrop of conservative talk radio, conservative think tanks, and Rupert Murdoch's various media properties. These existing sources of conservative political influence lead to divergent uses of new media. If we want to understand interest group digital communication practices, treating groups atomistically and lumping them within a single overarching population obscures far more than it reveals. Comparative analysis of right- and left-wing interest group mobilization must begin with intentionally tracing the two partisan networks.

Backchannels and Proprietary Data: Limits of the Dataset

There are two hidden problems with studying e-mail that confront every study: the *backend analytics* problem and the *dark social* problem. Interest groups have a tremendous amount of computational data at their disposal. The messages that appear in your inbox are a product of a lengthy production process that often remains obscured.

As one staff person of a netroots group noted to me, "The only way to see every message we send out to the membership is to be on staff." These organizations segment their lists, tracking which members respond to which sorts of appeals. They also engage in constant "A/B testing," sending out competing versions of the same mobilization appeals to randomized segments of their member list to determine which is more effective. This "culture of testing" creates a substantial problem for textual or rhetorical analysis of interest group communications: action appeals are shaped by passive member input. The e-mail "blasts" received by the full membership are more like a politician's poll-tested stump speech than off-the-cuff remarks.

As one example, out of the 2,162 messages in the Membership Communications Project dataset, only 70 (3.2%) featured requests for input from the membership. One might be tempted to interpret this data point as evidence that progressive advocacy groups continue to be expert-driven and lack interest in democratic input from their online supporters. But such a conclusion ignores the production process: these organizations have *tried* to solicit membership input, witnessed minimal response rates, and then adapted to the revealed lack-of-interest from the existing membership. Organizations do not share their analytics data with the public, so it can often be difficult to tell whether modern interest groups are *ignoring* potential member input or *adapting* to revealed member input. Likewise, when organizations select particular issue frames, this is often due to the *passive democratic feedback* obtained through A/B testing. Backend analytics and data visualization techniques play an increasing role in the production of organized political activism, but it remains out of sight for studies such as my own.

While analytics data is obscured from researchers' view, "dark social" refers to the large amount of online activity which the interest groups themselves cannot see. Alexis Madrigal of *The Atlantic* coined the term, writing,

> [the] vast trove of social traffic is essentially invisible to most analytics programs. I call it "dark social." It shows up variously in programs as "direct" or "typed/bookmarked" traffic, which implies to many site owners that you actually have a bookmark or typed in www.theatlantic.com into your browser. But that's not actually what's happening a lot of the time. Most of the time, someone Gchatted someone a link, or it came in on a big e-mail distribution list, or your dad sent it to you. The most important forms of online networked communication are obscured from view.[30]

For interest group analysis, this dark social problem takes the particular form of semi-formal, semi-secret backchannel lists organized through Google Groups or Yahoo Groups. These simple listservs allow cross-organizational stakeholders to speak freely without being observed by the broader public. There are hundreds (possibly thousands) of these Google Groups within the progressive advocacy community. Labor activists, immigration activists, and climate activists all have (multiple) invitation-only listservs where they can debate political strategy and engage in intra-movement arguments. Most of these listservs employ a "Fight Club Rule" (no discussing the existence of the list) to avoid the gaze of opposition conspiracy theorists or advocacy journalists. Backchannel lists provide a networked equivalent of the "inside" discussion occurring on organizational listservs. In the wake of media events like the Trayvon Martin shooting, advocacy professionals take to these lists to debate strategy and coordinate response among their peers. While interest group competition is clearly visible, interest group collaboration occurs behind digitally closed doors.

Finally, missing from this study is any indication of e-mail effectiveness. Data such as clickthrough rates, message tests, regional variation, and e-mail segmentation are kept proprietary by the advocacy groups themselves. Though these groups frequently contract with massive data vendors like Catalist for industry-wide analysis, those reports are conducted behind the veil of confidentiality. Do (some) organizations send different messages to Providence, Rhode Island, than to Tucson, Arizona? Do they make different action or funding requests? How closely do they track and respond to individual-level clickthrough rates? Which types of e-mail appeal are most and least effective? There is a wealth of private industry knowledge on this subject. At present, academic researchers can only access it through qualitative field research and interviews. Studying new media comes with thorny new analytic challenges.

Descriptive Findings

The MCP dataset spans six months of 2010 (January 21–July 21). Messages were clearly produced on an orderly and professional timetable—e-mail primarily was sent on weekdays, and there was little variance in the total number of messages sent per week. There were three weeks with a significant drop in e-mail output, and those weeks were marked by a major DC blizzard and two holidays (July 4 and Memorial Day). Organizational e-mail is a profession and obeys an underlying professional logic. Interest groups set benchmarks for the number of messages they send to supporters per week and attempt to rationalize the flow of member communications.

Though the weekly volume of messages displays an underlying organizational logic, there was substantial variance in how these organizations approached online member communication. Over the 26 weeks that the study was conducted, 6 organizations sent no messages (AFL-CIO, Young Democrats, Rock the Vote, National Security Network, American Progressive Caucus Policy Foundation, and American Constitution Society for Law and Politics) and another 12 organizations sent fewer than one message per month (Bus Project, Alliance for Justice, Democracia Ahora, Public Campaign Action Fund, Gathering for Justice, Amnesty International, League of Young Voters, Progress Now, Women's Voices/Women's Vote, 21st Century Dems, Center for Progressive Leadership, and FairVote). More than 2 messages per week were sent by 10 organizations (Brennan Center (57), Leadership Conference on Civil Rights (59), Progressive Change Campaign Committee (63), Organizing for America (75), Democracy for America (82), MoveOn (99), Center for Budget and Policy Priorities (110), Faith in Public Life (127), Sierra Club (145), and Campaign for Americas Future (288)). Campaign for America's Future alone sent out 13.3% of all messages in the dataset, primarily due to their twice-daily digest e-mails, "Progressive Breakfast" and "PM Update." These digest e-mails are part of a broader set of communications offerings, providing links to blog entries written at the organization's website. Faith in Public Life likewise sent out a daily digest, "Daily Faith News," while the Center on Budget and Policy Priorities sent out frequent report releases and the Sierra Club sent out a variety of e-newsletters, as well as e-mailed versions of Executive Director Carl Pope's blog posts.[31] Figure 7.1 provides the distribution of group e-mails.

I categorized these messages using a five-part, non-exclusive classification scheme. I categorized each message as a "digest/e-newsletter," "action alert," "fundraising ask," "event invitation," or "request for member input." Action alerts are e-mails that include a call-to-action—signing a petition, calling a representative, attending a rally, etc. Digest/e-newsletter was the most common category, with 1,049 messages in total (48.5%). The four most prolific organizations in the dataset—Campaign for America's Future, Sierra Club, Faith in Public Life, and Center on Budget and Policy Priorities—all frequently send informational updates to their membership, and those updates make up nearly half of the e-mail traffic from the organizations in the study. These e-mails generally do not attempt to mobilize the

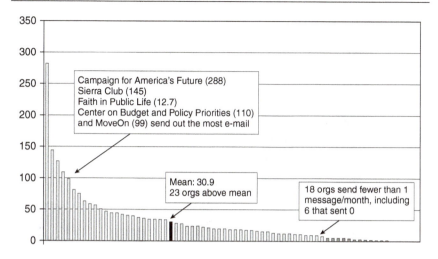

Figure 7.1 Total Messages Ordered by Group

resources of any members, with only 126 action alerts (12.0%) and 108 fundraising, member input, or event announcements (10.2%). They are mostly informational. Nearly all of those action alerts, input and fundraising requests, and event announcements appeared in heavily formatted e-newsletters that include sidebar columns inviting readers to take action or announced an upcoming event. In those cases, I coded the message as falling into both categories. Figure 7.2 displays the breakdown of the full MCP e-mail population.

In light of the common "clicktivism" critique, equating online interest group communication with a never-ending stream of e-petitions, it may be surprising to note that, at least during the six months of this study, progressive advocacy groups were more interested in urging their members to contact congress (271 requests to e-mail or call) than they were in signing online petitions (202). Furthermore, local action requests made up 10.2% of the total mobilization efforts (85), and creative tactics such as distributed get-out-the-vote calling systems (14) became a staple in the late moments of the 2010 primary campaigns. Figure 7.3 displays the full breakdown of action requests in the dataset.

The case against "clicktivism" is further undermined if we consider how professional online organizers themselves discuss online petitions. Chris Bowers of DailyKos writes, "The first goal of the petition is to use it to get meetings with Senators, or their staff . . . We need a list of which activists are, and are not, interested in order to conduct this campaign. That way, we will contact the right people for future actions on this topic."[32] The MCP dataset captures these initial e-mails, and is representative of the informational experience of a common member who reads-then-deletes the message without action. Members who take action are segmented into a different category, and receive additional invitations for political involvement.

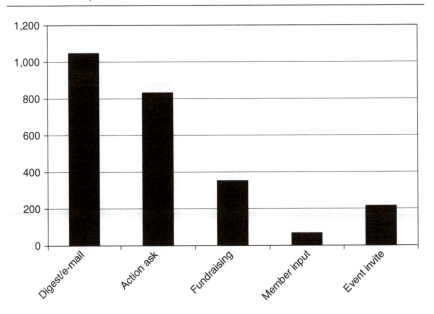

Figure 7.2 Total E-mails by Category

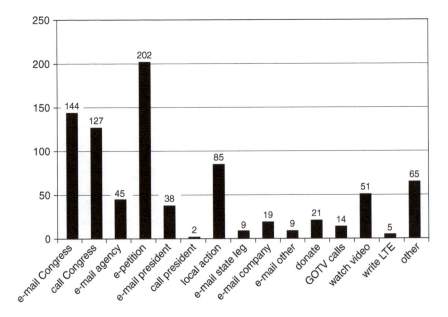

Figure 7.3 Action Requests by Type and Audience

The most revealing distinction between new and old interest groups appears in the distribution of fundraising e-mails. There are three classes of fundraising e-mail in the MCP dataset: general appeals, targeted appeals, and pass-through appeals. General appeals simply ask supporters to donate funds to the organization. No restrictions are placed on what the money can be used for, making the donations similar to gifts to a university's general fund. Historically, small donor fundraising through direct mail was directed toward these types of general donations. Organizations would build up a member base of reliable small donors, and this would provide a degree of freedom to senior staff in determining how, when, and where to invest in program and overhead. A broad trend toward online bill payment has produced an industry-wide decline of direct mail, leaving legacy interest groups with falling unrestricted revenues that they seek to replace through online donor appeals.[33] Targeted appeals, by contrast, request support for a specific action, such as giving $10 to put a television commercial on the air. Targeted fundraising is event-specific, introducing restrictions on its use for general organizational overhead costs. As a general rule, these restricted gifts are easier to raise but less useful to the organization.[34] The third type of fundraising, pass-through fundraising, was pioneered decades ago by EMILY's List. Here the organization urges members to donate to a political candidate, but to use the organization as a bundler so the candidate knows which advocacy group to thank.

Among the 350 fundraising e-mails sent by interest groups in the dataset, 214 were general fundraising appeals, 56 were targeted fundraising appeals, and 80 were pass-through fundraising appeals. Advocacy groups still rely heavily on general funding appeals, and many have directly exported their traditional direct mail expertise to the digital communications environment. Figure 7.4 and Table 7.1 display these funding appeals.

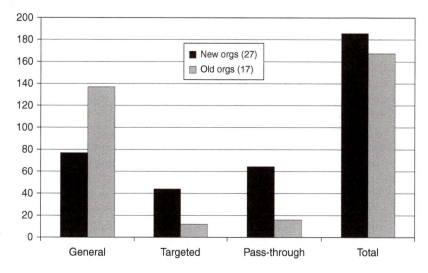

Figure 7.4 Fundraising Appeal by Organization Type

Table 7.1 Fundraising Appeal by Organization Type

	General	Targeted	Pass-through	Total
New (38 groups)	77 (42%)	44 (24%)	64 (35%)	185
Old (27 groups)	137 (83%)	12 (7%)	16 (10%)	165
Total	214 (61%)	56 (16%)	80 (23%)	350

Note: Null hypothesis of independence between Organization and Fundraising type is rejected with a Chi-Square value of 62.97 (2 df and p < .0001)

An important gap appears when we look at *which* organizations send the targeted and pass-through funding requests, however. The netroots generation of advocacy groups does send out general funding appeals (particularly in the wake of a major legislative victory like health care reform), but only 42% of their fundraisers adopt that format, compared to 83% of their legacy peers. Of the netroots fundraising e-mails, 24% adopt the targeted format, and 35% are pass-through candidate fundraisers. Among legacy organizations, a mere 7% of the fundraisers are targeted in nature, and 10% are pass-through fundraisers. Of the 16 pass-through fundraisers originating from legacy organizations, 12 came from EMILY's List, and 4 came from the League of Conservation Voters. By contrast, the Progressive Change Campaign Committee sent out 21 of these messages, Democracy for America sent out 18 of them, MoveOn sent out 16, and VoteVets sent out 7. Simply put, the new generation of political advocacy groups is raising money for different purposes and in different ways than its older peers.

This fundraising gap points to a larger problem for legacy advocacy organizations. Whereas netroots organizations have little organizational overhead costs, and thus can rely heavily on targeted fundraising, their peer organizations that emerged through the 1970s-era "interest group explosion" have spent decades building up large staffing and office expenditures. Direct mail membership provided a stable revenue stream for the archetypical single-issue advocacy group with a DC office and a large staff of policy experts and lobbyists. The new style of targeted online fundraising is less well-suited to this organizational model. Unless foundations or patron donors choose to fill in the gaps, many legacy organizations will soon face increasingly dangerous budgetary shortfalls.[35]

A final key finding emerges from the "media agenda" variable, the last column in the dataset. Through field observation and interview, I found that netroots interest groups appear to be "issue generalists," focusing member attention on calls-to-action associated with the political media agenda. Netroots groups engage in "headline chasing," running shorter-duration campaigns around a broader array of issues topics. To test this hypothesis, I tracked the two leading news programs on MSNBC in 2010—*The Rachel Maddow Show* and *Countdown with Keith Olbermann*—and recorded their nightly topical coverage. These two programs serve as an indicator for the progressive political media agenda in today's fragmented media environment.[36] Though network news attracts a larger overall audience, MSNBC's primetime programs are geared toward the same target audience of well-informed, politically engaged liberals that progressive advocacy organizations seek to attract. On a day-to-day basis, the two programs' editorial staffs and progressive advocacy groups are seeking content of interest to the same segment of society.

The issues covered by Maddow and Olbermann serve as a reminder of the dominant political issues of 2010. Health care reform dominated coverage on the two shows between January 21 and March 31, 2010, generally as the lead story. Maddow often covered Don't Ask, Don't Tell hearings, filibuster reform, and minor Republican congressional scandals. Olbermann focused more on rebutting Sarah Palin, Fox News, and the Tea Party movement. Both programs featured some coverage of financial reform, unemployment legislation, and breaking news stories on disasters (Haiti and Peru earthquakes, plane crash into Austin IRS building) and Republican scandals. Both programs turned central attention from health care to extreme rightwing responses to the bill's passage in late March and early April. The BP oil spill then took center stage, receiving top billing on almost every program from April 30 through mid-July.

I compared the topical coverage of these programs with the topics of advocacy group e-mails, recording a "1" if the topics had an adjacent overlap.[37] I then converted this measure into a "media agenda propensity score" by dividing the number of overlapping messages by the total messages sent by the organization. This places the organizations on a continuum from 0 to 1, as displayed in Table 7.2.[38] When we pool the sample into two generations, the netroots disjuncture again becomes clear: 50.4% of all messages sent by netroots advocacy organizations related to the issues discussed by Maddow and Olbermann, while 30.6% of the messages from legacy organizations exhibited such a connection, providing a Yates Chi-square of 83.79, significant at the 0.0001 level.[39] This is despite an incidental feature of the MCP data collection which artificially inflates the overlap for legacy organizations—environmental organizations were slightly oversampled at the outset for a companion study based on this dataset, and the occurrence of the BP oil spill put environmental issues as the lead story for two months of the study.

Some organizations founded after 1996 are not issue generalists. But single-issues groups founded in the past decade nonetheless borrow from the broader netroots tactical repertoire. Democracia Ahora, for instance, sent only five e-mails, all of them in response to the passage of a controversial state immigration law in Arizona. In the three months of data collection prior to the law's passage, Democracia Ahora sent no messages. Such activity resembles "headline reacting" rather than "headline chasing," but nonetheless demonstrates the greater attention paid by younger advocacy organizations to the political news cycle.

Table 7.2 Media Agenda Propensity Scores by Organization

New Org	Old Org	Media Agenda	Total Msgs	%
Progressive Congress		7	9	0.78
Campaign for America's Future		212	288	0.74
Organizing for America		54	75	0.72
350.org		9	13	0.69
MoveOn		63	99	0.64
Media Matters		22	35	0.63
PCCC		38	63	0.60
	Center for Community Change	11	19	0.58
True Majority		19	34	0.56
Color of Change		10	18	0.56
Courage Campaign		13	24	0.54
I Sky		9	18	0.50
Catholics in Alliance		12	24	0.50
Democracy for America		41	82	0.50
Moms Rising		8	17	0.47
	AFSCME	16	37	0.43
Demos		9	21	0.43
	Citizens for Tax Justice	11	28	0.39
Faith in Public Life		49	127	0.39
	Human Rights Campaign	15	40	0.38
Sunlight Foundation		6	16	0.38
	Leadership Council on Civil Rights	22	59	0.37
Repower America		7	19	0.37
	NAACP	15	42	0.36
	Sierra Club	51	145	0.35
	League of Conservation Voters	12	35	0.34
	National Organization for Women	8	24	0.33
	Environmental Defense Fund	7	22	0.31
VoteVets		6	19	0.32
	SEIU	3	10	0.30
	Planned Parenthood	8	27	0.30
	Defenders of Wildlife	15	51	0.29
	EMILY's List	12	45	0.27
	Center on Budget and Policy Priorities	29	110	0.26
	Economic Policy Institute	9	35	0.26
	Century Foundation	3	12	0.25

New Org	Old Org	Media Agenda	Total Msgs	%
Progressive Majority		3	12	0.25
	NARAL	9	40	0.23
	ACLU	8	36	0.22
	NRDC	10	45	0.22
Change Congress		3	15	0.20
Citizens for Responsibility and Ethics in Washington		2	10	0.20
Progressive States Network		9	47	0.19
Truman Project		2	11	0.18
	Greenpeace	2	12	0.17
Brennan Center		6	57	0.11
New Organizing Institute		1	11	0.09
	Human Rights First	2	30	0.07
Iraq and Afghanistan Vets of America		1	15	0.07
Free Press		1	17	0.06

Conclusion: Adapting to the Generation Gap

Six months of e-mail content analysis reveals one striking trend: there are distinct differences between how older and newer progressive interest groups make use of information technology. Previous researchers have presumed that established advocacy groups would lead the way in developing cutting-edge online engagement practices.[40] Instead, we are witnessing a disruptive pattern, as a new generation of advocacy groups, unburdened by the staffing and overhead costs that made their legacy peers influential, is now better situated to experiment with online mobilization. Influence within the progressive network is shifting from the interest groups with the largest lobbying budgets to those with the largest online membership list. Netroots groups are better able to raise large sums to influence politics when the media agenda is ripe. They are more likely to reward allied candidates through frequent pass-through fundraising appeals. They mobilize their members online and offline, constructing ladders of engagement out of simple, timely, rigorously tested action alerts.

This generation gap not only forces us to rethink the place of digital-native organizations in interest group politics. It also demands that we reassess some of the assumptions that ground our standard methodological choices. The interest group universe has long been treated as synonymous with the DC lobbying population. This was a safe assumption in the 1970s, 1980s, and 1990s, when direct mail membership and the growth of the business lobby afforded the rise of single-issue professional advocacy work. Today, the most prominent public-facing advocacy groups employ "campaign directors," "media campaigners," and technologists rather than policy experts and lobbyists. And as the Internet continues to alter fundraising streams, we should expect traditional interest group patterns to slowly change as well.

In the final tally, it is too soon to tell whether the new netroots organizations will outperform their legacy brethren. They are clearly more capable of building large member lists and pivoting to the most salient political issues of the day. But it may prove to be the case that large lobbying and policy staffs offer greater long-term impact in the halls of Congress. As with the 1960s/1970s era transition from cross-class membership federations to single-issue professional advocacy groups, the current generation shift is a response to the opportunity structure provided by media and government activity. But those new mobilization opportunities will not necessarily ensure better outcomes.

It is also too soon to tell how conservative organizations will adapt to the new media environment. At the time of this writing, there is still no conservative equivalent to MoveOn, DailyKos, Progressive Change Campaign Committee, or Organizing for Action. Networks of Tea Party–oriented advocacy groups have adopted different online practices and can rely on a wholly different set of allied media and policy organizations. The success of Tea Party mobilization in 2009–2010 should provide a warning that large netroots e-mail lists and fundraising totals only serve as operational measures of success. The end goal of influencing government policy outcomes remains as complex as ever.

The Internet is spurring changes to how major public interest groups structure and staff themselves. It is spurring changes to how they define membership and relate to supporters. This is not the overthrow of organized interests that some early theorists had hoped for. Nor is it a decline in the quality of citizen activism that others have feared. Rather, it is a shift in tactical repertoires, network structures, and public engagement practices. These new styles of communication and organization demand that we look at interest groups in America with a fresh lens.

Notes

1 For discussion of traditional constraints and the relative effectiveness of interest group lobbying and influence campaigns, see Frank Baumgartner, Jeffrey Berry, Marie Hojnacki, David Kimball, and Beth Leech, *Lobbying and Policy Change* (Chicago: University of Chicago Press, 2009). Also see Matt Grossmann, *The Not-So-Special Interests: Interest Groups, Public Representation, and American Governance* (Stanford, CA: Stanford University Press, 2012).
2 Clay Shirky, *Here Comes Everybody: The Power of Organizing without Organizations* (New York: Penguin Books, 2008).
3 David Karpf, *The MoveOn Effect: The Unexpected Transformation of American Political Advocacy* (New York: Oxford University Press, 2012).
4 David Perlmutter, *BlogWars* (Oxford, UK: Oxford University Press, 2008); Henry Farrell and Dan Drezner, "The Power and Politics of Blogs," *Public Choice* 134,

no. 1–2 (2008): 15–30; Antoinette Pole, *Blogging the Political: Politics and Participation in a Networked Society* (New York: Routledge Press, 2009); Eric Lawrence, John Sides, and Henry Farrell, "Self-Segregation or Deliberation? Blog Readership, Participation and Polarization in American Politics," *Perspectives on Politics* 8, no. 1 (2010): 141–57.

5 Girish Gulati and Christine Williams, "Congressional Candidates' Use of YouTube in 2008: Its Frequency and Rationale," *Journal of Information Technology & Politics* 7, no. 2–3 (2010): 93–109; Kevin Wallsten, "Yes We Can: How Online Viewership, Blog Discussion, Campaign Statements, and Mainstream Media Coverage Produced a Viral Video Phenomenon," *Journal of Information Technology and Politics* 7, no. 2–3 (2010): 163–81; Robert Klotz, "The Sidetracked 2008 YouTube Senate Election," *Journal of Information Technology and Politics* 7, no. 2–3 (2010): 110–23.

6 Christine Williams and Girish Gulati, "The Political Impact of Facebook: Evidence from the 2006 Midterm Elections and the 2008 Nomination Contest," *Politics and Technology Review* 1, no. 1 (2008): 11–24; Jody Baumgartner and Jonathan Morris, "MyFaceTube Politics: Social Networking Websites and Political Engagement in Young Adults," *Social Science Computer Review* 28, no. 1 (2010): 24–44; Chris Mascaro, Alison Novak, and Sean Goggins, "The Daily Brew: The Structural Evolution of the Coffee Party on Facebook During the 2010 US Midterm Election Season," *Journal of Information Technology and Politics* 9, no. 3 (2012): 234–53.

7 Bob Boynton, "Politics Moves to Twitter: How Big Is Big and Other Such Distributions" (paper presented at the Midwest Political Science Association Annual Meeting, Chicago, IL, April 2010).

8 Rasmus Kleis Nielsen, "Mundane Internet Tools, Mobilizing Practices, and the Coproduction of Citizenship in Political Campaigns," *New Media and Society* 13 no. 5 (2011): 755–71; Rasmus Kleis Nielsen, *Ground Wars* (Princeton, NJ: Princeton University Press, 2012).

9 Bruce Bimber, Andrew Flanagin and Cynthia Stohl, *Collective Action in Organizations* (New York: Cambridge University Press, 2012), p. 94.

10 Bimber, Flanagin, and Stohl, *Collective Action in Organizations*, pp. 42–43.

11 Ari Melber, "Year One of Organizing for America: The Permanent Field Campaign in a Digital Age," http://www.arimelber.com/?page_id=445.

12 David Karpf, *The MoveOn Effect: The Unexpected Transformation of American Political Advocacy* (New York: Oxford University Press, 2012).

13 Reported via Twitter, February 3, 2010, 8:43AM EST, by username @Salsalabs, the organizational account of Democracy in Action.

14 Malcolm Gladwell, "Small Change: Why the Revolution Will Not Be Tweeted," *The New Yorker*, October 4, 2010. http://www.newyorker.com/reporting/2010/10/04/101004fa_fact_gladwell?currentPage=all; Micah White, "Clicktivism is Ruining Leftist Activism." *The Guardian Online*, August 12, 2010, http://www.guardian.co.uk/commentisfree/2010/aug/12/clicktivism-ruining-leftist-activism.

15 David Karpf, "Online Political Mobilization from the Advocacy Group's Perspective: Looking Beyond Clicktivism," *Policy & Internet* 2, no. 4 (2010).

16 Hahrie Han, *Moved to Action: Motivation, Participation, and Inequality in American Politics* (Stanford, CA: Stanford University Press, 2009).

17 I discuss these methodological challenges and the "lobster trap"–style design employed in the MCP in David Karpf, "Social Science Research Methods in Internet Time," *Information, Communication, and Society* 15, no. 5 (2012): 639–61.

18 Jack L. Walker, *Mobilizing Interest Groups in America* (Ann Arbor: University of Michigan Press, 1991).

19 Karpf, "Social Science Research Methods in Internet Time."

20 "527" refers to a line in the tax code 527 groups are organizations that engage in Independent Expenditure Campaigns during election cycles, under guidance established by the Bipartisan Campaign Reform Act of 2002.

21 Julian Brookes, "An Interview With Erica Payne, Author of *The Practical Progressive.*" *Huffington Post*, October 23, 2008, http://www.huffingtonpost.com/julian-brookes/an-interview-with-erica-p_b_137206.html.

22 Erica Payne, *The Practical Progressive: How to Build a Twenty-first Century Political Movement* (New York: Public Affairs, 2008).

23 The 2008 Obama campaign was renamed Organizing for America and housed within the Democratic National Committee. After the 2012 Obama campaign, it was again renamed Organizing for Action and broken away from the Democratic National Committee.

24 Jennifer Earl, Katrina Kimport, Greg Prieto, Carly Rush, and Kimberly Reynoso, "Changing the World One Webpage at a Time: Conceptualizing and Explaining Internet Activism," *Mobilization* 15, no. 4 (2010): 425–46; Jennifer Earl and Katrina Kimport, *Digitally Enabled Social Change* (Cambridge, MA: MIT Press, 2011).

25 These terminology decisions reflect some important realities. First, it would be inappropriate to term the new generation "internet-mediated organizations" since, as Bruce Bimber in *Information and American Democracy* (Cambridge, UK: Cambridge University Press, 2003), Andrew Chadwick in "Digital Network Repertoires and Organizational Hybridity," *Political Communication* 24, no. 3 (2007): 283–301, and others have noted, older organizations have themselves adopted internet-mediated tools. Second, the "legacy" organizations include groups founded in the direct mail era and groups founded in the earlier era described by Theda Skocpol in *Diminished Democracy* (Norman: University of Oklahoma Press, 2003). Groups like the Sierra Club (founded 1892) underwent major structural adaptations in response to the new membership and fundraising regimes of the 1970s (Kenneth Andrews, Marshall Ganz, Matthew Baggetta, Hahrie Han, and Chaeyoon Lim, "Leadership, Membership, and Voice: Civic Associations That Work," *American Journal of Sociology* 115, no. 4 (2010): 1191–1242.

26 Paul Dimaggio and W. Powell, "The Iron Cage Revisited: Institutional Isomorphism and Collective Rationality in Organizational Fields," *American Sociological Review* 48, no. 2 (1983): 147–60.

27 This choice also alleviates some otherwise difficult classification problems. Should Color of Change, for instance, be considered a "civil rights organization" or an "internet-mediated organization" It was developed by a former MoveOn staffer, seeded through MoveOn's member list, as a spinoff of MoveOn to better respond to the particular interests of the African American community. A strong argument could be made for both.

28 Daniel Kreiss, *Taking Our Country Back: The Crafting of Networked Politics from Howard Dean to Barack Obama* (New York: Oxford University Press, 2012).

29 Karpf, *The MoveOn Effect*, chap. 6.

30 Alexis Madrigal, "Dark Social: We Have the Whole History of the Web Wrong," *The Atlantic Online*, October 12, 2012, http://www.theatlantic.com/technology/archive/2012/10/dark-social-we-have-the-whole-history-of-the-web-wrong/263523/.

31 Carl Pope ceased to be executive director of the Sierra Club midway through the data collection period but continued posting under his new position as chairman of the organization. Full disclosure: I was a member of the Sierra Club National Board in 2010.

32 Chris Bowers, "The Thinking Behind Our First Email," Blog post, Dailykos.com, August 17, 2010, http://www.dailykos.com/storyonly/2010/ 8/17/893956/-The-thinking-behind-our-first-email.

33 Monitor Institute, "Disruption: Evolving Models of Engagement and Support. A National Study of Member-Based Advocacy Groups," April 2011; also see Karpf, *The MoveOn Effect*, chap. 2.

34 Universities face an equivalent dilemma in fundraising, with alumni often wanting to donate to specific programs or new construction projects, and the Office of Development urging alumni to give to the General Fund so the donations can be put to their greatest use.

35 For a more complete discussion of this trend, see Karpf, *The MoveOn Effect*.

36 Kathleen Hall Jamieson and Joseph Cappella, *Echo Chamber: Rush Limbaugh and the Conservative Media Establishment* (Oxford: Oxford University Press, 2010); M. A. Xenos and N. Kim, "New Mediated Deliberation: Blog and Press Coverage of the Alito Nomination," *Journal of Computer-Mediated Communication* 13, no. 2 (2008): 485–503; Bruce Williams and Michael X. Delli Carpini, *After Broadcast News: Media Regimes, Democracy, and the New Information Environment* (New York: Cambridge University Press, 2012).

37 By "adjacency," I mean that the topic of the e-mail appeared on the news program within a one-day window. Sometimes the e-mail and news program would occur on the same day. Sometimes news would break on the program, leading to an advocacy e-mail the next day. Sometimes the news inspiring the action alert would not make it onto MSNBC until the following day.

38 Organizations which sent fewer than one e-mail per month are removed from Table 7.2 for visual clarity.

39 Computed using Richard Lowery's free online toolset: http://faculty.vassar.edu/lowry/newcs.html?.

40 Bimber, *Information and American Democracy*; Chadwick, "Digital Network Repertoires."

Chapter 8

Attack of the Super PACs?

Interest Groups in the 2012 Elections

Michael Franz

In the fall of 2012, voters in Wisconsin were asked to fill a Senate seat to replace the retiring Democrat Herb Kohl. Democratic Congresswoman Tammy Baldwin went up against former Republican Governor Tommy Thompson in the general election. In the 67 days between September 1 and Election Day (November 6), voters in the state were exposed to over 49,000 ads on broadcast television. Of those ads, 31%—over 15,000—were sponsored by interest groups. This included over 7,500 ads from the affiliated Crossroads GPS and American Crossroads (both of which had ties to former George W. Bush aide Karl Rove), 1,700 ads from Majority PAC (run by the former chief of staff to Senate Majority Leader Harry Reid), and almost 2,000 ads from the labor unions AFSCME and SEIU. Wisconsin was not unique, however. Across the country, voters in states with competitive Senate races were exposed to a deluge of spending from interest groups. This included Montana, with over 70,000 ads in the fall re-election campaign of Democrat Jon Tester, 24% of which were from outside groups; Indiana, where over 40% of 40,000 ads were from groups; and Virginia, where 35% of over 39,000 ads were group sponsored.

Most of this advertising can be traced to changes in campaign finance laws in the five years before the 2012 elections. The Supreme Court in 2007 in *Wisconsin Right to Life v. FEC* overturned parts of a 2002 campaign finance law that put limits on how interest group television ads could be funded. The Court expanded the scope of the case in 2010 in *Citizens United v. FEC*. A series of lower court cases and regulatory actions in 2010 and 2011 expanded the reach of the Court's decision in *Citizens United,* and by the fall of 2012, interest groups were largely unfettered in the way they could raise and spend money to advocate for federal candidates. This is in comparison to the fairly rigid fund-raising rules that remain in place for candidates and political parties.

By almost any measure, as will be demonstrated in this chapter, the role played by interest groups in 2012 exceeded anything witnessed in prior elections. But interest groups were not absent from previous elections, and the first goal of this chapter is to place 2012 in its proper context. First, citizens in 2012 have heard a lot about the development of "Super" PACs, which were sanctioned by the Federal Election Commission in the aftermath of *Citizens United.* But PACs— short for political action committees—have been around for decades. Traditional

PACs can contribute directly to candidates, something Super PACs cannot do, and they make up a non-trivial percentage of many candidates' war chests. This has concerned campaign finance reformers for years. Second, Super PACs are not the only means of trying to influence voters with campaign ads. In many senses, they are merely the latest in a long line of developments, from "sham" issue advocacy in the 1990s (where groups used gaps in existing election law to sponsor unregulated ads that bolstered candidates) to 527s in the 2004 elections (a type of group that collected large donations for the purpose of promoting candidates). Both prior developments (which are discussed in more detail later in the chapter) raised concerns about excessive influence of wealthy individuals and interests.

The chapter will also explore two key concerns surrounding the role of interest groups in elections. First, what effects have interest group ads had on the outcome of close elections? Can Super PACs and other groups tip close elections with their advertising efforts? Second, what types of issues do interest groups focus on when they advertise in an election? Does their issue focus diverge from what the candidates discuss? If so, this would suggest that interest groups have the potential to shift issue debates in an election away from the issues preferred by the candidates.

The development of Super PACs in 2011 and 2012 highlights once again the importance of elections to many organized interests, especially in a deeply polarized political environment where the outcome of these close elections determines who shapes public policies. And the rules that exist for Super PACs demonstrate that the Court may be willing to reduce the restrictions that currently remain for candidates and political parties. In that sense, 2012 was truly a momentous election, but it may only be the beginning.

Traditional PACs, 1976–2012

The role of interest groups in the funding of federal candidates is not new to the post–*Citizens United* context. Since the progressive era in the early twentieth century, activists and citizens have worried about the influence of money in politics. Major campaign finance reform efforts passed Congress in 1907, 1946, 1971, 1974, 1976, and 2002.[1] All of these efforts put fresh restrictions on the electioneering efforts of organized interests.

Since the campaign finance reform of the 1970s, campaign finance rules have allowed corporations, trade associations, membership groups, and unions to contribute to federal candidates but only through highly regulated political action committees (PACs). These traditional PACs are funded only by contributions from a group's members: union members for union PACs, for example, and corporate employees for trade association and corporate PACs.[2] Each donation by an individual is capped at $5,000 total per donor. PACs can contribute these pooled funds to candidates but with a maximum of $5,000 per election.

PACs are often viewed with suspicion, as tools of the corporate and union sponsor, for example. But it is important to remember that all PAC funds come from voluntary donations by individuals, and the total value of a single PAC contribution to a federal candidate is quite small. The average winning House member spent $1.4 million in 2010, and the average winning Senate candidate spent nearly $9 million.[3] The marginal value of a $5,000 maximum contribution then is not much to worry about. (Moreover, the average PAC contribution is much smaller. In 2012, it was a little less than $1,800.)

On the other hand, some candidates rely on PAC money more than others, and collectively, PAC contributions can provide substantial electoral benefits. As one might expect, incumbents tend to leverage their positions on important committees to raise a greater share of their war chests from PACs. The upper limit for contributions from individuals in 2012 was $2,500, meaning that a maximum PAC contribution was worth twice as much as an individual's.

To get a sense of how incumbents rely on a greater share of PAC dollars than challengers or open seat candidates, Figure 8.1 plots the percentage of donations that came from PACs for House and Senate candidates in 2012.[4] The graph shows the range separately for incumbents, challengers, and open seat candidates. The reported dots on the graph show the median candidate within type, and the shaded box shows the range from the 25th to 75th percentile.

It is clear from the graph that incumbents generally accept a far higher share of their overall totals from PACs. Challengers and open seat candidates for both the House and Senate generally cluster between 0% and 10% from PACs. Indeed, the median for both combined set of candidates is 0% and the mean is 6%. PAC contributions to such candidates are almost irrelevant then to these candidates' budgets. The mean and median for House incumbents, however, is 47%. And the vast majority of House incumbents raise between 35% and 60% of their

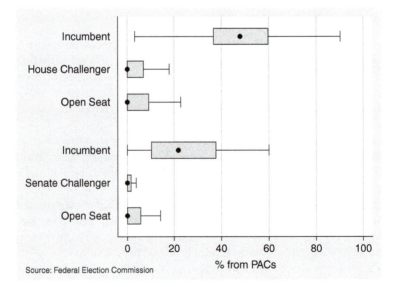

Figure 8.1 PAC Contributions to Congressional Candidates in 2012

campaign funds from PACs. Senate incumbents rely to a far lesser extent on PAC money—the mean and media for them is 22% and 24%, respectively—but they still accept a far higher share of PAC money that challengers and open seat candidates.

The efforts of PACs in funding incumbents has been a serious source of anxiety for many campaign finance reformers, and it does raise concerns that incumbents find it far easier to ride the fund-raising circuit in Washington, DC, than to raise contributions from constituents back at home. On the other hand, there is also nearly three decades of political science research in this area, and the consensus is that PAC contributions are not responsible for purchasing much more than access to the candidates.[5] That is, the money seems to flow from PACs to candidates that already share a similar position on public policies. It is very rare, in other words, for a corporate PAC to contribute to a liberal Democrat with the hopes of buying their vote. PAC contributions more often make securing a meeting with a candidate much easier. Meetings are valuable, of course, but they are not a guarantee that an interest group's public policy goals will be implemented. Indeed, any change in the status quo, whether for corporations, unions, or big lobbying efforts, is hard to initiate, regardless of how much campaign cash or lobbying pressure is applied.[6]

At the end of the day, the influence of PACs on candidates is a matter of some debate. It might be troubling that incumbents seem to have a built-in fund-raising mechanism that can facilitate the accumulation of a war chest, and that they grant more time to large donors. On the other hand, the money is rarely tied to the outcome of votes in the House and Senate, and the cap for each PAC is very low in comparison to what it costs candidates to run for office.

Beyond Traditional PACs to Super PACs

PACs do more than contribute to candidate coffers, however. Traditional PACs are also allowed to spend their resources on pro-candidate advocacy efforts. These are called independent expenditures, and Congress sanctioned them for PACs in 1974. Moreover, whereas contributions to a PAC are capped,[7] the group can spend an unlimited amount of these funds on independent expenditures. This means that PACs have the potential to invest considerably more in an election beyond their $5,000 contributions.

PAC independent expenditures were quite small, however, prior to the mid-1990s. Table 8.1 sums the amount of PAC contributions to candidates and their independent expenditures from 1980 to 1994, a time span covering eight elections. In that time period, PACs spent just below $100 million on independent expenditures, in comparison to over $1 billion on candidate contributions. (All totals in Table 8.1 are in nominal dollars.) It is quite clear that in the 1980s and early 1990s, PACs preferred the more limited efforts of candidate contributions.[8]

Since the mid-1990s, though, the role of outside groups has expanded considerably. This is a complex story to tell. It involves changes initiated by Congress and the government's election law regulator, the Federal Election

Table 8.1 Interest Group Contributions and Electioneering, 1980–2012

	PAC contributions to candidates	Independent expenditures	Electioneering Comm.	IG "Issue ads"*	Ratio of Contributions to Expenditures
1980–94 (8 elections)	$1,083,314,457	$99,322,733	n/a	n/a	$10.91 to $1
1996–2002 (4 elections)	$994,147,217	$68,849,580	n/a	$136,964,189	$4.83 to $1
2004–06 (2 elections)	$700,663,702	$107,264,094	$89,883,644	n/a	$3.55 to $1
2008–10 (2 elections)	$865,044,459	$365,439,674	$168,548,353	n/a	$1.62 to $1
2012	$435,357,578	$1,137,598,645	$26,371,598	n/a	$1 to $2.67

*Estimates for 1996 are from Deborah Beck, et al., 1997. "Issue Advocacy Advertising During the 1996 Campaign," Philadelphia: Annenberg Public Policy Center; totals for 1998–2002 are from the Wisconsin Advertising Project. All other totals in the table are from the Federal Election Commission. Dollars are not adjusted for inflation.

Commission (FEC). It involves changes in the law as mandated by the federal courts. And it involves changes in the way interest groups tried to test the limits of the law. It might be easiest to tell the story chronologically.[9]

In the early 1970s, Congress passed a series of campaign finance changes, in part triggered by the Watergate crisis. A 1974 law that updated a much weaker 1971 reform put in place much of the system we have today: imposing contribution limits for candidates, parties, and groups; formally legalizing PACs; and creating the Federal Election Commission to regulate the new law. Some changes were challenged and overturned in the 1976 Supreme Court case *Buckley v. Valeo*, and Congress responded in 1976 and 1979 with necessary tweaks in the law.[10]

For much of the 1970s, 1980s, and early 1990s, however, the campaign finance environment was somewhat quiet. Reformers moaned about the establishment and influence of PACs, but as noted above, much of the action for interest groups in elections concerned limited candidate contributions.[11] By the mid-1990s, however, politics in Washington started to become far more polarized. The Republicans in 1994 captured both houses of Congress for the first time since 1952, and the two parties moved apart ideologically.[12] Elections, as it were, became critically important to determining control of Congress. The cries of excessive partisanship that have been so characteristic of the Obama presidency really started back in the 1990s.

With such polarization came incentives for organized interests to invest more resources in elections. Contributions, as suggested, had too little "bang-for-the-buck" when it came to tipping the outcome of close contests. And independent

expenditures had a single weakness: they had to be funded by the capped donations to the PAC.

Lurking just below the surface for much of the 1980s, however, was a loophole
that opened the door to more resources for electioneering. The loophole was what
came to be called the "magic word" test of electioneering. The justices in *Buckley
v. Valeo* had struggled to answer an important question: When is an ad designed to
influence vote choice, and when is it designed to influence voters' opinions about
public policies? This was important because the Court argued that the former
could be regulated by Congress, but the latter could not.

That is, the former was considered an avenue by which to influence and
potentially corrupt elected officials; if a candidate were to win an election in part
because of interest group support, for example, might it not create an opportunity
for the group to leverage that influence for help in the passing of public policies?
Issue-related ads, however, were considered protected First Amendment speech.
Indeed, urging the public to support or oppose a policy is a right that lies at the
heart of the First Amendment. The justices provided a list of words and phrases
that they thought would clearly designate an election ad from an issue ad. These
"magic words," as they came to be colloquially identified, were: "vote for," "elect,"
"support," "cast your ballot for," "[Smith] for Congress," "vote against," "defeat," or
"reject."

As organized interests in the 1990s looked for ways to invest in elections, the
absence of "magic words" in ads seemed to offer a lot of potential. If a group aired
an ad that did not tell people how to vote, for example, could the ad be bank-
rolled by much larger contributions to the group? A number of lower court rulings
opened the door for this, and interest groups started to spend more resources on
such "issue advocacy."[13] During this time, the tagline of an ad might not say "Vote
for John Smith," but instead "Call John Smith and thank him for his hard work
on the environment." The two ads—but for the tagline—might be identical, and
the clear implication might be to help elect John Smith, but the absence of "magic
words" meant the issue ad was outside the purview of federal election laws.[14]

Table 8.1 shows PAC candidate contribution and pro-candidate expenditures
between 1996 and 2002, a timeframe of four elections. The expenditures in this
period cover both regulated independent expenditures from traditional PACs and
unregulated "issue advocacy" efforts by other groups.[15] Most notably, in these four
elections, the candidate contribution efforts no longer outpaced electioneering by
11 to 1, but by less than half that. The growing role of organized interests in the
conduct of campaigns grew considerably in this time period.

All of this inspired Congress to reform campaign finance again in 2002.
The legislation was the Bi-Partisan Campaign Reform Act (known also as
McCain-Feingold), and its single impact on interest group electioneering was to
broaden the "magic word" standard to include a "candidate mention" standard for
ads airing close to an election. Under this definition, if an ad mentioned or pic-
tured a candidate for federal office, regardless of whether it featured magic words,
the ad was considered an election-related ad if it aired within 30 days of a primary

and 60 days of a general election.[16] Congress said also that such ads could not be funded with corporate or union money.

The reform was a relatively simple fix to what had emerged as a glaring gap in the law. But as with most things involving campaign finance, a new loophole emerged in the elections following the law's passage. McCain-Feingold had been silent on whether a collection of individuals could pool their resources to air issue ads. Congress had redefined all such ads as "electioneering communications" and mandated that the Federal Election Commission track them. But it was not clear whether a group could accept unlimited contributions from individuals (without accepting union and corporate funds) and use those for electioneering communications without having to form as a traditional PAC.

With such loopholes, a number of groups in the 2004 elections (and to a lesser extent in 2006) formed as 527s under a section of the IRS tax code and flooded the airwaves with ads that were not regulated. The Section 527 option allowed a group to claim some interest in elections, freeing them to advertise about candidates. By not also filing as a PAC with the FEC, however, such groups could argue that their major purpose was not those candidates' election or defeat. Such groups included MoveOn.org, the Swift Boat Veterans for Truth, and the Progress for America Fund. Table 8.1 shows the collective electioneering efforts of these and other groups in 2004 and 2006 compared to the PAC candidate contribution totals in the same elections. Despite the efforts of Congress to slow the electioneering of organized interests, the expansion continued. In 2004 and 2006 PAC contribution totals only outpaced electioneering communications and independent expenditures by 3.55 to 1.

At this point in the story, the focus shifts from interest groups angling to uncover gaps in the law to a story where the Supreme Court modifies its perspective on the constitutional reach of campaign finance laws. This started in 2007 when the Supreme Court ruled in *Wisconsin Right to Life v. FEC* that part of the McCain-Feingold restrictions on issue advocacy were too broad. Recall above that Congress had broadened the "magic word" test to a "candidate mention" test, but the Court argued in *Wisconsin* that the new test was too inclusive. That is, some ads that mention federal candidates might not be intended to influence how voters cast ballots, but how constituents urge action on public policies. In other words, perhaps the "Call John Smith and thank him" ads were really about thanking Congressman Smith for his advocacy on a particular issue. Why should campaign finance laws govern the funding of such ads?

Such an argument is compelling, but the justices provided little guidance on how to implement the decision. How would one know if an issue ad was intended to influence an election or not? The justices posited a "reasonable person" test, in that if any reasonable viewer could consider the ad about policies and not elections, it would apply to the former. In practice this eviscerated the McCain-Feingold changes and allowed corporations and unions to fund issue advocacy.

The Court understood, however, that its decision was hard to implement, and so they went further in their 2010 *Citizens United v. FEC* decision. The case revolved around whether a documentary that was highly critical of presidential candidate Hillary Clinton and was produced by the group Citizens United (which solicited and received corporate donations) amounted to a campaign ad funded illegally with corporate funds. The justices could have decided the case on narrow grounds (e.g., exempting documentaries from campaign ad laws), but they chose instead to make a broad ruling. In their final decision, a 5–4 one, they overturned all restrictions on how interest group ads could be funded, even ones featuring "magic words." Table 8.1 shows the effects of these decisions in 2008 and 2010. The gap between candidate contributions and interest group electioneering continued to shrink, such that $1.62 in contributions produced $1 in independent expenditures and electioneering communications. These elections were dramatically different from the campaigns before 1996, when the ratio was nearly 11 to 1.

The decision in *Citizens United* was only the opening salvo, however. Much needed to be sorted out in terms of what was permissible in light of the decision. The Federal Election Commission devoted considerable effort to offering guidance on what interest groups could do with their resources. In a series of Advisory Opinions in 2011 and 2012, for example, they sanctioned what have come to be called "Super" PACs. These were PACs that registered with the FEC and that had no interest in contributing to federal candidates. Their sole goal was to advocate independently for federal candidates. The FEC allowed these groups to raise unlimited contributions from any individual (excluding foreign nationals), union, trade group, or corporation. They were identified as "super" because prior to *Citizens United*, such groups would have been required to raise limited contributions for their independent expenditures. That fund-raising limitation was no longer in place beginning with the 2010 elections.

The only requirement for Super PACs was that they register with the FEC and disclose their donors publicly. Another type of group, however, was not forced to be so transparent. 501(c)(4) non-profits are tax-exempt groups whose stated purpose is to advance the social welfare. They too were freed to spend their resources on campaign ads, though the IRS mandates that such groups spend less than the majority of their budget on such ads. The advantage to 501(c)(4) groups is that their donors are not released publicly. This means that a collection of wealthy investors (individuals, corporation, unions, etc.) can help bankroll an advertising campaign that attacks or promotes a federal candidate (or slate of candidates), and they can do so without having their name attached publicly to the organization. This type of shadow electioneering is a serious concern for many.[17]

By 2012, the limits on interest group electioneering had disappeared. There was almost no threat of legal sanction on any ads a group would air, and groups could form with the singular goal of electing or defeating a candidate; indeed, there was no need to pretend that issues or public policies were at the center of a group's mission.

As such, 2012 featured an unprecedented level of spending on independent expenditures and electioneering communications. As Table 8.1 shows in the last line, the ratio of contributions to candidate advocacy finally flipped in 2012, such that $1 in contributions now saw over $2.60 in pro-candidate advertising. It is no exaggeration to assert 2012 as a truly unparalleled election in terms of interest group participation.

One other concern in the aftermath of the 2010 *Citizens United* decision focused on whether corporate wealth would dwarf the efforts of liberal groups in advocating for federal candidates. The decision seemed to unleash wealthy investors (i.e., conservative corporate power) to spend on elections. Such a wealth-gap was fairly well contained in the 1980s and early 1990s when traditional PACs were the chief concern of campaign finance reform advocates. With no limits on corporations or business trade associations, however, it was possible that the collective efforts of pro-business, small government interests could overwhelm unions, which have been in decline in America.[18]

To some extent, the balance of spending by groups in 2010 and 2012 did favor the Republicans. Table 8.2 shows the efforts of pro-Democratic and pro-Republican groups in the congressional elections of 2010 and 2012 and in the presidential election of 2012. Using data from the Wesleyan Media Project—which tracks political ads on local broadcast stations in all 210 media markets in the country—the table shows television ads as a percentage of all ads aired in each race, and as a percentage

Table 8.2 Partisanship in Interest Group Television Advertising, 2010–2012

	% of all ads	% of ads in party
2010		
House		
Dem Groups	3.83%	7.31%
GOP Groups	9.17%	19.48%
Senate		
Dem Groups	3.82%	8.71%
GOP Groups	10.56%	19.81%
2012		
House		
Dem Groups	6.68%	13.69%
GOP Groups	11.07%	21.83%
Senate		
Dem Groups	8.55%	19.56%
GOP Groups	18.76%	33.95%
President		
Dem Groups	6.13%	11.86%
GOP Groups	24.92%	51.61%

Source: Wesleyan Media Project

of ads for each party. In all instances, pro-Republican groups dwarf the efforts of pro-Democratic interests, often at a rate of 3 to 1. Note specifically the efforts on behalf of Mitt Romney. Pro-Romney groups aired about 1 in every 4 ads in the entire general election campaign and more than half of all pro-Romney spots. This was a huge investment from interest groups, a presence in size and scope not before seen in American elections.[19]

On the other hand, we do not yet know how much of these pro-Republican efforts were backed by corporations or corporate wealth. For one, no corporation in 2010 or 2012 took advantage of the *Citizens United* decision to directly sponsor a pro-candidate ad. Corporations do not want to risk backlash from the public or shareholders for being too partisan in an election. This is what makes the limited disclosure required for 501(c)(4) groups so attractive, however. Corporations or corporate executives can donate significant sums to groups that can shield their identity. The inability to track such efforts limits what we can say about how much corporate money enters (and entered in 2012) federal elections.

Effectiveness of Outside Spending

The efforts of organized interests in the last few elections beg the question: Did any of this make any difference? There was much talk in the media following the 2012 election, for example, about whether the significant efforts of pro-Republican groups were for naught. Obama won a second term, after all, and Democrats gained eight House seats while also expanding their majority in the Senate. Dave Weigel at the online magazine *Slate* titled his article on the day after the election, "Take the Money and Lose." He asked, "Why did Republican [S]uper PACs waste so many millions on bad TV?"[20] That sort of macro-level assessment is suggestive, but it is not enough to declare ads from organized interests as ineffective.

There are really two ways to think about the efforts of organized interests on election outcomes. One is to count ads from groups as uniformly equal in power to ads from candidates or parties. In this approach, interest group expenditures in a campaign are added to all other pro-candidate dollars to assess the relationship between campaign spending and election results. We know from work on campaign effects that the outcome of elections—especially high profile ones like presidential contests—is in many cases highly predictable.[21] This suggests that campaigns do little to change voters' minds, except perhaps at the margins. And campaigns have their strongest marginal effects when one candidate can marshal more resources than the opposition.[22] In this first approach to measuring the impact of interest group efforts, interest group expenditures are counted in the overall pro-Democratic or pro-Republican totals to assess their role in shifting more resources to preferred candidates.

Consider the congressional elections of 2012. Figure 8.2 aggregates ad totals on behalf of House and Senate candidates by media market and state or congressional district for ads airing between September 1 and Election Day (November 6).

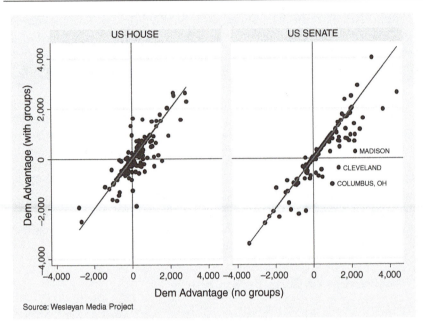

Figure 8.2 Advertising in 2012 House and Senate Media Markets

The x-axis counts all ads sponsored by candidates and parties and graphs the Democratic minus Republican totals in the market. That is, if the Democratic candidate and party aired 3,000 ads in the market but the Republican sponsored only 1,000, the advantage of ads aired is 2,000 for the Democrat. The y-axis adds interest groups into the totals, such that the balance of ads in the market now accounts for the level of support each candidate received from organized interests. In the plot, any point above the shown line is a market where interest group ads helped the Democrat with more ads on television; and any point below the line is one where pro-Republican groups moved the balance of ads in their candidate's direction.

The figure does not show these ads' impact, but shows merely how organized interests can help candidates in the overall tally of ads aired. There are lots of instances indeed where interest group ads tip the balance in the direction of their preferred candidate.[23] In some instances, in fact, the Democratic candidate might have more ads on the air than the Republican, but pro-Republican groups move the overall total to benefit the Republican. (Two media markets from the Ohio Senate race are highlighted on the graph. In Madison, Wisconsin, Democrat Tammy Baldwin heavily out-advertised Republican Tommy Thompson, but when the groups are included in the totals the candidates were at near parity.) To the extent that interest groups move the overall balance of resources in a race toward the candidate they prefer, they are able to likely move vote totals.[24] Indeed, research that measures the effect of ad advantages in presidential elections demonstrates the ability to influence overall vote share in just this fashion.[25] The effect is also present in congressional races, though it is rare that ad imbalances account for enough of an effect to determine the actual winner.[26]

This approach to measuring potential impact makes the strong assumption, though, that all ads in a market are similarly powerful. This is a strong assumption and probably a wrong one. As any close watcher of campaign ads (and commercial advertising, more generally) knows, ads can vary in their quality and appeal. Getting a good handle on what one would count as a persuasive or effective ad is very difficult, however. And the research is not clear on sorting out differences across ad types. Scholars of campaign advertising have committed considerable resources, for example, to addressing the tone of ads. From this rich scholarship we know less than we might expect, as evidence on whether negative or positive ads are more persuasive is simply inconclusive.[27]

Some scholars have exploited the increase in interest group advertising to test some specific hypotheses about advertising effects. For example, we know that the credibility of message senders can aid or inhibit a message's influence.[28] That is, the more credible a source is, the more likely receivers are to accept the underlying message. For interest group ads, this suggests that their ads might be more effective than candidate ads, in part because candidates are viewed as less credible (i.e., they want to win an election) than an unaffiliated interest group with ostensibly more sincere goals.[29] However, the success of group-sponsored ads may be moderated by how much information voters have about the group or its financial backing, such that groups known for being partisan or relying on large donors may lose credibility.[30]

All of this points to important differences in ad effects across ad types and ad sponsors. But more work is needed to sort out what makes an ad "powerful" or not. Much of this research often relies on experimental work to test for very specific manipulations in ads, but this can leave many other features untested. We often lack bigger sets of data that point to voters' perceptions of ads.

There is one exception, though, albeit an imperfect one. In 2012, a new iPhone app, SuperPACapp, allowed viewers to use their phones to identify the funding sources of ad sponsors. A user could point their phone at an ad on television or a video on YouTube, and the voice recognition software of the application would search for a match. If one was located, the app showed the user any campaign finance information reported by the video sponsor (if there was any). The application also asked users to rate the video on a four-point metric from "fail" to "fishy" to "fair" and "love." The resulting data set was made available on the application's website, and this allows one to aggregate average rankings by sponsor.[31]

I aggregated the tens of thousands of rankings into six sponsor types—the Romney and Obama campaigns, the two party committees, and pro-Democratic and pro-Republican interest groups. The mean rankings on the four-point scale are reported in Figure 8.3. The results point to important perception differences among the application's users.

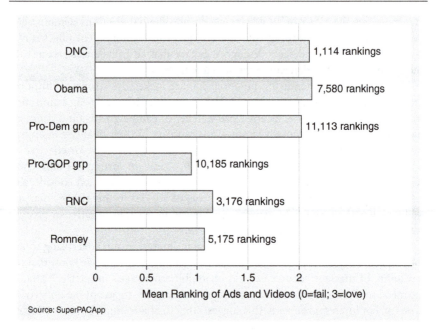

Figure 8.3 Rankings of Ads and Videos by Users of SuperPACapp, 2012

First, the Democratic ads and videos were consistently rated higher than the Republican ones. All three pro-Democratic ad sponsors scored on average above 2 on the 0–3 point scale. These were about 1 point higher than all of the pro-Republican sponsors. This is a substantively large difference and suggests that viewers were much more favorable to ads and videos that supported Obama or attacked Mitt Romney. Moreover, pro-Republican groups scored the lowest of all sponsor types (0.94 to 2.12 for Obama's ads); this finding is in line with the argument suggested earlier from media reports that Republican Super PAC money was wasted on ineffective ads.

One weakness in the data, though, is that the sample of users who rated ads is not random but self-selected. And it is likely that the universe of users was already pro-Democratic. Of the 59,000 user sessions that were identified by their state of residence, nearly 45,000 were from states that voted for Obama in 2012.[32] Excluding battleground states won by Obama still shows a blue state advantage, 21,000 sessions to 15,000 in red states.

Despite the limitations, however, the small differences within each party's set of sponsors are still instructive. All pro-Democratic ads and videos were rated high, including the DNC (2.10) and pro-Democratic groups (2.02). Users did not sort Obama's ads as being dramatically more effective than his allies. Similarly, Romney's ads were rated almost as low as pro-Republican groups (1.07 to 0.94). This suggests that there were some perceived differences in the ads within each party but not large ones. This might indicate more broadly that interest group ads are not uniformly more or less effective than candidate or party ads.[33] Message effectiveness, one might infer, is tied less explicitly to the sponsor of the ad. Of course, a data set with more pro-Romney users would help bolster the point. All told, it may not have been the case that Republican Super PAC ads were a drag on Romney, any more than if he had been able to sponsor all of the ads himself.

Issue Focus of Outside Spending in 2012

The discussion above leaves out one other issue: the content of the ads. What do interest groups bring to campaigns when they advertise? Do they introduce new issues into the debate or do they reinforce the discussions among candidates? There are positive and negatives to both potential outcomes. Interest groups could introduce new issues for consideration by voters, ones candidates might hope to avoid. Or they could be talking about a broader issue (i.e., the economy) in a way that candidates are not. This could be considered healthy from the perspective that "more debate is better." To that effect, one analysis of candidate and interest group advertising argued:

> In the post-*Citizens United* environment, an issue or theme has greater poten-tial to be promoted even where a candidate might prefer not to raise that issue. *This would suggest that meaningful political speech is in fact more open and more accessible than it once was. While the results may be messy for indi-vidual campaigns, they do auger well for political speech.*[34] (Emphasis added).

On the other hand, interest groups might be introducing a sort of cognitive dissonance that makes it harder for voters to sort out what the election is really about. Too many issues, that is, might be too much for voters to process. This can complicate interpretations of election outcomes. Did voters elect a candi-date because of attacks on the opposing candidate that were initiated by outside groups? Without such attacks, would the other candidate have won? If so, then the outcome of the election is not an affirmation of the campaign as waged by the candidate but a consequence of the issues raised by unaffiliated interest groups. Does that not complicate the candidate's hope that elections are referendums on their own campaign efforts?

Most scholarship on the question of issue debates in campaigns focuses on what opposing *candidates* talk about. One theory suggests that candidates in each party are advantaged on a set of issues—the Democrats on entitlements and the Republicans on taxes, for example.[35] If campaigns play to these strengths, we should witness issue divergence between opposing campaigns. Neither side would raise the issue on which they are perceived to have less of an advantage. The evidence for this expectation is weak, however. It seems that opposing campaigns often talk about a similar set of issues,[36] albeit from differing perspectives.[37] This is seen as healthy, in that voters are often asked to choose among candidates who are debating the direction of a similar set of public policies.

What happens when we put interest groups into the mix, however? Do they engage candidates on their terms? Or do they introduce new issues? The Wesleyan Media Project data are ideal for investigating this. The Project codes each ad aired in congressional and presidential elections on the issue content of the ads. Coders choose among a list of over sixty issues and identify as many issues in the ad that are mentioned.[38] Figure 8.4 aggregates the issues used in the 2012 presidential election as well as the 2012 Senate elections. Both graphs examine ads aired between May 2012 and Election Day in November. For the presidential election, this is essentially the entire general election period, since Romney was the presumed nominee after former Senator Rick Santorum dropped out in late April. The Senate graph lumps ads aired in all 30-plus Senate races. It would be more accurate to look at each Senate race separately, but the aggregation gives a general sense of whether any major disparities in issue focus are apparent.[39]

The graphs sort issues in descending order of mention by candidates, and they exclude any issue on the list of 60 that were not mentioned by either candidates or groups in at least 3% of their ads. An issue with a line is one where both candidates and groups devoted at least 3% of their ads to it; any issue without a line is one where only candidates or groups advertised at such levels.

The results suggest some notable differences. In the presidential election the candidates devoted significant attention to jobs and taxes, but interest groups devoted far more time to the former as opposed to the latter. Groups also focused more than half of their ads on the budget and federal debt, whereas the candidates devoted only about 1 in every 5 ads to the issue. (The heavy presence of pro-Romney interest groups—see again Table 8.2—is the primary culprit for these differences. Republican groups were far more active than Democratic groups, and the former was partial to an economic debate focused on government debt and slow job growth.) There were also disparities in the mention of government spending and the 2008 recession, where interest groups put more emphasis on both. The two candidates also made note of a host of issues that barely or did not register for groups, including education, Medicare, China, and women's health. Notably, however, we see no instances where interest groups spent considerable efforts promoting divisive social issues such as abortion or welfare. Indeed, it seems that interest groups in the presidential election put more spotlight on different types of economic questions, such as spending, the budget, and jobs.

There is a bit more consistency in the analysis of Senate ads. Here, it was interest groups that put more disproportionate focus on taxes than the candidates; and they also devoted more time to health care. But across most of the other top issues, there was a roughly proportionate level of attention for candidates and groups.

The evidence, all told, is perhaps comforting. Interest groups in 2012 injected new perspectives on some issues, namely the economy, while talking a lot about the issues on which the candidates were focused. In putting more attention on different aspects of the economy, then, interest groups may also have forced the candidates to engage with and respond to questions they may have wished to avoid. Such trends may not hold in future elections, or even if we disaggregate to

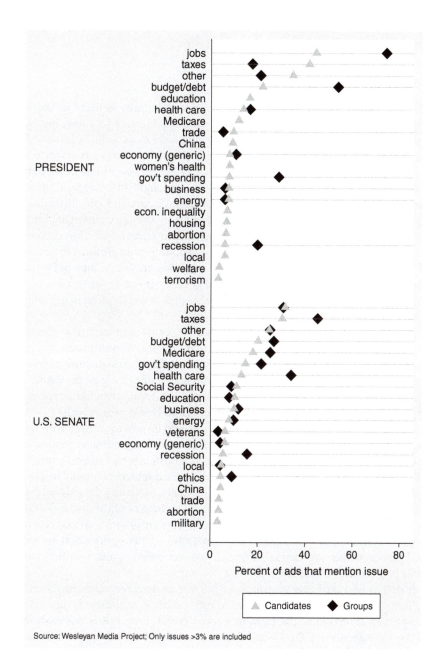

Figure 8.4 Issues Mentioned by Candidates and Groups in Ads, 2012

individual House or Senate races, but from this initial look at the data, we may have less reason to charge outside groups with upending campaigns and confusing voters with ads on random or less relevant issues.

Looking Forward

The role played by organized interest in federal elections is likely to be (and frankly, should be) a major topic of conversation in years to come, not only among scholars and policy-makers but among citizens as well. In just the last generation, the scale of interest group investments in elections has skyrocketed. It has also shifted in profile from an overwhelming focus on limited, regulated, and disclosed campaign contributions to an onslaught of campaign ads and candidate advocacy efforts often funded by large donors and with little disclosure. On the one hand, this may not represent a troubling or damaging impact on American elections. For one, as noted here, their effect on election outcomes is not yet known, but it is probably not the case that they determine the outcome of many elections. Additionally, while the ads from outside groups did refocus a lot of the debate in the 2012 presidential election, it was to other areas of the economy and fiscal matters (jobs and the debt) than it was to social issues or hot-button cultural issues.

There are reasons to be concerned, though, and they are significant. Two stand out in particular. First, many of these groups register as 501(c)(4) non-profits, and they do not disclose publicly their donors. Even Super PACs, who do disclose, can avoid it rather easily by accepting contributions from non-profits. Imagine the Center for American Democracy Super PAC claiming to be 100% transparent but accepting all of their contributions from the Center for American Democracy 501(c)(4).

Transparency is important because voters should be able to identify with some degree of precision the primary financiers of candidates, political parties, and political advocacy groups. This is primarily because democracy can only function efficiently and voters can only truly hold their elected leaders accountable if there is an abundance of information available to voters. Similarly, the existence and accessibility of these campaign finance reports can help diminish the appearance of corruption. When voters think that office holders are granting special access to large contributors, or making quid pro quo deals—all perceptions that are likely to skyrocket with fewer campaign finance laws on interest groups—voters could easily become demoralized.[40]

It should be noted that transparency is a widely accepted norm in American politics. Indeed, only one form of direct political advocacy is universally accepted as anonymous, the right to a secret ballot. Even this is not enshrined in the Constitution of the United States, however. Many other forms of campaign activity do not allow for anonymity: opinion columns and letters to the editor (which would almost never be published without author attribution), door-to-door campaigning (which requires the volunteer to appear in person), and party caucuses (which require supporters of a candidate to visibly stand with other supporters). Even candidates' aggressive use of voters' consumer data, which they purchase from credit card companies with the hopes of better targeting likely voters, represents a form of voter identification that no voter can reasonably hope to prevent.[41] All of these forms of identification are widely accepted in American politics, and are unlikely to change. What makes campaign contributions, simply another way for volunteers and interested voters to signal support for a political cause, unique enough to demand special protections?

There is another concern worth noting. The oversized presence of interest groups in many campaigns threatens to squeeze out the roles played by candidates and political parties. There is a long debate in political science about whether parties or candidate should be at the center of our electoral process. The proponents of parties envision the Democrats and Republicans as two opposing forces, where candidates fall in line as the foot soldiers in an ideological struggle for power. Under this argument, voters have a simple choice: a liberal or conservative direction in public policy. The candidate-centered theory argues that voters should be able to mix and match their preference to reflect the strengths of individual candidates. This is the "vote the person not the party" mantra, and it accepts that voters might want a Republican Congress and a Democratic president.

These two opposing democratic theories of elections stand in stark contrast to an emerging interest group-centered electoral process, where the party committees have fewer resources than interest groups and where candidates can be drowned out by the flurry of ads coming from numerous different groups. This interest group-centered system has little to recommend it, especially when so many groups disclose little to nothing about their donor base. The results from Figure 8.4 notwithstanding, the potential is there for shadow groups to drive the issue debates in a campaign, alter the balance of ads in a race, and even help elect candidates, all without providing the voting public any evidence for what it really hopes to accomplish. The goals of parties and candidates are crystal clear: win elections and implement a fairly transparent political philosophy. But what groups with generic names like Priorities USA, the Center for Individual Freedom, and American Crossroads hope to accomplish is simply unknown. Is it a set of public policies that run counter to the interests of the larger electorate? Only with a deeper discussion among the voting public can the influence of interest groups be sorted out. Are Americans comfortable with such groups being a large presence in elections, for example?

The 2012 election was a truly momentous one. In no election in modern times have interest groups been so involved in persuading voters to cast a ballot one way or the other. Only time will tell whether the groups' donors see this sort of investment as worthwhile. So long as the parties are polarized, however, and each side sees control of Congress and the White House as within grasp, we are likely to see heavy levels of interest group spending in the coming years. In that sense, 2012 may only be the beginning of a new phase in American elections.

Notes

1 For a review of these and other campaign finance laws, see Anthony Corrado. "Money and Politics: A History of Campaign Finance Law," in *The New Campaign Finance Sourcebook*, ed. Anthony Corrado, Thomas Mann, Daniel Ortiz, and Trevor Potter (Washington, DC: Brookings Institution Press, 2005).

2 Another type of PAC is a "non connected" PAC that does not have a union, membership, corporate, or trade association sponsor. They can accept contributions from the general public.

3 Values from a Campaign Finance Institute report: "The Cost of Winning a House Seat, 1986–2010," http://www.cfinst.org/data.aspx.

4 The reported amount from PACs also includes any contributions received from leadership PACs, which are maintained by other elected officials. These are not rightly understood as traditional PACs. However, these leadership PACs abide by the same $5,000 contribution limit, and so excluding them does very little to change the appearance of the graph. All figures here are from reports to the FEC at the beginning of 2013. Some figures will change as candidates amend their reports. The graph excludes any outside values from the visualization.

5 Stephen Ansolabehere, John M. de Figueiredo, and James M. Snyder, "Why Is There So Little Money in Politics?" *Journal of Economic Perspectives* 17, no. 1 (2003): 105–30.

6 Frank Baumgartner, Jeffrey Berry, Marie Hojnacki, and Beth Leech, *Lobbying and Policy Change: Who Wins, Who Loses, and Why* (Chicago: University of Chicago Press, 2009).

7 They remain capped for union, corporate, and trade association PACs. However, non connected PACs can run what are called "hybrid" PACs that accept limited donations for the purpose of contributions to candidates and unlimited contributions for the purpose of independent expenditures. This "hybrid" operation was first allowed in 2011.

8 This point is notwithstanding the presence of some high-profile independent expenditures in the 1980s, most especially from one group, the National Conservative Political Action Committee, which invested resources in some competitive Senate races in 1980 and 1982.

9 See also Michael Franz, *Choices and Changes: Interest Groups in the Electoral Process* (Philadelphia: Temple University Press, 2008).

10 Some of the overturned elements involved spending limits for candidates and PAC independent expenditures.

11 There were a number of court cases in the 1980s that involved the parameters of campaign finance laws. But these cases were not in response to a particularly large amount of spending by outside groups in the elections of the 1980s.

12 Nolan McCarty, Keith Poole, and Howard Rosenthal, *Polarized America: The Dance of Political Ideology and Unequal Riches* (Boston: MIT Press, 2006).

13 Some of these cases included *FEC v. Christian Action Network, Inc.* (1996, Fourth Circuit Court of Appeals) and *Maine Right to Life Comm. v. FEC* (1997, First Circuit Court of Appeals).

14 Parties used the same loophole, but to ostensibly fund party branding messages. As with interest groups, parties crafted pro-candidate messages funded with unregulated money that stopped short of directly calling for that candidate's election.

15 Traditional PACs were not the vehicles for issue advocacy in this time period. These groups, in registering with the Federal Election Commission, conformed to restrictions on all of their fund-raising. As a result, PACs' parent groups would often fund issue advocacy efforts—for example, trade associations, business leagues, and unions.

16 There were exceptions for ads distributed via mail or print media, and for peer-to-peer mobilization and Internet communications. These forms of voter outreach were still governed by the "magic word" test.

17 Two other non-profit classifications are relevant here as well: 501(c)(5) unions and 501(c)(6) business leagues. They follow the same set of rules for non-profit classification as the social welfare 501(c)(4)s.

18 For a nuanced take on union power in American elections, see Peter Francia, "Do Unions Still Matter in U.S. Elections? Assessing Labor's Political Power and Significance," *The Forum* 10, no. 1, Article 3 (2012).

19 With respect to Table 8.2, it should also be noted that many campaigns feature almost no ads from outside groups. These are mostly for races where the outcome is not very competitive. As such, the presence of groups in competitive campaigns can often be quite larger than the percentages indicated in the table. But conversely, interest groups are essentially absent from a majority of campaigns.

20 http://www.slate.com/articles/news_and_politics/politics/2012/11/gop_super_pacs_republican_donors_spent_millions_on_tv_ads_and_got_almost.single.html

21 See, for example, the research on presidential forecasting. For a forecast of the 2012 election, see James Campbell, "Forecasting the Presidential and Congressional Elections of 2012: The Trial-Heat and the Seats-in-Trouble Models," *PS: Political Science & Politics* 45, no. 4 (2012): 630–34.

22 Michael D. Jones and Jorgensen D. Paul, "Mind the Gap? Political Advertisements and Congressional Election Results," *Journal of Political Marketing* 11, no. 3 (2012): 165–88.

23 The graph does not scale the markets to reflect population size, and it should be remembered that not all media markets have similar numbers of voters.

24 Interest groups boost candidates, however, somewhat inefficiently. Interest groups essentially drive up election costs because they generally pay more for ads than candidates do. Federal candidates are required by law, specifically Section 315(b) of the Communications Act of 1934 (as amended), to get a discount on radio and television ads: the "lowest unit rate." This applies to ads aired by candidates within 45 days of a primary and 60 days of a general election. Interest groups do not similarly benefit, and it is understood that broadcast stations can use competitive elections to charge very high rates on interest group ads.

25 See, for example, Michael Franz, "Interest Groups in Electoral Politics: 2012 in Context," *The Forum: A Journal of Applied Research in Contemporary Politics* 10, no. 4 (2012): 62–79 Michael Franz and Travis Ridout, "Political Advertising and Persuasion in the 2004 and 2008 Presidential Elections," *American Politics Research* 38, no. 2 (2010): 303–29.

26 Jones and Jorgensen, "Mind the Gap?"

27 Richard Lau, Lee Sigelman, and Ivy Brown Rovner, "The Effects of Negative Political Advertisements: A Meta-Analytic Reassessment," *Journal of Politics* 69:4 (2007): 1176–1209.

28 David Sears and Richard E. Whitney, *Political Persuasion* (Morristown, NJ: General Learning Press, 1973).

29 Deborah Jordan Brooks and Michael Murov, "Assessing Accountability in a Post-Citizens United Era: The Effects of Attack Ad Sponsorship by Unknown Independent Groups," *American Politics Research* 40, no. 3 (2012): 383–418.

30 Christopher Weber, Johanna Dunaway, and Tyler Johnson, "It's All in the Name: Source Cue Ambiguity and the Persuasive Appeal of Campaign Ads," *Political Behavior* 34, no. 3 (2012): 561–84; Amber Wichowsky and Conor M. Dowling, "Who's Behind the Curtain? Interest Groups and Anonymity in Political Advertising" (paper delivered at the Annual Meeting of the Midwest Political Science Association, 2011).

31 The data are available also from the author on request.

32 54,000 uses of the application could not be identified by the state of the user. Not all users rated an ad. Only about 37,000 users rated an ad or video.

33 There are differences within the interest group categories when looking at specific ad sponsors. Among pro-Romney groups, American Crossroads' ads and videos scored the highest, with 1.11 on the 0–3 scale. The N for each sponsor declines significantly, however, when the data are disaggregated in this way.

34 Kenneth Goldstein, David A. Schweidel, and Mike B. Wittenwyler, "Lessons Learned: Political Advertising and Political Law," *Minnesota Law Review* 96, no. 5 (2012): 1753.

35 John R. Petrocik, William L. Benoit, and Glenn J. Hansen, "Issue Ownership and Presidential Campaigning, 1952–2000," *Political Science Quarterly* 118, no. 4 (2003: 599–626.

36 Noah Kaplan, David K. Park, and Travis N. Ridout, "Dialogue in American Political Campaigns? An Examination of Issue Convergence in Candidate Television Advertising," *American Journal of Political Science* 50, no. 3 (2006): 724–36.

37 John Sides, "The Origins of Campaign Agendas," *British Journal of Political Science* 36, no. 3 (2006): 407–36

38 If a coder noted an issue that was not on the pre-populated list of 60, they could enter it manually in a separate column, after selecting "Other." The data reported below use only the list of 60 issues, however. Coding of the 2012 election is not complete, though over 90 percent of the ads have been coded as of early 2013.

39 One could also separate out the candidates by party and compare against pro-Democratic and pro-Republican groups separately.

40 Such claims, of course, require evidence. The relationship between disclosure laws and trust in government or political efficacy is murky, and any positive effects are likely small. See, for example, David Primo and Jeffrey Milyo, "Campaign Finance Laws and Political Efficacy: Evidence from the States," *Election Law Journal* 5, no. 1 (2006): 23–39. Most studies on the question focus on state campaign finance laws, however. With the dramatic expansion of outside spending at the federal level in 2012, it is probably important to study the question more.

41 This is called "micro-targeting." See Sunshine Hillygus and Todd G. Shields, *The Persuadable Voter: Wedge Issues in Presidential Campaigns* (Princeton, NJ: Princeton University Press, 2008).

Chapter 9

When Does Money Buy Votes?
Campaign Contributions and Policymaking

Christopher Witko

In the midst of the Senate debate over the Patient Protection and Affordable Care Act (aka "Obamacare") in late 2009, Ben Nelson, a Democratic senator from Nebraska, was wavering on whether to support the bill. In what some humorously called the "Cornhusker Kickback," Nelson obtained federal funding for Nebraska to cover its Medicaid expansion required by the bill. Less notoriously, Nelson also bargained for a provision that resulted in Nebraska insurance companies paying tens of millions of dollars less in fees than they otherwise would have. A story on the website *The Huffington Post* pointed out that in the last several years Nelson's campaigns received $650,000 from the insurance industry.[1] The implication was clear—Ben Nelson rewarded his campaign contributors with millions of dollars in financial benefits. Did Ben Nelson make this deal because he received campaign contributions from the insurance industry? More generally, when and how do campaign contributions influence policy-making?

How campaign contributions influence government decisions and policy outcomes is a critical question. News stories suggesting that politicians exchange votes or other policy benefits for campaign contributions are common in the media and in the public consciousness and many critics view the system of campaign contributions as little more than "legalized bribery." If campaign contributions are simply legalized bribery, then a fundamental restructuring of the system of campaign finance is called for, since this makes a mockery of the ideal of political equality embodied in legal doctrines like "one person, one vote." But empirical studies of campaign contributions show that the effect is complex and inconsistent across different issues, decisions, and stages of the policy process. Campaign contributions are clearly not simple quid pro quos. In the Ben Nelson example discussed above, Nelson's help of home state companies can be viewed as helping out constituents, since large insurers provide many jobs. Considering the fact that Nelson decided to retire without another reelection campaign and therefore had no reason to continue to need insurance company money, it is extremely unlikely that he fought for this legislative provision because of campaign contributions. Nevertheless, based on numerous studies, it seems clear that campaign contributions can influence government decisions under some conditions, and I consider how campaign contributions may influence policy in this chapter.

I begin the chapter with a discussion of different theoretical perspectives on how campaign contributions may influence decisions and policies and a discussion of the scholarly literature on this subject, with an emphasis on my own research. Campaign contributions can influence policy outcomes by either influencing the types of candidates elected to institutions or by influencing decisions once people are elected. I do not focus very much on the former, because how interest groups influence elections is discussed in other chapters. Thus, I consider primarily how campaign contributions may influence the decisions of current policy makers. Next, I focus on one of the major limitations in the existing literature, which is a failure to systematically consider how the changing balance of power among business interests and labor in the campaign finance system over the past 30 years may have influenced policy. The increasing power of business may have important consequences for what policies government does enact and what problems do not even make it to the political agenda. I conclude by briefly considering how recent changes in the campaign finance system may shape the power of organized interests that contribute money to influence the policy process in the future.

When and How Campaign Contributions Influence Policy

In 2005 three social scientists, Stephen Ansolabehere, John M. de Figueireido, and James M. Snyder, published an article provocatively entitled "Why Is There so Little Money in U.S. Politics?"[2] This article provides strong arguments that campaign contributions are largely irrelevant to policy-making. The authors reject the idea that campaign contributions are able or even intended to purchase policy benefits from government. They show that only approximately one in four analyses of the effect of campaign contributions on Congressional roll-call voting conducted in the past find significant effects. In their own analysis of roll call votes important to the Chamber of Commerce they fail to find significant effects for contributions in their unusually large data set. They argue that campaign contributions should be viewed as a form of consumption spending, akin to spending money on tickets to a baseball game. Considering that the median campaign contribution is $1,000, contributing is not much more costly.[3]

Yet, one in four studies did find a significant relationship between campaign contributions and voting, and the potential exists for campaign contributions to influence many other types of decisions. And a number of studies do find that campaign contributions influence other types of policy choices besides roll call votes. Rather than indicating that one group of studies is incorrect, while the other is correct, these contradictory results likely reflect different assumptions about how campaign contributions influence decision making, and the reality that the effect of campaign contributions varies across the different types of issues, time periods, and policy-making venues that have been examined in different studies. Indeed, studies specifically designed to understand the contingency of the effect of campaign contributions show that the effect of contributions varies in sometimes predictable ways. While contributions are not a dominant consideration under many circumstances, some interest groups and organizations donate hundreds of thousands or millions of dollars to candidates, and these contributions can make a difference in the policy process at times.[4]

Early studies generally viewed contributions as part of a simple exchange relationship, which is not surprising since we are used to thinking of spending money to buy desired goods.[5] This view of a simple purchase also probably most closely resembles the image of campaign contributions held by the media and public. That is, there is an implicit contract that the contributor provides money in exchange for some tangible policy benefit. This contract must be implicit because otherwise a crime (bribery) is committed. Thus, campaign contributions are essentially legalized bribery from this perspective.

One difficulty with studying this exchange relationship is that, since we are not privy to communication between policy-makers and campaign contributors and any "contracts" cannot be recorded for legal reasons, we cannot be certain what policy benefits are desired by contributors in the first place. Therefore, early studies generally examined the effect of contributions on Congressional roll call votes that were known to be important to campaign contributors, either from media reports or the groups' own lists of "key votes." This was a reasonable approach, but the large number of early studies examining roll call votes makes it clear that there is simply not any consistent relationship between contributions and voting.[6] Furthermore, the fact that most contributions are given to politicians that already support group goals and are thus likely to vote with the contributing interest anyway indicates that groups are probably not generally trying to influence voting.[7]

Some scholars have taken the view that rather than discrete exchange there is a long-term investment in politicians, but others have argued that it is difficult to enforce these market "contracts" whether they are short term or long term.[8] Another variation on the exchange theme is that contributions should be viewed as gifts among friends rather than simple purchases.[9] These latter variants of exchange theory recognize that interactions between contributors and politicians take place in political and policy-making institutions that are very much unlike the typical economic marketplace. Parties, committees, ideology, and constituents all place significant constraints on policy-makers. Most studies now begin with the premise that rather than buying specific policy benefits, campaign contributions help organized interests to gain access to important decision-makers, and this access *sometimes* results in policy benefits.[10] Campaign contributions and lobbying are highly correlated, but relatively few studies attempt to determine whether campaign contributions or lobbying are more effective, and disentangling the effects of lobbying and campaign contributions is extremely difficult because almost all entities that contribute to politicians also lobby, though the opposite is not true.[11] Furthermore, many groups that contribute money to politicians already have some constituency relationships with them, providing some access.[12]

Contributors do not expect politicians to always do what they want, but they do expect them to listen to their concerns and help them out if possible.[13] For most interests, contributing money to politicians is an activity that reinforces broader lobbying strategies rather than a separate strategy or tactic.

Based on a number of existing studies it seems that campaign contributions are most effective when other factors that influence the decision-making of policy actors (whether elected or unelected, like bureaucrats) do not provide a clear guide to decision-making and when the public is not a constraint on decisions either due to indifference or because the decision is made out of public view.[14] This seems to be the case across different institutions (Congress and the bureaucracy) and different stages of the policy process (committee action, floor voting, and even the exercise of bureaucratic discretion).

My research on the Congress has examined how the issue context and stage of the policy process shapes how contributions affect decision-making. There is almost no research into how contributions may affect Presidential decision-making, but there is some recent research into how campaign contributions may influence bureaucratic decision-making. Though bureaucrats do not benefit directly from campaign contributions in the way that politicians do, according to my research they can still be influenced by these interest group expenditures. I organize the discussion below by studies examining the influence of campaign contributions across different stages of the policy process. But the effect of money does not only vary across stages of the policy process. As I note, the type of issue under consideration is important and the stage of the policy process can also condition the effect of campaign contributions. It is also possible that the effect of campaign contributions varies over time or across states. However, no studies examine how the effectiveness of campaign contributions varies across states, and few studies examine how the effectiveness of campaign contributions may vary over time, though my own research discussed below examines how the influence of campaign contributions in the bureaucracy varies across different periods of partisan control of government.

The Effect of Money in Different Stages of the Policy Process

Campaign Contributions and Pre-Floor Decisions

Some scholars argue that money is more likely to purchase beneficial activity in pre-floor stages of the legislative process because these activities (like altering the language of bills) are less visible to the public, reducing the probability of a public backlash against politicians' favors for campaign contributors. Less cynically, the lack of public knowledge of committee processes limits the utility of constituency opinion (which is an important influence on congressional behavior) as a guide to decisions, and campaign contributions can enter into decision-making to fill this void.

At least one study examines the relationship between campaign contributions and bill sponsorship and finds that money influences the propensity to sponsor bills for particular interests.[15] There are also recorded votes in committee and scholars have considered whether contributions influence these votes. In the U.S. Congress, it does not appear that campaign contributions influence committee voting in any consistent pattern.[16] In a study of California legislative committees, Gordon finds that campaign contributions do influence committee votes that are very important to organized interests but do not have a general effect. Other scholars find that campaign contributions predict the amount of effort that members of Congress expend on specific bills.[17]

Why is there variation in the effect of money in these different studies? My answer and that of some other scholars is that it may have to do with the type of issue being considered.[18] I argue that on non-partisan, non-salient issues (i.e., those of limited interest to the public) most politicians will not invest a significant amount of time on these issues, even in exchange for campaign contributions, because it will do little to benefit them in their own reelection campaigns or to increase their influence in the party or Congress. In contrast, on highly partisan, salient issues that define the major political conflicts of the day, politicians have a major incentive to be active because these activities can win acclaim with the electorate and party leaders, while also permitting an important impact on major policies. The problem with deciding among which of these issues to pursue for members of Congress is that there are many of them, but money from an organized interests can help tip the balance for involvement in an issue important to contributors. Thus, the effect of money is very subtle, and money does not influence outcomes by changing the issue preferences of politicians but rather by influencing the amount of effort they spend on different issues at the margin.

I examined these arguments by analyzing committee activity on 20 issues—10 that were highly partisan and salient and 10 that were non-salient and non-partisan. I found that involvement in committee action on non-partisan/non-salient issues is driven largely by a clear constituency interest or institutional factors (such as being a committee chair) and campaign contributions were irrelevant. For example, one issue I considered involved funding for a supercollider for scientific research and the committee deliberations on this issue were dominated by representatives from the districts near where it was located. No amount of money is going to make a politician from Seattle become deeply involved in supercollider funding in Texas. In contrast, on partisan/ideological issues member involvement is relatively more widespread, but money from affected organized interests is a significant predictor of committee "effort" on particular issues, supporting my argument.

Campaign Contributions and Roll Call Voting

The vast majority of existing studies of the effect of campaign contributions examine roll call voting, but as noted above the results of these studies are completely inconsistent. Most studies do not find any significant relationship between money and congressional voting, but some do.[19] Again, I argued that the inconsistencies in this research may reflect that different studies examine different types of issues. But in contrast with committee stages of the legislative process, I argued that on highly partisan, salient votes campaign contributions are less likely to influence voting behavior because party, ideology, and constituency opinion determine the vote. Indeed, because these factors tend to be highly correlated, these types of votes are "over-determined." In contrast, I argued that when votes are not highly partisan or ideological and these factors do not lead politicians to a particular decision, campaign contributions can influence roll call voting.[20]

In order to test these arguments, I collected roll call voting data on the 10 highly partisan/high salience issues and 10 low partisanship/low salience issues discussed above that I also used to examine committee behavior. I examined how money influenced the voting of members of the House of Representatives on these 20 issues, controlling for the effect of other influences on the vote like party and constituency preferences. I found that on the 10 highly partisan/salient issues campaign contributions had a minimal effect on roll call decisions, while on the other 10 votes campaign contributions were usually a statistically significant influence on roll call vote decisions. I also simulated what the vote outcomes might have been on these issues if no campaign contributions were made. A summary of these results are presented in Table 9.1. We see that on the non-ideological/non-visible issues campaign contributions usually influenced roll call voting outcomes, while on the other issues, this was seldom the case. In addition, in a couple of instances the campaign contributions appeared to influence the outcome of the vote based on simulations of how individual members' votes would have changed in the absence of any campaign contributions.

Campaign Contributions and the Executive Branch

What happens after legislation leaves the legislature? There is almost no research into how campaign contributions may influence the decision-making of elected executives. This may reflect that, because the president's policy positions are well-known and actions are very visible, it is probably difficult for campaign contributions to influence decision-making once presidents are elected. But the situation may be different for governors, who often receive less media attention.[21]

The states also provide interesting opportunities to learn about the effect of campaign contributions on elected executives because there are many more elected (from Attorneys General to Insurance Commissioners) along with more variation in campaign finance institutions.[22] And some of these elected officials head fairly obscure departments that are not subject to much media attention. Indeed, in recent decades some of these lesser executive branch officials have been involved in notable campaign finance scandals. For example, Megg Scott Phipps, Agricultural Commissioner of North Carolina, allegedly traded contributions for state fair contracts, which led to time in prison.[23] In another example, it was

Table 9.1 The Effect of Campaign Contributions on Voting and Outcomes across Different Contexts

Id/Vis	Subject	Side	PACS	Influence Voting?	Influence Outcome?
Yes	National Service Bill	Nay	Labor	No	No
Yes	Unemployment Benefits	Nay	Labor	Yes	No
Yes	California Desert Protection	Yea	Environmental	No	No
Yes	Elementary/Secondary Education	Nay	Teachers, Abortion Rights	No	No
Yes	Regulatory Moratorium	Nay	Business	No	No
Yes	Securities Litigation	Yea	Lawyers, Labor, Pub. Int. Groups	No	No
		Nay	Securities and Investment Firms	No	No
Yes	Product Liability	Yea	Business, Pharmaceutical, Medical	No	No
		Nay	Trial Lawyers, Pub. Int. Groups	No	No
Yes	Unfunded Mandates	Yea	Labor	No	No
Yes	Tax Limitation Amendment	Yea	Business, Anti-tax Groups	No	No
Yes	Gasoline Tax	Nay	Petroleum Refiners, Gas Marketer	No	No
No	Interior Appropriations	Yea	Taxpayer/ Environmental Groups	No	No
		Nay	Paper and Lumber Companies	Yes	No
No	Airport Improvements	Yea	Airlines	Yes	No
No	Energy and Water Appropriations	Nay	General Dynamics Corp.	Yes	No
No	Omnibus Crime Bill	Yea	Labor	Yes	No
		Nay	Large Business Groups	No	No
No	Interior Appropriations	Nay	Coal/Energy Producers	Yes	Yes
No	Agriculture Appropriations	Yea	Homebuilders	No	No
No	Agriculture Appropriations	Nay	Wine Producers, Brewers	Yes	No
No	Agriculture Appropriations	Yea	Food, Candy Companies	No	No
		Nay	Peanut farmers	Yes	Yes
No	Treasury Postal Appropriations	Yea	Insurance	Yes	No
		Nay	Banks	Yes	No
No	Immigration Reform	Nay	Miscellaneous Business	Yes	No

alleged that California Insurance Commissioner Chuck Quackenbush declined to fine insurance companies for illegal activities in exchange for campaign contributions.[24]

There is more research into how campaign contributions may influence the implementation of legislation by the bureaucracy. It may initially seem strange to consider whether campaign contributions influence the choices of unelected decision-makers that do not directly benefit from campaign contributions, but there are good reasons to do so. Many of the benefits that organized interests want from government are actually provided (or not) by public managers.[25] Campaign contributions might influence bureaucrats either indirectly or directly. In the indirect route, campaign contributions to elected officials might cause them to intervene in bureaucratic processes on the group's behalf.[26] Campaign contributions may directly influence bureaucratic decision-making by acting as a "signal" to public managers that an interest is heavily engaged in politics and would use their connections with elected officials to challenge unfavorable agency decisions.[27] As with politicians, a number of factors influence bureaucratic decisions, and contributions are likely to matter at the margin.

In my own research I have considered how campaign contributions may affect the awarding of government contracts and workplace safety Occupational Safety and Health Administration (OSHA) regulation. In my study of federal government contracting I collected information on the campaign contributions and contracts for a large number of companies (367) from 1981 to 2006. I found that even after controlling for important factors that influence contracting decisions (past contractor performance, past contracting relationships, etc.) the companies that contributed more money to federal candidates subsequently received more government contracts.[28] One state level study found a similar relationship between campaign contributions and the awarding of contracts to build and maintain highways in Wisconsin.[29]

In keeping with the themes of my other work I also considered how the effect of campaign contributions in the bureaucracy may depend on the decision-making context in a study of workplace safety regulation. I argued that the campaign contributions from business should be more effective when the Republican Party is in power because it is more hostile to regulation than the Democratic Party, and bureaucrats must also be responsive to their elected political principals. I examined this argument in an analysis of highly partisan OSHA (workplace safety) regulation, again using a large sample of firms from 1981 to 2006. I found that even after taking a number of other factors into account that can influence OSHA regulation, more campaign contributions resulted in fewer OSHA violations but that this effect was greatest when the Republicans controlled the Congress or Presidency.[30]

Campaign Contributions and the Courts

In America's system of separated powers the courts are also important policy actors. Can unelected judges be influenced by campaign contributions in the same manner as unelected bureaucrats? There have been no studies of whether groups that contribute more money to politicians are more likely to win judicial cases decided by appointed judges. This type of influence is probably quite unlikely in the U.S. Supreme Court because of the relatively high visibility of these decisions (at least to journalists), but other unelected courts may be more subject to this type of influence.

Unlike federal judges who are all appointed, however, the majority of state judges are actually elected. There is a growing concern that with the increasing costs associated with judicial elections, justice may be for sale. Because judicial elections and proceedings do not receive much media or public attention, most of the money contributed to judges is provided by either lawyers or firms that have a direct stake in cases. There is limited research into the effect of contributions on judicial decision-making, but it appears that money from lawyers results in more favorable decisions for their clients.[31]

After reviewing the effect of campaign contributions across different stages of the policy process, we can see that the image of "legalized bribery" is largely inaccurate. In fact, quite often campaign contributions buy nothing tangible. However, it is equally inaccurate to say that campaign contributions do not influence decisions and policy outcomes. In these studies, scholars have taken the issue context, level of partisanship, and other factors as a given. But many of these factors that I argued conditioned the influence of campaign contributions should not always be taken as given because they are also potentially subject to being influenced by campaign contributions. For instance, what if powerful interests are able to kill legislation before it ever gets a hearing in committee or even before it is introduced? What if parties develop their platforms in an attempt to maximize the contributions from different types of interests as some scholars have argued?[32] In addition, few studies consider the effect of campaign contributions on aggregate policy outputs because most research focuses on individual-level studies over a relatively short period of time. We tend to examine the effect of campaign contributions on discrete decisions, taking the issue agenda and member's ideological positions as fixed. But what if money influences the very composition of the agenda, and politicians' observed ideologies are formed with an eye toward fundraising? Then the predominant approach to understanding campaign contributions (including in my own studies) only tells us part of the story. The discussion below is more suggestive than definitive because so few studies have been done on the types of questions discussed, but based on recent research and data it seems that broad changes in the campaign finance system may have led to changes in what gets on the policy agenda in the first place, what policies parties pursue, and what policies are ultimately enacted.

Changing Sources of Campaign Contributions and Changing Policy Outcomes

In recent decades elections have become considerably more expensive and thus the amount of money contributed by organized interests has grown significantly. But contributions from business interests and wealthy individuals have increased dramatically, while those from unions have increased at a slower rate. Therefore, the balance of power in the campaign finance system has shifted toward business and the wealthy. National studies are inconclusive on whether campaign contributions from business influence aggregate policy outputs.[33] And because federal contribution data is only available since the late 1970s, we have limited data with which to perform powerful statistical analyses; however, I have examined how the business dominance of campaign finance systems influences policy outputs in the states, which provide more variation in the business dominance and a larger sample size. In this study, Adam Newmark and I found that states where business provided a larger proportion of total contributions had economic policies that were more favorable to business interests, but that business power did not affect non-economic policies like gun control and abortion.[34] Though only one study, it suggests that the business power in campaign finance system has important policy implications.

As business and wealthy individuals have become more dominant in the campaign finance system in the last 30 years, policy outcomes have more often reflected the interests and preferences of these actors according to observers.[35] But just as importantly, issues that are not important to these wealthy donors, or which by being raised may even harm the interests of business and the wealthy are ignored by politicians, meaning that policy fails to change in response to changing conditions.[36] It is difficult to prove that aggregate policy changes are a direct result of changes in patterns of campaign finance, and certainly many factors have led to changes in the direction of public policy in recent decades. The micro-level literature discussed above shows that campaign contributions influence only some decisions and usual has modest effects on policy, but when aggregated, these effects on policy can be important. In addition, the existing research which focuses mostly on how contributions to individual decision-makers influence their decisions neglects other means by which money may influence policy.

More Expensive Elections, More Reliance on Business

Increasingly expensive elections led politicians to pursue additional campaign funding from interests that had money to spare, which are mostly individual corporations and groups representing business.[37] According to data that I collected from the Federal election commission (FEC) detailed data files page, the amount of all campaign contributions from interest group PACs directly to candidate committees (in constant 2010 dollars) increased from just under $100 million in the 1979–80 election cycle to over $240 million in the 2009–10 election cycle. Total PAC expenditures (including contributions to party committees and for internal group communications to members, for example) increased by more than 10 times from just under $100 million to $1.16 billion.

Some scholars note that compared to other items Americans spend money on (potato chips, sneakers), campaign spending is fairly small.[38] This is true, but because only the wealthiest Americans can afford to pay for their own election campaigns (the cost of which can run anywhere from hundreds or thousands of dollars for some local offices to tens of millions for a U.S. Senate seat or billions for the presidency), they must rely on others to fund their campaigns. And by definition, the "others" are people and interests that have abundant financial resources. Furthermore, even relatively small gifts appear to generate a sense of obligation among participants in the exchange.[39] Because elections became much more expensive precisely when business was mobilizing into politics and organized labor was declining, politicians have become much more reliant on business interests for campaign contributions.

In order to get a quantitative sense of these shifts over time I calculated the gap in total expenditures between labor union PACs and corporate and trade, membership and health (TMH) PACs, in 2010 dollars. Most trade, membership, and health PACs represent business interests, so these contributions are often considered as coming from business in PAC studies. In the 1979–80 election cycle the gap between labor and business interest expenditures was relatively small at just below $113 million. At its largest, the gap was almost $324 million, and in 2010 it was over $244 million. So the gap has more than doubled in the last three decades adjusting for inflation.

And this increasing importance of business money is not limited to the Republican Party, which has traditionally represented business interests. The Democratic Party has also become much more reliant on business. Figure 9.1 presents the labor proportion of campaign contributions from Labor, Corporate, Trade, Membership, and Health (TMH) to federal Democratic candidates. The figures for the 1968 election and for the 1980 and all subsequent election cycles are known, and the values for the 1972, 1974, 1976, and 1978 cycles are imputed with a linear trend between our two known years. Based on research conducted by Herbert Alexander (1971) we know that as late as 1968, Democratic Party candidates for Congress raised 61 percent of their direct contributions from labor unions (see discussion in Wright 2000).[40] The next observed values can be seen for the 1980 election cycle.

We can see that, despite an uptick in the late 1990s and early 2000s, when the Democrats did not control either chamber of Congress (and therefore had less valuable access to trade to business interests for campaign contributions), at the end of the time period Democrats received substantially less as a proportion of their total receipts in contributions from labor. The most useful comparisons are during the periods that Democrats have had unified control of government. In each subsequent decade during periods of unified Democratic control there has been a dramatic decline in the proportion of money raised from labor. In 1968, it was approximately 60%; in 1978–79, it was just over 40%; in 1993–94, it was around 35%; and in 2009–10, it was barely over 30%. Therefore, money from business interests and associations has basically replaced labor unions in importance

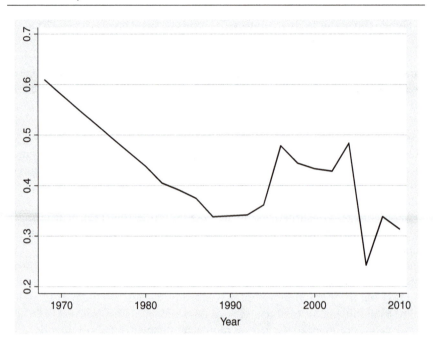

Figure 9.1 Labor's Proportion of Labor and Corporate/TMH Contributions to Democratic Congressional Candidates

for Democratic candidates since the 1960s. This may mean that both parties are very much beholden to business interests, with potentially important policy implications.

Business Contributions and Conservative Policy Shifts?

It is clear that just as the dominance of the campaign finance system by business and the wealthy increased, economic policy in America took a sharp "right turn."[41] In their outstanding book on the politics of income inequality, Jacob S. Hacker and Paul Pierson (2010) note that the shifting balance of power seen in the campaign finance system (and closely related lobbying) has coincided with increasingly conservative economic policies such as deregulation and tax cuts for the wealthy. Because these policies disproportionately benefit the wealthy and business, according to Hacker and Pierson (2010) the increasing dominance of campaign finance and lobbying by business and the wealthy has probably contributed to growing income inequality. There are many reasons why policy became more conservative in the 1980s, but the increasing importance of business campaign

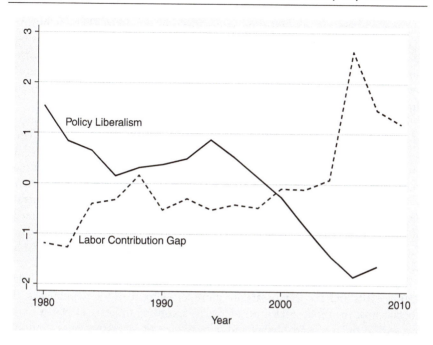

Figure 9.2 The Gap Between Labor and Corporate/TMH PAC Expenditures and Policy Liberalism

contributions, which is closely related to the surge in business lobbying, probably played an important role in this process.[42]

Hacker and Pierson (2010) provide an excellent qualitative discussion of how the increasing political mobilization of business produced more conservative policies. Figure 9.2 quantitatively shows the relationship between the gap between business and labor PAC expenditures (discussed above) and a measure of national policy liberalism created by Robert S. Erikson, Michael B. Mackuen, and James A. Stimson that is often used by political scientists in their studies. These data series have been standardized to appear on the same metric.[43] The number of cases is small, so we must be cautious in interpreting any statistics using these data, but the correlation between the two variables is -0.84.

As every student of research methods knows, correlation is not causation, but examining the figure we can see that movements in the two data series correspond fairly closely and these data are consistent with the qualitative interpretation of increasing business influence over public policy given by Hacker and Pierson (2010). While changes in policy liberalism clearly correspond to changes in party control of government (e.g., there is a major decrease in liberalism following the 1994 elections, which returned the Republicans to control of the Congress for the first time in decades), in the early 1980s, as business become more dominant in financing campaigns, policy became increasingly more conservative, despite a lack of change in the partisan control of institutions between 1981 and 1987. And we see similar opposite movements in the series in the 2000s, as we would anticipate if the power of business in campaign finance led to more conservative policy.

Because, as I showed above, Democrats are also reliant on business, the march of pro-business policy has continued when either party is in government. There is no doubt that there are party differences in economic policy, and Democratic presidential campaigns often still put economic fairness at the center of their messages. However, for much of the last 30 years bread and butter issues of importance to the working or middle class have arguably not been a major goal of Democratic presidents or Congresses, and many of the major conservative policy achievements of the last few decades were bipartisan efforts. For instance, Democratic President Jimmy Carter began the push toward deregulation and regressive tax cuts, and Bill Clinton very much continued on this trajectory.[44]

How can this be true in an era of extreme party polarization? While party polarization exists and the Democrats are more left-wing than the Republicans, the liberalism of the modern Democratic Party, according to Berry (1998) is not as focused on the traditional bread and butter issues of increasing wages and jobs but more concerned with issues like women's rights and the environment.[45] This probably partly reflects that, as noted above, labor unions are a less important source of campaign contributions for Democratic candidates and corporations and wealthy individuals have become a more important source of money for Democrats. Following Howard Dean's 2004 campaign for the Democratic nomination for president, individual small contributors were viewed as an important new source of money for campaigns. However, only relatively affluent people can contribute significant amounts of money to politicians. It would take hundreds of $20 contributions to equal a $10,000 check that a wealthy individual can write. This is important because affluent individuals have different policy views than their less affluent counterparts, even among Democrats.[46] Wealthy Democrats are much more likely to be associated with groups advocating for agendas like women's rights, gay rights, environmental issues, or even business interests than they are to be members of labor unions or groups advocating for the poor or working class. Thus, the Democratic Party can be more liberal on social issues, while staying in the same ideological space or even becoming more conservative on traditional economic issues.[47] Note that this does not mean that the Democrats have entirely abandoned issues important to working people. The Democrats are still much more likely to enact things like minimum wage increases, and my own research discussed above shows that when the Democrats are in power workplace safety regulations are more likely to be vigorously enforced. But the pursuit of these types of issues has perhaps been crowded out to some extent by issues concerning wealthier Americans.

The Dogs that Didn't Bark: Campaign Contributions and Policy "Non-Responses" to Growing Problems

Not only can the growing power of business in the campaign finance system be seen in observable policy outcomes, it may also explain things that did not happen. Determining why certain issues are kept off the policy agenda is a perennially vexing problem for social scientists. Nevertheless, it is important to address this issue because controlling what policies make it onto the policy agenda in the first place is central to the exercise of political power.[48] If politicians do not seriously consider policy options that would benefit the vast majority of citizens because they are unimportant to or opposed by business or wealthy contributors this would be a very powerful effect of campaign contributions.

Perhaps the best example of this is how policy-makers essentially ignored income inequality and its components parts, such as stagnant wages for low-income workers, which have been growing problems for decades. After the economic problems in recent years which prompted the Occupy Wall Street movement, income inequality emerged as a major political issue. But prior to this spasm of interest there was little discussion of these problems at all, with the exception of John Edwards' presidential campaigns in 2004 and 2008, which described "the two Americas." Even after Occupy Wall Street has thrust these issues onto the agenda, neither party has sought to develop a coherent program that would address the growing economic insecurity faced by most Americans. There are many reasons why this issue was not addressed—including the slow pace of increasing inequality, indifferent public opinion, and other factors—but if campaign contributions focus politicians on issues most important to donors, then it is not surprising that income inequality and stagnant wages for those at the bottom were not a priority.

The decline of organized labor's relative power in the campaign finance system has also probably contributed to the decline of organized labor itself. With fewer resources to offer politicians, organized labor's concerns have been largely absent from the national political agenda. When the Democrats took back both houses of Congress in 2006, they did so with labor providing the smallest share of campaign contributions since the FEC has kept records. Not surprisingly then, though the Democrats did a number of things benefiting workers (such as increasing the minimum wage), they failed to act on the most important priority for the flagging labor movement, a policy called "card check." "Card check" refers to a change in law that would allow organizers trying to create a new union to obtain member signatures on cards, rather than a drawn-out election process, which critics charge creates opportunities for employers to engage in propaganda and intimidation efforts to prevent workers from voting to form a union. In 2007 President Bush would likely have vetoed this legislation, but even with control of all three branches of government after the 2008 election, the Democratic Party did not seriously pursue this policy. Because union power is related to positive economic outcomes for most workers, the failure to act to strengthen unions goes well beyond the organizational interests of labor.[49] It is notoriously difficult to determine why things do not happen. But because parties assist groups in exchange for needed resources it seems likely that if labor provided a greater proportion of funds for Democratic candidates, as was the case prior to the 1980s and 1990s, this card check provision would have been more seriously pursued, even if not ultimately enacted.[50]

There is some tension between the idea that campaign contributions influence mostly non-salient, low-visibility issues which emerges from the existing research and the contention that campaign contributions may influence the ideological direction of major legislation. But this reflects different units of analysis and different mechanisms of campaign contribution influence. In most existing research, including my own, scholars examine how contributions influence individual decision-making, taking current policy makers, issue agendas, and party positions as a given. But who serves in government, which issues are on the agenda, and what positions parties adopt are *not* a given—they can also be influenced by campaign contributions. Campaign contributions may help to elect more conservative politicians in the first place, which importantly shapes policy outcomes. In addition, campaign contributions can shape party platforms and agendas. If both parties pursue more pro-business policies in the hopes of attracting more campaign contributions from business, then after controlling for an individual member of Congress' party affiliation we would not expect to observe an independent effect of campaign contributions on individual behavior. Finally, the balance of power in the campaign finance system may contribute to keeping certain liberal policy alternatives off of the agenda in the first place. This discussion of the possible effects of the growing bias in the campaign finance system was necessarily preliminary and more research needs to be done to examine these questions. Nevertheless, we can see potential ways that the growing business dominance of the campaign finance system may influence public policy.

There is currently a great deal of uncertainty regarding campaign finance regulation due to the de facto deregulation of campaign finance laws at the state and federal level by the Supreme Court. It has taken us a couple of decades to understand how the changes in the campaign finance system introduced in FECA passed in 1974 have affected the political world, and as we can see from the discussion above, we still have much to learn. Thus, it will probably take a number of decades to understand how the major changes that are currently taking place today are affecting policy outcomes. Many critics believe that recent Court decisions will have the effect of favoring those interests with the greatest financial resources, which are generally business interests. After the 2012 election results, it was often stated that Super PACs on the right did not have a major influence on election outcomes, and this seems to be correct. But over the last 30 years, factors that have increased spending overall have probably strengthened business in the policy process because they simply have more resources than labor unions or other organized interests that typically oppose business in the policy process.

Conclusion

It is often alleged by the media and other critics that campaign contributions are nothing more than "legalized bribery." I have argued in this chapter that this is far too simplistic an understanding of how campaign contributions influence policy decisions and outcomes. Yet, it is not correct to say that just because campaign contributions do not work in this blunt, simple manner, that they do not influence outcomes. Indeed, if we view the effect of campaign contributions as constrained by other factors in the policy-making environment and design our studies to identify the more subtle effects of campaign contributions in different policy and institutional contexts, we see clearly that campaign contributions do influence some decisions and policy outputs.

Most research has focused on individual-level decision-making. At the individual level, campaign contributions seem to be most influential when there is uncertainty in the decision-making environment. For members of Congress, this is when party, ideology, and constituency are weak guides to decision-making. For bureaucrats, campaign contributions can influence decision-making in subtle ways depending on the type of decision in question. There is limited research into how campaign contributions may influence aggregate policy outputs and as a result we do not have a good understanding of how the increasing business dominance of the campaign finance system has influenced policy. However, it is notable that just as business began to dominate the campaign finance system economic policy in the United States took a right turn. Though there are many reasons for this change in the direction of policy, some observers argue that changes in campaign finance played an important role in this process and the data are consistent with this interpretation. Even the Democrats have become more reliant on business and the wealthy, and the Democratic Party also embraced more conservative economic policies in recent decades. In addition, it may be that the need to raise money from these sources prevented particular issues, like income inequality, from being addressed at all.

The campaign finance system seems to undergo major changes about once a generation, and we are currently in the midst of what certainly appears to be a major change. The contributions of individuals have become more important, and there are a number of new types of groups that can spend virtually unlimited amounts of money on government and politics with a minimum of regulation. How these changes in the campaign finance system may change the influence of money in the policy process remains to be seen.

Notes

1 http://www.huffingtonpost.com/2009/12/21/how-nebraskas-insurance-c_n_400080.html.
2 Stephen Ansolabehere, John M. DeFigueiredo, and James M. Snyder, "Why Is There so Little Money in U.S. Politics?" *Journal of Economic Perspectives* 17, no. 1 (2003): 105–30.

3 This figure is based on analysis of all contributions from groups or individuals in the 2010 election cycle, available at the Federal Election Commission detailed files web page: http://www.fec.gov/finance/disclosure/ftpdet.shtml

4 John R. Wright, *Interest Groups and Congress: Lobbying, Contributions and Influence* (New York: Longman, 2003).

5 Cletus G. Coughlin, "Domestic Content Legislation: House Voting and the Economic Theory of Regulation," *Economic Inquiry* 23, no. 3 (1985): 437–48; Jonathan I. Silberman and Gary C. Durden, "Determining Legislative Preferences on the Minimum Wage: An Economic Approach," *Journal of Political Economy* 84, no. 2 (1976): 317–28; George J. Stigler, "The Economic Theory of Regulation," *The Bell Journal of Economics and Management* 2, no. 1 (1971): 3–21.

6 Frank R. Baumgartner and Beth L. Leech, *Basic Interests: The Importance of Interest Groups in Politics and in Political Science* (Princeton, N: Princeton University Press, 1998); Christopher Witko, "The Impact of Campaign Contributions on Congressional Behavior," in *Oxford Bibliographies in Political Science,* ed. Rick Valelly (New York: Oxford University Press, 2012).

7 Richard L. Hall and Frank W. Wayman, "Buying Time: Moneyed Interests and the Mobilization of Bias in Congressional Committees," *American Political Science Review* 84, no. 3 (1990): 797–818; John R. Wright, "PACs, Contributions, and Roll Calls: An Organizational Perspective," *American Political Science Review* 79, no. 2 (1985): 400–414.

8 Nolan McCarty and Lawrence S. Rothenberg, "Commitment and the Campaign Contribution Contract," *American Journal of Political Science* 40, no. 3 (1996): 872–904; James M. Snyder, "Campaign Contributions as Investments: The US House of Representatives 1980–86," *Journal of Political Economy* 98, no. 6 (1990): 1195–1227.

9 Dan Clawson, Alan Neustadtl, and Denise Scott, *Money Talks* (New York: Basic Books, 1992).

10 David Austen-Smith. "Campaign Contributions and Access," *American Political Science Review* 89, no. 3 (1995): 566–81.

11 Stephen Ansolabehere, James M. Snyder, and Micky Tripathi, "Are PAC Contributions and Lobbying Linked? New Evidence from the 1995 Lobby Disclosure Act," *Business and Politics* 4, no. 2 (2002): 135–55; Laura I. Langbein, "Money and Access: Some Empirical Evidence," *Journal of Politics* 48, no. 4 (1986): 1052–62.

12 John R. Wright, *Interest Groups and Congress: Lobbying, Contributions and Influence* (New York: Longman, 2003); Arthur T. Denzau and Michael C. Munger, "Legislators and Interest Groups: How Unorganized Interests Get Represented," *American Political Science Review* 80, no. 1: 89–106.

13 Laura I. Langbein, "Money and Access: Some Empirical Evidence," *Journal of Politics* 48, no. 4 (1986): 1052–62; Maureen Shea and Ellen Miller, *PACs on PACs: The View from the Inside* (Washington, DC: Center for Responsive Politics, 1988).

14 Frank L. Davis, "Balancing the Perspective on PAC Contributions: In Search of an Impact on Roll Calls," *American Politics Quarterly* 21, no. 2 (1993): 205–22; Diana M. Evans, "PAC Contributions and Roll-call Voting: Conditional Power," in *Interest Group Politics,* 2nd ed., eds. Allan J. Cigler and Burdette Loomis (Washington: Congressional Quarterly, 1986); Matthew C. Fellowes and Patrick J. Wolf, "Funding Mechanisms and Policy Instruments: How Business Campaign Contributions Influence Congressional Votes," *Political Research Quarterly* 57, no. 2 (2004): 315–24; Richard Fleisher, "PAC Contributions and Congressional Voting On National Defense," *Legislative Studies Quarterly* 28, no, 3 (1993): 391–409.

15 Jan Leith Schroedel, "Campaign Contributions and Legislative Outcomes," *Western Political Quarterly* 40, no. 3 (1986): 371–89.

16 Stacy B. Gordon, "All Votes Are Not Created Equal: Campaign Contributions and Critical Votes," *Journal of Politics* 63, no. 1 (2001): 249–69; Wright, "PACs, Contributions, and Roll Calls."

17 Richard L. Hall and Frank W. Wayman, "Buying Time: Moneyed Interests and the Mobilization of Bias in Congressional Committees," *American Political Science Review* 84, no. 3 (1990): 797–818.

18 See, for example, these two studies arguing that issue visibility conditions the impact of campaign contributions: Woodrow Jones Jr., and K. Robert Keiser, "Issue Visibility and the Effects of PAC Money," *Social Science Quarterly* 68, no. 1 (1987): 170–76; Alan Neustadtl, "Interest-Group PACsmanship: An Analysis of Campaign Contributions, Issue Visibility and Legislative Impact," *Social Forces* 69 (1990): 549–64.

19 Ansolabehere, DeFigueiredo, and Snyder, "Why Is There So Little Money in U.S. Politics?"

20 Christopher Witko, "PACs, Issue Context and Congressional Decision-Making," *Political Research Quarterly* 59, no. 2 (2006): 283–95.

21 Roland Zullo, "Public-Private Contracting and Political Reciprocity," *Political Research Quarterly* 59, no. 2 (2006): 273–81.

22 Christopher Witko, "Measuring the Stringency of State Campaign Finance Regulation," *State Politics and Policy Quarterly* 5, no. 3(2005): 295–310.

23 Patrik Jonsson, "A Family Legacy and the Threat of Scandal," *Christian Science Monitor,* May 27, 2003.

24 Ken Debow and John C. Syer, *Power and Politics in California* (New York: Longman, 2003), p. 166.

25 Jeffrey M. Drope and Wendy L. Hansen, "Purchasing Protection?: The Effect of Political Spending on US Trade Policy," *Political Research Quarterly* 57, no. 1 (2004): 27–37.

26 Drope and Hansen, "Purchasing Protection?"; Christopher Witko, "Campaign Contributions, Access and Government Contracting," *Journal of Public Administration Research and Theory* 21, no. 4 (2011): 761–78; Christopher Witko, "Party Government and Variation in Corporate Influence on Agency Decision-Making: OSHA Regulation, 1981-2006." *Social Science Quarterly* (forthcoming).

27 Sanford C. Gordon and Catherine Hafer, "Flexing Muscle: Corporate Political Expenditures as Signals to the Bureaucracy," *American Political Science Review* 99, no. 2 (2005): 245–61.

28 Christopher Witko, "Campaign Contributions, Access and Government Contracting."

29 Roland Zullo, "Public-Private Contracting and Political Reciprocity," *Political Research Quarterly* 59, no. 2 (2006): 273–81.

30 Christopher Witko, "Party Government and Variation."

31 Damon M. Cann, "Justice for Sale? Campaign Contributions and Judicial Decision-Making," *State Politics and Policy Quarterly* 7, no. 3 (2007): 281–97.

32 Thomas M. Ferguson, *Golden Rule: The Investment Theory of Party Competition and the Logic of Money-Driven Political Systems* (Chicago: University of Chicago Press, 1995).

33 Dennis P. Quinn and Robert Y. Shapiro, "Business Political Power: The Case of Taxation," *The American Political Science Review* 85, no. 3 (1991): 851–74; Mark A. Smith, *American Business and Political Power* (Chicago: University of Chicago Press, 2000), chap. 6; John T. Williams and Brian K. Collins, "The Political Economy of Corporate Taxation," *American Journal of Political Science* 14, no. 1(1997): 208–44.

34 Christopher Witko and Adam J. Newmark, "Business Mobilization and Public Policy in the U.S. States," *Social Science Quarterly* 86, no. 2 (2005): 356–67.

35 Larry Bartels, *America Unequal* (Princeton, NJ: Princeton University Press, 2010); Martin Gilens, *Affluence and Influence: Economic Inequality and Political Power in America* (Princeton, NJ: Princeton University Press, 2012).

36 Jacob S. Hacker and Paul Pierson, *Winner Take All Politics* (New York: Simon and Schuster, 2010).

37 John R. Wright, "Interest Groups, Congressional Reform and Party Government in the United States," *Legislative Studies Quarterly* 25, no. 2 (2000): 217–35.

38 Jeffrey Milyo, David Primo, and Timothy Groseclose, "Corporate PAC Campaign Contributions in Perspective," *Business and Politics* 2, no. 1 (2000): 75–88.

39 Ulrike Malmendier and Klaus M. Schmidt, "You Owe Me," unpublished manuscript.

40 Herbert E. Alexander and Caroline D. Jones, eds, *Contributions of National-level Political Committees to Incumbents and Candidates for Public Offices, 1968* (Princeton, NJ: Citizens' Research Foundation, 1971); Wright, "Interest Groups, Congressional Reform and Party Government in the United States."

41 Thomas Ferguson and Joel Ferguson, *Right Turn: The Decline of the Democrats and the Future of American Politics* (New York: Hill and Wang, 1986).

42 Bartels, *America Unequa*; Gilens, *Affluence and Influence.*

43 I utilize a measure of policy liberalism developed by Erikson, MacKuen, and Stimson (2002), which focuses on important, substantive changes in laws across a variety of policy areas. This is important since, as we argue, so many types of policy can potentially influence income inequality. This measure examines important policy change by focusing on the crucial public laws identified by Mayhew (1991) and coding them for liberalism and conservatism. See Robert S. Erikson, Michael B. MacKuen, and James A. Stimson, *The Macropolity* (New York: Cambridge University Press, 2002); David R. Mayhew, *Divided We Govern: Party Control, Lawmaking and Investigations, 1946–1990* (New Haven, CT: Yale University Press, 1991).

44 Jacob S. Hacker and Paul Pierson, *Winner Take All Politics* (New York: Simon and Schuster, 2010).

45 Jeffrey M. Berry, *The New Liberalism: The Rising Power of Citizen Groups* (Washington, DC: Brookings Institution Press, 1999).

46 Andrew Gelman, David Park, Boris Shor, Joseph Bafumi, and Jeronimo Cortina, *Red State, Blue State, Rich State, Poor State: Why Americans Vote the Way They Do* (Princeton, NJ: Princeton University Press, 2008).

47 Peter L. Francia, John C. Green, Paul S. Herrnson, Lynda W. Powell, and Clyde Wilcox, "Limousine Liberals and Corporate Conservatives: The Financial Constituencies of the Democratic and Republican Parties" *Social Science Quarterly* 86, no. 4 (2005): 761–78.

48 Peter Bacharach and Morton Baratz, "The Two Faces of Power," *American Political Science Review* 56, no. 4): 947–52 (1962); E.E. Schattschneider, *The Semisovereign People: A Realist's View of Democracy* (Hinsdale, IL: Dryden Press, 1975).

49 Bruce Western, "A Comparative Study of Working Class Disorganization: Union Decline in 18 Advanced Capitalist Countries," *American Sociological Review* 60, no. 2 (1995): 179–201.

50 Christopher Witko, "The Ecology of Party-Organized Interest Relationships," *Polity* 41, no. 2 (2009): 211–34.

Chapter 10

Understanding the Influence of Lobbying in the U.S. Congress

Preferences, Networks, Money, and Bills

Holly Brasher and Jason Britt

One of the central questions associated with lobbying is whether interest groups can influence outcomes in Congress through their lobbying activity. They are widely assumed to do so. In an interview about the legislative process associated with fiscal cliff negotiations, a senator made the following observation:

> Look, I'm not in the room so I can't say with certainty, but I am very hopeful that they are making progress. And look, it would be wise on their part not to come too quickly with a deal, because that would give all the interest groups a chance to get organized and try to kill it. And we know that on the right, on the left, special interest groups are just salivating at the chance to attack any agreement.[1]

Along with members of Congress, the American public also perceives interest groups to have an important influence. Currently a majority of the American public does not approve of the performance of the U.S. Congress and some of the cynicism toward the institution comes from the perception that Congress serves special interests rather than the public interest.[2]

For the functioning of American democracy, this question is of great significance. If lobbying does influence policy outcomes, then it shapes sweeping decisions about the allocation of federal money, legal rights, and monetary benefits for large groups in society as well as smaller and more narrowly targeted decisions about the development of solid oxide fuel cells by defense contractors, hospital payments for graduate medical education, and Grand Canyon air tour curfews.

A recent example of lobbying activity can be seen with the Marketplace Fairness Act, a bill that would require online retailers to collect sales taxes for state and local government from their Internet sales. The Marketplace Fairness Act attracted an array of interest groups lobbying on both sides of the issue with Wal-Mart and the National Retail Federation lobbying in favor of the legislation and online retailer eBay leading opponents of the bill.[3] Amazon received pressure from the states and ultimately joined the side of the brick-and-mortar businesses and state and local governments even though it is an online retail business. The bill divided Republicans who were split in by their desire to oppose new taxes but also to support Main Street businesses. This legislation would have a broad impact on consumers, businesses, and state and local governments. Because lobbying is an integral part of the process it is important to understand, in a systematic way, the role it has in shaping the outcome of legislation in Congress.

The empirical studies that directly address this question are curiously limited, however, relative to the centrality of the question. Lack of access to appropriate data provides at least a partial explanation for why there are not more studies on the influence of lobbying. This chapter makes a case for the data and approach that that are needed to advance our understanding of the nature of the influence, if any, that lobbying has. Lobbying is a complex process and much of it is conducted privately. However, we have currently have both data and methodology that when exploited fully will allow researchers to draw new empirically based conclusions about the relationship between lobbying, influence, and outcomes in Congress.

An advance in availability of data began in 1995 when the U.S. Congress passed the Lobbying Disclosure Act (LDA). This new law instituted a requirement that organizations lobbying Congress and the executive branch register with Congress.[4] This provides data to empirically research many of the popular claims and scholarly conclusions about interest group behavior and influence on congressional policymaking. Prior to this development, much of the research on interest groups and lobbying relied on sources such commercially available directories of Washington lobbyists that were incomplete, inconsistently produced, and that provided no information about the scope and the focus of interest group lobbying efforts beyond simply the listing of the organization. The reports required by the LDA in contrast, provide a detailed and systematic account of the lobbying organizations' activity, including a general description of organization's business or activities, lobbying expenditures, the target of the lobbying activity (the House, the Senate, or the executive branch agency) and the issue for which the organization lobbied.

The LDA data are not a perfect measurement instrument, however, and they present challenges. The purpose of this chapter is to present the ways in which some of the challenges in data and analysis can be overcome in order to develop a complete model of lobbying and influence. In the chapter we discuss ways to measure and utilize organization preferences, networks, and campaign contributions. First, we present the results of content analysis of the digitized text that was produced by Discovertext. This software enables the use of filters, searching, indexing, and annotation to facilitate the content analysis process that has been, in the past, a slow and labor intensive process. The data contain over a million entries that report the issues for which the organizations are lobbying. This text can be used to begin to identify the organizations' preferences for outcomes. Entries in the reports identify statements of preference within the text where organizations report their position on the bill or the issue. Second, we present results from social network analysis of the structure of the lobbying community. Social network analysis can be used to further establish preferences through an analysis of shared relationships among clients. While this methodology is now widely employed in political science, this chapter identifies the ways in which the features of the lobbying data can be used to create global network parameters that can be applied to the study of the policy process. Finally, in addition to the methodological approaches, we show the ways in which studies of the legislative process can fully exploit the features of the lobbying data that now connect campaign contributions with the organizations that lobby. The recent years of the data associate lobbying expenditures with campaign contributions through the registrants' identification number and therefore provide a way to model the relationship between the two types of influence strategies.

The chapter includes the following sections. It first briefly presents a review the relevant literature in both political science and economics. It then presents the different components of a comprehensive model of lobbying and the legislative process. Each of these sections proposes an approach to both data and methodology to capitalize on available data. Finally, following this, the chapter identifies ongoing limitations in the available data on congressional bills that is needed to evaluate lobbying influence in greater detail. In the conclusion, the chapter presents possibilities for empirically driven conclusions about the influence of lobbying in the U.S. Congress.

The Political Science Literature on the Influence of Lobbying in Congress

The absence of work that directly focuses on the influence of lobbying is apparent in a review of recent work in political science. Important empirical work on interest groups and lobbying often address questions that are not directly related to influence on outcomes. A number of recent studies employing sophisticated analytical tools focus on related questions including the function of lobbyists, whether lobbyists mislead legislators, whether organizations lobby, how organizations allocate their lobbying resources, and who they lobby.[5]

A limited number of other studies use the lobbying disclosure data but similarly do not directly address questions of influence. Aaron Dusso uses a random sample of bills from the 1996 lobbying disclosure filings.[6] Dusso's study and an earlier study using the same data source provide valuable conclusions and explanations of variations in levels of lobbying across bills, but they do not directly address the impact of this activity on outcomes or lobbying influence.[7] Another study using the LDA data evaluates the relationship between lobbying expenditures and firms' stock prices.[8] Other studies identify the reasons why organizations mobilize and become active in Washington.[9]

Studies that *do* directly address the question of interest group influence often do not use the lobbying disclosure data. Instead they have used campaign contribution data, companies' financial statements, or original data collected specifically for the purpose of the study.[10]

In a recent study that directly addresses the question of the relationship between lobbying and legislative outcomes, Matt Grossmann and Kurt Pyle use a variety of models and measures to evaluate the relationship.[11] Using interest group support for or opposition to bills, and levels of lobbying on bills, Grossmann and Pyle find only limited evidence that lobbying has an influence on bill outcomes. Grossman and Pyle preface their results by identifying two persistent impediments to establishing definitively the influence of lobbing on outcomes. The first is that the causal ordering of lobbying is difficult to establish because lobbying may cause a bill to advance, but lobbying activity may be caused by bills that are advancing as interests seek to capitalize on the action. Second, they note that it is difficult to establish the preferences for the lobbying organizations for outcomes. Some of those lobbying may oppose a bill, others may support it. These observations point to the additional work that must be done as we continue to try to specify more clearly the relationship between lobbying and outcomes.

The Economics Literature on the Influence of Lobbying in Congress

Economists do a better job than political scientists of using both the LDA data and of trying to quantify the relationship between lobbying and outcomes. However, while the relevant economics literature makes intriguing and important contributions, when economists write about politics, the politics is usually missing.

One body of literature in economics measures indirect relationships between lobbying and outcomes. In these studies, the dependent variable is not the influence on outcomes; it is the return on investment to the lobbying entity. Inputs in the form of lobbying go in, and results in the form of firm benefits come out. In the middle, the intervening political processes are not specified.

There are a wide variety of issues and industries analyzed in this literature. The following studies demonstrate the prevalence of this model. Frank Yu and Xiaoyun Yu find that higher levels of lobbying lower the likelihood of fraud detection.[12] Another study identifies the firm level determinants of lobbying and shows the benefits of lobbying in the form of firm performance.[13] John M. De Figueiredo and Charles M. Cameron assess the returns on lobbying in the form of earmarks received by universities, given legislator positions on House and Senate Appropriations Committees.[14] Another study assesses lobbying and immigration by sector, finding that lobbying does influence levels of temporary work visas within industries.[15] Researchers also used public comments to determine two general sides in the lobbying on Sarbanes-Oxley (SOX) during the implementation stage of the legislation at the SEC, finding that stock returns were higher for investors who lobbied for strict implementation.[16]

Finally, one set of authors report findings but also caution against drawing conclusions about causality. They find that lobbying by financial institutions is associated with lending behavior and with a higher probability of receiving funds during the bailout but state that the causality may be the reverse, with bailout funds being targeted to those who lend.[17]

There is an absence of congressional or agency processes in these models, and research is needed that will make an important contribution to the understanding of lobbying by analyzing the legislative process and clearly identifiable legislative inputs and outputs. Influence is difficult to claim absent any evidence that interests intended to influence that specific policy.[18]

Preferences, Networks, Money, and Bills: Modeling the Impact of Lobbying on Outcomes

First and foremost, a study of lobbying must include the elements of the policymaking process. These are well understood, and a significant literature has developed around models of legislative outcomes in Congress. However, in order to understand lobbying, and indeed, to fully understand legislative outcomes in general, it is important to complete these models of legislative outcomes by incorporating the role of interest groups, lobbying activity, and campaign contributions.

The lobbying data contain a large number of different types of information. It is important to incorporate the features of the lobbying activity that are appropriate to the research question. For example, levels of lobbying activity vary across issues and over time. Budgeting and Appropriations, Health Issues, Taxation and Internal Revenue Code, and Defense are listed on the largest number of reports out of the issue categories. In 2004, however, Torts moved from 46 overall to 26 in the number of reports listing it as the issue that was the subject of a given lobbying effort. A bill dealing with class action lawsuits was the target of extensive lobbying activity as business and insurance companies faced off against lawyers and consumer advocates and the category moved up in the attention it received from lobbyists in 2004. If the research question involves attention to issues it is important to incorporate the variation in attention that occurs over time.

Spending patterns also vary across issues. For example, spending in some categories is dominated by behemoth firms such as such as Medco Health Solutions, a large pharmaceutical interest which spends in both the Health Issues and Pharmacy categories. If the research question involves the impact of spending, instances of asymmetrical spending should be incorporated in the model.[19]

Because of the numerous types of information it contains the lobbying disclosure data allow us to fill in a number of missing pieces in models of lobbying and interest group influence in Congress. They provide information organizations' goals, preferences, expenditures, and characteristics that we do not have from any other source. Beginning with organization preferences, the following sections identify the ways in which the lobbying disclosure data can be used to reveal the connection between lobbying and results in the form of policy outcomes.

The Preferences of the Lobbying Interest Groups

Perhaps the greatest limitation in what we can conclude about the impact of lobbying is that we do not have a ready record of what interest groups *want* when they lobby a legislator or a staff member. The LDA data do not provide a perfect measure of preferences, but they contain more information that we have had before.

The lobbying disclosure forms include a general issue code for issue areas including Transportation, Banking, Accounting, and so forth. However, a second field in the lobbying reports asks the filer of the report to identify the specific issues for which the organization is lobbying. The filing guidelines ask filers to provide bill numbers where possible and even contextual information so that the layman can understand what the organization is reporting. The issue field is a much more specific statement of the lobbying issue than the general issue code. Along with bill numbers it sometimes includes specific provisions in bills, and in some cases the organization's stated intention for the lobbying effort.[20]

This component of the data provides one possibility for connecting *specific* lobbying objectives with policy outcomes. To use what is in these fields in the reports, some content analysis is necessary. Even with the guidelines on how to report specific issues, filers of the lobbying reports use their own language, without format, and some specific issues are reported in a detailed and lengthy way while other filers disregard the Senate's directive and report nothing but a bill number, standing alone.

We have greater capacity to analyze digitized text currently than in previous years. Because of the currently available tools, the task of mastering the volume and detail of data is no longer prohibitive. We executed this task using Discovertext, which is text analytic software.

The content of greatest value is those action words that provide a stated intent for an outcome by the organization. In other words, reports that include words such as *support, oppose, monitor,* and *advocate* should provide direct information about the organizations preferences for the outcome of a specific issue.

Table 10.1 is a frequency table with the distribution of the specific action words in the data along with number of reports that contain none of the identified action words. The number of items that contain any of the action words is relatively small. However, the action words provide one measurement strategy for identifying preferences and can be used to validate other measures.

The results are presented using a comparison between the stated intentions of new registrants for the 2007–2008 filing period to all organizations active for those years. The table also includes the result of a chi-square test and shows that the distribution for the words that indicate the organization preferences are different for those that are already active in lobbying and those that have newly registered.

One interesting thing to note is the relationship between these results to previous findings that a status quo bias dominates lobbying efforts.[21] Here the word "support" is by far the most prevalent of the action words. Although this is intriguing in light of earlier conclusions, further evaluation of the data is needed to determine whether this indicates that most lobbying interests are seeking change rather than the status quo. This distribution may be observed because of reluctance by the lobbying organizations to report, in writing, a blatant effort to thwart the legislative process. In other words, there may be a social acceptability bias in

Table 10.1 Distribution and Chi Square Test of Action Words by New Registrants and All Lobbying Organizations for 2007–2008

	All Reports	Reports from New Registrants
Advocate	978	90
Monitor	5,234	238
Support	10,848	814
Oppose	1,046	14
Other	235,551	21,305
	236,597	21,319

Note: Chi square 4 degrees of freedom Pearson: 214.1 (p<0)

the reporting. However, the finding does present a starting point for a conversation about what organizations are actually trying to achieve in their lobbying efforts.

Future research can benefit by fully mining these data. Because the data are not a perfect measure, however, the next section presents an additional method for measuring organizations' preferences for outcomes using other components of the LDA data in a different way.

Networks as Indicators of Preferences, Organization Strength, Centrality, and Interconnectedness

Applying social network analysis tools to the lobbying disclosure data also gives us analytical leverage to establish "sides" for an issue. Lobbying firms avoid taking clients where there is a conflict of interest with another client and are unlikely to lobby for a bill for one client and against the same bill for another. Information about sides and preferences for outcomes can be derived by defining networks of organizations lobbying on individual bills or within the lobbying community as a whole. We can use what we know about lobbying firms to discern organization preferences from the networks by modeling these shared associations to infer support for or opposition to a bill.

In addition, by using the shared associations we can produce global network parameters to evaluate the level of influence associated with particular network characteristics. We can use this approach to capitalize on earlier findings and conclusions about relationships among organized interests. For example, in the landmark study *The Hollow Core,* John P. Heinz and his colleagues thoroughly explore the question of whether there is a structure to interest group representation.[22] Specifically, they evaluate whether some of the participants, by virtue of their central location in policy networks, control or mediate the policy process. On the contrary, they find that no dominant central actors are evident and assert that there are no "hub" positions. Rather, they find that there are specialists operating in particular domains influencing outcomes on specific pieces of policy, and that there are no dominant players that cross policy domains.

There have been changes in the lobbying community since that time that make additional research on this question worthwhile. One important difference from this earlier study is that the authors found, at that time, that about two-thirds of the lobbyists they studied were in-house employees that worked for organizations rather than lobbyists working for contract lobbying firms with multiple clients.[23] The lobbying disclosure data indicate that only a small percentage of organizations are now represented by their own in-house lobbying apparatus. Of the 79,721 unique registrant-client relationships listed by the Secretary of the Senate, only 5% (3,949) list the registrant and the client as the same organization. In other words, this 5% are organizations lobbying on their own behalf. This new phase of representation may reflect significant consolidations of power, expertise, and connectedness. A handful of lobbying firms at the top such as Patton Boggs, Akin Gump, Cassidy and Associates, and Van Scoyoc and Associates report far more revenue than smaller firms in their industry.

Using the centrality concept from *The Hollow Core*, there are social network measures of centrality that can be used to replicate aspects of their study. Specifically, what we present in the Figures 10.1 through 10.3 are closeness and betweenness centrality parameters. Closeness centrality calculates the length of the path from an organization to other entities in the network. A large closeness measure indicates that the organization has the shortest path to others in the network, which can provide the organization the best opportunity to understand the activity throughout the network. Betweenness centrality measures the connection between organizations in the network and can serve as a measure of information flow from one part of the network to the other. Incorporating these parameters in a multivariate model would allow us to establish whether high levels of centrality are associated with lobbying success.

The contents of the LDA can provide numerous indicators to use as measures of connectedness. These include organizations' shared relationship from lobbying within the same issue categories or for the same bills and campaign contributions to the same candidates or political committees. Of course, the type of organization (such as professional associations, state and local governments, and corporations) can also be used to create similarity measures and identify subgroups.

We present an example of these measures in Figure 10.1. We use registrant and client identification numbers to identify state and local governments that have shared connections as clients of the same lobbying firm. These reflect the place of the lobbying firm within the lobbying community. Networks are generated using i2 Analyst's Notebook software with the 2007–2008 LDA data.[24] In Figure 10.1 Van Scoyoc Associates has a betweenness measure of 100%, while Marlowe & Company has a value of 85.7%.

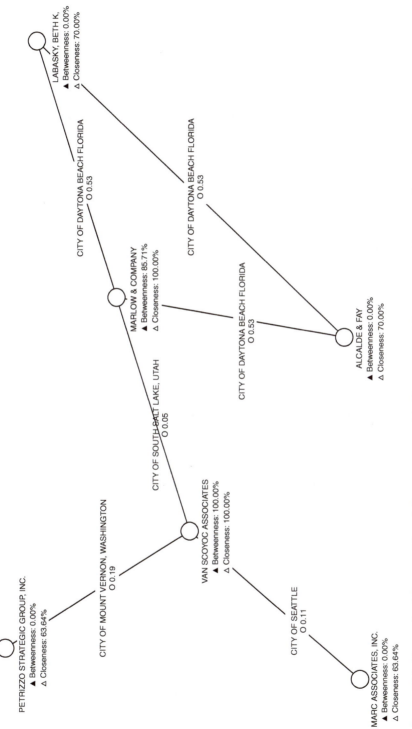

PETRIZZO STRATEGIC GROUP, INC.
▲ Betweenness: 0.00%
△ Closeness: 63.64%

CITY OF MOUNT VERNON, WASHINGTON
O 0.19

VAN SCOYOC ASSOCIATES
▲ Betweenness: 100.00%
△ Closeness: 100.00%

CITY OF SEATTLE
O 0.11

MARC ASSOCIATES, INC.
▲ Betweenness: 0.00%
△ Closeness: 63.64%

CITY OF SOUTH SALT LAKE, UTAH
O 0.05

MARLOW & COMPANY
▲ Betweenness: 85.71%
△ Closeness: 100.00%

CITY OF DAYTONA BEACH FLORIDA
O 0.53

CITY OF DAYTONA BEACH FLORIDA
O 0.53

LABASKY, BETH K.
▲ Betweenness: 0.00%
△ Closeness: 70.00%

CITY OF DAYTONA BEACH FLORIDA
O 0.53

ALCALDE & FAY
▲ Betweenness: 0.00%
△ Closeness: 70.00%

Figure 10.1 Network of State and Local Governments with Closeness and Betweenness Measures for Lobbying Organizations

Figures 10.2 and 10.3 show the network of all corporations lobbying in 2007–2008 along with link parameters based on the number of overlapping clients of all types. The figure shows one large and complex network, with a collection of subnetworks. On the lower right hand side of the figure are the relationships between only one registrant and one client. Figure 10.3 is an enlargement of one of the subnetworks from the full image.

A number of other metrics can be used with components of the LDA data. While here we have just used shared connections between clients to create the network, a set of measures used in network analysis, such as density (the edges in a subnetwork expressed as a proportion of the maximum possible number of edges in the same network), degree distribution (distribution of the number of edges associated with a node in a subnetwork), and average path length (the average of the distances between pairs of nodes in the network), can also be used to identify subgroups.[25] Subgroups are areas of the larger network that are densely connected and show some degree of separation from the rest of the network.

In many analyses of lobbying, lobbying expenditures are used as a measure of lobbying effort. But lobbying takes place in context with the other organizations that are also engaged in lobbying and spending alone modeled as a solitary action by each interest is insufficient. The network associations of all groups active on a bill along with a model of their relationships to one another will allow us to infer information about the preferences of clients and their relative position within the interest group community as a whole and what influence that has on the legislative progress of individual bills.

Campaign Contributions and Timing

So far we have argued for the inclusion of measures of organization preferences and information about the relationship of organizations to others in the lobbying community. We argue in this section for the inclusion of another component in the study of the exercise of influence—campaign contributions. In an interview on CNN, former Vice President Al Gore noted the relationship between the timing of campaign contributions and legislation, saying that "fundraisers are often scheduled by special interests, according to the legislative calendar when particular bills come up. The same conversations involve legislation and fundraising."[26]

Those who study interest group politics and the legislative process have incorporated campaign contributions into their models. However, evidence of the influence of PAC contributions is varied and inconsistent.[27] In a study using social network analysis, Matt Grossmann and Casey B. Dominguez show that networks of campaign contributions "appears multidimemsional and driven by a bipartisan core of diverse actors" and that "ties among interest groups in legislative debate do not match the picture of two competing party coalitions."[28] This conclusion produces the expectation that campaign contributions and lobbying expenditures by organizations are motivated by strategies that diverge in important ways. Efforts to model the relationship require an awareness of contribution patterns

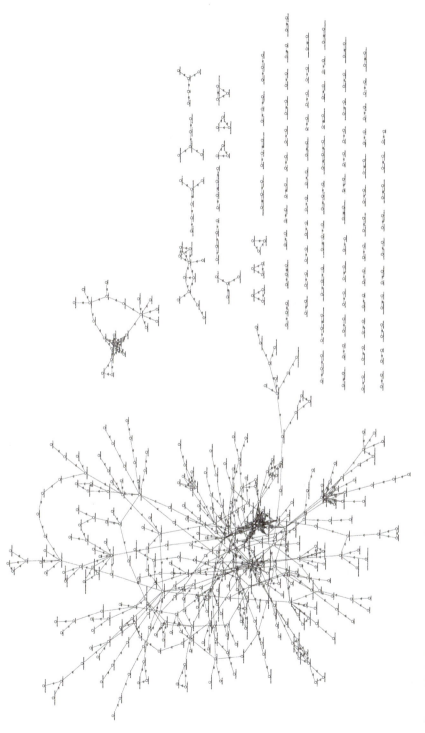

Figure 10.2 Connections between Registrants and Clients for Corporations: Corporations Network

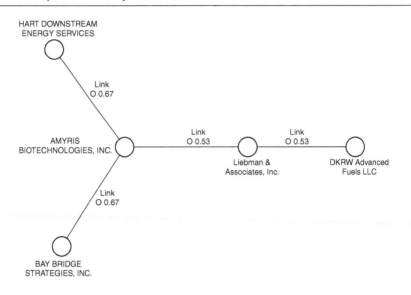

Figure 10.3 Corporation Subnetwork

combined with an expectation that organizations will vary in their utilization of campaign contributions as a component of their lobbying strategy.

In incorporating campaign contributions, the relationship between the timing of legislative action, lobbying, and campaign contributions will be important for establishing causality. The lobbying disclosure activity reports are filed quarterly and therefore are not particularly precise for determining the chronological order of lobbying behavior and congressional action. However, campaign contributions are reported with more precise dates in filings that accompany the lobbying reports and the contribution activity can be connected with the lobbying activity through registrants' unique identification numbers that are used in reporting both types of activity. How organizations shape, respond to, and influence the policy agenda are processes that are inherently temporal in character.

Figure 10.4 compares the contribution activity with the new registrants for 2007–2008 with those of all Federal Election Campaign Act (FECA) contributions from lobbying organizations for the same period. This is a first pass at making a comparison between two groups that, because of their different relationship with the lobbying community (one set is newcomers, the other set is already active), may have different strategies. The graph shows some variations but also similarities in the timing of contributions. Although these two categorizations may not reveal different strategies, other ways of categorizing differences between lobbying participants may. However, what Figure 10.4 does reveal is that there is an ebb and flow of campaign contributions over time. Contributing activity is not constant.

We can assume that the timing of campaign contributions is often meaningful. The second thing to consider is the relationship between levels of campaign

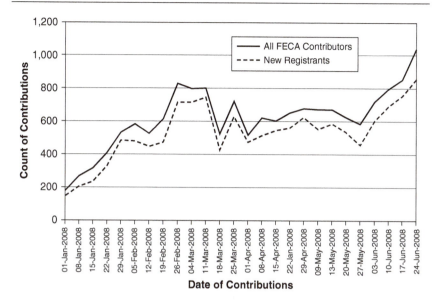

Figure 10.4 FECA Campaign Contributions for New Lobbying Registrants and All Contributors

contributions and lobbying. Figure 10.5 explores that relationship. It shows the relationship between the amount spent for campaign contribution and the amount spent on lobbying. Figure 10.6 shows the relationship between the number of lobbying reports (as a measure of activity) and the number of campaign contributions. Both of levels of spending and levels of activity may show a relationship between the two types of influence strategies.

Both figures contain two plots. The first shows the raw data. For both spending and activity, there are cases with extreme values. Some interests far out lobby and out contribute others to such an extent that the raw data are exponential. The second graph for each figure shows the logged values of the raw data. Logging values put the data on a more condensed scale and allows linear relationships to emerge when the data are plotted.

In the graph on the left in Figure 10.5, the extreme outlier at the top right is Patton Boggs LLC, one of the largest lobbying firms in DC. At the extreme lower right is the Chamber of Commerce of the United States with an extraordinary level of spending for lobbying but a very limited expenditure on FECA contributions.

In Figure 10.6 the case at the extreme top left is Deloitte, LLP, a financial services firm. The case at the extreme right hand side is again Patton Boggs, LLP. The raw data do not indicate a simple linear relationship between campaign contributions and lobbying expenditures; any modeling strategy must model the relationship between those two effectively or important aspects of the relationship will be missed. To fully assess the impact of lobbying, research must incorporate the

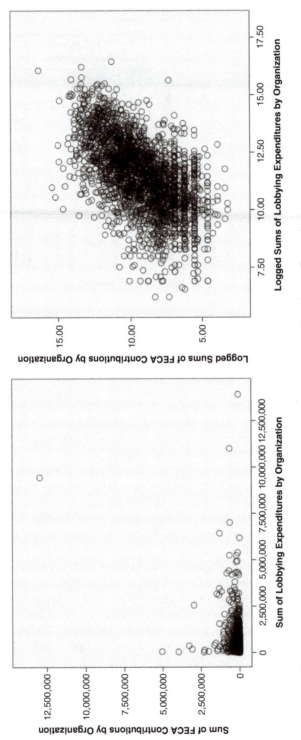

Figure 10.5 The Relationship between Sums of Campaign Contributions and Lobbying Expenditures

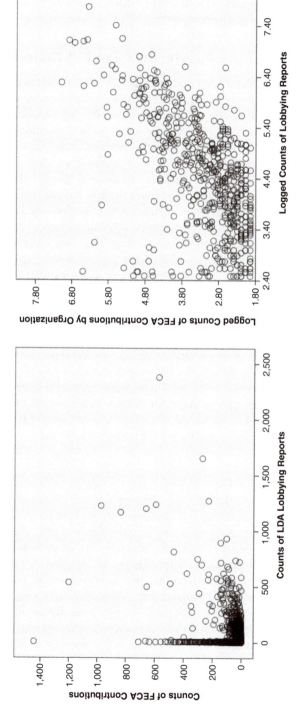

Figure 10.6 The Relationship between the Number of Campaign Contributions and Lobbying Activity

goal of the lobbying effort, the relationship of the lobbying organization to other organizations that lobby, and the relationship between lobbying expenditures and campaign contributions as core components of the lobbying effort.

The Last Piece of the Puzzle: Bills and Bill Content

Finally, the lobbying effort must be connected with bills and issues in Congress. Data from the Congressional Bills Project,[29] with comprehensive information about bills, bill topic codes, sponsors, and congressional committees, provide the best complement to the LDA. However, we know that organizations often seek to shape the content of the bill and specific provisions rather than just working on whether a bill passes or fails. A perfect model in an ideal world would include a detailed measure of the content of congressional bills and would provide some way to connect the lobbying effort with the specific provisions. With the general listing of bills by the lobbying organizations unaccompanied by information about the specific provisions that matter to the organization, both of these things are lacking. Many are omnibus bills of staggering complexity and it is difficult to discern with multiple provisions what is of interest to any individual lobbying organization. With new methodologies for analyzing digitized text, perhaps a future project will undertake the mammoth task of coding bill content at a detailed level, for this is an important missing piece of the puzzle. And perhaps new data or innovative data gathering strategies will reveal organizations' interests in the specific components of a bill.

Until such time as we have an ideal world and perfect data, the information in the Congressional Bills Project, the lobbying disclosure data, and information about the legislative process can be used to answer a significant number of questions about when interest groups shape outcomes, which groups shape outcomes, and why they are able to do so. We currently have the informational resources to add significantly to our understanding of the impact of lobbying.

Conclusion

Why is the exercise of influence through lobbying an understudied phenomenon? This chapter makes the argument that challenges of data have presented obstacles that have not yet been overcome. It also presents the argument that appropriate methodologies now exist to make the available data effect tools for answering this bedrock question about the functioning of Congress. We should now be able to address the popular perception that lobbyists control policymaking. Future work can draw strongly supported empirical conclusions about whether this is true, conditionally true, or not true. The legislative process includes large legislative battles with extraordinary sets of interests configured into competitive networks, smaller policy areas that produce bills that are only of interest to the relevant professional associations, and narrow pieces of legislation that are only of interest to one or a few groups. Dynamic models that include organization preferences, networks, and campaign contributions can accommodate these variations. Particularly with open source databases capable of handling and manipulating millions of observations, software tools for text analytics, and various types of software for network analysis, the challenges can be overcome.

A more cynical view suggest that perhaps the prosaic question of the influence of lobbying and interest groups on outcomes is not a sufficiently recondite or sophisticated topic to be of interest to political scientists. Legislators, the media, and the public have already concluded that special interests have a significant influence on outcomes. Perhaps it is a forgone conclusion. In this chapter, we encourage a renewed focus on this topic. It is as yet understudied, incompletely understood, and at the same time of great interest for what we can say about the functioning and effectiveness for the policymaking process in the U.S. Congress.

Notes

1 Senator Kent Conrad (D-ND) in an interview on *Andrea Mitchell Reports* on MSNBC, December 11, 2012.
2 The American National Election Studies (www.electionstudies.org) reports a survey item that asks whether "the government is pretty much run by a few big interests looking out for themselves or that it is run for the benefit of all the people?" The percentage of those answering "a few big interests" was 69% in 2008, up from about 56% in 2004.
3 Shawn Zeller, "With Sales Tax on the Line, Lawmakers Weigh Options," *CQ Weekly*, April 8, 2013, 614–15, http://library.cqpress.com/cqweekly/weeklyreport113-000004251304.
4 Legislation was passed in 1946 in an early effort to provide some accountability and transparency for lobbying. The Regulation of Lobbying Act of 1946 provided for some record of lobbying activity, however it applied only to those organizations lobbying Congress and only for those who solicited and received contributions where the primary purpose was lobbying. In response to the widely acknowledged limitations of the 1946 Act, Congress began to act on new lobbying legislation beginning in 1967. In 1983, the Justice Department determined that the existing law was unenforceable. As reported in "Lobbying Disclosure Bill Dies," efforts to reform the system were made periodically from 1967 until 1994 and finally succeeded in 1995. *CQ Almanac 1994*, 50th ed. (Washington, DC: Congressional Quarterly, 1995), 36–42, http://library.cqpress.com/cqalmanac/cqal94–1102367.
5 Richard L. Hall and Alan V. Deardorff, "Lobbying as Legislative Subsidy," *American Political Science Review* 100, no. 1 (2006): 69–84; Peggy Lopipero, Dorie E. Apollonio, and Lisa A. Bero, "Interest Groups, Lobbying, and Deception: The Passage of the Airline Smoking Acts." *Political Science Quarterly* 122, no. 4 (2007): 635–56; Jeffrey M. Drope and Wendy L. Hansen, "New Evidence for the Theory of Groups: Trade Association Lobbying in Washington, D.C.," *Political Research Quarterly* 62, no. 2 (2009): 303–16; R. Kenneth Godwin, Edward J. Lopez, and Barry J. Seldon, "Allocating Lobbying Resources Between Collective and Private Rents," *Political Research Quarterly* 61, no. 2 (2008): 345–59; Marie Hojnacki and David C. Kimball, "Organized Interests and the Decision of Whom to Lobby in Congress," *American Political Science Review* 92, no. 4 (1998): 775–90.
6 Aaron Dusso, "Legislation, Political Context, and Interest Group Behavior," *Political Research Quarterly* 63, no. 1 (2010): 55–67; the filings were compiled by Frank R. Baumgartner and Beth L. Leech, "Studying Interest Groups Using the Lobbying Disclosure Reports," *VOXPOP* 17, no. 3 (1999): 1–3.

7   Dusso, "Legislation, Political Context, and Interest Group Behavior"; Frank R. Baumgartner and Beth L. Leech, "Issue Niches and Policy Bandwagons: Patterns of Interest Group Involvement in National Politics," *Journal of Politics* 63, no. 4 (2001): 1191–1213.

8   Timothy Werner, "The Sound, the Fury, and the Nonevent: Business Power and Market Reactions to the Citizens United Decision," *American Politics Research* 39, no. 1 (2011): 118–41.

9   Baumgartner and Leech, "Issue Niches and Policy Bandwagons"; Beth L. Leech, Frank R. Baumgartner, Timothy La Pira, and Nicholas A. Semanko, "Drawing Lobbyists to Washington: Government Activity and Interest-Group Mobilization," *Political Research Quarterly* 58, no. 1 (2005): 19–30.

10 Robert S. Chirinko and Daniel J. Wilson, "Can Lower Tax Rates Be Bought? Business Rent-Seeking and Tax Competition Among U.S. States," Federal Reserve Bank of San Francisco Working Paper; Brian Kelleher Richter, Krislert Samphantharak, and Jeffrey F. Timmons, "Lobbying and Taxes," *American Journal of Political Science* 53, no. 4 (2009): 893–909; Frank R. Baumgartner, Jeffrey M. Berry, Marie Hojnacki, David C. Kimball, and Beth L. Leech, *Lobbying and Policy Change* (Chicago: University of Chicago Press, 2009).

11 Matt Grossmann and Kurt Pyle, "Lobbying and Congressional Bill Advancement," *Interest Groups & Advocacy* 2, no. 1 (2013): 91–111.

12 Frank Yu and Xiaoyun Yu, "Corporate Lobbying and Fraud Detection," *Journal of Financial and Quantitative Analysis* 46, no. 6 (2011): 1865–91.

13 Matthew D. Hill, G. Wayne Kelly, G. Brandon Lockhart, and Robert A. Van Ness, "Determinants and Effects of Corporate Lobbying," working paper, Social Science Research Network (2010).

14 John M. De Figueiredo and Charles M. Cameron. "Endogenous Cost Lobbying: Theory and Evidence," working paper, Social Science Research Network (2006).

15 Giovanni Facchini, Anna Maria Mayda, and Prachi Mishra, Working Paper 244, International Monetary Fund (2008).

16 Yael V. Hochberg, Paola Sapienza, and Annette Vissing-Jorgensen, "A Lobbying Approach to Evaluating the Sarbanes-Oxley Act of 2002," *Journal of Accounting Research* 47, no. 2 (2009): 519–83.

17 Deniz Igan, Prachi Mishra, and Thierry Tressel, "A Fistful of Dollars: Lobbying and the Financial Crisis," Paper Presented at the Jacques Polak Annual Research Conference, International Monetary Fund (2009). Other literature from economists echoes the topics of the political science literature in that it does not directly address influence. There is an economics literature on information provision in lobbying. See Marianne Bertrand, Matilde Bombardini, and Francesco Trebbi, "Is it Whom You Know or What You Know? An Empirical Assessment of the Lobbying Process," Working Paper 16765, National Bureau of Economic Research (2011). They frame this as a question of whether lobbyists rely on expertise or connections. The preponderance of their evidence supports the conclusion that lobbying is driven by connections rather than expertise.

18 These studies by economists use elements of the Lobbying Disclosure Act (LDA) data. De Figueiredo and Cameron, "Endogenous Cost Lobbying" use originally collected LDA data, but the data are from only two years, 1997–99. In their study of trade policy, Matilde Bombardini and Francesco Trebbi use LDA data from 1999 to 2001. See Matilde Bombardini and Francesco Trebb, "Competition and Political Organization: Together or Alone in Lobbying for Trade Policy?" Working Paper 14771, National Bureau of Economic Research (2009). The most significant data compilation effort is that of Bertrand, Bombardini, and Trebbi, "Is it Whom You Know or What You Know," who use LDA data from 1999 to 2008. Whereas this study focuses on the lobbyist as the unit of analysis, research on lobbying would be better served by a focus on influence at the

organization level. Organizations are the meaningful unit, given that the preferences of the interest group are reflected at the group level and not at the level of the lobbyist.

19 The characteristics of the lobbying disclosure data present challenges and they must be accordingly handled with awareness that the files contain duplicates, missing values, complex relational database associations, variation in client and registrant names, and many other elements that require expertise in working with data. For example, each report includes a registrant and a client. In the majority of cases the registrant is a contract lobbying firm and the client is the interests for which the contract lobbying firm lobbies. The Senate assigns unique numbers for registrants but not for clients, nor is there consistency in the completeness of the organization names or the way names are abbreviated or punctuated. A technique such a clustering algorithm can be used to ensure that a collection of reports all are appropriately attached to a single client rather than being attributed to more than one client that simply represent variations in the name that exist in the data.

20 The reporting instructions for the lobbying disclosure reports issued by the secretary of the Senate demand reasonably thorough statements about the focus of the lobbying activity from the filers. In the instructions to those who submit the lobbying forms the directions make clear that the listing of a bill number alone is not sufficient and that filers are to provide information about the specific issue on which they lobby. The instructions state that "the disclosures on Line 16 must include bill numbers, where applicable, but must always contain information that is adequate, standing alone, to inform the public of the specific lobbying issues." See: http://www.senate.gov/legisla tive/common/briefing/lobby_disc_briefing.htm#6. Even with the directions to be thorough, filers in many cases list only a bill title along with the bill or other preference-neutral information. The filers vary in the compliance with the instructions, and some entries in this field are quite thorough while others fail to heed the instructions and list only a bill.

21 Baumgartner et al., "Lobbying and Policy Change," p. 7.

22 John P. Heinz, Edward O. Laumann, Robert L. Nelson, and Robert H. Salisbury, *The Hollow Core: Private Interests in National Policy Making* (Cambridge, MA: Harvard University Press, 1993).

23 Heinz et. al, *The Hollow Core*, p. 369.

24 The connections in Figures 10.1 and 10.2 are the amount of client overlap between the registrants using a Kulczynski 2 coefficient calculation to arrive at a number between 0 and 1. The Kulczynski 2 coefficient calculation is (1/2 (# shared clients /# registrant 1 clients)) + (1/2 (# shared clients/ # registrant 2 clients)).

25 Laing Xiong, Fei Wang, and Changshui Zhang, "Multilevel Belief Propagation for Fast Inference on Markov Random Fields," Proceedings of the 2007 IEEE International Conference on Data Mining, Omaha, NE, 2007.

26 *Fareed Zakaria GPS*, February 3, 2013.

27 David Lowery and Holly Brasher, *Organized Interests and American Government* (Boston, MA: McGraw-Hill, 2005), pp. 171–73.

28 Matt Grossmann and Casey B. Dominguez, "Party Coalitions and Interest Group Networks," *American Politics Research* 37, no. 5 (2009): 793.

29 Congressional Bills Project. http://congressionalbills.org/

Chapter 11

Interest Groups, the White House, and the Administration

Heath Brown

While constitutionally limited in authority, the presidency—the institution of the presidency, including the president, White House officials, and all of the associated offices—has steadily grown in public stature, political power, and actual size since the founding of the nation. This would not have come as a surprise or disappointment to Alexander Hamilton, who mused in *Federalist* No. 70: "Energy in the executive is a leading character in the definition of good government." Woodrow Wilson seconded this opinion a century later in his reflection on the presidency of Theodore Roosevelt—the embodiment of the muscular White House—that "Our President must always, henceforth, be one of the great powers of the world, whether he act greatly and wisely or not. . . We can never hide our President as a mere domestic office... He must stand always at the front of our affairs."[1]

Within the separation of powers, the White House has emerged as first among equals. Running parallel to this evolution of government has been the rise of interest groups. Once a spectator to executive governance and an occasional source of influence for the moneyed, industrial elite, groups now number into the tens of thousands for every vocation, issue, and industry. As other chapters in this volume attest, these groups provide a voice for diverse interests, though perhaps not at the same level of decibel and not always in an equal fashion. But interest groups are also valued sources of information, knowledge, and expertise, and today are staffed with former elected officials, trained scientists, and communication and technology specialists. As is the case for members of Congress, interest groups are a trusted ally for many federal and White House officials, providing help as often as they ask for favors.

Curiously muffled, though, in both the study of the presidency and the study of interest groups has been a full body of knowledge about their interactions.[2] There are many unanswered questions about the extent to which interest groups view lobbying the president as a priority and whether lobbying the president and executive branch is a sound strategic use of group resources. The aim of this chapter is to synthesize the major theoretical and empirical contributions of scholars on this issue. By foregrounding this excellent, but relatively sparse empirical literature, both fields of study can be advanced. The chapter presents a case study of the role interest groups played during the 2008–2009 presidential transition. In particular, by examining the ways that interest groups and the presidency—and by extension the executive branch of government—check and balance each other through personnel, policy, and implementation, a richer understanding will emerge of their symbiotic relationship.

Design, Change, and Learning

By constitutional design, the president and executive branch are shielded from many of the pressures Congress faces. With infrequent elections faced by the commander-in-chief, the president is less subject to the need to seek campaign donations, one of the most typical tools used by interest groups to curry favor. Moreover, high ranking officials are appointed by the president, not by voters, and approved by the insular Senate, not the free-wheeling House. And the federal bureaucracy is even more protected from influence, because most federal officials are hired through a system of merit and advance in their careers based on the quality of their work, rather than political allegiance or popular appeal. Federal law (The Hatch Act) also restricts the opportunity for federal officials to blatantly involve themselves in politics and elections, shutting another door to outside influence.[3] The president, cabinet secretaries, and federal officials can then work in the public interest, immune to the requests for special treatment by a variety of outside interests.

As we all know, the design of the U.S. system is not always practiced in such a pure form. The president, the White House, the Cabinet, and the thousands of officials in the federal government, each interact with interest groups, many on a daily basis. Walker showed that the largest percentage of trade associations (80.1%) listed "administrative lobbying" as "important" or "very important," a larger percentage than "legislative lobbying," "litigating," and "electioneering."[4] And Frederick Boehmke et al. found that groups that lobbied Congress also heavily lobbied the bureaucracy, perhaps fearing that successful efforts during legislative policy-making could be lost during the enactment phase.[5] Thomas Holyoke also found that groups that chose to lobby within the executive branch were often motivated by expectations of opposition to their interests.[6] These frequent executive group interactions help implement difficult decisions by government through the studied expertise of interest group professionals while at the same time opening the executive branch up to the potentially pernicious influence of special interests. Rather than adhering to the constitutional design, the practice of presidency is one defined by deep symbiosis between groups and federal executives.

One of the reasons for this close relationship is what scholars have referred to as the institutionalization of the presidency or "institutionalized presidency."[7] From the founding, when the presidency was just a skeleton of its current self, the White House has grown over the twentieth century not only in terms of the size of the staff and number of offices but also in ambition.[8] Government reforms of the 1920s and 1930s led to new presidential responsibilities for producing a budget, expectations about initiating a policy agenda, and the need for expert advice. A president with ambitious policy agendas cannot simply rely on a vast federal bureaucracy with competing goals to carry out their agenda.[9] By empowering ever-growing numbers of White House staffers with policy responsibilities, the president can increase the likelihood that the agenda is carried out. And by using the power of appointment, presidents can further their agenda aided by loyal and ideologically aligned allies throughout government.[10] Terry Moe tracks this evolution up to the Reagan presidency, but subsequent presidents have built on Reagan's mantra of "personnel is policy."[11] According to Robert Maranto, political appointees are now "more carefully vetted than in the past to assure their ideology, integrity, and relative competence."[12] In short, the White House and the presidency adopted a complex set of institutions and formalized or institutionalized this branch of government.

The effect of institutionalization could be to further shield the president and federal officials from outside influence. Rather than make decisions informally, an institutionalized system standardizes procedures, potentially reducing the chance of personal loyalties and existing relationships to steer decision-making. In fact, however, numerous scholars have demonstrated the ways that groups use the very institutions of government—rule making,[13] the appointment process,[14] and service on advisory boards[15]—to advance their interests. John Chubb wrote: "Through 'advisory' incorporation, selective cooperation, 'biased' ground rules for participation, and outright co-optation, the administration structures group-access and influence as assuredly as does any so-called corporatist system".[16]

One of the reasons for this is that interest groups have evolved alongside the presidency and executive branch of government. Ken Collier and Michael Towle contended that "interest groups often copy the techniques used by Presidents, and frequently are more successful at using them."[17] Influence may then be tied to adaptability as much as to interest group money, size, and resources. Paul Herrnson wrote: "The most successful groups readily adapt to changes in the political environment, including shifting partisan circumstances and political reform."[18] This process of strategic learning has changed the way interest groups behave, and these changes appear to lead to success. Indicative of this, Matt Grossmann showed that institutionalized interest groups are often the most successful in the policy process, though that success is not just limited to the executive branch.[19]

But at the same time institutionalization has occurred across the executive branch and within the operations of individual interest groups, the presidency has also grown increasingly politicized. Moe argued that presidents have used *politicization* to achieve their increasingly ambitious policy aims.[20] The president is not a neutral executor of the wishes of Congress. Rather, the president has increasingly been expected to boldly direct the country forward and is judged by the quality of policy proposals, all despite the Constitutional authority to legislate being housed across Washington. In order to meet heightened expectations, successful presidents have had to engage in increasingly clever political strategy.

One way presidents have politicized the White House is through interactions with interest groups. Joe Pika showed the politicization of the outreach efforts to various constituencies, including interest groups.[21] And Kathryn Dunn Tenpas referred to "institutionalized outreach" to describe the work of the White House Office of Public Liaison, Office of Intergovernmental Affairs, Office of Legislative Affairs, and Office of Political Affairs.[22] The president, since the 1950s, has had various offices in place to interact with outside groups; at times responsive to their demands, at others solicitous of their support and allegiance. Indicative of the importance of this office, President Barack Obama entrusted one of his closest friends and advisers, Valerie Jarrett, to oversee his Office of Public Engagement.[23] This office (first established as the Office of Public Liaison by President Ford) has functioned as central location for groups to contact White House staff with grievances, advice, and recommendations, and for the White House to mobilize groups around particular policy proposals.[24] During the initial years of the Obama administration, the office has also served as a hub of social media and outreach to the public in general, not just those organized into groups.

The fate of an interest group also seems to relate to these increasingly political and partisan dimensions of the presidency. Thomas Gais and Jack Walker found that after the 1976 election of Jimmy Carter, nearly 50% of citizen interest groups reported an increase in cooperation with federal agencies versus 27% of occupational associations who said cooperation had decreased.[25] For these citizen groups, the incoming Carter administration represented an opportunity that they had not had with President Ford to collaborate with the federal government to meet their interests. Similarly, Kay Schlozman and John Tierney showed that nearly every interest group believed that the 1980 election of Ronald Reagan affected their organization, though the effect differed by group type, as 93% of unions and 75% of citizen groups but only 2% of ideologically conservative groups claimed that their influence declined.[26] Peterson supported this finding on the Reagan administration with survey data that showed that conservative groups were much more likely to have meetings and contact with the White House than moderate or liberal-leaning groups.[27] What seems apparent is that the success of interest groups lies in their ability to adapt to the institutional changes in the White House, but that success also is prone to factors out of their control, such as the ideology or party affiliation of the latest occupant of the Oval Office.

Appointments and Confirmation

If we bore down more deeply into the presidency, below the White House, the complex role of interest groups can be better observed. As suggested above, one of the most important areas of presidential power is the power of appointments. Hugh Heclo opined: "Presidents and department heads make few choices that are more important than those concerning the type of people who will serve with them in the administration".[28] A newly elected president oversees a federal government of 2.5 million civilian employees. Nearly a thousand of these positions these require Senate approval.[29] Hundreds of other so-called Schedule C appointments are made on a patronage basis for less powerful but politically significant positions. Turnover of policy makers offers the opportunity for new ideas to enter the policy debate and new political pressures to influence the policy agenda. New officials may downplay issues that had previously been high priorities for government or elevate once dormant issues. For instance, Moe showed that presidents have used the appointment power for the National Labor Relations Board to shift their decisions from pro-labor or pro-business, depending on the attitude of the new president to either side of that dichotomy.[30]

In the textbook version of how a president fills the cabinet, the president nominates and the Senate holds a confirmatory vote on that nomination following a public hearing. The Senate infrequently rejects a nominee, but the public hearing does permit interest groups to voice agreement or disagreement with the president's choice, either in person or through writing. Interest groups also look to the appointment power of the president as an opportunity, sometimes to foment change and at others to maintain the status quo. Schlozman and Tierney found that in the 1980s a majority of groups employed the tactic of influencing appointments.[31] Groups can use the appointment process in at least three ways: influencing who is chosen, securing appointments for their own officials, and capitalizing on the wide attention paid to confirmation hearings to demonstrate their importance.

An interest group would certainly benefit from having one of their own officials chosen to serve the president or many interest groups later hire former presidential appointees. Robert Salisbury et al. showed some evidence of the extent to which this actually happens.[32] They demonstrated with survey data that around half of interest group officials had previously worked for government, yet most had left government a decade earlier. Schlozman and Tierney found similar results: 63% of trade associations, 31% of unions, and 55% of citizen groups had government affairs staff that had previously worked for the federal government.[33]

A persistent question is whether this a problem? Does the awarding of federal appointments to former interest group officials or the access of interest groups to appointees themselves pervert government policy? Anecdotes abound about former lobbyists gaining positions of power within the government and diverting federal policy in the direction of former employers and friends. Some of the most egregious examples occurred recently in the Department of Energy when one of the most powerful officials in the Bush administration, former lobbyist Steven Griles, used his high-ranking appointment to tilt land-management decisions toward developers. Despite his appointment by President Bush, and his own pledge to cut ties with his former employer and clients, Griles continued to be paid thousands of dollars by old lobbying firm. Griles ended up in jail for other crimes he committed related to the lobbying scandal of Jack Abramoff, but many still hold Griles accountable for the change in government policy toward corporate energy interests. But did Griles' former employment or his own ideological beliefs about oil and gas exploration dictate his regulatory decisions? In general, are lobbyists who serve in government prone to put special interests ahead of public interests? The answer to this is empirically difficult to reach a conclusion. How would we know which decision a federal official would have reached if they had no background in lobbying? The counter-factual is hard to investigate. Research, though, has demonstrated that some of the deep concerns about the influence of special interests on federal officials should be tempered. Joe Aberbach and Bert Rockman, for instance, used survey data to demonstrate that federal officials believe interest groups are the *least* influential groups with which they interact and further that their limited influence has been waning over time.[34] Perhaps the system works and is now working better than we fear?

Another way that groups can use the appointment process is through demonstrations of their importance. During a confirmation hearing held in the Senate, any interested party (individuals, groups, and elected officials) can give testimony and submit letters of support or opposition. Research by Lauren Cohen Bell showed that more interest groups are submitting letters to confirmation hearings and giving testimony than in the past.[35] This change has taken place as the confirmation process has grown increasing contentious and lengthy— not necessarily a causal result of interest groups' participation but certainly an interesting correlation. With the public broadcasting of certain confirmation hearings on C-SPAN and available on numerous public websites, an interest group that gives public testimony can be given a nationwide audience not only to debate the merits of their nominee but also to promote their own name.

Illustrative of this trend is an exchange that occurred during the confirmation hearing of President George W. Bush's nominee to become his first Attorney General, John Ashcroft, between Senator Orrin Hatch (R-UT) and the Chair of the Senate Judiciary Committee, Senator Patrick Leahy (D-VT).

As Leahy suggests, Planned Parenthood Federation of America, National Women's Law Center, and the Leadership Conference on Civil Rights lined up

---

HATCH: John Ashcroft, like many of us, is a man of strongly held views. I have every confidence, based on his distinguished record, that as attorney general he will vigorously work to enforce the law, whether or not the law happens to be consistent with his personal views. Finally, Mr. Chairman, you know that I would have preferred a format similar to that followed for President Clinton's nominees and prior nominees for the last four attorney general nominees: no more than a two-day hearing with outside interest groups submitting their testimony in writing. But I'm sure that you will endeavor to be fair as we proceed with this hearing. I have confidence in that. And I look forward to these proceedings and look forward to participating in them. Thank you, Mr. Chairman.

LEAHY: Thank you, Senator Hatch. And I can assure you the hearings will be fair. There are 280 million Americans who have views on who should be attorney general. There will be interest groups to the left or the right who may have suggestions. Ultimately, there's only 100 Americans who'll get to vote on that issue, and that's the 100 members of the Senate. And it will be—the whole tone of the debate and all will be decided by us.[53]

Figure 11.1 Senate Confirmation Hearing Exchange between Senators Hatch and Leahy

to oppose Ashcroft, and the Fraternal Order of Police, National Association of Wholesaler-Distributors, and National Baptist Convention argued in support. Indicative of this split, Robert Woodson, President of the National Center for Neighborhood Enterprise, beamed: "I am here to vigorously support the nomination of Senator John Ashcroft for U.S. Attorney General, and to explain to you the reasons why more than 150 leaders of faith-based organizations across the country came here Tuesday at their own expense to show their support for Senator Ashcroft. Most of these leaders, for the record, are minority and low-income." Conversely, Kate Michelman, President of NARAL, the pro-choice interest group, implored the committee to consider the policy implications of Ashcroft's nomination: "The right to safe, legal abortion hangs by a slender thread. That threat could be cut by just one Supreme Court Justice or by an Attorney General not committed to its protection. The women NARAL represents all across this country cannot afford to have that thread severed." And Senators took to defending the nominee by referencing Ashcroft's own work with prominent interest groups. Senator Charles Grassley (R-IA) said, "Would the National Association of Attorneys General and the National Governors' Association, two national associations representing both Republican and Democratic Attorneys General and Governors, name such a biased man to lead their organization? I don't think so, but the smear goes on."

The Judiciary Committee ultimately voted 10–8 to support the nomination, and Ashcroft was soon confirmed by the full Senate for the position. Senators voted largely along party lines, suggesting that the testimony and letters given by interest groups in support and opposition may have done little other than confirm pre-existing notions. To be sure, members of the committee extend invitations to particular interest groups to participate, especially to give the prized public testimony. Senators know in advance what views each group will express, and the contentiousness surrounding a confirmation hearing is therefore a type of Kabuki theatre: a way to construct a visible debate about the policy issues that the eventual appointee will address. Senators, even from the president's opposition party, typically will grant the president the Cabinet of his choosing, even if they disagree with the beliefs of nominees. Only in the rare circumstance will a nominee be turned down by a Senate vote: only twice since 1950 has the Senate rejected a Presidential Cabinet nominee.[36] The invitation to give testimony or submit letters, then, may also have to do with the exchange relationship between members of the Senate and allied interest groups. Testimony may not change votes, but it can represent a reward that a Senator can give to an interest group that has supported them during an election campaign or provided them with information on an upcoming legislative battle. For the interest groups, testimony permits them to cement a relationship with the nominee and demonstrate to members their influence. For those groups that oppose nominees, they likely have already written-off a sound working relationship with the eventual appointee, and the testimony and letters can remind their members that they are still fighting for their interests, even in a losing battle.

Federal Bureaucracy

Once ensconced in their position at the top of a federal agency or buried more deeply as the head of an unknown division of the agency, interest groups can look to their earlier support for the appointee as a way to set up a meeting or call in a favor. An interest group might meet with new deputy assistant secretary of transportation or the new administrator of the National Oceanic and Atmospheric Administration (NOAA) to discuss a pending regulation or offer suggestions for how to re-organize the division. More often, though, interest groups engage the bureaucracy through formal and institutionalized channels such as: the rule making process, the allocation of federal funds, or the implementation of programs. This formulation of the way the federal policy works has also long been associated with the "Iron Triangle" theory.[37] The cozy and stable relationships between the three corners of the triangle (congressional committees, federal agencies, and interest groups) promote a mutually supportive and status-quo oriented approach to policy making where favors are exchanged for access and influence. Hugh Heclo later argued that, rather than an Iron Triangle, policy making might be better thought of as operating in issue networks defined less by stability and more by fluidity and openness.[38]

More recent research aims to empirically test the Iron Triangle theory and other theoretical notions of how federal policy actually works. Scott Furlong and Cornelius Kerwin investigated the ways interest groups participate in federal rule-making; the process of determining particular rules about how the federal government will implement laws passed by Congress.[39] They found, as they had a decade earlier, that groups do engage in federal rule-making by submitting their opinions during the required period of open comment. As a group would during the legislative process, by influencing the wording of a final rule, the group can make certain that regulations are written to their advantage. This tactic has increased for interest groups even as other advocacy tactics, such as campaign and grassroots advocacy, have played an increasing role in their political strategy. For some, this type of influence poses serious problems for sound government regulations. Concerns for the role of outside influence over the bureaucracy were famously championed by notable economists. The "agency capture" critique emerged to examine anti-trust regulations and the potentially corrosive influence of industry on governmental regulations.[40] A "captured" federal agency might be so closely linked to industry through interest groups, think tanks, and lobbyists that federal policy-making cannot be distinguished from industrial policy making. The threat of the same officials cycling between government and industry has been called the "revolving door" and relates to the issues raised earlier about personnel and appointments.

Conclusive evidence to support these concerns about too close a relationship between interest groups and bureaucrats—deemed Iron Triangles or agency capture—are empirically hard to find. Some interest groups are able to gain formal access to the bureaucracy. Steve Balla and John Wright investigated the way Congress helps to institutionalize interest group influence by requiring that group representatives be appointed to boards established to oversee federal agencies.[41] By gaining a seat on one of these boards or influencing who is chosen, a group can maintain a very close eye over agency activities. In general, there is also some evidence that interest groups can work to increase federal spending. William Niskanen contended that interest group influence has inflated federal appropriations, and Robert Lowry and Matthew Potoski showed that, in the aggregate, interest groups do influence federal spending on federal grants related to agriculture, income security, and employment and training.[42] Other evidence from William West and Connor Raso showed that economic interests are highly influential during the rule-making process, and Susan Yackee found that groups that participate in rule-making do tend to steer rules to their preferred outcome.[43] On the micro-level, another widely held concern is that lobbying might direct specific federal funds toward certain causes or groups. Lobbying has long been connected to appropriations awarded by law makers, but Beth Leech showed that non-profit organizations which actively lobby are no more likely to receive federal grants than those who lobby minimally.[44]

Interest Groups and Presidential Transitions: A Case Study

One way to appreciate the variety of ways an interest group might seek to influence the executive branch is by focusing on a single point in time or phase of the policy process. The transition between administrations—called the Presidential Transition—provides a convenient lens through which one can observe a variety of tactical choices made by interest groups. Transitions across party occur infrequently—just three (George W. Bush to Barack Obama, Bill Clinton to George W. Bush, and George H.W. Bush to Bill Clinton) in the last thirty years—so the opportunity for interest groups to take advantage of the massive overhaul of government is a rare one. When such a transition does happen, as it did in 2008, the newly elected president has the power to make fundamental change in hundreds of policy areas, big and small, in just eleven weeks. By changing personnel, issuing executive orders, and altering the structure of the federal government, the president-elect can shift the direction of U.S. policy or maintain the status quo. Interest groups stand to gain or lose as much during this time as during any other period of a president's term in office, and yet the president is not even yet sworn in to office.

In early 2009, the first bill newly inaugurated President Barack Obama signed into law was the *Lilly Ledbetter Fair Pay Act*. During his announcement in the East Room of the White House, President Obama remarked that the pay equity issue was more than just a women's issue, but also a family issue, related to principles of fundamental fairness and American freedom. The president praised Lilly

Ledbetter, who was in attendance, congressional leaders, and "the advocates who are in the audience who worked so hard to get it passed."[45]

The act arose from a 2007 Supreme Court decision in *Ledbetter v. Goodyear Tire and Rubber Company*. In the pay discrimination case filed by Ms. Ledbetter, the court ruled that, because of the late filing of the claim, her employer would not be found in violation of the law and not required to pay damages. Congress soon took up the broader pay discrimination issue with the introduction of the *Lilly Ledbetter Fair Pay Act*. The bill aimed to amend the 1964 Civil Rights Act, and became a visible point of policy disagreement between Senators Obama and McCain during the 2008 campaign: Obama came out strongly in support and McCain in opposition. Obama pledged to support passage of the bill, and Ledbetter was invited to speak at the Democratic National Convention where she proclaimed to the audience, "Barack Obama is on our side."

As the president indicated, the issue was also a major priority for interest groups, including the National Partnership for Women and Families (NPWF), a prominent women's advocacy group. While the organization provided little in the way of financial contributions to the Obama campaign, it was able to advise the Obama transition team in a November 2008 report titled "Turning Promise into Progress: Key Priorities for Women and Families."[46] The organization candidly explained its approach this way: "We work in public and behind the scenes; leading coalitions and building individual relationships; providing technical assistance and strategic counsel; advising decision makers and transition teams; developing policy proposals; educating the public; and engaging women, men, advocates, policymakers, and the media—all to advance concrete policy changes that will improve the lives of women and families across the nation."[47] Perhaps there is no clearer explanation given for how groups operate in the policy process in the twenty-first century.

NPWF representatives met with the transition team on December 5, at the mid-point of the transition, to address the pay discrimination issue and other health and work policy proposals the organization supported. The organization had an advantage during the transition that other groups did not possess. Their senior advisor, Judith Lichtman, was serving on the transition team's advisory group for justice and civil rights. Lichtman was one of sixteen individuals chosen to coordinate justice issues and advise the president. Further, the former president of the organization (under its old name, the Women's Legal Defense Fund), Sally Katzen, was chosen to be one of twenty-one leaders of the transition of the executive office of the president. Katzen was elected president of the organization in 1990 and later served in senior positions in the Clinton administration.

Such high-level access on the Obama transition team coincided with numerous positive outcomes for the priorities of the NPWF. The NPWF applauded the reversal of Bush decisions (such as the ban on the U.S. funding of global family-planning initiatives) and the re-establishment of the White House Office on Women and Girls. That office later organized meetings on issues of maternal health, and the NPWF was invited to participate in those discussions.[48] Yet perhaps most significantly, President Obama soon named Jocelyn Frye to be deputy assistant to the president and director of policy for the First Lady. Frye, like Lichtman, had long worked at the Partnership, in her case as general counsel. Frye was a registered lobbyist and had lobbied for the Ledbetter bill and other legislation prior to her appointment to the White House. This appointment necessitated the White House granting Frye a waiver to the anti-lobbyist ethics pledge that the president had issued just a week before signing the Ledbetter bill into law. Similar waivers were granted for a handful of other former lobbyists whose expertise was deemed essential by the White House, including Cecilia Munoz who lobbied for the National Council of La Raza before being appointed to run the Office of Intergovernmental Affairs. Viewed from one perspective as a reversal on his strident stance on lobbyists, these waivers also indicate how inextricably linked lobbyists are from federal policy making.

Would the Ledbetter Act been passed without the active transition advocacy on part of the NPWF? Probably. Would it have been the very first Act signed by the President without Lichtman, Katzen, and Frye's active involvement in the transition? Maybe. In either case, it is difficult to empirically connect the dots between lobbying and policy outcomes. There is also no evidence that Frye has served the president with anything other than integrity. One does wonder, though, how prevalent this type of activity was during the 2008–09 transition. Was the NPWF's access to positions and policy decision-making unique or typical of groups? Survey data collected during that time period can help answer these questions.[49]

In 2008, only 12% of groups which responded to the survey employed not one of the transition tactics queried about in the survey, while 7% employed six or seven, the maximum. Joining a coalition was a favored activity during the transition, employed by 71% of the respondents (See Table 11.1). Conversely, planning for the upcoming congressional elections was the least popular (15%), most likely because it was too early for many groups to begin such planning.

Meetings with transition teams are one of the clearest tactics a group can use to advance their ideas about policy and personnel. Meetings may be arranged at the request of the interest group or at the request of the various inner- or outer-circle transition teams. A former president of the American Bar Association (ABA), Bob Evans, argued that meeting with the transition team is the most effective way to share policy recommendation documents.[50] A large portion of groups were in fact able to arrange for meetings with the Obama transition team. In 2008–2009, 58% of survey respondents claimed they had met with a transition team or the new president. This is a remarkable finding given the very short time period in which meetings could be held. To be sure, many meetings were held with dozens of groups at the same, so many these meetings were not of the private variety, only a very special interest groups would have been given exclusive access to President Obama.

But if a group was unable to secure a meeting, all was not lost. In 2008, the Obama administration made it possible through their "Seat at the Table" policy for any individual or group that wanted to submit recommendations to do so on

Table 11.1 Specific Transition Tactics (from 2008 Survey), n = 72

Question: Following the 2008 election, does your organization expect to (mark all that apply):	Percentage Responding "Yes"
a. Meet with the new president or officials from a presidential transition team	58
b. Publicly recommend individuals to be appointed to federal agencies or other senior positions	26
c. Publicly endorse individuals after they are nominated by the White House	30
d. Issue policy recommendations for the new administration	67
e. Join a coalition of organizations to advocate for your issues with the new administration	71
f. Change your legislative strategy or congressional priorities	28
g. Begin planning for the 2010 midterm election	15
h. Pursue other strategies or activities (please describe briefly)	11

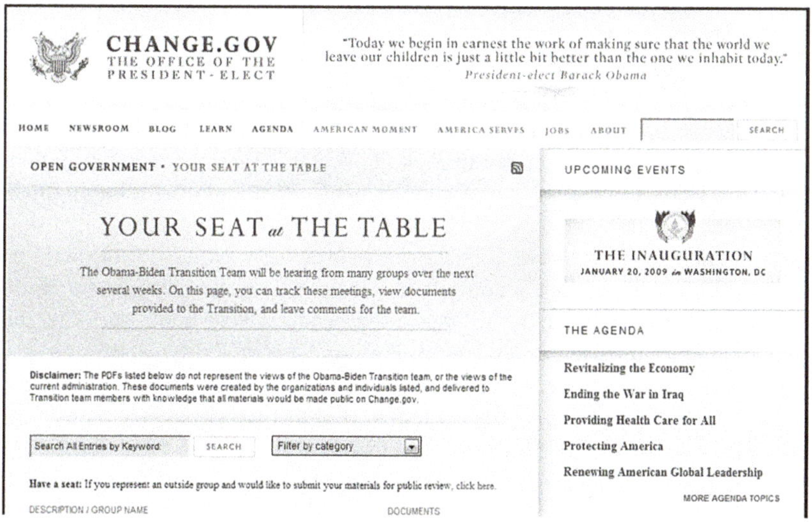

Figure 11.2 Screenshot from Obama Transition Public Website

a public website (See Figure 11.2). This policy represented a concerted effort on the part of the new president to avoid accusations of favoritism toward particular interest groups and increase public participation. Each letter was also open for public viewing, also increasing the transparency of the transition period. The transition team also forbade lobbyists from serving on transition teams and placed steep hurdles in front of a former lobbyist serving in the administration, though many exceptions were given shortly upon taking office.

While the Obama transition required groups to submit recommendations and advice via the web, policy recommendations were also delivered personally at transition meetings, submitted by mail, fax, e-mail, or released publicly to the media. Two-thirds (67%) of respondents to the survey claimed to make policy recommendations during the 2008–2009 transition. The survey results also showed that a quarter (26%) of respondents "publicly recommended individuals." As was demonstrated earlier in terms of nomination hearings in general, by using this tactic, groups may be able to influence who is chosen or at least the list of candidates that are under consideration.

More common was to make theoretical personnel recommendations, typically focusing on ideal job qualifications, rather than specifics. Of groups that submitted letters to the Obama transition team, 16% made this type of recommendation. For instance, the National Association of Crime Victim Compensation Boards (NACC) submitted a recommendation that "[t]he director of the (Office of Victims of Crime) needs to be highly qualified, with experience and expertise in issues relating to crime victims, and knowledge of VOCA [Victims of Crime Act] grants."

Is It Worth It?

Judging whether or not it is worth it for an interest group to expend energy and resources during such a short time period is difficult to answer definitively. Policy change happens slowly, so even if a group was very influential during the transition, the policy change they recommended might not occur for years into the administration. Another way to look at success is whether many groups had short-term gains in various types of appointments. An appointment for an interest group official to a transition team, to a political office, or some other related position, might catapult an organization into the center of policy making. Of course, in past transitions, some groups felt left out of the transition process. A leader of a national disability group, referring to the difference between the 1992 Clinton and 2000 Bush transitions, was quoted as saying: "Last time around, the disability [community] was lucky to have some long-term disability advocates involved early on in the transition . . . . [In 2000] I don't have a sense that a lot of that has gone on to date."[51] Such is the case with service on transition teams: opportunities are often shrouded in the mystery and chaos of the transition, frequently sought, but often resulting in disappointment.

In response to the survey, in 2008–2009, 10% of the responding organizations had an official chosen to serve on a transition team. This is not surprising since there are hundreds of groups in each policy area and a much smaller number of seats on each team. Moreover, there were only minimal differences between transportation and criminal justice. The percentage of groups on a transition team within the transportation policy area was slightly higher (14%) than criminal justice (8%), but this was not a statistically significant difference. In addition, 13% of survey respondents claimed that following the transition an official from their organization was hired into a non-political position in the federal government (see Figure 11.3), and 11% of survey respondents claimed that following the transition an official from their organization received a political appointment in the federal

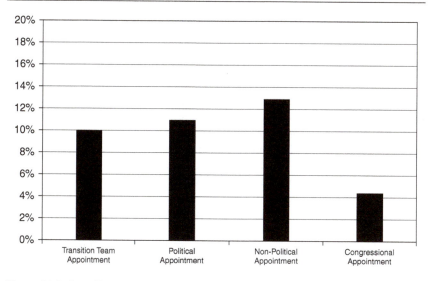

Figure 11.3 Post-Transition Appointments

government. Finally, less than 5% of survey respondents claimed that one of their officials had received a position working in Congress following the transition, yet another potentially fruitful outcome. This is an interesting finding because one would expect a transition to produce more positions for political appointments. The survey respondents suggested that the opposite is true: a larger percentage of groups report non-political appointments following the 2008–2009 transition.

Whether or not these post-transition appointments are problematic gets back to the quality of the appointee and their ability to pursue the public interests embodied in their new position. Former interest group lobbyists have served in U.S. government for decades, very few with any of the legal concerns raised by Steven Griles. Yet even if a former lobbyist maintains a stiff professional ethic and avoids criminality, they still are likely to bring the ideological and policy views of their former employers to federal decision making. For some, this will always be a problem; for others, the extent of concern will be determined by how closely they agree or disagree with that particular ideology.

Conclusion

So what is one to do with this evidence of interest group interactions with the president, White House, and federal bureaucracy? Like many other aspects of the U.S. political system, the practice of democratic governance does not match the theory and aspiration of the Framers. It is also unsurprising that as the presidency and interest groups have grown in stature, they have become increasingly intertwined in each other's lives, shared institutional practices, ideas and staff, and viewed success as symbiotic. Yet the evidence collected by researchers does not lead one to a single-minded conclusion that these interactions are always harmful. In numerous situations, interest groups help make better federal policy and insure the White House is informed, educated, and responsive to the needs of constituencies they may not fully understand. The net influence of interest groups on the presidency, whether during a transition, an appointment, or rule-making, is ambiguous at best. More research is certainly called for to plumb more deeply into these relationships, but simple cause-and-effect relationships between self-interested groups courting bureaucrats who cater to their needs are likely to remain elusive.

Despite the paucity of damning evidence, concerns remain and improvements to the system can be found. Change is worthwhile if for no other reason than to assuage concerns held by the public that the system is rigged. If reform can increase the legitimacy of federal governance in the eyes of the public, then it is justified. For example, a nonpartisan-panel made up of practitioners and scholars called the "Task Force on Transparency and Public Participation" convened in 2008 to make recommendations about federal rule-making.[52] Two of their most convincing recommendations were to increase transparency and public participation. Specifically, the Task Force called on agencies to streamline Freedom of Information Act (FOIA) request procedures, improve electronic access, and involve all interested parties in important federal decisions. These same recommendations for the rule-making process could be applied more broadly to all federal activities. Some of these very steps were adopted during the 2008 transition of President Obama. Future presidential transitions will grapple with many of these same concerns, and whether transparency and public participation procedures, such as the "seat at the table" online system, are fully institutionalized may determine not only the ways interest groups will influence a newly-elected president but also the level of cynicism held by the public at large.

Notes

1 Ronald J. Pestritto, *Woodrow Wilson: The Essential Political Writings* (Lantham, MD: Lexington Books, 2005).
2 Marie Hojnacki, David C. Kimball, Frank R. Baumgartner, Jeffrey M. Berry, and Beth L. Leech, "Studying Organizational Advocacy and Influence: Reexamining Interest Group Research," *Annual Review of Political Science* 15 (2012): 379–99.
3 For more information about the Hatch Act, see: http://www.osc.gov/hatchact.htm#.
4 Jack Walker, *Mobilizing Interest Groups in America: Patrons, Professionals, and Social Movements* (Ann Arbor: University of Michigan Press, 1991).
5 Frederick Boehmke, Sean Gailmard, John W. Patty, "Business as Usual: Interest Group Access and Representation Across Policy-Making Venues," *Journal of Public Policy* 33, no. 1 (2013): 3–33.
6 Thomas Holyoke, "Choosing Battlegrounds: Interest Group Lobbying Across Multiple Venues," *Political Research Quarterly* 56, no. 3 (2003): 325–36.
7 Richard Neustadt, *Presidential Power and the Modern Presidents: The Politics of Leadership from Roosevelt to Reagan* (New York: Free Press, 1997); Francis Rourke, "The Institutional Presidency," in *Understanding the Presidency*, ed. James P. Pfiffner and Roger H. Davidson (New York: Longman, 1997), pp. 196–204.
8 Bradley Patterson and James P. Pfiffner, "The White House Office of Presidential Personnel," *Presidential Studies Quarterly* 31, no. 3 (2001): 165–92.

Charles E. Walcott, Shirley Anne Warshaw, Stephen J. Wayne, "The Office of Chief of Staff," in *The White House World*, ed. Martha J. Kumar and Terry Sullivan (College Station, TX: Texas AM University Press, 2003), pp. 111–29.

9 Hugh Heclo, "Political Executives and the Washington Bureaucracy," *Political Science Quarterly* 92, no. 3 (1977): 395–424.

10 David E. Lewis, *The Politics of Presidential Appointments: Political Control and Bureaucratic Performance* (Princeton, NJ: Princeton University Press, 2008); G. Calvin MacKenzie, "The Real Invisible Hand: Presidential Appointees in the Administration of George W. Bush," *PS: Political Science and Politics* 35, no. 1 (2002): 27–30.

11 Terry M. Moe, "The Politicized Presidency," in *The Managerial Presidency*, ed. James P. Pfiffner (Pacific Grove, CA: Brooks/Cole, 1991), 135–57.

12 Robert Maranto, *Beyond a Government of Strangers: How Career Executives and Political Appointees Can Turn Conflict to Cooperation* (Lanham, MD: Lexington Books, 2005), pp. 25.

13 Suzanne J. Piotrowski and David H. Rosenbloom, "The Legal-Institutional Framework for Interest Group Participation in Federal Administrative Policymaking," in *The Interest Group Connection*, ed. Ronald G. Shaiko and Paul S. Herrnson (Washington, DC: CQ Press, 2005), pp. 258–81.

14 Lauren Cohen Bell, *Warring Factions: Interest Groups, Money, and the New Politics of Senate Confirmation* (Columbus: Ohio University Press, 2002).

15 Steve J. Balla and John R. Wright, "Interest Groups, Advisory Committees, and Congressional Control of the Bureaucracy," *American Journal of Political Science* 45, no. 4 (2001): 799–812.

16 John E. Chubb, *Interest Groups and the Bureaucracy: The Politics of Energy* (Palo Alto, CA: Stanford University Press, 1983).

17 Ken Collier and Michael Towle, "Winning Friends and Influencing the People: The President vs. Interest Groups," *White House Studies* 2 (2002): 185–99.

18 Paul Herrnson, "Interest Groups and Campaigns: The Electoral Connection," in *The Interest Group Connection: Electioneering, Lobbying, and Policymaking in Washington*, ed. Paul Hernnson, Ronald G. Shaiko, and Clyde Wilcox (Washington, DC: CQ Press, 2005), p. 45.

19 Matt Grossmann, *The Not-So-Special Interests: Interest Groups, Public Representation, and American Governance* (Palo Alto, CA: Stanford University Press, 2012).

20 Moe, "The Politicized Presidency."

21 Joseph Pika, "The White House Office of Public Liaison," *Presidential Studies Quarterly* 39, no. 3 (2009): 549–73.

22 Kathryn Dunn Tenpas, "Lobbying the Executive Branch," in *The Interest Group Connection*, ed. Paul S. Herrnson, Ronald G. Shaiko, and Clyde Wilcox (Washington, DC: CQ Press, 2005), pp. 249–57.

23 See: http://www.whitehouse.gov/engage/office.

24 Pika, "The White House Office of Public Liaison."

25 Thomas L. Gais and Jack L. Walker, "Pathways to Influence in America," in Jack L. Walker, *Mobilizing Interest Groups in America* (Ann Arbor: University of Michigan Press, 1991), pp. 103–21.

26 Kay L. Schlozman and John. Tierney, *Organized Interests and American Democracy* (New York: Harper and Row, 1986).

27 Mark A. Peterson, "The Presidency and Organized Interests: White House Patterns of Interest Group Liaison," *American Political Science Review* 86, no. 3 (1992): 612–25.

28 Hugh Heclo, "Political Executives and the Washington Bureaucracy," *Political Science Quarterly* 92, no. 3 (1977): 395–424.

29 David E. Lewis, *The Politics of Presidential Appointments: Political Control and Bureaucratic Performance* (Princeton, NJ: Princeton University Press, 2008).

30 Terry M. Moe, "Regulatory Performance and Presidential Administration," *American Journal of Political Science* 26, no. 2 (1982): 197–224.

31 Schlozman and Tierney, *Organized Interests and American Democracy*.

32 Robert H. Salisbury, Paul Johnson, John P. Heinz, Edward O. Laumann, Robert L. Nelson, "Who You Know versus What You Know: The Uses of Government Experience for Washington Lobbyists," *American Journal of Political Science* 33, no. 1 (1989): 175–95.

33 Schlozman and Tierney, *Organized Interests and American Democracy*.

34 John D. Aberbach and Bert A. Rockman, "The Political Views of U.S. Senior Federal Executives, 1970–1992," *Journal of Politics* 57, no. 3 (1995): 838–52.

35 Lauren Cohen Bell, *Warring Factions: Interest Groups, Money, and the New Politics of Senate Confirmation* (Columbus, OH: Ohio University Press, 2002).

36 See Senate Historical Office: http://www.senate.gov/artandhistory/history/minute/Cabinet_Nomination_Defeated.htm.

37 Ernest Griffith, *Impasse of Democracy* (New York: Harrison-Hilton, 1939).

38 Hugh Heclo, "Issue Networks and the Executive Establishment," in *The New American Political System*, ed. Anthony King (Washington, DC: American Enterprise Institute, 1978).

39 Scott Furlong and Cornelius Kerwin, "Interest Group Participation in Rule Making: A Decade of Change," *Journal Public Administration Research and Theory* 15, no. 3 (2005): 353–70.

40 Gary S. Becker, "A Theory of Competition Among Pressure Groups for Political Influence," *Quarterly Journal of Economics* 98, no. (1983): 371–400; George J. Stigler, "The Economic Effects of the Antitrust Laws," *Journal of Law and Economics* 9, October (1966): 225–58.

41 Steve J. Balla and John R. Wright, "Interest Groups, Advisory Committees, and Congressional Control of the Bureaucracy," *American Journal of Political Science* 45, no. 4 (2001): 799–812.

42 William A. Niskanen, *Bureaucracy and Representative Government* (Chicago: Aldine-Atherton, 1971); Robert C. Lowry and Matthew Potoski, "Organized Interests and the Politics of Federal Discretionary Grants," *Journal of Politics* 66, no. 2 (2004): 513–33.

43 William F. West and Connor Raso, "Who Shapes the Rulemaking Agenda? Implications for Bureaucratic Responsiveness and Bureaucratic Control," *Journal of Public Administration Research and Theory* (2012); Susan W. Yackee, "Sweet-talking the Fourth Branch: The Influence of Interest Group Comments on Federal Agency Rulemaking," *Journal of Public Administration Research and Theory* 16, no. 1 (2006): 103–24.

44 Beth L. Leech, "Funding Faction or Buying Silence? Grants, Contracts, and Interest Group Lobbying Behavior," *Policy Studies Journal* 34, no. 1 (2006): 17–35.

45 John Woolley and B. Gerhard Peters, "President Barack Obama: Remarks on Signing the Lilly Ledbetter Fair Pay Act of 2009," http://www.presidency.ucsb.edu/ws/index.php?pid=85704#axzz1RRPe86wU.

46 To read the full report: http://www.nationalpartnership.org/site/DocServer/turning_promise_into_progress.pdf?docID=4341.

47 Ibid, 2.

48 Ibid.

49 The findings are drawn from a survey of 300 interest groups in two policy areas: criminal justice and transportation.

50 Based on interview with Bob Evans on September 24, 2008.

51 Paul Singer, "Disability Advocates Say Bush Transition Has Ignored Them," United Press International, January 11, 2000.

52 To read the full report: http://www.hks.harvard.edu/hepg/Papers/transparencyReport.pdf.

Chapter 12

Interest Groups in the Judicial Arena

Paul M. Collins Jr.

On June 26, 2003, the U.S. Supreme Court handed down its decision in *Lawrence v. Texas*,[1] declaring that a Texas law that criminalized homosexual sodomy ran afoul of the Fourteenth Amendment's Due Process Clause, and was thus unconstitutional. To many, the decision in *Lawrence* was a surprise. After all, it was unusual for a conservative Court to support the privacy interests of same-sex couples. To others, the decision was not nearly as shocking as it verified the ability of interest groups to shape judicial decision making. The case was litigated by Lambda Legal, one of the nation's premier LGBT public interest law firms, and numerous organizations filed amicus curiae briefs urging the Court to strike down the sodomy law, including the American Civil Liberties Union, the American Psychological Association, and the Cato Institute.

Though *Lawrence* is a particularly high-profile example of how groups use the judicial arena to pursue their policy goals, it is far from alone. Indeed, interest groups have been active on a wide range of issues facing courts, including how police officers question suspects, the rights of same sex couples to marry, the constitutionality of affirmative action and health care programs, and prayer in public schools. The purpose of this chapter is to explore the role of interest groups in the courts. I begin by discussing why interest groups opt to lobby in the judicial arena, as opposed to pursing their influence in other venues. Following this, I examine the methods organizations utilize to influence the courts, focusing on the primary means of judicial lobbying—the amicus curiae brief. Building on this, I then consider why groups target specific courts and participate in certain cases. Next, I provide an examination of the ability of groups to shape various aspects of judicial politics. Here, I demonstrate a novel and promising method for investigating the influence of amicus curiae briefs on Supreme Court opinion content. I close with a discussion of profitable avenues for future research on interest group activity in the courts.

Why Interest Groups Lobby the Courts

When an interest group determines that it wants to attempt to influence government, one of the first decisions it must make is where to pursue its goals. While not all groups choose to involve themselves in the legal system, there are a variety of qualities that make the courts attractive to organizations. Before turning to these reasons, it is imperative to note that these explanations are typically not mutually exclusive. Rather, groups may target the judiciary for a variety of often interrelated reasons. It is likewise important to acknowledge that, for many organizations, litigation is one of many tools at their disposal. That is, a particular organization may pursue its goals in an array of venues, including mounting litigation campaigns, engaging in legislative lobbying, participating in electioneering, and testifying before regulatory boards, to name but a few of the techniques available to organized interests.[2]

A range of factors motivate groups to participate in the judiciary. Some organizations turn to the courts because they perceive that the elected branches of government, such as congress and the executive, are inhospitable environments. For example, Clement E. Vose[3] and Richard C. Cortner[4] demonstrated that in the 1950s and 1960s, civil rights organizations faced a hostile Congress that was controlled by Southern Democrats who opposed equal rights policies. As a result, these groups promoted their agendas in the federal courts, which were viewed as more welcoming to their causes. While African American civil rights organizations no longer find hostile environments in federal or state legislatures, the same cannot necessarily be said for organizations that promote the interests of lesbian, gay, bisexual, and transgender (LGBT) Americans. As a result of the perception that congress and state legislatures are unwilling to promote their rights, many LGBT organizations have sought to advance their agendas in the judicial system. For example, in *Goodridge v. Department of Public Health,*[5] Gay and Lesbian Advocates and Defenders, a public interest law firm, successfully persuaded the Massachusetts Supreme Judicial Court that the state cannot deny the protections, benefits, and obligations conferred by marriage to same-sex couples. As a result, Massachusetts became the first state in the nation to recognize same-sex marriages.

Organizations also participate in the legal system because they believe that the judicial branch can supply them with long lasting benefits.[6] For instance, while success in Congress may be short lived because legislation can be altered by a differently composed Congress at a later date, judicial decisions tend to be more stable because of the norm of stare decisis ("let the decision stand"). This holds that judges should respect and affirm prior court decisions involving the same subject matter. Because of this deference to precedent, judicial decisions are very rarely reversed and are thus typically long-lasting. As a result, if a group is able to establish a favorable precedent in the legal system, it is likely that such a victory will be more permanent than successes in executive and legislative institutions, which can be affected by electoral turnover.

A third reason interest groups participate in the court system is to counterbalance the lobbying efforts of their opponents. This form of counteractive lobbying occurs when organizations observe (or anticipate) the actions of their opponents and attempt to neutralize their adversaries' advocacy efforts.[7] For example, conservatives enhanced their litigation strategies in the 1970s after witnessing major victories in the courts by liberal organizations like the American Civil

Liberties Union.[8] These tactics included founding conservative public interest law firms, such as the Pacific Legal Foundation, and establishing organizations aimed at promoting conservative legal philosophies and increasing the number of conservative attorneys, judges, and law school faculty, the most notable of which is the Federalist Society.[9]

Organizations further engage the judiciary to protect victories they won in other branches of government.[10] For example, if an organization successfully lobbies congress to pass legislation beneficial to the organization, it is likely the group will defend any legal challenges to the law in the court system. To illustrate, the American Hospital Association lobbied heavily in support of what would become the Patient Protection and Affordable Care Act ("Obamacare"), the comprehensive health care reform bill passed in 2010.[11] When the law was challenged in the U.S. Supreme Court, the organization filed an amicus curiae brief supporting key provisions of the Act, including the individual mandate and the expansion of Medicaid coverage.[12]

Finally, some groups target the courts because their objectives predispose them to litigation.[13] That is, organizations may recognize that their goals are best pursued in the legal system. For example, the Equal Employment Advisory Council was founded in 1976 in part for the purpose of filing amicus curiae briefs in cases involving affirmative action and equal employment opportunity law.[14] Similarly, one of the primary goals of Americans for Effective Law Enforcement is to overturn the U.S. Supreme Court's decision in *Mapp v. Ohio*,[15] which applied the exclusionary rule—the principle that illegally obtained evidence is inadmissible in criminal prosecutions—to state courts. The organization does this by filing amicus curiae briefs in cases involving search and seizure law.[16] In essence, these groups recognize that their goals may be best pursued by attempting to influence both federal and state court precedents by ensuring conservative voices are well represented in such litigation.

How Interest Groups Lobby the Courts

For organizations that opt to use the legal system, there are a variety of tools at their disposal. While some groups choose to participate only in concrete legal disputes, others attempt to influence the makeup of the bench.[17] This is in recognition of the fact that the identity of the decision-maker affects the decisions that are made.[18] Thus, groups advocate for the appointment, confirmation, or election of like-minded jurists, while opposing those with divergent judicial philosophies.

At the state level, most judges are chosen by some form of election. Given this, groups pursue strategies akin to the electioneering techniques they employ in the other branches of government. Organizations contribute money and resources to judicial campaigns, endorse candidates, run media advertisements for or against candidates, mount voter education campaigns, hold rallies, and organize get-out-the-vote drives. For those state judges that are appointed by governors, legislatures, or nominating commissions, groups will often attempt to influence those making the appointments, including placing representatives from the organization on nominating commissions.[19] Generally speaking, the higher the level of judgeship, the more involvement from interest groups.

Judges at the federal level are appointed by the president and confirmed by the Senate. As a result, there are both similarities and differences as compared to state judicial selection. Akin to state systems, organizations work with and lobby the president and his advisors to appoint judges who will be favorable to the groups' causes, endorse presidential appointees, mobilize their members in support of or in opposition to a potential judge, hold demonstrations, and run ads for and against nominees. Distinct from state elections, federal judicial nominees require confirmation by the Senate. Consequently, organizations lobby senators to vote for or against particular nominees, work with senators to promote or oppose appointees, provide written and/or oral testimony at Senate Judiciary Committee confirmation hearings, and submit letters into the record.[20] In addition, the American Bar Association plays a formal role in the process, rating nominees on the basis of their qualifications for federal judgeships.[21] As with state courts, appointments to higher levels of the federal judiciary, particularly the Supreme Court, tend to attract more organizational involvement.

Turning now to group involvement in litigation, organizations can participate in two general ways. First, groups can act as direct parties to litigation by filing lawsuits themselves or by sponsoring lawsuits filed by individuals. The primary consideration as to whether a group will act as a litigant or a sponsor of litigation is whether or not the group has standing to bring a lawsuit. If an organization can demonstrate that an actual controversy exists that will directly impair the group's interests (a basic definition of standing), it is then authorized to file a lawsuit on behalf of the organization.[22] To obtain standing, a group typically has to show that the organization has a direct stake in the outcome of the case, not merely a political interest in its result. If a group can obtain standing, it becomes a named party in the lawsuit, bound by the judgment of the court. For example, the National Federation of Independent Business (NFIB), a trade association representing the interests of small businesses, was able to obtain standing to challenge the constitutionality of the Patient Protection and Affordable Care Act since its members were directly impacted by provisions in the legislation requiring certain small business to provide health insurance to their employees. Although the U.S. Supreme Court upheld most of the health care law, the NFIB was nonetheless successful at limiting the scope of Congress' Commerce Clause authority.[23]

If an organization cannot obtain standing, it will frequently sponsor lawsuits on behalf of individuals who have standing to sue. As sponsors, groups orchestrate the entire litigation effort, providing the individuals named in the lawsuit with attorneys, research and clerical staff, publicity, and other resources in exchange for using the lawsuit to further the group's goals. In some instances, often referred to as test cases, groups become involved in the litigation from the moment the law is challenged, often recruiting individuals to serve as plaintiffs or defendants in lawsuits. In other instances, groups wait until a case has reached the appellate stages to become involved in the litigation, working with, or taking over the case over from, the attorneys who initially filed the suit.[24] For example, in *Brown v. Board of Education*,[25] the NAACP Legal Defense and Education Fund (LDF) successfully challenged racial segregation in public schools, ending decades of racially disparate educational environments. The LDF sponsored the suit, as opposed to appearing as a named party to the litigation, because standing was limited to individuals with children attending racially segregated public schools.

Class action lawsuits are a special form of sponsorship, in which a group of individuals' grievances are combined into a single lawsuit that the organization brings on their behalf. Such class action lawsuits signal the breadth of an issue by combining the claims of hundreds of individuals and often result in much larger monetary damage awards than would be expected from a single lawsuit brought by a sole person.[26] For example, in 1999, Trial Lawyers for Public Justice (now Public Justice), a public interest law firm, filed a class action lawsuit against Chevy Chase Bank for breaking its pledge to never charge its customers more than 24% interest on credit cards. As a result of the suit, the Bank paid more than $16 million dollars to those affected and repaired any damages to its customers' credit reports.[27]

The second general means for group participation in litigation involves an organization's involvement as a third party, rather than appearing as a direct litigant or sponsoring a direct party to the case. Groups do this by becoming intervenors or by filing amicus curiae briefs. In the federal courts, organizations can achieve intervenor status if they are able to demonstrate that they are statutorily authorized to do so as a matter of right or if their interests would be impaired and they can show they would not be adequately represented by the direct parties to litigation.[28] Though not technically a direct party to the litigation, intervention allows groups to function similar to litigants, including making motions, introducing new legal arguments, and presenting evidence and witnesses at trials. In practice, however, judges are often unwilling to grant interest groups intervenor status as there are no firm guidelines constituting exactly how much of an interest a prospective intervenor must have to participate. As a result, groups denied the opportunity to intervene frequently turn to the amicus curiae brief to have their positions represented.[29]

The most common method interest groups use to lobby the courts—at both the state and federal levels—is the amicus curiae brief.[30] Though this phrase translates literally to "friend of the court," suggesting a form of neutrality, these briefs are in fact tools of advocacy.[31] In these legal briefs, organizations present the courts with alternative and reframed legal arguments, relay the concerns of the executive and legislative branches of government, highlight the policy ramifications of a decision, and inform judges of relevant social scientific evidence. All of this is done in an effort to persuade the judges to endorse the position advocated by the organization. For example, in *Brown v. Entertainment Merchants Association*,[32] a case involving a ban on the sale of violent video games to minors, 31 amicus briefs were filed from a diverse set of organizations, including the American Booksellers Association, the Eagle Forum Education and Legal Defense Fund, the International

Game Developers Association, the Motion Picture Association of America, and the U.S. Chamber of Commerce. Attesting to the ability of these briefs to influence the Court's decisions, eight separate amicus briefs were cited in the justices' opinions.

How Interest Groups Choose Tactics, Venues, and Cases

To understand why groups choose certain litigation tactics over others, it is useful to think in terms of control and resources. Control refers to the extent to which groups are in command of the litigation, while resources relate to the costs (such as attorney, staff, and research fees) that accompany a particular technique. The methods of direct involvement—filing lawsuits, sponsoring cases, engaging in class actions—offer a great deal of control over the litigation, but are also resource intensive. For instance, a group that sets up a test case can control the entirely of the litigation, including who is the named plaintiff, the choice of legal venue(s), the legal argument strategies, and the decision(s) to appeal. At the same time, this technique is very time consuming and expensive. For example, the NAACP LDF and a local attorney who assisted the group were awarded $2.3 million and $1.7 million, respectively, for their work on a school desegregation case they litigated over the course of more than half a decade.[33]

In contrast to direct involvement in litigation, the amicus curiae brief provides a lesser degree of control over the litigation but requires fewer resources.[34] In terms of control, groups participating as amici are bound by the facts of the case and the lower court record, neither of which they had the opportunity to mold.[35] Despite this, amici frequently present the courts with new legal arguments that can change the course of the litigation in the appellate stages.[36] In terms of costs, amicus briefs are much more accessible than forms of direct litigation. Estimates for amicus briefs range from a few thousand dollars up to $100,000, and some lawyers and law professors are willing to file them pro bono (for free) to gain experience, publicize their practices, and promote the public interest by shaping the direction of law.[37]

Once an organization decides on a method of litigation, it next must choose a venue in which to participate. Some of these "choices" are not really choices in that they are dictated by the factual circumstances surrounding a case. For example, if an organization sets up a test case in which the plaintiff it supports challenges a municipal policy, the lawsuit would necessarily be filed in a court with jurisdiction over the locale. Note, however, that even when an organization is geographically constrained, it is not necessarily totally without options. For instance, an organization challenging a local law for violating both the state and federal constitution will typically have the option of filing the suit in either federal or state court.[38]

When groups select a venue in which to participate, they are primarily motivated by two factors: the receptivity of the court to their claims and the potential impact of the decision. If an organization perceives that a court shares similar policy positions as the group, this makes the venue particularly attractive, as compared to a court that opposes the group's positions.[39] Accordingly, groups tend to seek out venues that allow them the best opportunity to establish favorable precedents. For instance, many LGBT organizations believed that state courts would be more amenable to their arguments than federal courts. Consequently, these groups turned to state judiciaries as their primary venues for litigating gay rights issues, such as those involving adoption, marriage, and hospital visitation.[40]

In addition, groups will weigh the potential impact of a ruling when deciding on a venue.[41] All else equal, organizations prefer to establish precedents that affect broad swaths of the American polity. In other words, they seek out the venue with the most reach over public policy. Of course, it is important to recognize that following this strategy has risks. While establishing a favorable precedent in a court with nationwide jurisdiction is a huge victory, failing to do so is a major defeat. Accordingly, an organization must carefully consider a court's receptiveness to the group's positions, along with the scope of its impact when selecting a venue.

To illustrate how the breadth of a precedent's impact influences venue choice, consider Figure 12.1, which compares the percentage of cases with amicus curiae briefs in the U.S. Supreme Court, the U.S. courts of appeals, and state courts of last resort from 1995 to 1998.[42] As this figure makes clear, the percentage of cases with amicus activity in the Supreme Court positively dwarfs that in the other venues. During this time period, more than 90% of Supreme Court cases were accompanied by amicus briefs, compared to only 8% in the courts of appeals and 7% in state courts of last resort. In light of the impact theory of venue selection, these differences make perfect sense. U.S. Supreme Court precedents are binding on the nation as a whole; courts of appeals decisions are binding on the relevant

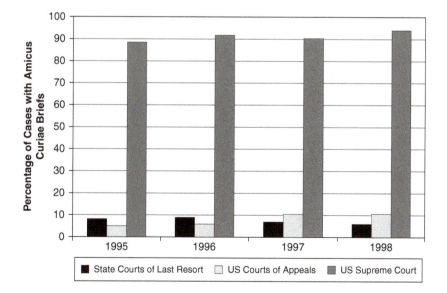

Figure 12.1 The Percentage of Cases with Amicus Curiae Briefs, 1995–1998

circuit in which they were decided (which includes three or more states); while state court of last resort precedents are binding only in the state where the court is located. Thus, Figure 12.1 provides empirical evidence that groups are especially attracted to judicial venues with broad influence over public policy. Of course, it is important to note that, in terms of the sheer volume of amicus activity, more amicus briefs are filed in state courts of last resort and the U.S. circuit courts since those venues decide substantially more cases than the U.S. Supreme Court, which has rendered fewer than 100 decisions per term in recent years.

Having chosen a venue, groups next must select cases to bring on behalf of the organization or to participate in as amicus curiae. Organizations setting up test cases or sponsoring cases in the appellate stages seek out disputes with clean factual circumstances. Such cases lack messy technical issues, such as whether the plaintiff has standing or the controversy is moot, that might result in the case being decided on grounds unrelated to the central issue in the case. In addition, groups are attracted to plaintiffs with sympathetic stories who can help attract media attention to the case.[43] This can raise the profile of the organization and help draw new members and patrons, as well as assist in maintaining the group's current base of support. For example, *District of Columbia v. Heller*,[44] in which the Supreme Court determined that the right to keep and bear arms was an individual right, was a test case initiated and financed by Robert Levy of the Cato Institute, a public policy research foundation. In order to exert maximum control over the quality of the case, Levy personally orchestrated the legal arguments and interviewed dozens of potential plaintiffs who would challenge the handgun ban. Levy modeled this strategy on the tactics used by civil rights organizations, such as the NAACP LDF, in the 1950s and 1960s.[45]

Organizations that file amicus curiae briefs are attracted to cases for a variety of often interrelated reasons. First, groups are more likely to file amicus briefs in cases that they believe will enhance their prospects of influencing judges' decisions. Often, this involves targeting cases in which the information environment is relatively poor, such as those involving complex legal questions or inexperienced counsel.[46] Note, however, that there is conflicting evidence as to whether interest groups are especially likely to file amicus briefs in cases in which the position they support is likely to prevail regardless of the groups' participation.[47] Second, groups seek out cases that will have far-reaching policy impact, such as those involving salient constitutional issues, the exercise of judicial review, and civil rights and liberties policies.[48] In addition, membership organizations seek out high-profile cases, such as those generating media attention, in order to foster organizational maintenance concerns.[49] Finally, groups file amicus briefs as a form of counteractive lobbying. That is, amici anticipate or respond to the lobbying efforts of opposition organizations in order to neutralize their opponents' potential to shape judicial outcomes.[50]

The Influence of Interest Groups on the Courts

In assessing the impact of interest group lobbying efforts, it is imperative to first consider the goals of organizations. For those groups that participate in the selection of federal or state judges, their objective is to influence the makeup of the bench. That is, they want to promote the appointment or election of judges who will further the groups' causes, while opposing those with divergent perspectives. This is in recognition of the fact that attributes of individual judges, particularly their ideological preferences, can result in outcomes that are favorable or unfavorable to the organizations' desired policies. At the state level, it is clear that interest groups donate to judicial campaigns and that these donations can shape the outcome of elections.[51] In addition, there is growing evidence that campaign finance donations can translate into favorable decisions.[52] At the federal level, numerous scholars have demonstrated that interest groups influence the confirmation of lower federal court and Supreme Court judges, most notably by lobbying senators, testifying before the Senate Judiciary Committee, and taking public positions for or against nominees.[53]

For organizations that participate directly in litigation, either by filing lawsuits themselves or sponsoring cases on behalf of individuals, the primary goal is to establish favorable precedents.[54] Through these planned litigation efforts, groups attempt to influence not only the outcome of the case in terms of winners and losers but also the policy announced in the judicial opinion. Extant research documents plentiful examples of successful litigation campaigns.[55] For example, Vose[56] provides a compelling account of the NAACP's monumental victories that resulted in the end of racial covenant laws that prohibited African Americans from living in certain neighborhoods. Yet, it is not entirely clear if victories such as these are attributable primarily to the efforts of interest groups. In particular, Lee Epstein and C. K. Rowland[57] found that interest groups were no more successful than non-interest groups in terms of having their positions adopted by federal district courts. Likewise, Jeffrey A. Segal and Harold J. Spaeth point out that the oft-touted success of the NAACP LDF in school desegregation cases, such as *Brown v. Board of Education,* is not necessarily indicative of the influence of that organization since the "liberal Warren Court most likely would have supported desegregation with or without the support of the LDF."[58]

The evidence as to the influence of amicus curiae briefs is more consistent in comparison to the aforementioned research on direct forms of litigation. While there is a general agreement that the goal of interest group amicus participation is to influence judicial decisions,[59] scholars have conceptualized amicus influence in a variety of ways. At the onset, it is imperative to note that amicus curiae briefs can be filed at two phases of litigation: the agenda setting stage and the decision on the merits stage. Most courts of last resort, such as the U.S. Supreme Court, have discretion as to which cases they hear, meaning they set their own agendas. Due to this, many groups choose to file amicus briefs to urge the court to accept a case for review or to pass on it. At the U.S. Supreme Court, there is compelling evidence that the presence of amicus briefs heavily influences the justices' agenda setting decisions, making review more likely.[60] In essence, because amicus briefs are relatively rare at this phase of decision making (appearing in about 10% of petitions for review), and because they are somewhat costly, they send a reliable signal to the justices that a case has economic, legal, political, and/or social significance and is thus worthy of the Court's attention.

The second phase of decision making, the merits stage, results in judges deciding the outcome of the case (i.e., determining winners and losers) and releasing the opinions that make policy and explain the reasoning behind their decisions. Much of the work examining the influence of amicus briefs at this stage focuses on whether amicus briefs influence the outcome of cases in terms of winners and losers. The presumption is that the goal of amici is to have courts render decisions that are favorable toward the litigant supported by the amicus briefs. There is a substantial body of evidence that supports this view, demonstrating that amicus briefs can influence case outcomes in state courts of last resort,[61] federal courts of appeals,[62] and the U.S. Supreme Court.[63] This research illustrates that, by providing the courts with argumentation that can buttress that of the direct parties to litigation, judges can be persuaded to rule in favor of the litigant supported in the amicus curiae briefs.

A second way to conceptualize amicus influence for decisions on the merits focuses on the ability of amici to shape the ideological direction of the judges' votes or the courts' decisions. This follows from the perspective that organizations are not primarily concerned with the outcome of the case in terms of winners and losers, but are rather principally interested in securing policies favorable to the groups' interests.[64] In other words, liberal amici seek to promote liberal causes, such as advocating for broad interpretations of core civil rights doctrines, while conservative amici advance conservative causes, such as limiting the scope of federal regulatory power. Paul M. Collins Jr.,[65] demonstrates that amici can successfully influence both the ideological direction of the U.S. Supreme Court's decisions and that of the individual justice's votes. This shows that amici are capable of persuading justices to endorse the ideological position advocated in the briefs by providing them with persuasive information regarding the legal, political, and social ramifications of a decision.

A third way of examining the influence of amicus briefs involves investigating the opinions that accompany legal decisions, which have great significance. For example, U.S. Supreme Court majority opinions set precedents that constrain the behavior of lower federal and state courts, the executive and legislative branches, and the public at large. These opinions establish acceptable norms of behavior, provide guidelines as the constitutionality of particular policies, and supply guidance to lower court judges who are charged with adjudicating lawsuits with similar factual circumstances.[66] Due to the broad power of precedent, amici actively seek to influence the language used in judicial opinions, hoping to contribute to the development of a judicial opinion that promotes the groups' interests. Existing research demonstrates that amici can serve this function, particularly at the U.S. Supreme Court. For instance, amicus curiae briefs are cited in approximately 30% of majority opinions in which at least one brief was filed.[67] Further, in-depth case studies reveal that the arguments made by amici contribute to the content of judicial opinions, regardless of whether the amicus brief was actually cited by the Court.[68]

Thus, by providing the justices with information that enhances their ability to make efficacious law—particularly with regard to better understanding the broad impact of a decision—amici can contribute to the language of judicial opinions.[69]

I now turn to demonstrating a new and promising method to investigate the ability of amicus briefs to influence the content of judicial opinions. In particular, I use plagiarism detection software to study the extent to which U.S. Supreme Court justices incorporate language from amicus briefs into their majority opinions. This is a very useful technique for a variety of reasons. First, it is consistent with one of the main goals of amici: to shape the development of federal law by influencing the language used in the Supreme Court majority opinions that act as precedents for the nation as a whole. Second, it illuminates the ability of amici to contribute to the content of the Court's opinions beyond merely counting citations to amicus briefs in those opinions. Consequently, it provides an especially nuanced means to evaluate amicus influence by focusing on the similarities between the language appearing in amicus briefs and the Court's opinions. Finally, it allows me to investigate the content of relatively large number of Supreme Court opinions, something that is very difficult to do without the assistance of computers. In particular, I explore the extent to which the justices adopted the arguments made in 524 amicus briefs in the 67 majority opinions released during the Court's 2004 term.[70]

Figure 12.2 is a box plot of the percentage of Supreme Court majority opinions that directly incorporate language from amicus curiae briefs, demarcated by the justice who authored the majority opinion. To allow for comparisons, this figure also reports the overall average for all majority opinions, labeled SC. The shaded area within the box represents the 25th (lower value) to 75th (higher value) percentiles, and the line in the middle of the graph indicates the median percentage of majority opinions that borrows language from amicus briefs. The lines outside of the box report adjacent values, and extreme outliers are represented by the circles that appear above these lines.

On average, about 3% of Supreme Court opinions are taken directly from amicus curiae briefs. This figure is lower than the average percentages of language from lower court opinions (4.3%) and litigant briefs (9.8%) that are directly incorporated into Supreme Court opinions.[71] Thus, it appears that the justices rely less on amicus briefs in their majority opinions as compared to the opinions of the lower courts who initially handled the case and the briefs of the direct parties to litigation. This is not surprising in that the core of the case record is established by the lower courts whose decisions are being reviewed, along with the arguments advanced by the litigants. Because most amici enter the case only when it reaches the Supreme Court, interest groups have more limited opportunities to shape how cases are framed.[72]

Notably, Figure 12.2 reveals that there is a good amount of variation among justices and amici. For example, majority opinions authored by Justices Thomas (4.8%) and Rehnquist (4.6%) incorporate the highest amount of amicus language, while opinions by Souter (1.2%) and Stevens (2.5%) rely least on amicus briefs. Regarding individual briefs, the language used in 15% of all amicus briefs never

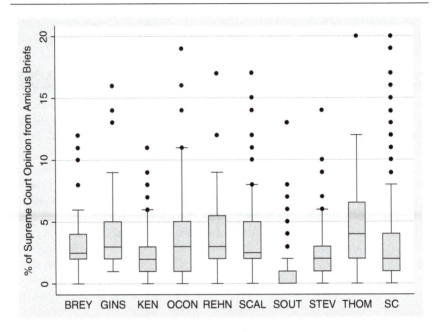

Figure 12.2 The Percentage of U.S. Supreme Court Majority Opinions from Amicus Curiae Briefs, by Justice (2004 Term)

Note: BREY = Justice Breyer; GINS = Justice Ginsburg; KEN = Justice Kennedy; OCON = Justice O'Connor; REHN = Chief Justice Rehnquist; SCAL = Justice Scalia; SOUT = Justice Souter; STEV = Justice Stevens; THOM = Justice Thomas; SC = Supreme Court. N = 524 amicus brief–majority opinion dyads.

made its way into a single majority opinion. Yet, several majority opinions relied substantially on amicus briefs. For example, 16% of the language used in the majority opinion in *Koons Buick Pontiac v. Nigh*[73] was adopted from the National Automobile Dealers Association's (NADA) amicus brief. The NADA was able to successfully contribute to the Court's decision to uphold limits on statutory damage awards for personal-property loans found to be in violation of the Truth in Lending Act. Similarly, 12% of the majority opinion in *Leocal v. Ashcroft*[74] was based on the joint amicus brief filed by the National Association of Criminal Defense Lawyers, the American Civil Liberties Union, the American Immigration Lawyers Association, Defending Immigrants Partnership, and the New York State Defenders Association. The coalition was able to persuade the Court to adopt its argument that driving under the influence and causing serious bodily injury in a resulting accident is not a "crime of violence" for the purpose of establishing deportable offenses under the Immigration and Nationality Act. Given the leverage this type of computer assisted content analysis offers over understanding interest group influence on opinion content, it is clear that there are a wide range of applications for future research, such as exploring why courts rely more or less on certain amicus briefs and whether the courts favor particular interest groups over others.

Conclusion

Despite the fact that Americans do not typically think about the judicial branch when we consider interest groups, it is clear that organized interests are active participants in the legal system. At the state level, groups play a major role financing judicial campaigns and engaging in electioneering techniques more broadly, seeking to contribute to a bench composed of jurists favorable to the organizations' causes. At the federal level, groups are likewise intimately involved in the selection of judges and devote substantial resources to lobbying senators, mobilizing their members for or against particular appointees, and testifying before the Senate Judiciary Committee. Moreover, in terms of litigation, interest group involvement was at the heart of many of the U.S. Supreme Court's land-mark decisions, ranging from racial discrimination, to Second Amendment rights, to search and seizure law. Indeed, it is not hyperbolic to say that one would have a difficult time understanding judicial politics without a solid knowledge of the role interest groups play in the legal arena.

While this essay has made it evident that we know a great deal about how interest groups use the legal system to pursue their goals, there still remains a variety of areas where our collective knowledge is lacking. For example, the literature on group involvement in the federal courts is much more extensive than that at the state level, as is research on the U.S. Supreme Court compared to other federal judicial venues. In terms of litigation strategies, the areas of class action lawsuits and intervention are relatively understudied, as is venue selection, particularly as it relates to how groups choose between and among federal and state court systems. While there has been a substantial body of research devoted to investigating amicus curiae participation, there has been scant attention devoted to how amicus briefs influence what is arguably the most important aspect of legal decision making: the content of judicial opinions. Thus, while we have made major inroads regarding interest group involvement in the judicial arena, there is still a host of research questions awaiting future study.

Notes

1 *Lawrence v. Texas*, 539 U.S. 558 (2003).
2 Thomas T. Holyoke, "Choosing Battlegrounds: Interest Group Lobbying Across Multiple Venues," *Political Research Quarterly* 56, no. 3 (2003): 325–36.
3 Clement E. Vose, *Caucasians Only: The Supreme Court, the N.A.A.C.P., and the Restrictive Covenant Cases* (Berkeley: University of California Press, 1959).
4 Richard C. Cortner, "Strategies and Tactics of Litigants in Constitutional Cases," *Journal of Public Law* 17, no. 2 (1968): 287–307.
5 *Goodridge v. Department of Public Health*, 798 N.E. 2d 941 (Mass. 2003).
6 Stephen L. Wasby, *Race Relations Litigation in an Age of Complexity* (Charlottesville: University of Virginia Press, 1995).
7 David Austen-Smith and John R. Wright, "Counteractive Lobbying," *American Journal of Political Science* 38, no. 1 (1994): 25–44; Lisa A. Solowiej and Paul M. Collins Jr., "Counteractive Lobbying in the U.S. Supreme Court," *American Politics Research* 37, no. 4 (2009): 670–99.
8 Lee Epstein, *Conservatives in Court* (Knoxville: University of Tennessee Press, 1985).

9 Steven M. Teles, *The Rise of the Conservative Legal Movement: The Battle for Control of the Law* (Princeton, NJ: Princeton University Press, 2009).

10 Paul M. Collins Jr., *Friends of the Supreme Court: Interest Groups and Judicial Decision Making* (New York: Oxford University Press, 2008).

11 Medicare News Group, "The American Hospital Association and Its Health Care Reform Lobby," http://www.medicarenewsgroup.com/news/medicare-faqs/individual-faq?faqId=a7693994-8416-4824-ab6f-ab93ab3e7246.

12 American Hospital Association, "Legal Resources: Amicus Briefs," http://www.aha.org/advocacy-issues/legal/legal-amicus-briefs.shtml.

13 Collins, *Friends of the Supreme Court.*

14 Karen O'Connor and Lee Epstein, "The Rise of Conservative Interest Group Litigation," *Journal of Politics* 45, no. 2 (1983): 479–89.

15 *Mapp v. Ohio*, 367 U.S. 643 (1961).

16 Epstein, *Conservatives in Court*, p. 163.

17 Lauren Cohen Bell, *Warring Factions: Interest Groups, Money, and the New Politics of Senate Confirmation* (Columbus: Ohio State University Press, 2002); Anthony Champagne, "Interest Groups and Judicial Elections," *Loyola of Los Angeles Law Review* 34, no. 4 (2001): 1391–1409; Nancy Scherer, *Scoring Points: Politicians, Activists, and the Lower Federal Court Appointment Process* (Palo Alto, CA: Stanford University Press, 2005).

18 Paul M. Collins Jr. and Wendy L. Martinek, "The Small Group Context: Designated District Court Judges in the U.S. Courts of Appeals," *Journal of Empirical Legal Studies* 8, no. 1 (2011): 177–205.

19 Champagne, "Interest Groups and Judicial Elections"; Michael E. Solimine and Rafael Gely, "Federal and State Judicial Selection in an Interest Group Perspective," *Missouri Law Review* 74, no. 3 (2009): 531–54. Further, some groups participate in the formulation of state judicial selection systems.

20 Bell, *Warring Factions*; Scherer, *Scoring Points.*

21 Susan Navarro Smelcer, Amy Steigerwalt, and Richard L. Vining Jr., "Bias and the Bar: Evaluating the ABA Ratings of Federal Judicial Nominees," *Political Research Quarterly* 65, no. 4 (2012): 827–40.

22 Karen Orren, "Standing to Sue: Interest Group Conflict in the Federal Courts," *American Political Science Review* 70, no. 3 (1976): 723–41.

23 *National Federation of Independent Business v. Sebelius*, 132 S. Ct. 2566 (2012).

24 Collins, *Friends of the Supreme Court*; Wasby, *Race Relations Litigation in an Age of Complexity.*

25 *Brown v. Board of Education*, 347 U.S. 483 (1954).

26 John C. Coffee Jr., "Class Wars: The Dilemma of the Mass Tort Class Action," *Columbia Law Review* 95, no. 6 (1995): 1343–1465.

27 Chris Kirkham, "Chevy Chase Bank Settles Credit Card Suit," *Washington Post*, July 28, 2006.

28 At the state level, the exact requirements for obtaining intervenor status vary from state to state, though they generally reflect those at the federal level. Matthew I. Hall, "Standing of Intervenor-Defendants in Public Law Litigation," *Fordham Law Review* 80, no. 4 (2012): 1539–84.

29 Kerry C. White, "Rule 24(A) Intervention of Right: Why the Federal Courts Should Require Standing to Intervene," *Loyola of Los Angeles Law Review* 36, no. 1 (2002): 527–63.

30 Collins, *Friends of the Supreme Court*; Sarah Corbally, Donald C. Bross, and Victor E. Flango, "Filing of Amicus Curiae Briefs in State Courts of Last Resort, 1960–2000," *Justice System Journal* 25, no. 1 (2004): 39–56.

31 On rare occasions, interest groups file seemingly neutral amicus briefs supporting "neither party." For example, during the 1995 term of the U.S. Supreme Court, 400

amicus briefs were filed, only 2 of which supported "neither party." Paul M. Collins Jr. and Lisa A. Solowiej, "Interest Group Participation, Competition, and Conflict in the U.S. Supreme Court," *Law & Social Inquiry* 32, no. 4 (2007): 955–84.

32 *Brown v. Entertainment Merchants Association*, 180 L. Ed. 2d 708 (2011).

33 Wasby, *Race Relations Litigation in an Age of Complexity,* p. 97.

34 Rorie Spill Solberg and Eric N. Waltenburg, "Why Do Interest Groups Engage the Judiciary? Policy Wishes and Structural Needs," *Social Science Quarterly* 87, no. 3 (2006): 558–72. I am unaware of studies that examine the costs associated with organizational intervention, likely due to the reality that groups are rarely granted this status. I suspect that the resources needed for intervention are similar to those necessary for case sponsorship, and are dependent on the stage at which the intervention occurs.

35 Epstein, *Conservatives in Court,* p. 148.

36 Collins, *Friends of the Supreme Court.*

37 Gregory A. Caldeira and John R. Wright, "Organized Interests and Agenda Setting in the U.S. Supreme Court," *American Political Science Review* 82, no. 4 (1988): 1109–27; Madeleine Schachter, "The Utility of Pro Bono Representation of U.S.-Based Amicus Curiae in Non-U.S. and Multi-National Courts as a Means of Advancing the Public Interest," *Fordham International Law Journal* 28, no. 1 (2004): 88–144; Gary F. Smith and Beth E. Terrell, "The Amicus Curiae: A Powerful Friend for Poverty Law Advocates," *Clearinghouse Review* 29, November-December (1995): 772–92; Stephanie Francis Ward, "Friends of the Court Are Friends of Mine," *ABA Journal,* November 1, 2007.

38 Mark Moller, "The Checks and Balances of Forum Shopping," *Stanford Journal of Complex Litigation* 1, no. 1 (2012): 107–69.

39 Thomas G. Hansford, "Lobbying Strategies, Venue Selection, and Organized Interest Involvement at the U.S. Supreme Court," *American Politics Research* 32, no. 2 (2004): 170–97.

40 Daniel R. Pinello, *Gay Rights and American Law* (New York: Cambridge University Press, 2003); William B. Rubenstein, "The Myth of Superiority," *Constitutional Commentary* 16, no. 3 (1999): 599–626.

41 Wasby, *Race Relations Litigation in an Age of Complexity.*

42 The data in Figure 12.1 comes from the following sources: U.S. Supreme Court (Collins, *Friends of the Supreme Court*); U.S. courts of appeals (Ashlyn K. Kuersten and Susan B. Haire, *Update to the Appeals Court Data Base [1997–2002]* [Department of Political Science, Western Michigan University, 2011]; Donald R. Songer, *The Original U.S. Appeals Courts Database 1925–1996* [Columbia, SC: Department of Political Science, University of South Carolina, 2008]); state courts of last resort (Paul Brace and Melinda Gann Hall, *State Supreme Court Data Project* [Department of Political Science, Rice University, 2006]). It is important to note that the level of amicus activity also varies among states and circuits. Generally speaking, more populous states and circuits, and those with greater levels of interest group density, attract more amicus participation. See, e.g., Lee Epstein, "Exploring the Participation of Organized Interests in State Court Litigation," *Political Research Quarterly* 47, no. 2 (1994): 335–51.

43 Wasby, *Race Relations Litigation in an Age of Complexity.*

44 *District of Columbia v. Heller*, 171 L. Ed. 2d 637 (2008).

45 Adam Liptak, "Carefully Plotted Course Propels Gun Case to Top," *New York Times,* December 3, 2007.

46 Hansford, "Lobbying Strategies, Venue Selection, and Organized Interest Involvement at the U.S. Supreme Court"; Wendy L. Martinek, "Amici Curiae in the U.S. Courts of Appeals," *American Politics Research* 34, no. 6 (2006): 803–24; Solowiej and Collins, "Counteractive Lobbying in the U.S. Supreme Court."

47 Compare, for example, Hansford, "Lobbying Strategies, Venue Selection, and Organized Interest Involvement at the U.S. Supreme Court," with Paul M. Collins Jr., "Friends of the Court: Examining the Influence of Amicus Curiae Participation in U.S. Supreme

Court Litigation," *Law & Society Review* 38, no. 4 (2004): 807–32, and Paul M. Collins Jr., "Lobbyists before the U.S. Supreme Court: Investigating the Influence of Amicus Curiae Briefs," *Political Research Quarterly* 60, no. 1 (2007): 55–70.

48 Martinek, "Amici Curiae in the U.S. Courts of Appeals"; Solowiej and Collins, "Counteractive Lobbying in the U.S. Supreme Court."

49 Hansford, "Lobbying Strategies, Venue Selection, and Organized Interest Involvement at the U.S. Supreme Court"; Solberg and Waltenburg, "Why Do Interest Groups Engage the Judiciary?"

50 Solowiej and Collins, "Counteractive Lobbying in the U.S. Supreme Court."

51 Champagne, "Interest Groups and Judicial Elections"; David Goldberger, "The Power of Special Interest Groups to Overwhelm Judicial Elections: The Troublesome Interaction Between the Code of Judicial Conduct, Campaign Finance Laws, and the First Amendment," *University of Cincinnati Law Review* 72, no. 1 (2003): 1–43; Matthew J. Streb, ed., *Running for Judge: The Rising Political, Financial, and Legal Stakes of Judicial Elections* (New York: New York University Press, 2007).

52 Damon M. Cann, "Justice for Sale? Campaign Contributions and Judicial Decisionmaking," *State Politics & Policy Quarterly* 7, no. 3 (2007): 281–97; Stephen J. Ware, "Money, Politics and Judicial Decisions: A Case Study of Arbitration Law in Alabama," *Journal of Law & Politics* 15, no. 4 (1999): 645–86.

53 Bell, *Warring Factions;* Gregory A. Caldeira and John R. Wright, "Lobbying for Justice: Organized Interests, Supreme Court Nominations, and United States Senate," *American Journal of Political Science* 42, no. 2 (1998): 499–523; Nancy Scherer, Brandon L. Bartels, and Amy Steigerwalt, "Sounding the Fire Alarm: The Role of Interest Groups in the Lower Federal Court Confirmation Process," *Journal of Politics* 70, no. 4 (2008): 1026–39; Jeffrey A. Segal, Charles M. Cameron, and Albert D. Cover, "A Spatial Model of Roll Call Voting: Senators, Constituents, Presidents, and Interest Groups in Supreme Court Confirmations," *American Journal of Political Science* 36, no. 1 (1992): 96–121.

54 In addition, organizations participating in the judiciary may also be attentive to organizational maintenance concerns, such as attracting new members and retaining their current base of support. Collins, *Friends of the Supreme Court,* 28–29; Scott A. Comparato, *Amici Curiae and Strategic Behavior in State Supreme Courts* (Westport, CT: Praeger Publishers, 2003); Lee Epstein and C. K. Rowland, "Debunking the Myth of Interest Group Invincibility in the Courts," *American Political Science Review* 85, no. 1 (1991): 205–17; Solberg and Waltenburg, "Why Do Interest Groups Engage the Judiciary?"; Wasby, *Race Relations Litigation in an Age of Complexity,* p. 116.

55 Epstein, *Conservatives in Court;* Karen O'Connor and Lee Epstein, "Beyond Legislative Lobbying: Women's Rights Groups and the Supreme Court," *Judicature* 67, no. 3 (1983): 134–43; Rubenstein, "The Myth of Superiority"; Teles, *The Rise of the Conservative Legal Movement;* Wasby, *Race Relations Litigation in an Age of Complexity.*

56 Vose, *Caucasians Only.*

57 Epstein and Rowland, "Debunking the Myth of Interest Group Invincibility in the Courts."

58 Jeffrey A. Segal and Harold J. Spaeth, *The Supreme Court and the Attitudinal Model* (New York: Cambridge University Press, 1993), p. 237.

59 Caldeira and Wright, "Organized Interests and Agenda Setting in the U.S. Supreme Court"; Collins, *Friends of the Supreme Court;* Hansford, "Lobbying Strategies, Venue Selection, and Organized Interest Involvement at the U.S. Supreme Court."

60 Caldeira and Wright, "Organized Interests and Agenda Setting in the U.S. Supreme Court"; Kevin T. McGuire and Gregory A. Caldeira, "Lawyers, Organized Interests, and the Law of Obscenity: Agenda Setting in the Supreme Court," *American Political Science Review* 87, no. 3 (1993): 746–55.

61 Donald R. Songer and Ashlyn Kuersten, "The Success of Amici in State Supreme Courts," *Political Research Quarterly* 48, no. 1 (1995): 31–42; but see Comparato, *Amici Curiae and Strategic Behavior in State Supreme Courts.*

62 Paul M. Collins Jr. and Wendy L. Martinek, "Friends of the Circuits: Interest Group Influence on the U.S. Courts of Appeals," *Social Science Quarterly* 91, no. 2 (2010): 397–414.

63 Collins, "Friends of the Court"; Joseph D. Kearney and Thomas W. Merrill, "The Influence of Amicus Curiae Briefs on the Supreme Court," *University of Pennsylvania Law Review* 148, no. 3 (2000): 743–853; but see Donald R. Songer and Reginald S. Sheehan, "Interest Group Success in the Courts: Amicus Participation in the Supreme Court," *Political Research Quarterly* 46, no. 2 (1993): 339–54.

64 Collins, "Lobbyists before the U.S. Supreme Court."

65 Collins, "Lobbyists before the U.S. Supreme Court"; Collins, *Friends of the Supreme Court.*

66 Pamela C. Corley, Paul M. Collins Jr., and Bryan Calvin, "Lower Court Influence on U.S. Supreme Court Opinion Content," *Journal of Politics* 73, no. 1 (2011): 31–44.

67 Kearney and Merrill, "The Influence of Amicus Curiae Briefs on the Supreme Court"; Ryan J. Owens and Lee Epstein, "Amici Curiae During the Rehnquist Years," *Judicature* 89, no. 3 (2005): 127–32.

68 Lee Epstein and Joseph F. Kobylka, *The Supreme Court and Legal Change: Abortion and the Death Penalty* (Chapel Hill: University of North Carolina Press, 1992); Suzanne Uttaro Samuels, *First among Friends: Interest Groups, the U.S. Supreme Court, and the Right to Privacy* (Westport, CT: Praeger Publishers, 2004). See also James F. Spriggs, II and Paul J. Wahlbeck, "Amicus Curiae and the Role of Information at the Supreme Court," *Political Research Quarterly* 50, no. 2 (1997): 365–86.

69 In addition, Collins shows how amicus briefs contribute to the frequency with which the justices write concurring and dissenting opinions. While not precedential, these opinions are nonetheless significant in that they highlight weaknesses in the majority opinion, making it more likely that it will be reversed at a future date. Paul M. Collins Jr., "Amici Curiae and Dissensus on the U.S. Supreme Court," *Journal of Empirical Legal Studies* 5, no. 1 (2008): 143–70.

70 More specifically, the data under analysis include all orally argued, signed Supreme Court majority opinions released during the 2004 term. The unit of analysis is the amicus brief-majority opinion dyad, meaning that each amicus brief is compared to the Supreme Court majority opinion corresponding to the case in which the brief was filed. I followed the protocols used by Corley, Collins, and Calvin, "Lower Court Influence on U.S. Supreme Court Opinion Content," to set the parameters for the plagiarism detection software.

71 Pamela C. Corley, "The Supreme Court and Opinion Content: The Influence of Parties' Briefs," *Political Research Quarterly* 61, no. 3 (2008): 468–78; Corley, Collins, and Calvin, "Lower Court Influence on U.S. Supreme Court Opinion Content."

72 Paul M. Collins Jr. and Wendy L. Martinek, "Who Participates as Amici Curiae in the U.S. Courts of Appeals?," *Judicature* 94, no. 3 (2010): 128–36.

73 *Koons Buick Pontiac v. Nigh*, 543 U.S. 50 (2004).

74 *Leocal v. Ashcroft*, 543 U.S. 1 (2004).

Chapter 13

Evaluating Reforms Lobbying and Money in Politics

Lee Drutman

The preceding chapters have detailed the many ways in which organized interests participate in the political process. This chapter asks what, if anything, should be done to reform these ways? In particular, we will focus on campaign finance and lobbying.

The first step in answering this question is trying to define the problem. A poll taken right after the 2012 election summarizes the basic public concern about the current system. To the question of "who has the most influence on Congressional votes," 59 percent identified "special interest groups and lobbyists" and 46 percent said "campaign contributors." "Constituent views" and "conscience" ranked at the very bottom (14 percent and 12 percent, respectively). Additionally, almost two-thirds responded that democracy was being "undermined" by big donors and secret money.[1]

But such diagnoses call for more specificity. If democracy is being "undermined," how is it being undermined? If lobbyists, special interests, and campaign contributors have too much influence, how is that influence wielded and manifested? And what would a democracy not undermined by such forces look like?

Though Americans generally hold complicated and sometimes conflicting attitudes toward fairness and equality, large majorities hold the ideal of political equality. As Kay Lehman Schlozman, Sidney Verba, and Henry E. Brady explain, "they are committed to the fundamental equality among persons and to equal citizenship—equal political rights and equal political influence for all."[2]

An idealized democracy in which voice and access are equally distributed is in most respects hard to square with the ways in which campaign finance and lobbying resources are distributed. In campaign finance, the very tiniest slice of Americans account for an outsized share of contributions. In 2010, for example, less than 1 percent of the top 1 percent of Americans (26,783 individuals to be exact) contributed one-quarter of all individual campaign donations.[3] In the 2012 election, 32 Super PAC donors gave a combined $313 million—the equivalent of what the two presidential candidates (Obama and Romney) earned from almost 4 million small donors giving less than $200 million. And in 2012, 40 percent of contributions to Senate candidates came from the 0.02 percent of donors who gave at least $2,500.[4]

Lobbying is similarly imbalanced. By Schlozman et al.'s count, business groups make up 53 percent of the organizations with lobbyists in Washington, hire 64 percent of the outside firms, and make 72 percent of the lobbying expenditures. They also give half of the PAC donations. Moreover, Schlozman et al. estimate that 10 percent of adults in the United States could be classified as executives, about 74 percent of the organizations in Washington represent the interests of executives. Another 10 percent of adults they classify as professionals, and 17.3 percent of Washington organizations represent them. That means that less than 10 percent of organizations represent the other 80 percent of Americans.

While the imbalances are relatively straightforward to document, political science has had a more difficult time pinning down the exact ways in which heavily resourced political participants wield influence. In earlier decades, this stemmed from conceptual difficulties in defining exactly what one meant by words like "power" and "influence."[5] More recently, scholars struggled with statistical tests of whether higher levels of campaign and lobbying spending improve groups' chances of success. In campaign finance, the meta-conclusion of more than 40 studies is that there is no statistically reliable relationship between PAC contributions and votes,[6] nor do lobbying resources reliably correlate with success.[7] But even if resources do not determine outcomes on any particular issue, there is substantial evidence resources do shape the attentions and priorities of members of Congress, providing both access, particular at key stages of agenda formation.[8] Access matters because, as the old Washington adage goes, "If you are not at the table, you are probably on the menu." Participation doesn't guarantee victory, but it's pretty difficult to win when you are not even in the game.

The preceding chapters have highlighted the many ways in which interest groups target all branches of government, working with and against each other, using multiple strategies across multiple venues, and with varying degrees of effectiveness. While any individual strategy on its own cannot guarantee success, "the general pattern is that doing more of anything produces greater success than doing less, regardless of the strategy."[9] In lobbying there is much wisdom to the old bromide about persistence: "if it first you don't succeed . . ." Influence may be hard to demonstrate in any one case, but aggregate levels of resource imbalances are likely to matter.

In campaign finance, the reformer's task is complicated by recent jurisprudence. Courts have considered political spending a form of free speech and have thus been wary of restrictions on it. Since the 1976 *Buckley v. Valeo* decision, courts have generally viewed quid pro quo corruption as the only legitimate reason for limiting money in politics, though *Buckley* did also consider the "appearance of corruption stemming from public awareness of the opportunities for abuse." The lone exception to this standard was the 1992 *Austin v. Michigan State Chamber of Commerce* case, which went beyond quid pro quo corruption and considered distortion as a form of corruption, arguing that state had a legitimate interest in preventing the unequal resources gained in the marketplace from spilling over into politics. However, the *Citizens United* court overruled *Austin*.

The legal focus on quid pro quo corruption as the only legitimate justification for limiting campaign finance has no doubt helped push reformers to think about campaign finance in terms of quid pro quo corruption, seeking the elusive evidence that would convince the Supreme Court that restrictions on campaign finance are acceptable. Yet this runs up against the fact that empirically, the case for systematic quid pro quo corruption is generally weak. Rather, if money matters, it most likely matters by providing access to contributors, who in turn use that to command attention and to shift the views of lawmakers though the self-interested worldview osmosis that comes from repeated sympathetic listening to campaign contributors.

Exclusive focus on quid pro quo campaign finance corruption ignores what is likely a more significant source of influence: the fact that congressional staff have come to increasingly depend on lobbyists to explain and frame the increasingly complicated policy questions that Congress faces. As Lorelei Kelly puts it: "Many contemporary and urgent questions before our legislators require nuance, genuine deliberation and expert judgment. Congress, however, is missing adequate means for this purpose and depends on outdated and in some cases antiquated systems of information referral, sorting, communicating, and convening."[10]

One reason for the lack of expertise is that turnover is high, and working in Congress is more often a job for enthusiastic 20-somethings than for more established professionals who bring genuine policy expertise. According to a 2009 Congressional Management Foundation survey, 27 percent of House legislative directors are under 30 years old, and 87 percent are under 40 years old. More than half (55 percent) have only a bachelor's degree, and only one in six (16 percent) have a law degree. Typically, they have two to three legislative aides working under them, and 80 percent of those aides will have less than three years' experience in Congress.[11] Committee staffers tend to have more experience than personal office staff, and Senate staff are likewise tend to be more experienced than their House counterparts. Still, turnover everywhere in the government is high because of relatively low pay and long hours and difficult work conditions, with only a handful of truly dedicated staffers making a career of it.

At the same time, legislation has grown ever more complex. The 111th Congress passed the two longest non-appropriations bills in Congressional history: the Dodd-Frank Wall Street Reform and Consumer Protection Act at 383,013 words and the Patient Protection and Affordable Care Act at 327,911 words. (For the sake of comparison, the Oxford World's Classics edition of Leo Tolstoy's *War and Peace* is 561,093 words.) Congressional offices also have to deal with a remarkable range of issues. As one measure of the diversity, since 2009, the Library of Congress has used 1,023 unique codes to identify legislation. Yet, the big transformation in Congress is that despite the ever-increasing complexity, offices have shifted more staff to deal with constituent concerns, and committees (where expertise tends to concentrate) have actually reduced their staffing levels. In 1979, 75 percent of Senate staff were based in DC; in 2005, only 61 percent of staff were. More significantly, the number of Senate committee staff fell from 1,410 in 1979 to 957 in 2005.[12] The House has witnessed similar trends.[13]

The practical implication is that the average staffer is constantly scrambling to make informed decisions. As Kevin Esterling puts it: "It is difficult for Congress to know about the current research-based state of knowledge for the full array of policies before it."[14] This is where lobbyists frequently step in. As Esterling continues, "In contrast, it is relatively easy for specialized interest groups to know about the state of knowledge for a policy."[15] Esterling finds that demonstrated technical expertise improves access, echoing John Wright's contention that lobbyists gain access by providing valuable policy information.[16] In one recent survey, two-thirds of staffers described lobbyists as "necessary to the process" as either "collaborators" or "educators." Staffers also frequently referred to lobbyists as "partners." As Nicholas Allard argues, lobbyists assist staffers "by sifting information and noise, putting information into a coherent framework, and by challenging or checking facts on impossibly short time deadlines."[17] The increasing reliance on outside expertise is particularly acute in the area of technology policy. In 1995, Congress cut off funding for the Office of Technology Assessment, killing the 23-year-old agency that had become a trusted and valuable source for neutral policy expertise.[18]

Strategies of Reform

Numerous reforms have been proposed to improve our campaign finance and lobbying systems. This chapter breaks them into four categories, with a focus on federal legislation. Two of these are what Heather Gerken has usefully called *Leveling Down* and *Leveling Up*. I add two additional categories: *Independence* and *Transparency*. We will discuss these approaches first here in summary form, and then in more detail, exploring reforms (both enacted and proposed) that would fall into these categories.

Leveling Down reforms involve restrictions on campaign finance and lobbying activities. Samuel Issacaroff off neatly sums up the thinking underlying such reforms: "The intuition is that at some level money must be corrupting of the political process and that something must be done to limit the role of money in that process.... It is the logic of constricting the effects of money that has defined the modern era of campaign finance reform."[19] The general view of such "Leveling Down" reforms is that activity is to be restricted. This view has historically dominated thinking about campaign finance and lobbying reform in American politics.

Leveling Up reforms take a different view. The goal here is to have *more* democracy. These reforms build from the Madisonian assumption that the best approach to limiting the power of a particular faction is to counter it with another faction, but that there are structural reasons why certain factions will not on their own be adequately represented. Thus, this perspective argues that the government should take affirmative steps to ensure that factions are equally represented, building a vibrant and competitive politics.

Independence reforms build from the premise that when lawmakers depend on outside sources for both policy expertise and campaign funding, this compromises their ability to come to their own conclusions. The goal here is to empower law-makers to be minimally dependent on lobbyists. They can utilize their support and resources when helpful without relying excessively on them.

Transparency reforms build on Brandeis' aphorism that "sunlight is the best disinfectant" and Madison's idea that "a popular government without popular information or the means of acquiring it, is but a Prologue to a Farce or a Tragedy or perhaps both." The argument here is that the more information available about lobbying and campaign finance activities, the more that actors within the system will be held accountable because they will know that somebody is probably watching. Citizens will be able to make more informed decisions, and the self-correcting mechanisms of proper political competition will place limits on what actors can get away with.

Leveling Down

The history of campaign finance and lobbying reform has largely been a history of leveling down, of placing limits on lobbying and campaign finance in order to limit activities that reformers felt were corrupting or unfair. In our purview are the most recent reforms in this area: the 2002 Bipartisan Campaign Finance Reform Act (aka BCRA, McCain-Feingold), the 2007 Honest Leadership and Open Government Act (HLOGA), and Obama's 2009 executive order on limiting the role of lobbyists in his administration.

BCRA

The 2012 election cycle marked the ten-year anniversary of the Bipartisan Campaign Finance Reform Act (BCRA). There was, however, little celebrating (or even any notice). The 2002 legislation banned "soft money"—the then large unregulated sums of money that went directly to political parties for "party-building" activities, a broad category that included such activities as getting out the vote. ("Hard money" is money given directly to candidates.) It also placed limits on express advocacy by unions and corporations. Ten years later, unlimited money remained an issue, and unions and corporations were again free to engage in express advocacy.

The reformers' view leading up to the legislation was that soft money, because of its unlimited nature, was corrupting the political process. Thus it should be banned.[20] But as Justices O'Connor and Stevens predicted in upholding McCain-Feingold a year later in *McConnell v. FEC*, "money, like water, will always find an outlet." They were correct. By the 2004 election, big donors had discovered so-called "527" groups. Large sums of unregulated money simply went to a more loosely jointed set of organizations with more particularized agendas than the parties. As Ray La Raja noted in 2008, "Recent elections confirm that we have paid a high price for this latter-day 'prohibition' law.... As a result, we currently possess a campaign finance system that manages to retain the vices of the former regime while jettisoning its virtues."[21]

Post-*Citizens United*, unlimited contributions from wealthy donors, corporations, and unions have found a new home in the proliferating Super PACs, and less traceably, in a new breed of "dark money" organizations that do not even have to report any donors and only limited campaign advertising to the Federal Elections Commission, since they are technically not "political committees" and are instead organized under sections 501(c)(4–6) under the tax code. In 2012, Super PACs spent $633.5 million dollars. Prominent 501(c) organizations in the 2012 campaign included Crossroads GPS ($70.7 million in *reported* expenditures), Americans for Prosperity ($33.5 million), and the U.S. Chamber of Commerce ($32.6 million), though these numbers only represent disclosures in the weeks leading up to the campaign when these groups have to report (see Chapter 8).

McCain-Feingold did put an end to one particular vehicle for unlimited money—so-called "soft money." To the extent that many reformers at the time viewed soft money as particularly nefarious, that is progress. The fact that unlimited money did find other conduits should not invalidate the progress that was made in limiting this particular conduit. But it should highlight the difficulties in limiting the many-headed Hydra of campaign contributions, and the challenges inherent in Leveling Down approaches.

Still, limits on campaign money continue to poll well. In one 2012 poll, 67 percent of respondents wanted limits on individual contributions, and 83 percent wanted limits on corporate and union contributions, while 89 percent of respondents said that there was too much corporate money in politics.[22]

Honest Leadership and Open Government Act

In 2007, Congress passed the Honest Leadership and Open Government Act (aka HLOGA). The bill was passed into law shortly after Democrats had taken back the House and the Senate, riding back into power on, among other things, then-Speaker Nancy Pelosi's 2006 rallying cry to "Drain the swamp" and on day one "break the link between lobbyists and legislation." The villain in mind as the bill passed was Jack Abramoff, the former lobbyist who had, in January 2006, been sentenced to prison for mail fraud, conspiracy to bribe public officials, and tax evasion after becoming famous for taking members of Congress on golf trips, giving them free tickets to sporting events, and letting them eat for free at his upscale Washington, DC, restaurant, Signatures.

HLOGA did a number of things to change the way lobbying worked. It put an end to meals, travel, and other gifts from lobbyists and special interests. (Campaign contributions, however, did not count as "gifts.") It upped lobbying disclosure filings to quarterly instead of bi-annually, and upped disclosure requirements for lobbyists who "bundled" multiple campaign contributions. It also slowed the revolving door: Senators would have to wait two years to lobby Congress upon retirement, instead of just one. It also prevented retiring top-level Senate staff (defined as those making 75 percent of a member's salary) from lobbying the entire Senate for a whole year, and prevented retiring top-level House staff from lobbying their former office or committee for an entire year. However, since lobbying is defined by direct contacts, it said nothing about retiring members and staffers who left to lead teams of lobbyists without lobbying themselves.

Did it make a difference? Lee Drutman and Bruce Cain find that as compared to "high-level" staffers who were not covered under HLOGA, top "covered" staff (those earning a salary that is at least 75 percent of what a member earns) were less likely to become lobbyists following the 2007 reform.[23] The effect was stronger among former Senate staffers which was to be expected since the law prevented departing Senate staff from having any contacts with *any* Senate office, whereas departing House staff were prevented only from contacting the office for which they worked. However, it is unclear whether these individuals are simply finding ways not to register by organizing their time to avoid working as a registered lobbyist. Meanwhile, among registered lobbyists, Tim LaPira and H. F. Thomas found that more than half of lobbyists (57 percent) still do not disclose in their lobbying forms that they previously worked in the federal government even though they had.[24]

Five years later, more than half of lobbyists surveyed said the law had made it more difficult to do their job (52.4 percent) and interact with congressional staff (53.4 percent). Most of the remaining lobbyists said it had made no difference, and only a handful said it had made their job easier. Additionally, the survey found that 51.9 percent thought it has increased transparency (24.9 percent disagreed); 41.8 percent thought it has increased outside campaign activities (15.3 percent disagreed); 34 percent thought it had increased accountability (31.6 percent) disagreed; 20.8 percent thought it had improved ethical standards (42.9 percent disagreed). (The remainder in all cases were neutral or had no opinion.) Roughly half of lobbyists also said that the law had hurt Congress's ability to gather information and understand different perspectives. Overall 81.4 percent of lobbyists said the law had either made it "much more" (33.7 percent) or "slightly more" (48.7 percent) difficult to lobby on behalf of their clients.[25]

If lobbyists are to be taken at their word, HLOGA made life slightly more difficult for lobbyists. But there's little evidence that it did anything more than clean up lobbying on the margins. Most lobbyists would argue that Abaramoff was an outlier, and that very little lobbying depended on the crude favor-trading that he exemplified.[26] Political science generally supports this view. So it's not surprising that lobbying looks largely the same as it did pre-Abramoff, with only the most minor changes to the balance of power.[27] For what it's worth, 81 percent of respondents in a recent poll say they would do more to close the revolving door.[28]

The Obama Lobbying Rule

On his first day in office in 2009, President Obama signed an executive order prohibiting registered lobbyists from serving in his administration. While it sent a powerful political signal, there were some practical problems. Many in the nonprofit advocacy world who had registered as lobbyists (including some who had registered out of extreme caution) were disqualified from administration positions that they were otherwise qualified for. The Obama administration was also forced into a position of hypocrisy when it granted a waiver to William Lynn, the former lobbyist for defense contractor Raytheon, so that he could serve as the deputy secretary of defense. Moreover, the consensus in Washington was that many who might otherwise have registered as lobbyists decided not to (or adjusted their time to avoid the legal definition of lobbying) for fear that such registration would prohibit them from future administration jobs.[29] The number of registered lobbyists in Washington has decreased every year since 2008 (from 14,849 in 2007 to 11,702 in 2012) after steadily increasing every year (save one) between 1998 and 2007 (*growing* from 10,408 to 14,849). Many in Washington attributed this change in direction to the Obama order.

Other than the optics, there was little evidence that executive branch lobbying changed in measurable ways in the Obama administration. As James Thurber concluded: "[Obama] has limited those who can be appointed to executive positions, but it has had little impact on those who actually influence the decision-making process. Moreover, President Obama has worked closely, often in a nontransparent way, with networks of "special interests" (lobbyists/advocates) in crafting the economic stimulus funding, health care reform, financial regulatory reforms, the federal budget deficit and debt, climate change legislation, education reform, immigration policy, and a wide array of other issues on his public policy agenda in 2009–10."

The three reforms discussed above all restricted activity. The problem is that those who wish to influence public policy are rarely discouraged so easily. If one road is blocked off, they will find another. Blocking only those activities that appear to be the most corrupting does little to address the fundamental gaps between our democratic ideals of equality and the imbalances of representation and access in our campaign finance and lobbying systems. Certainly, our democratic sensibilities urge us to do all we can to make sure that public policy is based on the merits of the policy arguments, as opposed to as a system of rewards for favors done, and that nobody has "undue influence." To that end, we have every reason to make sure that our political processes leave little space for the trading of favors.

But there is a challenge here. The issues that come before Congress and the executive branch are rarely the easy issues, where one approach is clearly superior. There are usually legitimate arguments on both sides, and hard choices that will leave some set of interests unhappy. Politics is always going to have winners and losers, and the losers will often cry that the other side had undue influence or that the process was somehow unfair.

Our democratic ideals want politics to be a "fair" fight, but fairness can mean many things. It can mean more than just making all attempts to decide policy based on the merits (as opposed to based on special favors). It may also mean that all sides can participate with some level of equality, that the referees themselves understand enough to be honest brokers, and that the process is transparent enough so that all participants and observers are able to hold all parties account-able. It is to these three goals that we now turn.

"Leveling Up"

Washington lobbying is dominated by businesses, rather than citizen groups, for two main reasons. One is the simple fact that it is relatively easy for businesses to mobilize politically since they already exist, and can, with just a few executive decisions, allocate some of their already existing budgets to political activity.[30] Interested citizens, by contrast, must find a way to overcome the collective action problem, pulling together resources and commitments.[31] Thus forming groups, especially when they rely on the contribution of many far-flung individuals, is notoriously difficult. Secondly, the nature of much political conflict, in which a particular policy affects a handful of companies greatly while it affecting most citizens only marginally, also skews political activity toward companies, who have the most incentive to remain vigilant and active.[32] All of this helps to explain the persistence of the participatory imbalance. Corporations and wealthy individuals both have the means and the motive to make large contributions. Both their personal stake in political outcomes and their ability to mobilize resources are greater than the average citizen.

The logical implication is that without active intervention by government, there will always be imbalances in participation. If we believe in a democratic system in which all sides are entitled to a fair hearing (as we do with our judicial system) then we ought to take affirmative steps to boost the voices of those who are unlikely to muscle the resources to do this on their own. Leveling Up approaches take these structural imbalances seriously and urge government to facilitate ways for those interests who are currently marginalized in lobbying and campaign finance to be more competitive. In this spirit, we discuss reforms that would expand the voice of those whose voice is currently marginalized, leading to a politics where fights are more balanced.

Campaign Vouchers and Matching Funds

On federal campaign finance, a series of reforms have been developed around the ideas of providing matching funds for small donors and campaign finance vouchers for everybody. When asked, 56 percent of respondents say that they would support a system that relies on small contributions.[33] The most prominent federal small-donor proposal in recent years is the "Fair Elections Now Act," which would set up a system where candidates who raised substantial sums from small donors would quality for larger sums of federal matching funds. House candidates who collected 1,500 in-state contributions and raised at least $50,000 in under $100 contributions would get $1,050,000. Senate candidates would qualify based on their state and get appropriately-sized matching grants. Candidates could also qualify for additional 5-to-1 matching for additional contributions under $100.

Such a system would be voluntary (any mandatory system would run afoul of constitutional concerns).

The logic behind small-donor matching approaches is that if candidates can raise money from small donors, it makes them less dependent on the more limited number of wealthy donors. This enhances the voice of ordinary voters in the campaign finance system. Michael Malbin, Peter Brusoe, and Brendan Glavin find that when New York City gave candidates a matching multiplier (a 4-to-1 match up to $250 per city resident starting in 2001, and a 6-to-1 match up to $175 in 2009), both the number and proportion of small donors increased, and the overall demographic and class profile of citywide campaign donors increased, bringing in more non-whites and higher levels of non-college educated voters.[34] As Malbin et al. conclude: "Increasing the number of small donors has been more than a means to dilute the power of the major givers. It has also led candidates to reach out to and engage a more representative set of constituents as they raise their campaign funds."[35] Malbin et al. also find that in Minnesota, which provides partial public funding to candidates who agree to abide by rules (and limits contributions to $3,500 per cycle for gubernatorial candidates and $600 for legislative candidates), 57 percent of funds came from small donors who gave $250 or less, and 44 percent of funds came from donors of $100 or less (the highest of any state).[36]

One caveat on the role of small donors is that candidates who rely on small donors tend to be more highly ideological because small donors tend to be more ideological than large donors.[37] Thus, one concern with any small-donor system is that it will attract even more polarized candidates. Adam Bonica's solution is to limit the matching funds to only the candidates' constituents, thus preventing out-of-state ideological money from distorting the balance.[38] He also suggests privileging first-time donors over repeat donors by reducing the match for donors who give more.

Another intriguing proposal comes from Bruce Ackerman and Ian Ayres.[39] They envision a system whereby every voter gets $50 to spend anonymously on federal candidates. Critics, however, have wondered whether the $50 would be enough to motivate otherwise apathetic citizens to bother to get involved.

In 2012, Congressman John Sarbanes (D-MD) introduced legislation called "The Grassroots Democracy Act" that would include both a matching system and a $50 voucher program. The matching program would give candidates who refuse to take PAC contributions a 5-to-1 match for under-$100 contributions, and candidates who agree to only rely on the under-$100 "grassroots donations" a 10-to-1 match. The legislation would also establish a "citizen-owned" People's Fund that would serve as a way to balance the outside money (i.e. Super PAC and 501(c)(4) groups) who spent hundreds of millions of dollars in the 2012 elections.

Small donor matching funds are a particularly promising example of the leveling up principle. The government match magnifies the importance of small donors, giving them greater voice. It may also have an added benefit of making small donors feel like their contributions matter more, and encouraging more small donors to participate.

On the lobbying side, Dorie Apollonio, Bruce Cain, and Lee Drutman have proposed providing a public defender analogue for lobbying. As they note,

> The goal should not be to eliminate lobbying but to increase lobbying, particularly for underrepresented and disadvantaged groups. This might mean adopting a public defender model, with publicly-funded lobbyists for groups that can demonstrate a sufficiently broad membership base and non-corporate funding. The funding could be matching or complete subsidy.[40]

The obvious challenges here involve developing mechanisms for what would count as a threshold for qualifications, and how to protect it from abuse. But at the very least, such an approach would serve to increase the diversity of perspectives represented, and diversity of perspectives often improves decision-making.[41]

The logic here is that both because of the Constitutional protections of lobbying (the right "to petition the *Government* for a *redress of grievances*") and because of the diversity of ways for organized interests to make their case in Washington, constraints on lobbying tend to be either unconstitutional, counterproductive, or both. Thus, the best we can hope for is for faction to counteract faction, in the spirit of James Madison. But for that to happen, the factions must be reasonably balanced, and decision-makers must have adequate resources to understand the arguments on both sides. It is very unlikely for this to happen of its own accord, given the unequal distribution of resources and wealth in society, the problems of collective action, and the distributions of costs and benefits inherent in most political fights. The natural distribution of resources in lobbying will heavily tilt toward business interests. But proactive approaches to leveling the playing field can make for better and more vibrant democracy.

Independence

A third strain of reform argues that what we should prize most in our lawmakers is independence, and most of all independence from lobbyists and special interests. This requires affirmative changes to the current system.

Such thinking would suggest that candidates should have access to full public funding, which would allow them to run without any need to for outside funding support, relying only on the most evenly distributed political resource of all: votes.

In the late 1990s, Arizona and Maine enacted the most comprehensive systems of public funding for state elections. In both states, candidates who can demonstrate certain threshold levels of support gain access to a fixed grant to fund their campaigns, as long as they do not raise any private money. Neil Malhotra found that both states benefited from more competition in races where the challengers accepted public funding by encouraging more candidates to challenge entrenched incumbents.[42] Peter Francia and Paul Herrnson show that candidates spend less time raising money when they accept full public funding.[43]

In many respects, running for office in the modern campaign environment more and more resembles high-end telemarketing, with candidates spending usually at least a few hours each day "dialing for dollars"—calling up prospective donors and asking for their support.[44]

However, public funding of elections tends to not go over well with voters. As Ray La Raja and Brian Schaffner note: "Americans would rather not pay for politics, and reform proposals must avoid incurring transparent costs on individual citizens to pay for reform."[45] Some critics have even called public funding of elections "welfare for politicians."[46]

More Resources for Congress to Develop its Own Sources of Expertise

One reason that lobbyists have influence in policymaking is because congressional offices rely on them for information and expertise, since congressional staff often lack their own expertise and have few institutional sources for it. It follows that one way to reduce the influence of lobbyists would be for Congress to develop more of its own expertise.

This could include expanding the resources for the independent sources of expertise that Congress does have—the Congressional Research Service (CRS) and Government Accountability Office (GAO), and the Congressional Budget Office (CBO)—as well as bringing back a modernized version of the Office of Technology Assessment (OTA). It could also mean improving the compensation and working conditions of congressional offices and providing more compensation to maintain a staff of policy experts. Academia could also do more to encourage and incentivize academics to devote time and resources to serving as a source of neutral expertise on a wide variety of subjects.

Heather Gerken argues for more permanent corps of researchers (going beyond the existing limited support from the Congressional Research Service) could help Congress to legislate without relying extensively on outside lobbyists. As she writes: "The best option, in our view, is to fund research consultants: people who could provide McLegislation, McTalkingpoints, and McResearch, plus all of the politically relevant advice congressional members could want."[47]

Dependence creates a power asymmetry. If members of Congress depend on private money, this may constrain them to advocate only those positions that maintain the support of a sufficient number of donors. If members and their staff must significantly depend on lobbyists to explain the complexities and impacts of policy, it makes it difficult for them to form independent assessments. On lobbying in particular, more resources for lawmakers and their staff has the potential to make them better and more informed consumers of information, which will almost certainly result in more thoughtful approaches to public policy.

Transparency

A final category of reform is Transparency. The idea here is relatively straight-forward: lobbying and campaign contributions are much more likely to be inappropriately effective if they occur in secret. But if they are fully disclosed in a timely manner, lobbyists and donors will know that others may be watching. Many Washington lobbyists unofficially abide by the *Washington Post* rule, which is that you don't want what you are doing to wind up as a scandal on the front page of the *Washington Post*. The easier it is for *Washington Post* reporters (and other watch-dogs) to keep track of lobbying and campaign finance activities, the less likely it is that lobbyists and donors will engage in approaches that would ruin their reputa-tions were they to grace the headlines.

A second reason for transparency and timely disclosure is that, even regardless of behavioral propriety, they help facilitate Madisonian competition. The more information adversaries have about each other, the better they can respond to each other and keep each other honest. Nicholas Allard argues that among lobbyists, "There is an intense competition to be right .... Competition is too strong among vigilant adversaries for the quick fix to work."[48] This is almost certainly true on issues where there is adequate competition.

Campaign Finance

As Justice Kennedy wrote in the *Citizens United* decision (arguing that adequate transparency would tame the impact of the unlimited sums of money the decision made possible), "transparency enables the electorate to make informed decisions and give proper weight to different speakers and messages." Put more directly, a voter who knows an ad has been funded by ExxonMobil may view it differently than a voter who sees an ad funded by another anonymous group promising some anodyne version of a better America.

Disclosure has been an important part of our campaign finance system for four decades now. Citizens can, with relative ease, now learn about the campaign finance records of any candidate. While this disclosure has not notably changed the balance of funds, it has continued to make money an issue. However, the 2012 election revealed limits to this disclosure, as 501(c) organizations became major players.

In July 2012, Senator Sheldon Whitehouse (D-RI) told gathered reporters, "The flood of secret money unleashed by the Supreme Court's *Citizens United* deci-sion threatens to drown out the voices of middle class families in our democracy. The DISCLOSE Act will uphold every citizen's right to know where this secret money is coming from."

The bill never got a full floor vote, as Senate Republicans filibustered the legislation. Had it been passed, the DISCLOSE (Democracy is Strengthened by Casting Light on Spending in Elections) Act would have required Super PACs,

501(c) organizations, and any other outside group spending $10,000 or more on election-related activities, to disclose within 24 hours any donor who has given more than $10,000 to the organization. It would have also required groups to include disclaimers in their ads from the heads of such groups, among other disclosure provisions.

The practical logic of the bill rested on the faith that knowing the source of spending is essential to helping citizens critically evaluate campaign advertising. Knowledge of who is contributing to whom can also empower watchdogs and opposing factions as to where to do direct their resources. While transparency by itself does not facilitate change, it often makes it significantly easier for others to facilitate change.

But while Congress stalled, in the wake of *Citizens United* Alaska, California, and North Carolina passed legislation requiring that independent expenditure advertising list the group behind the ad's top donors,[49] while Massachusetts required that if a corporation or other group pays for an ad, the person in charge of a group has to include a statement as part of the ad.[50] Additionally, Oregon requires that campaign committees must disclose large contributions within a week of receiving them during election season. Senators Wyden (D-OR) and Murkowski (R-AK) have proposed drawing on the Alaska and Oregon laws to put in place a federal law that would require "any organization engaging in federal political activity of any kind, from candidacy to advocacy, to disclose their donors in real time."[51] In a 2012 poll, 81 percent of respondents said that full disclosure should be required of corporations that spend money on political campaigns.[52]

Lobbying

Under the current disclosure rules, anyone who spends at least 20 percent of their time for a paying client in direct lobbying activities (i.e., meeting and preparing to meet with lawmakers and their staff) and makes two contacts for that client must register as a lobbyist. Like most arbitrary cut-off lines, there are many who are careful to skirt it, given that many in Washington would prefer not be labeled as a "lobbyist"—a problem that the Obama rules likely exacerbated. During the 2012 campaign, for example, Republican candidate Newt Gingrich insisted that mortgage lender Freddie Mac had paid the former House Speaker more than $1.6 million for his services as a "historian." Much back-and-forth ensued as to whether Gingrich's advocacy on behalf of Freddie Mac (as well as some other clients) met the definition of lobbying. But what was clear from all the back-and-forth was that the legal definition of lobbying left out much activity that sure looked to many people like lobbying.[53]

The simple answer is to expand the definition of lobbying, which is something that even lobbyists are now calling for. In 2012, American League of Lobbyists recommended that outside consultants that firms hire would have to register after one contact, and in-house lobbyists would have to report if 10 percent of their time were spent lobbying. The proposal would also introduce mandatory ethics trainings and up enforcement and oversight. It also encourages a wider definition of lobbying. As the ALL states:

> In today's lobbying environment, grassroots and public relations firms are an integral part of many advocacy efforts. Very large sums of money are spent on the services of those providing these services, as well as those engaged to prepare testimony, studies or op-eds. For full transparency, it is important that the public be aware of both the money being spent as well as the recipients of the funds. Determining how to craft a proposal that accomplishes that goal is a complex task that must be dealt with as these proposals are transformed into legislative language.[54]

The American Bar Association has also argued for a more expansive definition of disclosure to include "lobbying support activities"—such things as public relations, coalition building, polling, and other ancillary support services that are part of an advocacy campaign. The task force also supports more thorough enforcement of existing lobbying disclosure rules, arguing that the Department of Justice should have jurisdiction.[55]

An even more comprehensive proposal, known as the Lobbyist Disclosure Enhancement Act, was introduced in the 112th Congress. The legislation would call for lobbyists to get specific and include in their lobbying disclosure forms what congressional and executive offices they lobbied and when and what they discussed. Under current disclosure rules, lobbyists do not have to list which member offices they lobby. They are required to list the bills and issues they lobbied on, but only very rarely do they state their position.

Going even further, we could build a platform where all lobbyists would post their arguments and positions, in real time, in an online clearinghouse to which the public has full access.[56] The public and other interested parties would see who is advocating for what, what their arguments are, and what information they are basing those arguments on. Rather than endless reporting speculating about who is saying what behind closed doors and how special interests are twisting arms, this could shift public debate more to the actual arguments by making those arguments and facts more easily accessible and comparable. Public interest groups who can't afford to hire enough lobbyists to schedule multiple meetings with every office will now have a more level playing field on which to compete. They also will be able to see what corporations are arguing, and will more easily be able to respond to these allegations. Likewise, corporations can respond to any unfounded allegations their critics might be spouting.

In 2012, Rep. Darrell Issa (R-CA) launched a project he called "Madison" which was designed to "open the legislative and treaty process" by posting bills and treaties in progress on line so that different interests can publicly comment. The Sunlight Foundation also developed a Public Markup project at PublicMarkup. org. John Wonderlich makes that case for a term familiar to computer coders, "version control," which "means seeing what changes, and who changes it.

It means accountability forced very precisely into the processes of representation, and it means gaining a new ability for substantive contributions and oversight from a broadly empowered public."[57]

Conclusion

Lobbying and campaign finance both represent billions of dollars spent annually to influence federal policymaking, primarily on behalf of businesses and wealthy individuals. This fact alone leads many to be very cynical about how policy is made in Washington. But democracy is not a vending machine in which money poured in leads predictably to results. As the preceding chapters have explored, attempts by outside groups to influence government policy are incredibly varied, and their success is highly contingent. They are interests in society petitioning their government for the redress of grievances, engaging in political activity to pursue their idea of good public policy by convincing others to share that view, and in the process adding valuable information about policy and public opinion.

From a reform perspective, then, we must be cautious. We must not be afraid of politics simply because it is sometimes messy or because it involves expressions of self-interest. Rather we must do our best to encourage politics to be fought on a level and transparent playing field, with decision-makers who have the resources and independence they need to adequately evaluate competing arguments. And while we certainly want decisions to be made on the basis of merit as opposed to connections and favoritism, we must not let a narrow focus on quid pro quo corruption distract us from bigger questions of fairness, balance, and accountability. Ultimately, we should strive for the most vibrant, transparent, and competitive democracy we can build.

Notes

1 Democracy Corps Poll, 2012, http://www.democracycorps.com/National-Surveys/Page-2/.
2 Kay Lehman Schlozman, Sidney Verba, and Henry E. Brady, *The Unheavenly Chorus: Unequal Political Voice and the Broken Promise of American Democracy* (Princeton, NJ: Princeton University Press, 2012), p. 68; Douglas W. Rae and Douglas Yates, *Equalities* (Cambridge, MA: Harvard University Press, 1981); Jennifer L. Hochschild, *What's Fair: American Beliefs About Distributive Justice* (Cambridge, MA: Harvard University Press, 1986); Larry M. Bartels, *Unequal Democracy: The Political Economy of the New Gilded Age* (Princeton, NJ: Princeton University Press, 2010).
3 Lee Drutman, "The Political One Percent of the One Percent." *Sunlight Foundation,* 2011, http://sunlightfoundation.com/blog/2011/12/13/the-political-one-percent-of-the-one-percent/.
4 Blair Bowie and Adam Lioz, *Billion Dollar Democracy: The Unprecedented Role of Money in the 2012 Elections* (New York: Demos, 2013).
5 Robert Alan Dahl, *Who Governs?: Democracy and Power in an American City* (New Haven, CT: Yale University Press, 1961); Peter Bachrach and Morton S. Baratz, "Two Faces of Power," *The American Political Science Review* 56, no. 4 (1962): 947–52; William

H. Riker, "Some Ambiguities in the Notion of Power," *The American Political Science Review* 58, no. 2 (1964): 341–49.

6   Stephen Ansolabehere, John M. de Figueiredo, and James M. Snyder Jr., "Why Is There so Little Money in U.S. Politics?" *Journal of Economic Perspectives* 17, no. 1 (2003): 105–30.

7   Frank R. Baumgartner, Jeffrey M. Berry, Marie Hojnacki, David C. Kimball, and Beth L. Leech, *Lobbying and Policy Change: Who Wins, Who Loses, and Why* (Chicago: University of Chicago Press, 2009).

8   Richard L. Hall and Frank W. Wayman, "Buying Time: Moneyed Interests and the Mobilization of Bias in Congressional Committees," *American Political Science Review* 84, no. 3 (1990): 797–818; Dan Clawson, Alan Neustadtl, and Denise Scott, *Money Talks* (New York: Basic Books, 1992); Richard L. Hall and Alan V. Deardorff, "Lobbying as Legislative Subsidy," *American Political Science Review* 100, no. 1 (2006): 69–84.

9   John P. Heinz, Edward O. Laumann, Robert L. Nelson, and Robert H. Salisbury, *The Hollow Core: Private Interests in National Policy Making* (Cambridge, MA: Harvard University Press, 1993), p. 348.

10   Lorelei Kelly, *Congress' Wicked Problem: Seeking Knowledge Inside the Information Tsunami* (Washington, DC: New America Foundation, 2012), p. 1.

11   Congressional Management Foundation. *2009 House of Representatives Compensation Study,* http://www.scribd.com/doc/24769228/2009-House-of-Representatives-Compensation-Study.

12   Daniel Schuman and Alisha Green, "When It Comes to Pay, All Feds Aren't Created Equal" (Washington, DC: Sunlight Foundation, 2012).

13   Daniel Schuman, "Keeping Congress Competent: Staff Pay, Turnover, and What It Means for Democracy" (Washington, DC: Sunlight Foundation, 2012).

14   Kevin M. Esterling, *The Political Economy of Expertise: Information and Efficiency in American National Politics* (Ann Arbor: University of Michigan Press, 2004), p. 9.

15   Esterling, *The Political Economy of Expertise.*

16   John R. Wright, *Interest Groups and Congress: Lobbying, Contributions, and Influence* (Boston: Allyn and Bacon, 1996).

17   Nicholas W. Allard, "Lobbying Is an Honorable Profession: The Right to Petition and the Competition to Be Right," *Stanford Law and Policy Review* 19, no. 1 (2008).

18   Bruce Allen Bimber, *The Politics of Expertise in Congress: The Rise and Fall of the Office of Technology Assessment* (Albany: SUNY Press, 1996).

19   Samuel Issacharoff, "On Political Corruption," *Harvard Law Review* 124, no. 118 (2010): 118.

20   "I did not march across the bridge in Selma," former civil rights activist Rep. John Lewis (D-GA) said at the time, "to become a part of a political system so corrupt." Rep. James Greenwood (D-PA) (later to be head of the biotechnology industry trade group BIO) told the Congress: "It is about access and influence and it corrupts our process."

21   Raymond J. La Raja, *Small Change: Money, Political Parties, and Campaign Finance Reform* (Ann Arbor: University of Michigan Press, 2008).

22   Morgan Little, "Poll: Americans Largely in Favor of Campaign Spending Limitations," *Los Angeles Times,* September 16, 2012, http://articles.latimes.com/2012/sep/16/news/la-pn-poll-citizens-united-20120916; Liz Kennedy, *Citizens Actually United: The Bi-partisan Opposition to Corporate Political Spending and Support for Common Sense Reform* (New York: Demos, 2012).

23   Lee Drutman and Bruce Cain, "Congressional Staff and the Revolving Door: The Impact of Regulatory Change," *SSRN eLibrary,* http://papers.ssrn.com/sol3/papers.cfm?abstract_id=2107220.

24   Tim LaPira and H.F. Thomas, "Revolving Doors: Lobbyists' Government Experience, Expertise, and Access in Political Context," *SSRN eLibrary,* http://papers.ssrn.com/sol3/papers.cfm?abstract_id=2107222.

25   Lobbyists.info, 2012, http://www.lobbyists.info.

26 Allard, "Lobbying Is an Honorable Profession."

27 Schlozman et al, *The Unheavenly Chorus.*

28 Democracy Corps Poll.

29 James A. Thurber, "The Contemporary Presidency: Changing the Way Washington Works? Assessing President Obama's Battle with Lobbyists," *Presidential Studies Quarterly* 41, no. 2 (2011): 358–74.

30 Robert H. Salisbury, "Interest Representation: The Dominance of Institutions," *American Political Science Review* 78, no. 1 (1984): 64–76.

31 Mancur Olson, *The Logic of Collective Action: Public Goods and the Theory of Groups,* 2nd ed. (Cambridge, MA: Harvard University Press, 1971).

32 James Q. Wilson, *The Politics of Regulation* (New York: Basic Books, 1980).

33 Democracy Corps Poll.

34 Michael J. Malbin, Peter W. Brusoe, and Brendan Glavin, "Small Donors, Big Democracy: New York City's Matching Funds as a Model for the Nation and States," *Election Law Journal* 11, no. 1 (2012): 3–20.

35 Malbin et al., "Small Donors, Big Democracy."

36 Malbin et al., "Small Donors, Big Democracy," p. 11.

37 Adam Bonica, "Small Donors and Polarization," *Boston Review,* 2011, http://bostonreview.net/bonica-small-donors-polarization.

38 Bonica, "Small Donors and Polarization."

39 Bruce Ackerman and Ian Ayres, *Voting with Dollars: A New Paradigm for Campaign Finance* (New Haven, CT: Yale University Press, 2002).

40 Dorie Apollonio, Bruce E. Cain, and Lee Drutman, "Access and Lobbying: Looking Beyond the Corruption Paradigm," *Hastings Constitutional Law Quarterly* 36, no. 1 (2008): 13.

41 Scott E. Page, *The Difference: How the Power of Diversity Creates Better Groups, Firms, Schools, and Societies* (Princeton, NJ: Princeton University Press, 2008).

42 Neil Malhotra, "The Impact of Public Financing on Electoral Competition: Evidence from Arizona and Maine," *State Politics and Policy Quarterly* 8, no. 3 (2008): 263–81.

43 Peter L. Francia and Paul S. Herrnson, "The Impact of Public Finance Laws on Fundraising in State Legislative Elections," *American Politics Research* 31, no 5 (2003): 520–39.

44 Lawrence Lessig, *Republic, Lost: How Money Corrupts Congress—and a Plan to Stop It,* 1st ed. (New York: Twelve, 2011).

45 Raymond J. La Raja and Brian F. Schaffner, "Explaining the Unpopularity of Pubic Funding for Congressional Elections," *Electoral Studies* 30, no. 3 (2011): 525–33.

46 John Curtis Samples, *Welfare For Politicians: Taxpayer Financing Of Campaigns* (Washington, DC: Cato Institute, 2005).

47 Heather Gerken, "Leveling Up: A Public Finance Analog for Lobbying," Election Law Blog, 2011, http://electionlawblog.org/archives/018736.html.

48 Allard, "Lobbying Is an Honorable Profession."

49 In Alaska, it required disclosure of the top three donors; in California, the top two over $50,000; in North Carolina, the top five.

50 Robert M. Stern, *Sunlight State By State After Citizens United: How State Legislation Has Responded to Citizens United* (Washington, DC: Corporate Reform Coalition, 2012).

51 Ron Wyden and Lisa Murkowski, "A Federal Blueprint for Transparent Campaign Financing," *Washington Post,* December 27, 2012.

52 Liz Kennedy, *Citizens Actually United* (Washington, DC: Demos, 2012).

53 Glenn Kessler, "Newt Gingrich and Freddie Mac: Is He Being Misleading?" *The Washington Post,* 2011.

54 American League of Lobbyists, "Recommendations for Improving the Regulation of Federal Lobbyists, American League of Lobbyists," April 9, 2012, http://www.alldc.org/press/lda_wg_report_04-09-12.pdf.

55 American Bar Association, "Lobbying Law in the Spotlight," http://www.americanbar. org/content/dam/aba/migrated/2011_build/administrative_law/lobbying_task_force_ report_010311.authcheckdam.pdf.

56 Drutman, "The Political One Percent of the One Percent."

57 John Wonderlich, "On Legislative Collaboration and Version Control," *Sunlight Foundation,* 2012, http://sunlightfoundation.com/blog/2012/09/27/on-legislative-collab oration-and-version-control/.

Chapter 14

Conclusion

Matt Grossmann

In the wake of the December 2012 shootings at Sandy Hook Elementary School in Newtown, Connecticut, many political observers predicted that gun control legislation was on its way. Yet immediate and significant opposition scuttled attempts to revisit a ban on "assault" weapons and high-capacity magazines. Policy change looked more likely in the area of background checks designed to avoid gun sales to criminals and the mentally ill. The bipartisan team of Senators Joe Manchin (D-WV) and Pat Toomey (R-PA) advocated an expansion of background checks to purchases over the Internet and at gun shows; they obtained quick support from President Barack Obama and Majority Leader Harry Reid. When the bill failed to advance through the U.S. Senate, Obama blamed the National Rifle Association (NRA). Senators voted no on the bill, he said, because "they worried that the gun lobby would spend a lot of money and paint them as anti-Second Amendment."[1] He called it a "shameful day for Washington" and insinuated that members of Congress ignored the vast majority of their constituents because they feared the wrath of an interest group.

This type of claim is commonplace in American politics. Whenever politicians fail to achieve their policy goals, they blame the "special interests" for standing in the way. Views of interest groups as all-powerful and malevolent reflect widespread public disenchantment with government. Nearly 70% of Americans believe that the "government is pretty much run by a few big interests looking out for themselves" rather than for "the benefit of all the people."[2] Does this public cynicism match the facts about American interest groups? Does Obama's story of NRA influence tell the whole story? After all, Republican senators may oppose gun control due to their ideological preferences, their beliefs about its lack of efficacy, or their lack of incentives to cooperate with Obama. The failure to pass gun control may reflect the success of the NRA, the failure of their opponents (such as the Brady Campaign to Prevent Gun Violence), or simply the power of the status quo. Perhaps the White House lacked a compelling argument that the new legislation would have prevented the tragedy or had nothing of value to trade with Republicans in exchange for their support.

This book has systematically assessed common claims about interest groups by subdividing the investigation into several key questions. First, which sectors of the American society and economy mobilize interest organizations (Chapters 1–4)? In other words, why are gun control opponents better represented than supporters and just who does the NRA leadership speak for? Second, how do interest groups operate in the political system (Chapters 5–8)? Did the battle over gun control reflect an electoral threat by the NRA, a lobbying campaign, or a broader competition between partisan coalitions? Third, how do interest groups influence policy decisions in political institutions (Chapters 9–13)? Did the particular lobbying and contributing strategies of the NRA or the Brady Campaign make a difference? Would things have turned out differently if the same battle took place in other venues or with different rules?

Even if citizens cannot be sure about the NRA's influence in this particular case, the research that interest group scholars are conducting can certainly add much to the public discussion. Gun control supporters may be much less politically engaged than opponents, contributing to the disproportionate role of a small number of prominent groups like the NRA (Chapter 1). Business interests like gun manufacturers may be able to stimulate grassroots lobbying, in addition to the greater mobilization of gun rights supporters (Chapter 3). The NRA's success may depend on its support for current policy (Chapter 10) or its permanent place in the Republican Party coalition (Chapter 5). The failure to compromise between gun control supporters and opponents may have helped doom the legislation (Chapter 6).

On the other hand, the gun control case may not be representative of broader patterns of interest group mobilization and influence. Perhaps the central finding is a basic economic divide: interest groups tend to represent the well-off rather than more general public interests, even among groups with members (Chapter 2) and those speaking on behalf of social justice (Chapter 4). Beyond the stable advantages of some groups, a few organizations may take better advantage of the Internet (Chapter 7) or new campaign finance rules (Chapters 13) to influence elections or policy. Final votes in Congress, such as the one that angered Obama, may be the worst place to look for the influence of lobbying and campaign contributions, which may have influence at early stages of the legislative process (Chapters 9 and 10). Interest groups may have just as many, if not more, opportunities to influence administrative and judicial decisions (Chapters 11 and 12) or state-level policymaking.

This final chapter reviews a few broad lessons from *New Directions in Interest Group Politics* and comments on several paths forward for interest group research. Rather than blindly accept or reject Obama's complaint that the NRA killed gun control legislation, your goal should be to use the findings of interest group research to inform your observation of the next critical vote in Congress. Rather than accept the claim that the special interests rule government, scholars hope to provide a better empirical basis for evaluating the role of interest groups in American democracy.

A Third Generation of Interest Group Scholarship

After reading several examples of contemporary research, I hope that you share my optimism about our growing knowledge of interest group mobilization, operations, and influence. Yet sometimes scholars learn more by realizing where our previous models went astray than by confirming our previous ideas. The patterns of interest group behavior may be more complicated than scholars or citizens originally supposed. Researchers in what I call the third generation of interest group scholarship now make more constrained claims about what we do and do not know.

The first generation of scholarship began with a discipline-wide clash between pluralists, who argued that diverse social and economic groups were the base units of political competition, and elitists, who argued that one dominant socio-economic class controlled political decisions.[3] Both claims faced a challenge from collective action theory, which posited that groups and classes of all kinds would face difficulty pursuing their joint interests.[4] All three views assumed that the relative political mobilization of different interest groups would be reflected in government institutions and public policy: politicians would face tremendous pressure to appease interest group concerns. Interest group scholars claimed to be debating who rules America, but they generally avoided close assessments of the process by which organizations influenced specific government decisions.

The second generation of scholarship focused on the interest group community, monitoring how each organization mobilizes and maintains its resources as well as their strategies to influence policy. Scholars learned that most interest groups are institutions like businesses or universities, rather than associations of individuals, and even many associations rely on financing from a few rich patrons, rather than their members.[5] Interest groups in state capitals show these same patterns, but vary dramatically in their composition based on state economies and institutions.[6] Scholars studied a wide array of tactics that organizations use to influence government, including when, where, and who they lobby and how they contribute money. Yet the voluminous literature has been unable to show that lobbying or campaign contributions consistently move votes in Congress or change policy outcomes.[7] The latest research shows no overall pattern between the amount of resources spent on each side of policy disputes and who wins and loses.[8]

What I call the third generation of scholarship, including the chapters highlighted in this volume, share two assumptions: (1) interest organizations arise from a variety of social groups and economic sectors but are highly unrepresentative of the American population, and (2) their influence is highly conditional on their relationships to other political actors and what they want to achieve. Scholars seek to identify which social and economic groups and political perspectives mobilize organizations to speak on their behalf as well as the circumstances under which these organizations influence American government. At its best, this generation of scholarship engages some of the deep questions of democracy associated with the first interest group scholars but does so with the tools that the second generation provided. It seeks nuance, observing differences across interest group sectors, policy areas, branches of government, and states. It avoids presuming that interest groups are any more central to politics than other political actors like parties or legislators. It sees some consistent advantages of some groups over others but also engages with changes brought by technology or regulation.

The third generation of scholarship generally avoids grand theories meant to apply to all groups at all times (even as it undermines some of the claims of previous theories). That leaves two theoretical frameworks commonly used in interest group research, neither of which are fully compatible with contemporary findings. The first, pluralism, is the baseline from which interest group theory began and has been repeatedly updated under the label "neopluralism."[9] The updated version still sees politics as a competition between stakeholders, but incorporates the primary role of government institutions: interest groups influence government officials, who are hardly passive responders to their demands. The second framework, rational choice theory, is the most popular method of theoretical modeling in political science; it explains why rational individuals would join organizations or respond to their concerns. Interest group behavior is described as two types of exchanges: one between members and organizational leaders that gives both an incentive to form a group; another between group leaders and policymakers that provides the reason why government responds to interest group demands.[10] The research highlighted in the previous chapters show that both pluralism and rational choice theory are in need of significant revision but points to productive methods for updating each framework.

Updating Pluralist Theories of Interest Groups

Pluralist theories start from the premise that many different social and economic groups will compete to influence public policy by developing formal organizations to speak on their behalf before government. Pluralist scholars expect each issue area and policymaking venue to be associated with a different subset of these organizations, with new groups mobilizing in response to social, economic, and political change. Policymaking, in this view, is a battle over who gets what, when, and how; interest groups are its primary combatants.[11]

Several findings highlighted in *New Directions in Interest Group Politics* could make pluralism a more useful framework for understanding contemporary politics. First, scholars now recognize endemic inequalities in all stages of interest group mobilization. Interest groups represent economic interests, especially businesses, much more than social groups or political viewpoints. Individuals of high socio-economic status are more likely to participate and lead groups (Chapter 2) and more likely to have their interests advanced even within organizations speaking on behalf of the disadvantaged (Chapter 4). Organizations with more resources can better intervene in election campaigns (Chapter 8) and policymaking (Chapter 10).

Second, many interest groups are not archetypal membership associations. A staff of paid lobbyists for General Electric, for example, may not be properly seen as an interest group; it certainly raises different concerns than a group of citizens pursuing their civil rights. Most organizations that lobby government are more like the former than the latter (Chapter 10). Most organizations involved in contemporary elections are even less likely to fit our classic vision of collective civic action. Campaign finance laws have stimulated an array of entities designed to skirt the law; their primary purpose is to funnel money toward political advertising; they sometimes exist only on paper (Chapters 8 and 13).

Third, interest groups often work in permanent or temporary coalitions. Their capacity to work together with other groups may depend on the overall ideological structure of American politics; whether they win or lose may be a product of Republican or Democratic ascendance, rather than their own behavior (Chapter 5). Their capacity to reach a compromise with other interests may depend on their ideological position, the availability of alternative moderate positions, the willingness of their opponents to compromise, and the views of policymakers (Chapter 6). Rather than compete as independent stakeholders, groups may compete as party coalitions or arrangements of convenience between typical opponents.

Fourth, the rules and procedures for influencing government are different in the legislature, the administration, and the courts. Interest groups that win in one forum may lose in another. Campaign contributions may be effective only for groups with few opponents who pursue separable economic benefits (Chapter 9). Groups with ties to an incoming White House may have an advantage in shaping administration policy even before the new president takes office (Chapter 11). Groups with the experience to influence the courts may have sections of their submitted materials written into judicial decisions (Chapter 12). Each branch has its own agenda, culture, and rules; it is not merely a venue for interest groups to fight it out. Procedures for influence may also need to adapt to changes in technology (Chapter 7) or lobbying and campaign regulation (Chapter 13).

Pluralism must thus incorporate critiques from two opposing angels. On the one hand, it fails to fully account for the many sources of change in interest group communities, including the rise of new methods of communication (Chapter 7), new types of vehicles for intervening in campaigns (Chapter 8), and changes in practices in the administration or the courts (Chapters 11 and 12). On the other hand, pluralism avoids the conclusion that the same types of well-off interests might consistently benefit from most organized attempts to influence government. Businesses may dominate interest group communities (Chapter 1), engage in more lobbying (Chapter 10), and pay for mobilization strategies to look like broad social movements (Chapter 3). The same inequalities may extend to mass associations of individuals (Chapter 2) and organizations representing minorities (Chapter 4). Given these modifications, the pluralist view of interest groups as primary stakeholders in political decision-making may still be a useful starting point for research.

Updating Rational Choice Theories of Interest Groups

Theories of interest groups based on the rational decisions of individuals are also in need of revision. Initial models of collective action supposed that most large groups would have trouble forming any organizations to speak on their behalf. Updated versions suggested that individuals could be motivated by solidarity with others or the mere act of expression, in addition to the material side benefits of organizational membership.[12] Likewise, the initial model of direct vote buying, with interest groups providing campaign contributions in exchange for support, has also been modified. Interest groups may provide other goods to legislators, such as information about policy debates or potential electoral gains from adopting policy positions.[13] They may merely provide a staffing subsidy to allied policymakers, providing additional resources to pursue shared interests.[14]

The research in *New Directions in Interest Group Politics* could further update this rational choice perspective on interest group organizing and influence. First, quite a few types of interest groups appear on the scene at the state and national levels. Group size and industry concentration, two factors highlighted in collective action theory, appear to be poor guides to which groups mobilize (Chapter 1). Most groups do not need to worry about membership at all—even the minority of groups with members relies on a small, well-off subset (Chapter 2). Mobilization may be a product of professional organizing firms (Chapter 3) or better use of contemporary technology (Chapter 7), rather than traditional collective action. Given the variety of institutional arrangements that serve as solutions to collective action problems, the height of this hurdle is not clear.

Second, the direct contributions of interest groups to policymakers often signal their shared ideological or partisan goals, rather than an exchange. Many interest groups ally permanently with one of the two major political parties (Chapter 5), and interest groups usually directly intervene in elections to support candidates from the same party (Chapter 8). Businesses may try to become part of both parties' coalitions, while labor becomes a diminishing portion of the Democratic coalition (Chapter 9). Some interest groups directly provide administrative staff when a new party comes to power in Washington (Chapter 11). The lines between parties, interest groups, and government officials are thus a little blurrier than initially expected.

Third, policymakers appear to heed the advice of interest groups without receiving anything directly for their support. Most interest groups spend more on lobbying legislators than trying to buy their support (Chapter 10) and the most prolific election spenders appear to be party appendages (Chapter 8). Interest groups may be at least as influential with administrators and judges as with legislators, even though administrators and judges have no electoral incentive to respond (Chapter 11 and 12). Policymakers may respond directly to arguments made by interest groups, incorporating them into their own statements (Chapter 12), absent any direct exchange. The most prized interactions may be early meetings with new officials (Chapter 11) or alliances between unlikely partners (Chapter 6).

To be effective for analyzing contemporary interest groups, rational choice theory needs to acknowledge some limitations. The collective action problem, individuals deciding whether to join a group effort on the basis of their individual gains, may not be typical of interest mobilization. Quid pro quo exchanges, deals where groups provide goods to policymakers for their support, may not be the typical path to interest group influence. Chapters 5 and 6 of this volume provide illustrations of how rational choice modeling could incorporate new findings, enlarging our perspective about when individuals and organizations will act collectively to support shared interests. Yet they come to somewhat distinct conclusions; one chapter argues that most groups should rationally join a party coalition and another argues that they should try to find common ground with their opponents. The rational choice approach has already shown its flexibility in incorporating critiques. As scholars unpack the circumstances under which organizations and individuals are likely to pursue different types of collective action, it could continue to be a useful method of modeling group behavior.

Connecting Unequal Group Mobilization with Conditional Influence

In addition to updating previous theoretical frameworks, the evidence compiled in *New Directions in Interest Group Politics* points to more original possibilities for future theory and research. Its story of interest group mobilization suggests that many groups mobilize, but at vastly different levels with unequal capabilities (Chapters 1 and 2). The interest group population is broad and widening but the opportunities for fruitful participation are narrow. The book's story of interest group strategy suggests that, although groups emulate one another in terms of their tactics (Chapter 3), they also pursue quite different organizational forms (Chapter 7) and different policymaking venues for their several constituencies (Chapter 4). The story of influence is even more complicated, with many distinct routes in each branch and level of government. In all cases, group influence seems conditional on factors well outside an individual organization's control, such as the behavior of their competitors, the alignment of the parties, and the winners of the last election.

Traditionally, three strands of interest group research proceed in isolation: scholars study how the population of interest groups mobilized, how they operate and behave strategically, and whether they succeed in influencing government. Each stage of research builds upon the findings of the previous stage. Among the mobilized groups, scholars ask, what subset participates in each venue. Then, among participants, what side wins each dispute? This volume mirrors that step-by-step approach, but the findings suggest that a more productive view of interest groups would combine these steps. It would explore how inequalities among groups build on one another, avoiding the assumption that all groups or participants are similarly likely to be influential. We know that the financially well off are more likely to participate in interest groups (Chapter 2), but we know less about whether their interests generate a better response from policymakers because their organizations are more influential. We know that businesses can emulate grassroots advocacy groups (Chapter 3), but we know less about whether policymakers in each branch of government respond equivalently to their efforts. We know that new interest groups arise via new communications technology (Chapter 7) and loopholes in campaign finance regulation (Chapter 13), but we know less about whether they succeed in competition with older interest groups.

Future interest group research should continue to tackle the broad questions that concerned early scholars, even if the answers are less definitive than expected. Combining studies of group mobilization, operations, and influence should lead to better answers. A key question is which social and economic groups win political battles most often. Simply counting organizations or studying whether money consistently buys votes cannot answer this question. We need to know whether the extent of a group's mobilization predicts its influence on policy and whether interest groups are the primary reason that highly involved constituencies like gun owners win their political battles. Do the groups that benefit most from group mobilization also usually face the conditions that enable policy influence? How much does their success depend on the ebb and flow of partisanship and the venues where policymaking takes place?

If the second generation of interest group research had found that interest group mobilization is consistent and that influence is direct and easily predictable, subdividing research between studies of mobilization and influence would not be a detriment to answering important questions. Because research finds complexity in both processes, full answers to age-old questions will require more holistic research. Scholars might follow groups like gun control supporters and opponents as they develop organizations, stimulate opponents, and seek to influence policy.

Where Interest Groups Fit in American Governance

Interest group scholars often bemoan that their subfield has lost its prominence within studies of American government. Scholars of public behavior and each government institution previously assumed that interest groups were central to governance, this story goes, but now they treat the research area as a backwater. This view is oversold; interest groups are prominent in research on Congress, administrative politics, judicial politics, and state policy. Nonetheless, pluralist theory did suffer a discipline-wide decline in influence and it was indicative of a more circumscribed role for interest groups in studies of American government.

The decline may also be a product of a successful and necessary narrowing of the aspirations of interest group research. Interest organizations are only one important subset of the actors trying to influence American policymaking. We should not expect to build a theory of who gets what, when, and how that focuses only on interest organizations rather than political parties, elections, and the operations of each branch of government.

One positive signal from the chapters in *New Directions in Interest Group Politics* is the willingness of contemporary scholars to combine studies of interest groups with research on other actors and institutions. One potential area of productive overlap is between studies of interest groups and America's two major political parties. Both differences in the party coalitions and changes in the relative power of the two parties are likely to condition nearly all of the relationships between interest group tactics and their influence. Just like parties play quite different roles in the three branches of government, scholars are finding that interest group behavior and influence is quite distinct in the courts and the administration.

Even as our theoretical aspirations have narrowed, we have accumulated evidence of several potential routes toward interest group influence. Interest groups may affect American politics in many small ways that add up to a significant role, rather than have one dominant role. In trying to assess whether particular tactics are consistently influential or whether the side with the most money wins most often, scholars have mostly reached dead ends. This is not for lack of trying, but likely because there is no simple and consistent relationship between resources directed to lobbying and campaign contributions and policy outcomes. This volume presents evidence that the text of interest group briefs show up in Supreme Court decisions (Chapter 12), that interest groups are able to place preferred workers in administrative positions (Chapter 11), and that interest groups change the balance of advertising in congressional elections (Chapter 8). Combined, the research suggests that interest groups have many potential routes to influence, even if buying votes in Congress is not usually one of them.

Several of these routes to influence may depend on trends separate from interest group behavior. Changes in campaign finance laws, communication technology, or the rules of standing in court cases may affect group influence even if groups were not responsible for the changes. The value of connecting interest group research to other fields is to provide a better view of the many routes to affect policy outcomes, the roles that interest groups play alongside myriad other actors, and differences across policy issues and institutional venues.

Trends in Interest Group Behavior

Interest group research advances through sustained interaction by a community of scholars, but it also responds to changes in interest group behavior in the real world. *New Directions in Interest Group Politics* has showcased several examples of important recent transformations in interest group activities. The rise of specialty professional firms allows corporations to simulate the behavior of grassroots activists and social movements (Chapter 3). This capacity may give corporations what was once one of the major relative advantages of advocates: their perceived public support. It may also change how policymakers view interest groups, making it harder to stand out in the crowd. The massive expansion of the interest group community, after all, has been accompanied by a continued concentration of opportunities for influence among a small subset of groups (Chapter 1).

New communications technology also seems to be altering the mobilization strategies of interest groups. It may be changing how groups raise money, providing a scarce advantage to new upstarts over veteran organizations that rely more on direct mail (Chapter 7). The evidence so far suggests that liberal and conservative groups are responding quite differently to the opportunities provided by the Web and social media, with fortuitous consequences for the relative mobilization of the American left and right (Chapter 7). Because it is still early in the transformation, we do not yet know whether the changes will accelerate. Perhaps veteran organizations will fend off the challenge from new upstarts. Since the changes are affecting how organizations define their membership as well as how they interact with the public and policymakers, they have the potential to have quite an impact.

Changes in campaign finance law and lobbying regulation are also changing interest group behavior. The recent liberalization of campaign finance law means that interest groups can now outspend candidates in critical elections and change the issues discussed in campaigns (Chapter 8). Some of the changes may be superficial, as the new breed of interest groups look more like vehicles for party activists than single-issue groups trying to change the agenda. Attempts to monitor and reform lobbying have provided copious data for researchers (Chapter 10) but have also led fewer people to consider themselves lobbyists (Chapter 13).

Because these changes in regulation affect both interest group behavior and the types of data that researchers have at their disposal, we sometimes confuse trends in what we learn about groups with real changes in their behavior. Observers must be careful in assessing changes in the total number of lobbyists or organizations if new rules provide incentives to split organizations into multiple parts or avoid registering as lobbyists. Likewise, influence may be easier to establish in cases where we have more complete data. Two studies of lobbying in Wisconsin show that bills with support from lobbyists move further through the legislative process; the phenomenon is unlikely to be unique to one state government, but Wisconsin happens to have the most extensive records on lobbyist support and opposition.[15] The new sources of data—as long as they are taken with a grain of salt—should remain an advantage for future interest group research.

Informed Evaluation of Interest Groups

The primary goals of this volume are those of traditional subject-based learning: the chapters cover the components of interest group behavior, allowing you to see how researchers investigate interest groups. The volume should enable better-informed observation and participation in American politics. The next time you hear President Obama or another politician blame an interest group for a specific legislative failure, you now have the tools to evaluate whether things would have turned out differently if the interest group had not been involved.

You can also assess whether interest group roles are productive or destructive. Is the NRA merely representing the views of its membership, effectively allying in a successful coalition with other Republican-leaning groups and providing information to inform public policy? Alternatively, is it an example of a narrow organizational leadership, speaking only on behalf of a small subset of its members and thwarting the will of a majority of Americans? It is likely doing some combination of the two; research helps discern how much each vision is supported by the evidence.

Just as importantly, research allows generalization beyond any one specific case. The NRA may be an outlier in its influential role, enabled by its focus on keeping the law unchanged in one policy area. As a membership organization unconcerned with economic policy, it is not even a representative case of the interest group population. Observing its outsized role is certainly not enough to conclude that a few big interests dominate the American government.

Although interest group research challenges blanket claims that "the special interests" control government, it includes plenty of evidence that groups play significant roles in political decision-making. Groups also represent some social and economic interests much better than others, providing an important source of imbalance in American democracy. The benefit of scholarship is to subject the claims of politicians and the assumptions of the American public to assessment: are common ideas consistent with the evidence? There are plenty of questions left unanswered in interest group research, but we have managed to eliminate some views as less likely than others. After your exposure to research, I trust that your view of "the special interests" will be a little more nuanced and informed.

Notes

1 Transcript of remarks by Barack Obama and Mark Barden at the White House, April 17, 2013, http://www.nytimes.com/2013/04/18/us/politics/obamas-remarks-after-senate-gun-votes.html? For a useful review of the competition between gun control supporters and opponents and the failure of the movement for gun control, see Kristin A. Goss, *Disarmed: The Missing Movement for Gun Control in America* (Princeton, NJ: Princeton University Press, 2008).

2 National Election Studies 2008 Survey, http://www.electionstudies.org/nesguide/toptable/tab5a_2.htm.

3 These debates mostly took place concerning local-level politics. They are reviewed in Nelson W. Polsby, *Community Power and Political Theory* (New Haven, CT: Yale University Press, 1963). At the national level, the key contributors were David B. Truman, *The Governmental Process: Political Interests and Public Opinion* (New York: Knopf, 1951), and E. E. Schattschneider, *The Semisovereign People: A Realists View at Democracy in America* (New York: Holt, Rinehart and Winston, 1960).

4 Mancur Olson, *The Logic of Collective Action: Public Goods and the Theory of Groups*, 2nd ed. (Cambridge, MA: Harvard University Press, 1971).

5 Jack L. Walker, *Mobilizing Interest Groups in America: Patrons, Professions, and Social Movements* (Ann Arbor: University of Michigan Press, 1991); Robert H. Salisbury,

Interests and Institutions: Substance and Structure in American Politics (Pittsburgh: University of Pittsburgh Press, 1992).

6 Virginia Gray and David Lowery, *The Population Ecology of Interest Representation: Lobbying Communities in the American States* (Ann Arbor: University of Michigan Press, 2000).

7 Frank R. Baumgartner and Beth L. Leech, *Basic Interests: The Importance of Groups in Politics and Political Science* (Princeton, NJ: Princeton University Press, 1998).

8 Frank R. Baumgartner, Jeffrey M. Berry, Marie Hojnacki, David C. Kimball, and Beth L. Leech, *Lobbying and Policy Change: Who Wins, Who Loses, and Why* (Chicago: University of Chicago Press, 2009).

9 Andrew S. McFarland, *Neopluralism: The Evolution of Political Process Theory* (Lawrence: University of Kansas Press, 2004).

10 Robert H. Salisbury, "An Exchange Theory of Interest Groups," *Midwest Journal of Political Science* 13, no. 1 (1969): 1–32; John R. Wright, *Interest Groups and Congress: Lobbying, Contributions, and Influence* (Boston: Allyn and Bacon, 1996).

11 Harold Lasswell, *Politics: Who Gets What, When, How* (New York: World Publishing, 1958).

12 Salisbury, "An Exchange Theory of Interest Groups."

13 Wright, *Interest Groups and Congress.*

14 Richard L. Hall and Alan V. Deardorff, "Lobbying as Legislative Subsidy," *American Political Science Review* 100, no. 1 (2006): 69–84.

15 Daniel C. Lewis, "Advocacy and Influence: Lobbying and Legislative Outcomes in Wisconsin," *Interest Groups & Advocacy* (forthcoming); Nathan Grasse and Brianne Heidbreder, "The Influence of Lobbying Activity in State Legislatures: Evidence from Wisconsin," *Legislative Studies Quarterly* 36, no. 4 (2011): 567–89.

Index

5
501(c) groups 151, 160, 243, 250

9
9/11 69, 77

A
AARP (American Association of Retired Persons) 1, 13, 119
ABA (American Bankers Association) 107–8, 113, 114–16
ABA (American Bar Association) 214, 224, 252
Aberbach, Joe 209
Abramoff, Jack 208, 243–4
accountability of candidates 88
Ackerman, Bruce 247
action alerts 132, 139
activism 47, 50. *see also* mobilization
   armchair 124
   and e-mail 125
   listservs for cross-organizational communications 131
activity levels of organizations 65–7
advertising
   and candidate advocacy spending 152
   candidate mention standard in 149–50
   issue-related 149
   and loopholes in IRS tax code 150
   magic words used in 149
   and outside spending 153–7
   Section 527 effect on 150
   and Super PACs 144
   television 152–3
Advisory Opinions of FEC 151
advocacy
   and communication 125
   explosion 4, 53

express 242
   independent 151
   PACs spending on 147
advocacy groups
   consultants for 51–2
   digitally-based 123
   e-mail use by 123–4, 140
   funding appeals by 135
   and the generation gap 139–40
   legacy 124
   and marginalized constituencies 60
   membership in 124
   policy issues of 63–5
advocacy organizations 6, 22, 46, 49, 60
   institutional targeting by 67–72
   professionalization of 124–5
affirmative advocacy 60, 80
Affirmative Advocacy (Strolovitch) 62, 68, 76, 77, 79
AFL-CIO 105, 113
African Americans 10, 61–2, 90–1, 222, 229
AFSCME 144
agency capture critique 211
Aldrich, John
   Why Parties 87–9
ALL (American League of Lobbyists) 251–2
Allard, Nicholas 241, 250
alliances. *see* coalitions
always hard times 77
Amazon 185
America Coming Together 527 effort 127
American Association of Retired Persons (AARP) 1, 13, 119
American Bankers Association (ABA) 107–8, 113, 114–16
American Bar Association (ABA) 214, 224, 252

American Cancer Association 99
American Civil Liberties Union 128, 221, 222–3, 232
American Crossroads 144
American Hospital Association 1, 223
American League of Lobbyists (ALL) 251–2
American Legion 13, 26
American Medical Association 1, 51
American Muslim Political Coordination Council PAC 97–8
American Political Science Association 86
American Psychiatric Association 47
American Psychological Association 221
Americans for Effective Law Enforcement 223
Americans for Prosperity 143
amicus curiae briefs 67, 223, 225–6, 229–30
Amnesty International 128
Ansolabehere, Stephen
    "Why is There so Little Money in U.S. Politics?" 165
anti-lobbyist ethics pledge 214
Anti-Saloon League, The 100–1
anti-trust regulations 211
Apollonio, Dorie 248
appeals for funds 135
appearance of corruption 160, 239
appointments, presidential 207–10
appropriations, allocation of 212
Arab American Political Action Committee 97–8
Arab Americans 97–8
armchair activism 124
Ashcroft, John 209–10
assault weapons ban 257
associations 38, 124
astroturf lobbying 46, 55
Atlantic, The 131
Augusta National Golf Club 47
Austin v. Michigan State Chamber of Commerce 239
Ayres, Ian 247

B
backchannel lists 130–1
backend analytics problem 130
Backyard Revolution 50
Baldwin, Tammy 144, 154
Balla, Steve 212
bank reserve requirements 106–8, 113

Baptist and bootlegger coalitions 55
Bawn, Kathy 88–9
    Theory of Political Parties 88
BCRA (Bipartisan Campaign Finance Reform Act) 242–3
Beard, Charles 68
Bell, Lauren Cohen 209
Bentley, Arthur 3, 23
Berry, Jeffrey M. 178
biases
    against marginalized groups 60, 80
    mobilization of 61
    in representation 76
Bickel, Alexander 68
Bimber, Bruce
    Collective Action 124
    Collective Action in Organizations 124
Bipartisan Campaign Finance Reform Act (BCRA) 242–3
Bi-Partisan Campaign Reform Act 149–50
Blades, Joan 124
blogs 122, 123
Blue State Digital 125, 129
Boehmke, Frederick 205
Bonica, Adam 247
Bowers, Chris 133
Boyd, Wes 124
BP oil spill 137
Brady, Henry E. 238
Brady Campaign to Prevent Gun Violence 12, 257
Brandeis, Louis 242
bread and butter issues 178
Brown v. Board of Education 225, 229
Brown v. Entertainment Merchants Association 225
Brusoe, Peter 247
Bryan, William Jennings 89
Buckley v. Valeo 147, 149, 239
bureaucracy
    and campaign contributions 170–2
    and support for federal appointees 211–12
Bush, George H. W. 97, 212
Bush, George W. 95, 97–8, 179, 209–10, 212
business donors 173–6
business elites 50
business organizations 48
    mobilization of 8–10, 18–19, 258
    political representation of 29, 126

C

Cain, Bruce 244, 248
Cameron, Charles M. 188
campaign activity and anonymity 160–1
campaign contributions
  and bill sponsorships 169
  and the courts 172–173
  distribution of 238
  influence on executive branch 170–2
  outside spending effects on 153–7
  from PACs 146–7
  studies about 166–9
  timing of 194–200
campaign contributions and policymaking
    165–84
  business participation in 174–8
  courts, effect on the 172–3
  executive branch, effect on 170–2
  influences 166–9
  outcome of votes on 259
  problems in 179–80
  and roll call voting 169–70
  sources of financing 173–6
campaign finance laws 145, 149–50, 258
  changes in 144, 266
  court decisions on 239–40
  entities designed to avoid 261
  and transparency 150
candidate mention standard 149–50
candidates
  accountability 89
  contributions from PACs 146–7
  fund-raising rules 144
  influence of PACs on 147
  PACs contributions to 146–7
  public funding for 248–9
  spending averages on campaigns 146
card check 179–80
Carter, Jimmy 178, 207
case selection for litigation 228
Catalist 129, 131
Cato Institute 221, 228
CBO (Congressional Budget Office) 249
Center for American Democracy 501(c)(4)
    160
Center for American Democracy Super
    PAC 160
Center for American Progress 1
Center for Voting and Democracy 128
Center on Budget and Policy Priorities 28
CFSI (Citizens for Fire Safety Institute) 54
Change Congress 128

checkbook and mailing list associations
    31, 49
checks and balances 120
Chevy Chase Bank 225
Children's Hospital of Philadelphia 22
Chubb, John 206
citizen activity 122
citizen associations 27, 35, 48–9
citizen interest groups 207
Citizen Participation Study (1990)
    22–3
Citizens for Fire Safety Institute
    (CFSI) 54
Citizens United v. FEC 144, 239, 250
City of Los Angeles 22
civic organizations and public policy 61
civil liberties 101
Civil Rights Act (1964) 213
civil rights organizations 27
class action law suits 67, 225
clicktivism 124, 125, 133
Clinton, Bill 76–7, 95, 124, 178, 212
Clinton, Hillary 151
coalitions 261
  conditions 108–9
  gay rights 95–6
  ideological 100–1
  interest groups 72–6, 87–9
  joining during transition 214
  and new technologies 129
  party 100–2
  permanent alliance 87
Cohen, Marty 90, 95–6, 97
  Party Decides, The 88
collective action 3, 9, 12, 259
Collective Action (Bimber, Flanagin, Stohl)
    124
colleges and gainful employment rule
    44–5
Collier, Ken 206
Collins, Paul M., Jr. 230
color-blind approach to policy 97–8
Commerce Clause 224
communications
  and advocacy campaigns 125
  cross-organizational listservs for 131
  electioneering 152
  left-right divide in 129–30
  and member e-mail analysis 130–1
  with members 132
  organizational membership 124
  research 126–9

communications technologies 122, 123,
125. *see also* Internet and interest
group change
and growth of consulting firms 53
and mobilization strategies 266
Communications Workers of America 26
community-based organizations 50
Community Reinvestment Act (1977) 50,
115
compensatory representation of
marginalized groups 60, 65
competing interest groups 106–7
compromises on issues 258, 261
conferences 129
congregation-based organizations 50
Congressional Bills Project 199
Congressional Budget Office (CBO) 249
congressional candidates, contributions
from PACs 146–7
Congressional Management Foundation
240
Congressional Research Service (CRS)
249
congressional staff 240–1
conservative
donors 90, 127
network professionals 129
new media, use of 130
policy approach 97–8
policy shifts 176–8
Conservative Message Machine Money
Matrix 127
Conservative Political Action Committee
96–7
conspiracy theorists 131
constituencies, interests of 31
consultants
clients of 52–3
e-mail 129
fees 53–4
and grassroots mobilization 51–5
history of 52–3
industry 44
contacts sharing 111
contributions
contributions from interest groups 146–7,
176–8
Convio 125, 129
Cornhusker Kickback 165
corporate interests 6
corporate spending 152
corporations 48

associations of 4
election spending by 153
and grassroots mobilization 51
issue advocacy 53–4
and issue advocacy 150
and political spending 151
Cortner, Richard C. 222
costs
fundraising 136
of joining a coalition 111–12
litigation 226
Countdown with Keith Olbermann 126–37
counter-majoritarian difficulty 68
Courage Campaign 128
courts
activism of 69
and campaign contributions 172–3
and free speech issues 239
institutional targeting of 67–8
lobbying of 47, 223–6
courts of appeals decisions 227
Crenshaw, Kimberlé 62
cross-class membership federations 125,
140
Crossroads GPS 144, 243
CRS (Congressional Research Service) 249
C-SPAN 209
culture of testing 122

D
DA (Democracy Alliance) 127
Dahl, Robert 3, 61
DailyKos 122, 133
dark money 243
dark social problems 130
data analysis of interest group e-mails
130–1
DC lobbying community 126, 127, 139
Dean, Howard 129, 178
Deardorff, Alan 102
Defenders of Wildlife 110
Defending Immigrants Partnership 232
Defense of Marriage Act 77
De Figueiredo, John M. 165, 188
"Why is There so Little Money in U.S.
Politics?" 166
Deloitte, LLP 199
Democracia Ahora 137
Democracy Alliance (DA) 127
Democracy and the Internet's Politics
Online Conference 125
Democracy for America 136

Democracy in Action 125
Democratic National Convention 213
Democratic Party
    and contributions from business
        interests 175
    and ethnic minorities endorsements
        97–8
    International Brotherhood of Police
        Officers 95
    spending on advertising 154–7
    spending on causes 152
    and wealthier contributors 178
    and women's issues 97
democrats
    and gender gap advantage 97
    and gun control legislation 89
    and labor union support 90–1
Department of Energy 208
deregulation of campaign finance laws 180
descriptive representation 80
Dimaggio, Paul 128
Diminished Democracy (Skocpol) 124
direct contributions 262
direct mail 124, 135, 136
disadvantaged groups. see also
        marginalized groups
    and the courts 68
    economically 29
    and mass politics 44
    organizations speaking on behalf of 61
    and public participation 50
DISCLOSE Act 250–1
disclosure requirements 153
Discovertext software 186, 190
distributive politics 87
District of Columbia v. Heller 228
doctors, organizations of 12
doctors organizations 2
Dodd-Frank Wall Street Reform and
        Consumer Protection Act 240
Dole, Bob 95, 96–7
Dominguez, Casey B. 194
donations
    appeals for 135
    to incumbents 146–7
donors
    changing source of 173–4
    of 501(c)(4) groups 151
    unrestricted revenues appeals 135
Don't Ask, Don't Tell 77, 137
Drutman, Lee 244, 248
Dusso, Aaron 187

E
Earl, Jennifer 128
EarthFirst! 110
Earthjustice 49, 110
economic matters 28–9, 31, 179
Edelman (PR firm) 55
Edwards, John 179
elderly 30–1. see also AARP
elected officials, effect of campaign
        contributions on 170–3
electioneering 150–2
elections
    and campaign finance rules 258
    costs of 174–6
    influences on 258
    interest group participation in
        90–4
    investments in 148–9
    and outside spending 153–7
    and PACs 144–5
elites 3, 46, 50
    and agenda manipulation 61
    defined 259
    and mass politics 44
e-mail 122, 123–6
    analysis of 130–1
    best practices 125
    cost of 123
    fundraising 135–6
    studying 130–1
    volume of 132–4
emerging technologies 123
EMILY's List 135
endorsements 91
Engage DC 29, 129
environmental advocacy 110
Environmental Defense Fund 110, 124
e-petitions 123, 133
Epstein, Lee 229
Equal Employment Advisory Council
        223
equitable representation 80
Erikson, Robert S. 177
Esterling, Kevin 241
ethics 119–20
Evans, Bob 214
exclusionary rule 223
executive branch 67–8, 170–2
expert knowledge 45
express advocacy 242
extremists 12
ExxonMobil Corporation 22

F
Facebook 122
Fair Elections Now Act 246
FairVote 128
Family Research Council 98
farm groups 29
favors and legislative policy 87
FEC (Federal Election Commission)
    147–8, 150, 151, 174
(FECA) Federal Election Campaign Act
    196
federal campaign finance reforms 246–7
Federal Election Campaign Act (FECA)
    196
Federal Election Commission (FEC). *see*
    FEC (Federal Election Commission)
federal funding 5
federal government 5
    and budget impact on low-income
        Americans 28
    collaboration with interest groups 207
    contractors and campaign contributions
        172
    regulations and grassroots lobbying 46
Federalist No. 70 204
Federalist Society 223
Federal Marriage Amendment 97
Federal Reserve Act of 1913 115
federal spending, influence of interest
    groups on 212
federated organizations 48
feedback 122–3, 131
filibuster reform 137
Financial Reform 137
financial resources, sharing of 111–12
financial-supporter relationship 124
First Amendment speech issues 149
First Amendment to the Constitution 120
Flanagin, Andrew *Collective Action in
    Organizations* 124
FOIA (Freedom of Information Act) 218
FOP (Fraternal Order of Police) 95, 210
Ford, Gerald 207
for-profit economic entities 26
foundations 49
Fourteenth Amendment's Due Process
    Clause 221
Fox News 137
Francia, Peter 248
Fraternal Order of Police (FOP) 95, 210
fraud in campaigns 46
Freddie Mac 251

Freedom of Information Act (FOIA) 218
Frye, Jocelyn 213–14
Frymer, Paul 8, 68
funding sources, iPhone application to
    identify 155
fundraising 135, 136, 144
Furlong, Scott 211

G
gainful employment rule 44–5
Gais, Thomas 207
GAO (Government Accountability Office)
    249
Gay and Lesbian Advocates and Defenders
    222
gay rights 96–7
generation gap 139–40
Gerken, Heather 241, 249
get-out-the-vote (GOTV) 52
get-out-the-vote campaigns 91
Gingrich, Newt 251
Gladwell, Malcolm 125
Glavin, Brendan 247
goals of organizations
    affected by War on Terror 77–8
    of identity groups 27
    and individual interests 3
    policy 88
Goodridge v. Department of Public Health
    222
Google groups 131
GOProud 96
Gordon, Stacy B. 169
Gore, Al 95, 194
GOTV (get-out-the-vote) 52
government. *see also* federal government;
    state governments
    and interest groups 13–16
    spending and increase in lobbying
        15
Government Accountability Office (GAO)
    249
government contracts, campaign
    contributions effects on 172
Grassley, Charles 210
grassroots 129
Grassroots Democracy Act 247
grassroots lobbying 44–59, 258
    by consultants 44, 51–5
    defined 45–7
    and the Internet 122
    mass participation, sources of 47–51

persuasion techniques used for 35
  tactics 48
Gray, Virginia 16–17
Greenpeace 110
Griles, Steven 208–9, 217
Grossmann, Matt 187–8, 194, 206
  *The Not-So-Special Interests: Interest
    Groups, Public Representation, and
    American Governance* 6
group mobilization 1–21
  business mobilization 8–10
  government action and interest
    mobilization 13–16
  national interest group population 4–5
  skew of interest group participation
    6–7
  social, economic, and political 17–19
  social constituency mobilization 10–13
  state-level interest mobilization 16–17
  theoretical perspectives on 2–4
groups
  identity of 90–1
  and lobbyists persuasion 119
  and public representation 12
  research into communication methods
    of 126–9
gun control legislation 89, 257

H
Hacker, Jacob S. 176–7
Hall, Richard 102
Hamilton, Alexander 204
Hamlet (Shakespeare) 119
hard money 242
Hatch, Oren 209–10
Hatch Act 205
Headstart 31
Health Care Reform 137
Heaney, Michael 100
Heclo, Hugh 207, 211
Heinz, John P.
  The Hollow Core 191–2
Herrnson, Paul 206, 248
high-capacity magazines, ban on 257
Hispanic Business Roundtable 98
Hispanic organizations 27
(HLOGA) Honest Leadership and Open
    Government Act 242, 243–4
Hollow Core, The (Heinz) 191–2
Holyoke, Thomas 205
Honest Leadership and Open Government
    Act (HLOGA) 242, 243–4

House members, PACs contributions to
    146–7
housing and foreclosure policy 50
Huffington Post 127, 165
Hula, Kevin 111
Human Rights Campaign 96, 98
human rights organizations 27

I
IBPO (International Brotherhood of Police
    Officers) 95
identity groups 4, 29–30, 48
ideology 89–90
  and interest groups 86
  and matching funds 247
  and presidential appointments 207
Immigration and Nationality Act 232
immigration reform legislation 105
income gaps 76–7
income inequality 176, 179
incumbents, donations to 146–7
independence reforms 241, 248–9
independent advocacy 151
independent expenditures 147–8, 151–2
individual-membership associations 26,
    28–31, 50
Industrial Areas Foundation 49
inequality and interest group
    representation 60–85
influence
  of campaign on policy 166–8
  of PACs on candidates 146–7
information revolution 124
information sharing 111
inside lobbying 45–6
Institute for Politics 125
Institute for Politics, Democracy and the
    Internet's Politics Online Conference
    129
institutes 49
institutional isomorphism theory 128
institutionalization of the presidency
    206–7
institutional targeting 67–72
institutions
  associations of 26, 28
  built by conservative donors 127
  intense policy demanders 95–6
  interest advocacy associations 128
  interest group behavior 258–9, 265–6
    collaboration 131
    coordination 98–100

endorsement patterns 90
membership numbers 105
networks 98
participation in elections 90–4
pluralism 23–5
support for candidates 91
interest group communications
advertising 155
costs 153–7
e-mail use 123
tools 122
interest group costs
for advertising 153–7
expenditures on campaign funding
174–6
spending by SuperPacs 144
interest group electioneering 151
election issues 158, 160
group-centered electoral process 161
limits on 151
interest group explosion 48, 125, 136
interest group formation
and business groups 8–10
defined 23
organization 88
population of 4–5
single-issue 100–1
and social groups 10–13
interest group mobilization 258–60
interest group PACs
contributions to candidate committees
178
expenditures 144–5, 174–6
and fund-raising by SuperPACs 144–5
interest group regulations
and FEC 147–8
on hiring former government appointees
208
interest group representation 60–85
coalitions 72–8
competing interests of 106–8
independence from political parties 90
and inequality 60–85
and institutional targeting 67–72
levels of activity 65–7
in not-so-good times 76–9
interest group research 126–9, 186–7
interest groups, the White House, and the
administration 204–21
appointments and confirmation 207–10
design, change, and learning 205–7
federal bureaucracy 211–12

interest groups and presidential
transitions 212–16
presidential appointments 208
interest groups and the judiciary 221–37
influence of 228–32
litigation tactics of 226–8
and lobbying 221–6
interest representation 26
International Brotherhood of Police
Officers 95
Internet and interest group change
122–43, 258. see also communications
technologies
costs of e-mail 123
descriptive findings 132–9
e-mail, focus on 123–6
generation gap, adapting to 139–40
Internet Marketplace Fairness Act 185
Internet Membership Communications
Project 126–31
intersectionality 11, 39, 60
intersectionally marginalized groups 62–3,
65, 69, 71–80. see also marginalized
groups
iPhone application to identify funding
sources 155
Iron Triangle theory 211
IRS tax code 150
Issa, Darrell 252
Issachar, Samuel 241
issue advertising 149
issue advocacy 53, 149
funding for 150
groups 4
McCain-Feingold restrictions on 150
sham 145
issue networks 211

J
Jarrett, Valerie 207
Jewish organizations 11, 13
judiciary. see also courts
decision-making and campaign
contributions 172–3
interest groups and 221–37

K
Karol, David 88
Katzen, Sally 213
Kelly, Lorelei 240
Kennedy, Anthony 250
Kenney, Sally 68

Kerry, John 97–8
Kerwin, Cornelius 211
key votes 167
knowledge sharing 129
Koger, Gregory 98–100
Kohl, Herb 144
Kollman, Ken 50
Koons Buick Pontiac v. Nigh 232
Kreiss, Daniel 129

L
Labor, Corporate, Trade, Membership, and
   Health (TMH) 175
labor unions. *see* unions
ladder of engagement 125
Lambda Legal 221
LaPierre, Wayne 89
LaPira, Tim 244
La Raja, Ray 242, 249
Latino organizations 11
law and order 95–6
lawmaker independence 248–9
lawmaker pressure 116–18
Lawrence v. Texas 221
lawyers organizations 12
LDA (Lobbying Disclosure Act of 1995) 4,
   36–7, 186–7
LDF (NAACP Legal Defense and
   Education Fund) 225, 228–9
Leadership Conference on Civil and
   Human Rights 27
Leadership Conference on Civil Rights
   209–10
League of Conservation Voters 136
League of United Latin American Citizens
   27
Leahy, Patrick 209–10
Ledbetter, Lilly 212–14
*Ledbetter v. Goodyear Tire and Rubber
   Company* 213
Leech, Beth 212
leftwing organizations 128, 129
legacy organizations 124, 128, 135–6, 137
legalized bribery 173
legal mobilization 68
legislation, complexity of 240
legislators 15, 45
legislatures 87
Leocal v. Ashcroft 232
lesbian, gay, bisexual, transgender, and
   queer (LGBTQ) people 60
Leveling Down reforms 241, 242

Leveling Up reforms 241, 246
Levy, Robert 228
LGBTQ (lesbian, gay, bisexual, transgender,
   and queer people) 60
liberal media bias 130
liberals 90
libertarian ideology 96
Lichtman, Judith 213–14
Lilly Ledbetter Fair Pay Act 212–14,
   213
listservs 131
literature 18–19, 187–8, 187–9, 233
litigation tactics 226–8
lobbying. *see also* mobilization
   activity 189
   and appropriations 212
   astroturf 46, 55
   behavior of interest groups 4
   business spending on 8, 9, 177
   and Congressional registration data
      14–15
   and deal-making 105
   definition of 251–2
   disclosure regulations 4, 36–7, 186–7
   expenses 8
   and interest group participation in 6
   recruiting for 108
lobbying and money in politics, reforms of
   238–56
   BCRA 242–3
   Bipartisan Campaign Finance Reform
      Act (BCRA) 242–3
   campaign finance 250–1
   campaign vouchers and matching funds
      246–8
   HLOGA 243–4
   independence 248–9
   leveling down 242
   leveling up 246
   lobbying 251–3
   Obama lobbying rule 244–6
   resources for Congress 249
   transparency 250
Lobbying Disclosure Act of 1995 (LDA).
   see LDA (Lobbying Disclosure Act of
   1995)
lobbying groups
   and business share 4
   expenditures 8, 239
   identifying 126
   registration requirements 14–15
   regulations 266

lobbying in the U.S. Congress 185–203
  bills and bill content 200
  campaign contributions and timing
    194–200
  limits set by HLOGA 243–4
  literature on the influence of 187–9
  networks as indicators of preferences
    191–4
  preferences 189–91
Lobbyist Disclosure Enhancement Act 252
lobbyists
  access to congressional staff 239–40
  assessing changes in the total number 266
  and coalition benefits 111–12
  and deal-making 105
  and lawmaker pressure 116–18
  and lawmakers 116–18
  as legislative subsidy 102
  for membership organizations 35–9
  numbers of 105–6
  professional grassroots 48
lobbyists, cooperation among 105–21
  competing interests 106–8
  and ethics 119–20
  lawmakers and lobbyists 116–19
  long term coalitions 109–13
  multi-dimensional-trade-offs 113–15
  short-term issue coalitions 113
  status quo sticking points 115–16
lobbyists for competing interest groups
    106–7
local community-based organizations 50
local governments 12–13, 26
Log Cabin Republicans 96
logroll 87
long-term coalitions 87, 88, 109–13, 119
Lowery, David 16–17
low-income people 28, 60–2
Lowry, Robert 212
Lynn, William 245

M
Mackuen, Michael B. 177
McCann, Michael 68
McClurg, Scott 102
Maddow, Rachel 136–7
Madison, James 242, 248
Madison project 252
Madrigal, Alexis 131
magic words 149, 151
mailing lists 98, 124, 131
Main Street businesses 186

Majority PAC 144
Malbin, Michael 247
Malhotra, Neil 248
managerial occupations 29–30
Manchin, Joe 257
Mapp v. Ohio 223
Maranto, Robert 206
marginalization 62, 79
marginalized groups 60. *see also*
    disadvantaged groups
  advocacy for in not-so-good times 76–9
  biases against 60
  coalition for 72–3
  compensatory representation of 65
  and the courts 68
  evaluating advocacy group
    representation of 62–3
Marketplace Fairness Act 185
Martin, Trayvon 131
Masket, Seth 98–100
Massachusetts Supreme Judicial Court 222
mass membership organizations 47–51
matching funds 246–8
McCain, John 213
McCain-Feingold act 149–50, 242–3
McConnell v. FEC 242
(MCP) Membership Communications
    Project 123, 125–6
measures of connectedness 192
media. *see also* social media
  agenda of netroot groups 136–7
  campaigners 40
Medicaid 31
Medicare 13
meetings with transition team 213–15
member communications, approach to 132
membership, redefinition of 124–5
membership associations 28, 48
  and advocacy interests 29
  and communication analysis 130
  internal operations of 31–3
  lobbyists for 35–9
  professional management of 262
  and representation in Washington 22–43
  status of citizen groups 27
membership communications 124
Membership Communications Project
    (MCP) 123, 125–6, 130
membership organizations 110
  direct mail 136
  and the Internet 122
members of coalitions 110

Michelman, Kate 210
military associations and political
    representation 29
minorities organizational representation
    for 60, 61
mobilization. *see also* lobbying
    and business 177
    conservative grass roots 129
    effect on outcome of votes 259
    and government policies 17
    increases during rulemaking 46
    interest groups 3
    and Internet influence on 123
    and issue areas 14
    online 139
    spending on 38–9
    on state level 16–17
    tactics 122
mobilization of bias 61
Mobilizing Interest Groups in America
    (Walker) 126
Moe, Terry 206, 208
money influence on politics 174–6
money in politics 146–7, 236–56. *see also*
    lobbying and money in politics
motivation 262
MoveOn.org 122, 124, 127, 129, 136, 150
M+R 129
MSNBC 136
mundane Internet tools 125
"Mundane Internet Tools: the
    Coproduction of Citizenship in
    Political Campaigns" (Nielsen) 125
mundane mobilization tools 123
Munoz, Cecilia 214
Murdoch, Rupert 130
Murkowski, Lisa 251
Muslims 98

N
NAACP Legal Defense and Education Fund
    (LDF) 49, 225, 228–9
NADA (National Automobile Dealers
    Association) 232
NARAL 210
Nation, The 127
national advocacy associations 49
national advocacy organizations 60–1
National American Woman Suffrage
    Association 61
National Association for the Advancement
    of Colored People 61, 128

National Association of Attorneys General
    210
National Association of Criminal Defense
    Lawyers 232
National Association of Wholesaler-
    Distributors 210
National Automobile Dealers Association
    (NADA) 232
National Baptist Convention 210
National Center for Neighborhood
    Enterprise 210
National Council of La Raza 1, 214
National Federation of Independent
    Business (NFIB) 224
National Governors' Association 210
national interest groups 4–5, 48–9
National Labor Relations Board (NLRB)
    50, 208
National Oceanic and Atmospheric
    Administration (NOAA) 211
National Organization for Women 97, 128,
    129
National Partnership for Women and
    Families (NPWF)
    "Turning Promise into Progress: Key
        Priorities for Women and Families"
        213
national policymaking, involvement in 6
National Resources Defense Council 129
National Retail Federation 185
National Review 98
National Rifle Association. *see* NRA
national security 101
National Women's Law Center, 27,
    209–10
Nation magazine 99
Nature Conservancy 110
Nelson, Ben 165
neopluralism 259
netroots groups 128
    fundraising 136
    and media agenda 136–7
netroots interest groups and e-mail agenda
    136–7
Netroots Nation conference 129
Netroots Nation convention (2010) 125
netroots organizations 122, 125, 136
netroots political associations 127
networking sites 123
networks
    analysis of 98–100
    analysis tools 191–4

communication 129
for organizational learning 129
new generation organizations 128
Newmark, Adam 174
new media 122–3
New Organizing Institute (NOI) 129
New Organizing Institute's "Rootscamps" 125
New York State Defenders Association 232
NFIB (National Federation of Independent Business) 224
niche groups 110
Nielsen, Rasmus Kleis 123
"Mundane Internet Tools: the Coproduction of Citizenship in Political Campaigns" 125
Niskanen, William 212
NLRB (National Labor Relations Board) 50, 208
NMAOs (Non-Membership Advocacy Organizations) 49
NOAA (National Oceanic and Atmospheric Administration) 211
Noel, Hans 98–100
NOI (New Organizing Institute) 129
Non-Membership Advocacy Organizations (NMAOs) 49
non-membership associations 48
non-partisan environment 89
nonprofit organizations 124
not-for-profit economic entities 26
Not-So-Special Interests: Interest Groups, Public Representation, and American Governance (Grossmann) 6
NPWF (National Partnership for Women and Families) 213
"Turning Promise into Progress: Key Priorities for Women and Families" 213
NRA (National Rifle Association) 89, 129
and gun control legislation 257
and influence on legislation 267
supporters of 12

O
Obama, Barack 90, 101, 153, 156, 207, 212, 214, 218, 245
and gun control legislation 257
and health care reform 1
Obamacare (Patient Protection and Affordable Care Act) 165, 223
Obama lobbying rule 242, 244–6

occupational associations 4, 6
and political representation 29
Occupational Safety and Health Administration (OSHA) 172
Occupy Wall Street movement 179
O'Connor, Sandra Day 242
Office of Intergovernmental Affairs 207, 214
Office of Legislative Affairs 207
Office of Political Affairs 207
Office of Public Engagement 207
Office of Public Liaison 207
Office of Public Records 15
Office of Technology Assessment (OTA) 241, 249
Olbermann, Keith 136–7
Olson, Mancur 3–4, 9, 12, 18, 23–4
Olson critique of pluralism 18
one person, one vote 165
online mobilization 139
online-to-offline engagement 123
Operation Desert Storm 76
opinions, extreme 12
organizational communications 124, 129–30
organizational layer of American politics 126
organizational listservs 131
organizational representation of disadvantaged populations 62
organizations 27. *see also* coalitions
activity levels of 65–7
for disadvantaged populations 61–2
nonprofit 124
population definition of 126–9
organized interests 22
and campaign contributions 173–8
campaigns, influence on 149
policy process, influence on 165
organized labor. *see* unions
organized representation 2, 11–13, 24
Organizing for Action 124
Organizing for America/Organizing for Action 128
organizing processes 47–51
organizing without organizations 123
OSHA (Occupational Safety and Health Administration) 172
OTA (Office of Technology Assessment) 241, 249
outside lobbying. *see* consultants; grassroots lobbying

outside spending
  effectiveness of 153–7
  issue focus of 157–60
oversight boards 212

P
Pacific Legal Foundation 223
PACs 126. *see also* Super PACs
  contributions effect on votes 238
  contributions to candidates 145, 146–7,
    174–6
  contributions to incumbents 146
  independent expenditures 147–8
  influence on candidates 147
  regulations regarding funding 145–6
  traditional 145–7
Palin, Sarah 137
parties
  coalitions 100–2
  as interest group coalitions 87–9
  interests of 88
  strategies 89
partisan environment 89
partisan identity 91
partisanship 53, 148–9
Party Decides, The (Cohen) 88
party polarization 178
passive democratic feedback 122–3
pass-through fundraising 135, 139
Patient Protection and Affordable
    Care Act (Obamacare) 165, 223,
    224, 240
PATRIOT Act 101
Patton Boggs, Akin Gump, Cassidy and
    Associates 192, 199
pay equity issues 212–14
Payne, Erica 127
  Practical Progressive, The 127
Pelosi, Nancy 243
Personal Democracy Forum conference
    125, 129
Peterson, Mark A. 207
petitions 133
Pew Internet and American Life Project
    Tracking Survey (2008) 22–3
Philips, Jeremy 102
Phipps, Meg Scott 170
PhRMA 1
Pierson, Paul 176–7
Pika, Joe 207
PIONM (Public Interest Organizations in
    the New Millennium) 77

PIRG (U.S. Public Interest Research
    Group) 107–8
Planned Parenthood Federation of
    America 209–10
pluralism 3, 18, 23–5, 86, 259, 260–1
pluralists 61
polarization. *see* partisanship
policies
  goals and special interests 257
  legislative 87
  planning organizations 49
  state-level 50
policy
  advocating for 89
  color-blind approach to 97–8
policy demanders 88–9, 90, 95–6
policy domains 108
policy issues of advocacy groups 63–5
policy outcomes 107
political access, inequalities in 61
political action committees. *see* PACs
political activism and e-mail 125, 131
political advertising and campaign finance
    laws 261
political agendas 179
political appointees, vetting 206
political consultants 51–5
Political Dictionary (Safire) 45
political news cycle 122, 137
political organizations 86
political parties
  fund-raising rules for 144
  and ideology 86–104
  and interest groups 86
  relationships to allied interest groups 91
political policy demands 95
politicians
  and interest group concerns 259
  investments in 167
politics
  biases in 76
  and business groups 8–10, 29
  connecting people to 48
  and election support 262
  and the elites 3
  and growth of consulting industry 53
  individual participation in 24, 31–2
  influence of money on 145
  and interest groups 86
  and Internet influence on 123
  and marginalized groups 60
  and netroot group influence 139

organizations and representation in
    33–5
organized out of 61
pressure 29
process in 3
poor people, advocacy for 31
population definition of organizations
    126–9
Potoski, Matthew 212
Powell, W. 128
Practical Progressive, The (Payne) 127
preferences for policy outcomes 107
pre-floor decisions and campaign
    contributions 168–9
presidential appointees hired by interest
    groups 208
Presidential Transition 212
presidential transitions 212–16
presidents
    and Congress 206
    institutionalization of office 205
    and interest group interactions 204, 207
    and political appointments 206
pressure political system 22–3, 25, 29, 31,
    39, 61
pressure to cooperate 116–18
prioritization of interests 60
pro-business groups 152
pro-business policy 178
professional advocacy organizations
    124–5
professional occupations 29–30
professional organizations 26, 31, 48, 51
Progress for America Fund 150
progressive advocacy community 129, 131
Progressive Change Campaign Committee
    122, 128, 136
progressive donors 127
progressive political media 136–7
prohibition 100–1
public affairs consultants. *see* consultants
public comment 46
public funding of candidates 248–9
public interest groups 4, 6, 29, 48
    individuals in 29
    mobilization 10–13
    and organized representation 11–12
    representation of 10–12
Public Interest Organizations in the New
    Millennium (PIONM) 77
public interest political associations 127
Public Justice law firm 225
Public Markup project 252

public mobilization techniques 35
public opinion shaping 36
public policy, shaping of 145
push medium 123
Pyle, Kurt 187–8

Q
Quackenbush, Chuck 172
quid pro quos 160, 165, 239–40
quiet politics 44

R
Rachel Maddow Show 136–7
racial covenant laws 229
racial segregation in public schools 225
Raso, Connor 212
rational choice theories 259, 262–3
Raytheon 245
reaching across the aisle 102
Reagan, Ronald 206, 207
Reagan administration 50
recession 76
recruiting 108
reform strategies 241–2
regulations 259
regulations and business mobilization
    9–10
Reid, Harry 144, 257
religious associations 48
representation
    biases in 76
    compensatory 60
    descriptive 80
    equitable 80
Republican
    causes, spending on 152
    color-blind approach to policy 97–8
    and conservative MoveOn 130
    conservative woman voters 97
    gun control legislation 89, 257
Republican congressional scandals 137
Republican National Committee 98
Republican National Conventions 97
Republican Party
    and contributions from business
        interests 175
    and gay conservatives 97
    law and order platform and 95
    and Log Cabin Republicans 96
    spending on advertising 154–7
Republican super PACs 153
research into campaign contributions
    influence 179–80

research into communication methods of groups 126–9
Resource Mobilization 44
resource sharing 90, 111
revolving door between government and industry 211
right to bear arms litigation 228
Rockman, Bert 209
Rojas, Fabio 100
roll call voting 166, 169–70
Romney, Mitt 153, 156–7
Roosevelt, Theodore 204
Rootscamp conference, 129
Rother, John 119
Rove, Karl 144
Rowland, C. K. 229
rulemaking 46, 211, 218

S
Safire, William
    Political Dictionary 45
Salisbury, Robert 3–4, 26, 106, 208
SalsaLabs 129
same-sex marriages 222
Sandy Hook Elementary School shooting 257
Santorum, Rick 158
Sarbanes, John 247
Sarbanes-Oxley (SOX) 188
Saudi Arabia 98
Schaffner, Brian 249
Schattschneider, E. E. 3, 23–4, 44, 61
Schedule C appointments 208
Schlozman, Kay Lehman 207, 208, 238–9
school desegregation cases 229
Schumer, Charles 105, 116
scope of conflict 44
search and seizure law 223
seat at the table policy 214–15
SEC (Securities and Exchange Commission) 188
Section 527 145, 150
Securities and Exchange Commission (SEC) 188
Segal, Jeffrey A. 229
Service Employees International Union (SEIU) 1, 144
SES (socio-economic status) 25, 32–5
shadow electioneering 151
Shakespeare, William
    Hamlet 119
shared identity organizations 31

short-term issue coalitions 113–16, 120
Sierra Club 49, 129
single-issue groups 18–19, 49, 100–1, 127
Skocpol, Theda 31, 49, 124
small-donor matching funds 247
small government interests 152
SNAP 31
SNESJO (Survey of National Economic and Social Justice Organizations, 2000) 63, 69, 73
Snyder, James M.
    "Why is There so Little Money in U.S. Politics?" 165
social group mobilization 18
social justice 258
social media 122, 207
social networks. *see* networks
Social Security 13
social welfare organizations 28
social welfare tax exempt groups 151
socio-economic status (SES) and public representation 12, 25
sodomy laws 221
soft money 242, 243
sources of campaign contributions 173–4
SOX (Sarbanes-Oxley) 188
Spaeth, Harold J. 229
special interests 77
    and blame for failure to achieve policy goals 257
    influence on federal officials 209
    and Obama lobbying rule 245
specialized communication tools 125
specialty professional firms 265–6
spending patterns 189
staffing of non-member organizations 48
standing to bring a lawsuit 224–5
stare decisis 222
state capitals, interest groups in 2, 259
state court of last resort precedents 228
state governments 13–14, 16–17, 26
state-level interest mobilization 16–17
state-level lobbying 15
status quo, maintaining 44
status quo position 115–16
STB (U.S. Surface Transportation Board) 46–7
Stein, Rob 127
Stevens, John Paul 242
Stimson, James A. 177
Stohl, Cynthia *Collective Action*
    Collective Action in Organizations 124
strategies, party 88–9

Strolovitch, Dara 31
  Affirmative Advocacy 62, 68, 76, 77, 79
structural inequalities 77
subnational governments 26
Sunlight Foundation 252
SuperPACapp 155
Super PACs 144–64
  compared to traditional PACs 145–7
  influence on election outcomes, 180
  and post-*Citizens United* spending 243
Survey of National Economic and Social
    Justice Organizations, 2000 (SNESJO)
    63, 69, 73
surveys of individuals 22–3
Susan B. Anthony's List 97
Swift Boat Veterans for Truth 150

T
targeted appeals for funds 135
targeting for public policy issues 71
Target Point 129
targets for consultant campaigns 54–5
Task Force on Transparency and Public
    Participation 218
tax code, loopholes in 150
tax-exempt groups 151
Tea Party 90, 129
  activists 101
  movement 137
  online practices 140
technology 259
  and grass roots lobbying 46
  uses in mobilization 262
television advertising 152–3
Tenpas, Kathryn Dunn 207
Tester, John 144
testing culture 122
Theory of Political Parties, A (Bawn) 88–9
think tanks 49
Thomas, H.F. 244
Thompson, Tommy 144, 154
Thurber, James 245
Tierney, John 207, 208
Time magazine 99
timing and campaign contributions
    194–200
TMH (Labor, Corporate, Trade,
    Membership, and Health) 175
Tocqueville, Alexis de 47, 61
Toomey, Pat 257
Towle, Michael 206
Tracking Survey 2008 (Pew Internet and
    American Life Project) 22–3

trade associations 48, 50, 205
trade-offs for lobbyists 113–15, 119–20
transparency 160–1, 242, 250
Trial Lawyers for Public Justice 225
Truman, David 3, 23, 61
Truth in Lending Act 232
"Turning Promise into Progress: Key
    Priorities for Women and Families"
    (NPWF) 213
Twitter 122, 123

U
UCLA School approach 88
under-representation 6
undocumented immigrants, support
    for 50
unemployment legislation 137
uninsured, coverage for 50
unions 4, 6, 29, 48, 90–1
  and campaign support 90–1
  contributions to candidates 175–6
  decline of power 179–80
  and grassroots mobilization 48, 50
  and issue advocacy 150
  membership 29
  and political policy demands 95
  and political representation 29
  power decline 179
  and spending limits 152
University of Maryland 91
unregulated money 242
unskilled workers underrepresented in
    advocacy organizations 30
urban politics 50
U.S. Chamber of Commerce 105, 113, 166,
    199, 243
U.S. Congress
  and campaign finance 147, 149–50
  and e-petitions 133
  and gun control legislation 257
  independent expenditures sanctioned
    by 147–8
  institutional targeting of 67
  lobbying 15, 105–6, 118, 140
  and presidential policy 206–7
U.S. House of Representatives 170
U.S. Public Interest Research Group
    (PIRG) 107–8, 113
U.S. Senate
  candidates and matching funds 246–7
  and confirmation of presidential
    appointments 207–10
  confirmations hearings 207–10

and gun control legislation 257
PACs contribution to members of 146–7
U.S. Senate Judiciary Committee 224, 229
U.S. Senators, e-mail petitions to 133
U.S. Supreme Court 221, 224
  Buckley v. Valeo case 147–8
  and campaign finance laws 144, 180
  Citizens United v. FEC 144, 151
  District of Columbia v. Heller 228
  effect of amicus curiae briefs on 229–32
  Koons Buick Pontiac v. Nigh 232
  precedents 227, 231
  restrictions on candidates and political
    parties 145
  Wisconsin Right to Life v. FEC ruling 144,
    150
U.S. Surface Transportation Board (STB)
    46–7

V
Van Scoyoc and Associates 192
venue selection 226–7, 233
Verba, Sidney 238
voluntary associations 25, 38
Vose, Clement E. 222, 229
voter identification 161
voters
  and campaign ads 145
  and candidate support 91
  and gender 97
  and issue-related adverstising 149
  partisan patterns of 91
  transparency, need for 160–1
voter turnout rate and organized
    representation 12–13
VoteVets 136
voting 24, 97
vouchers, campaign 246–8

W
waivers to the anti-lobbyist ethics pledge
    214
Walker, Edward 52–3, 205
Walker, Jack 207
  Mobilizing Interest Groups in America
    126
Wal-Mart 54, 55, 185
War on Terror 60
Warren Court 229
Washington-based associations 49
Washington Post rule 250
Washington Representatives Directory 4, 23,
    25, 36

Washington Representatives Study
    22–3
Watergate 148
WCTU (Woman's Christian Temperance
    Union) 100–1
weak groups and political agenda,
    exclusion from 61
wealth-gap 152
websites 122, 215
Weigel, David
  "Take the Money and Lose" 153
Weingast, Barry 87
Weiser, Mark 124
welfare reform legislation (1996)
    76–7
Wesleyan Media Project 152, 158
West, William 212
White, Micah 125
Whitehouse, Sheldon 250
White House Forum on Health Reform
    (2009) 1, 6
White House Office of Public Liaison
    207
White House Office on Women and Girls
    213
"Why is There so Little Money in U.S.
    Politics?" (Ansolabehere, De
    Figueiredo, Snyder) 165
Why Parties (Aldrich) 87–8
Wilderness Society 110
Willard, Francis 100–1
Wilson, Woodrow 204
Wisconsin Right to Life v. FEC 144, 150
Woman's Christian Temperance Union
    (WCTU) 100–1
women
  courts 68
  groups for 97
  representation of 27, 60, 61, 62
Women's Legal Defense Fund 213
Wonderlich, John 252–3
Woodson, Robert 210
workplace safety regulations 172
World Wide Web 123
Wright, John 212, 241
Wyden, Ron 251

Y
Yackee, Susan 212
Young, McGee 108
YouTube 122, 123
Yu, Frank 188
Yu, Xiaoyun 188

CPSIA information can be obtained
at www.ICGtesting.com
Printed in the USA
FFHW012035091118
49329096-53601FF